Family, Love, and Work in the Lives of Victorian Gentlewomen

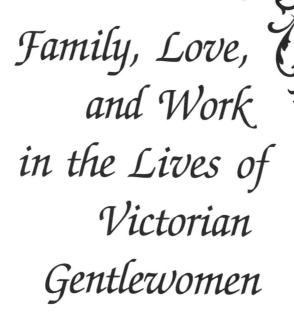

Family, Love, and Work in the Lives of Victorian Gentlewomen

M. Jeanne Peterson

Indiana University Press
Bloomington & Indianapolis

Manufactured in the United States of America

Library of Congress Cataloging-in-Publication Data

Peterson, M. Jeanne (Mildred Jeanne)
Family, love, and work in the lives of Victorian
gentlewomen.
Bibliography: p.
Includes index.
1. Middle class women—England—Social conditions.
2. Middle classes–England–History–19th century.
I. Title.
HQ1599.E5P48   1989   305.4'0942   88-45389
ISBN 0-253-34427-1
ISBN 0-253-20509-3 (pbk.)

1 2 3 4 5 93 92 91 90 89

To Teri, Kris, and Scott,
and some friends

CONTENTS

Preface

You will find her everywhere, once you begin to look for her. She sits on the ground at a camp site high in the Mexican mountains, dark skirt wrapped about her, white blouse crisp, fashionable hat neatly in place. She is on horseback, fording a river, skirt and hat still in place. She is playing cricket on a summer holiday. She is in the study, too, editing her husband's scientific writings or reading the galley proofs of her own latest article. The Victorian lady makes morning calls, sips tea, walks in the park. She is at home, caring for husband and children. She is also studying, teaching, working.

The exceptional gentlewomen of the age—from Queen Victoria and Florence Nightingale to Harriet Martineau and George Eliot—have long dominated our attention. More recently middle-class activists and heroines like Josephine Butler and Emily Davies, and now the wives of famous men, have come to scholars' attention.[1] Much as we have come to know about these exceptional women, we still have much to learn about the ordinary, obscure gentlewomen who lived in the Victorian age. We have already begun to suspect that they were no angels. To continue the venture of exploring Victorian ladies' lives, I have chosen to focus on one circle of upper-middle-class women, linked to each other by ties of family, friendship, and work. Their families were involved in the professions—the law, the Church, the universities, and the upper ranks of medicine—and occasionally in business or land-owning. None were in retail trade, none were craftsmen, none were clerks or petty bureaucrats.[2] The social world of these women, their personalities, education, family life, and work will also be explored.

The impetus for studying these women's lives arises out of the powerful and persistent stereotypes of the Victorian lady that survive, despite all the recent research and writing about women.[3] The existence of these powerful (and often false) images is itself a puzzle. Much of our "knowledge" of the Victorians has come from their children—Samuel Butler, Lytton Strachey, Virginia Woolf, and other, lesser writers—in what must be the most successful attack of children on their parents in the modern world. Their half-true portraits of the Victorian age have shaped the twentieth century's vision of the Victorians until our own time. Their twisted pictures of Victorian women, in particular, as badly educated, somewhat silly girls, evolving into docile or dominated wives, devoted mothers, and meddlesome ladies bountiful, have survived for two reasons. First, because (as recent cognitive research has established) we see what we want, expect, or need to see.[4] And it has been a comfort to think of the Victorian era as a golden age when, at least for the upper-middle class, the ideal nuclear family really existed:

there was a man in charge and an angel in the house; he led, she followed, he was active, she was passive, he was strong and she was weak, he took care of public life and she of the private sphere, and out of such order came at least a modicum of peace if not always happiness.

A further source of our flawed image of Victorian women has been the nature of the sources we have used. We have relied heavily on the testimony of reformers for our knowledge of women's lives. The gloom of Florence Nightingale's "Cassandra," the negative female experiences described in John Stuart Mill's *Essay on the Subjection of Women*, the bleak perspective of Virginia Woolf's *Room of One's Own* all have been taken as objective accounts of women's plight in the nineteenth century. Take, for example, Lady Frances Balfour's description of gentlewomen's role in the nineteenth century: "there was very little in England that was outside the scope of what used to be called 'Church work.' Women were not asked to do any political work, there were no Local Bodies on which they might sit, they were not even permitted to be guardians of the poor, only men were capable of dealing with the nurseries of the State, and the poverty or lapses of young women."[5] These sentences are untrue for much of the nineteenth century, but Lady Frances's overstatement justified her involvement in the newly formed Women's Liberal Unionist Association. Her words cannot be read as an objective description of Victorian women's activities. The writings of Mill, Nightingale, and the others were, in fact, political statements, polemics in favor of change, polemics that often presented (of necessity) the worst cases of Victorian women's experience as the norm in order to strengthen the case for reform. We have mistaken Victorian rhetoric for reality.

A third reason for the survival of our distorted picture of Victorian gentlewomen in particular arises from the fact that students of Victorian society have tended to see the Victorian middle class(es) as a relatively coherent group. As a result, data pertaining to the lower-middle-class female, often aspiring to a higher social rank, has been misread as descriptive of all of the "middle classes," including gentlewomen. Instead, we must recognize that the distinction between gentlefolk and the rest of Victorian society is the largest rift in the Victorian social structure.[6] Finally, our recently acquired consciousness of the facts of sexual inequality in the present has resulted in a major emphasis on gender as a determinant of autonomy and power in the past as well. Such emphasis may be warranted in the study of contemporary American society but not of nineteenth-century England: there, rank may have mattered more than sex. It will be the burden of this book to explore Victorian upper-middle-class women's characters, their private lives, their work, their experience of public action. The goal will be a re-vision, a new view, of those women ignored until now.

Acknowledgments

Primary thanks for help with research for this book must go to the staffs of libraries and archives: the British Library, the Cambridge University Library, the Bodleian Library, the Principal Registry of the Family Division (Somerset House), St. Catherine's House, the Cheshire Record Office, Glasgow University Library and Archives, and Pusey House (St. Cross College, Oxford). Mrs. Edith Moore, the former principal of the Burlington Danes School, kindly allowed me to see the Victorian records of the school. Thanks are also due to the Huntington Library for permission to use materials from their British history collection. Special thanks go to Mr. Eustace Cornelius, librarian of the Royal College of Surgeons, whose earliest interest in, and support of, my work has been crucial to its existence at all. The reference staff of the library at Indiana University, Bloomington, deserves special kudos: they were efficient and cheerful throughout.

I also want to express my appreciation for the cooperation, kindness, and help of many individuals. For their assistance in my research and for permission to use their family papers, my thanks to Lord Mayhew, Sir Julian and Lady Paget, Mr. and Mrs. Paul Paget, Dr. Oliver Paget, Mr. David Thomson, Mrs. Joan Thomson Charnock, the late Sir George Paget Thomson, Col. Humphrey Paget, Mrs. Henry (Alice) Thompson, and Mr. Simon Heywood. The late Mrs. James M. (Mari) Thompson gave me help from the earliest days of my research. She became a friend whose loss I mourn.

For their reading of the manuscript at one stage or another, for helpful suggestions, and other sorts of assistance and support, I want to thank the following friends, students, and colleagues: George Alter, Walter Arnstein, Ellen Berkowitz, Judith Berling, William Burgan, Moureen Coulter, Laura Gordon, Ann R. Higginbotham, Catherine Hoyser, Linda Kerber, David Kohn, Rick Railsback, Anya Peterson Royce, Anka Ryall, Zuzanna Lady Shonfield, Barbara Sicherman.

Finding out about Victorian women is extremely difficult, for they are often lost to history. Many times in the course of this work I found myself relying on the careful work of an army of unnamed and unsung researchers, librarians, and bibliographers—those who prepared such important research tools as the *British Museum Catalogue* and the *Wellesley Index to Victorian Periodicals*. They were important sources for my research. I salute them.

Good editorial work is a joy forever. I had that, and more, from my editors at Indiana University Press. Janet Rabinowitch believed in the idea of this book; she also attended to the details. I am grateful to her for all her skills and for all the benefits her intelligent editing gave me.

Some of the material presented here appeared previously in the *American Historical Review*. At that stage and since I have benefited from the advice of the then-editors of the *Review*: Otto Pflanze, Helen Nader, and Michelle Mannering. Earlier versions of parts of this work were presented to the Women's Studies Program and the West European Studies Program, Indiana University, Bloomington, the Departments of History and Women's Studies at the University of Hawaii at Manoa, the Anglo-American Conference of Historians, University of London, and the Indiana University Institute for Advanced Study, Bloomington.

Financial support for my work on the history of the family has come from the Office of Research and Graduate Development and the Institute for Advanced Study, Indiana University, Bloomington, the American Council of Learned Societies, and the National Endowment for the Humanities. The Guggenheim Foundation provided me with a leave of absence and the freedom to work on this and other projects. Anya Peterson Royce and Morton Lowengrub, the Dean of the Faculties and the Dean of Research and Graduate Development respectively, have created an environment at Indiana University fully supportive of the faculty's research. They deserve the praise and thanks of all the faculty here. To all these individuals and organizations I am deeply grateful. Needless to say, the errors of fact and of judgment in this book are mine alone.

For permission to reproduce illustrations in this book, I want to thank: the Aberdeen Art Gallery and Museums, the Forbes Magazine Collection, Dr. Oliver Paget, Mrs. James M. Thompson, and Mrs. Joan Charnock.

Part of the title (although not the analytical structure) of this work derives from Sigmund Freud. It was he who codified the notion that the good life may be found in the exercise of *lieb und arbeit*, love and work.

Family, Love,
and Work
in the Lives of
Victorian Gentlewomen

CHAPTER ONE

Backgrounds and Personalities

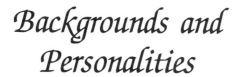

In the winter of 1871 Catharine Paget, the twenty-five-year-old daughter of a successful London surgeon, found herself in the usual rounds of duties, calls, and social life. In the morning, she later recalled,

> The boys & I went early to the Botanical with Carrie Gull & had a short time for skating (Agnes Twining & Miss Bence Jones were learning) then I drove with her to the Station to meet Gertrude Rowden coming to stay at Dr. Gull's. In the evening Stephen & Mary went to Mrs. Busk's, & I to dine at Dr. West's, to meet & talk French to a young refugee, who was pleasant enough. I met 3 Miss Wards, rather handsome & most picturesque. . . . heard Mrs. Liddell abused by some Ch.Ch. men, & the Prussians by the general company.[1]

The ladies who populated drawing rooms like those Catharine Paget described—those of thousands of upper-middle-class business and professional families—are largely unknown to us. *Punch* cartoons depicted them as pretty young women, leisured and well-to-do, who spent their days in calling, walking in the park, going to balls, or reclining on *chaises longues*.[2]

Although the type is familiar enough, upper-middle-class women are, as individuals, faceless and without a history. Without distinction, they lived the ordinary lives of daughters, wives, mothers, and sisters. They came from the social milieu that produced the famous few, but the great achievers among women were atypical (as they were among men) and thus they cannot offer us any clues to the lives of the average females of their rank in the last century. The goal of this book is the understanding of these ordinary Victorian ladies' lives.

To give focus to this study, I have chosen to center my investigations on one set of women who were linked by ties of family, friendship, and profession, as well as by membership in a single social stratum. The nucleus of the group consists of the women of the Paget family in three nineteenth-century generations. Their story spans the period from 1778, when the first was born, to 1958, when the last survivor of the third generation died, but this study is limited to the nineteenth century; it begins with Betsey Tolver's marriage to Samuel Paget in 1799 and ends with the coming of war in 1914, when the Victorian age began to crumble. The Paget family is an apt focus for this study because the Pagets and their friends were in touch with much that was happening in science, arts, letters, and university and professional life in the Victorian age. Moreover, they and their friends experienced a pattern of social mobility within the professional classes that seems typical of the Victorian experience: in the course of the century many of them moved from the world of business into the minor professions and, by 1914, into the upper reaches of the professional classes. They and their circle were not, by and large, descendants of the landed gentry. Nor did they move into landed society on the basis of their successful upward mobility. Instead, they became a new, urban gentry made up of professional families—gentlefolk firmly placed in the hierarchy of metropolitan and industrial society.

The inner circle of women included those born or married into the Paget family. Next came the mothers, sisters, sisters-in-law, and nieces of those women who married into the family. Beyond family, the Paget women's social world consisted of their connections and friends, those of their parents, siblings, and children, and the colleagues of fathers, brothers, and husbands. Together the Paget women, their relatives, and their friends constitute one slice of the Victorian upper-middle classes. These women were the mothers, sisters, wives, and daughters of the rising professional men of Victorian England. Their circle included many quintessential Victorians—George Eliot, Florence Nightingale, and Charles Darwin, for example—but this study will avoid their famous associates in order to examine the more ordinary members of their circle.[3]

Geographically this study begins in Great Yarmouth, Norfolk, where Betsey and Samuel established their home. Their own activities and their children's marriages and mobility widened their circle to include Cambridge, Shrewsbury, and London, and, in the third generation, Oxford and numerous points around the urban and, only occasionally, rural landscape of Victorian England. A study of this ever-widening circle of women gives us at least one window on the lives of the females of this rank, and understanding them brings us to a better understanding of their status group and of Victorian society as a whole. We begin by examining the socio-economic environment and professional milieu in which the women of this study lived and by introducing the individual women who will populate this book. Where possible, personalities will be examined. Unfortunately, not all are equally visible at this historical distance. Some left no documentary evidence of their existence; others left only fragments—a few letters, a photograph, a sentence or two in the biography of a husband or brother. Some can be seen at only one point in their lives—here a girlhood portrait, there a view of a woman in middle age. Few left extensive records and fewer still were the subjects of biographies or memoirs. The record is spotty, and this account necessarily reflects to some degree that limitation.[4]

The goals of this book are several. Chapter two will explore the educational achievements of Victorian women. Then, given the special place of sex and money in the Victorian ethos, gentlewomen's relations to these topics will be examined. Attention will also be given to the other facts of Victorian family life: conflict within families, health problems of husbands and children, and women's confrontations with death. The final chapters of this book will explore how these "leisured ladies" spent their days—in particular their roles in a variety of unpaid occupations and their relationship to professional life. Of special interest will be the ways that women ventured out of the so-called "private" sphere of women and into the "public" sphere of men.

The Nucleus of the Circle: The Paget Women

Great Yarmouth was a rude, coarse town. Its inhabitants won their livelihood from the sea, from shipping, ship building, fishing, and commerce, and to a lesser extent brewing and manufactures. It was the town where the Victorian Pagets' story begins. The matriarch of the Paget family of Great Yarmouth was Sarah Elizabeth (Betsey) Tolver (1778–1843), the eldest daughter of Ann Capps and Tom Tolver of Chester, a self-made gentleman. Betsey was brought up in the comfortable home of her Aunt Godfrey in Yarmouth, and in 1799, when she was twenty-one, she married Samuel Paget, also of Great Yarmouth. A young man of modest origins, Sam made a fortune as a provisioner of ships during the Napoleonic Wars. Later he diversified his economic activities to include shipping and brewing, a business in which three of his sons became his partners. His ventures prospered so well as to permit the construction of a fine house on the Yarmouth quay and the purchase of works of art.[5]

Betsey Paget was "handsome, tall, and graceful." Her portrait, done in middle life, presents a buxom matron with the direct gaze of a woman who has a mind of her own. Betsey was as independent a wife and mother as her portrait suggests. Although she was the first-born daughter, her father preferred her sisters. Her parents allowed her aunt to take her away from Chester to bring her up in Yarmouth. She had a romance with a naval officer but he died at sea. All these circumstances may have contributed to her strength of character. To her marriage she brought financial resources (whether in the form of a settlement or an inheritance) that helped make

Sam's business ventures possible and that underpinned her sense of authority. Also, she was Sam's social superior: he was the son of an "idle and disso-
lute" artisan, while she came from a monied and reasonably genteel family.
From whatever cause, Betsey Paget was an authoritative woman, with views
of her own and the liberty to express them.[6] Her son James described her
as "somewhat hasty in temper, resolute, strong-willed and strong in speech."
She was given to expletives like "Good God!" and to sarcasm when she was
displeased. She may also have been a bit of a snob. Her father rebuked her
for aspiring to a coat of arms when the family did not have a right to one.
Perhaps, too, her choice not to breast-feed her babies reflected a certain
level of social pretension.[7]

More? Wet nurse?

One of Betsey's sons was critical of the "irreligion" of the house on the
Yarmouth quay; neither Betsey nor Sam made any claims to piety. On the
other hand, Betsey had an eager interest in politics, and she propounded
her own brand of "ultra-Toryism." Most characteristic of Betsey was the enthusiasm with which she plunged herself into the family's work, life, and
aspirations. Such energy and activity waned only when she was in her sixties
and suffered a stroke. Though "speechless from paralysis," she continued
to express her views, communicating, by way of a slate, "the wit, the pun-
gent sarcasm, [and] the daring high spirit" that were still hers.[8]

Betsey's social world in Yarmouth included her two younger sisters, Maria
Jane and Frances Sarah. Maria Jane was the wife of Henry Moor, an officer
in the Royal Navy, who died at sea in 1805. Frances Sarah married Charles
Bagnall, occupation unknown. Through her marriage to Sam, Betsey had
two sisters-in-law, Mary Paget Wiseman and Anne (Nancy) Paget Bracey.
All formed part of the Yarmouth circle; none had as prosperous or respectable a family life as Betsey.[9]

The second generation in the Paget family was a large one: Betsey bore
seventeen children in the first twenty-five years of her married life. Two
daughters and seven sons survived to adulthood. Martha (Patty) (1800–81)
and Katherine (Kate) (1825–85) were the oldest and youngest of Betsey's and
Sam's offspring. Patty enjoyed her parents' prosperity and took pride in the
fine house her father built on the quay. But in the late 1820s financial trouble
came to the Paget house: Paget ships were lost at sea, and the brewery failed
to bring in hoped-for returns. These troubles grew worse over the next decade and ended in a last-ditch sale, at auction, of all the family's belongings,
part of a desperate (and successful) attempt to ward off bankruptcy.[10] The
family's financial crisis meant there was no money for daughters' dowries nor
for their financial independence. After the death of their hopes for the future, Patty and Kate settled down to life with their parents in reduced circumstances, in a rented house in Yarmouth. The two Paget daughters never

married, nor did four of the sons. Daughters and sons alike had their prospects damaged by the financial collapse of their parents.[11]

In the 1850s, when both parents were dead, Patty and Kate went to live with their one surviving bachelor brother, schoolmaster and clergyman Alfred Paget. The three watched from the enclosed world of Kirstead rectory as their brothers in London and Cambridge went from success to success. Alfred died in 1863 and the two sisters moved yet again, to Woodridings, in the drab environs of petty-bourgeois Pinner, where they stored the memorabilia of their Yarmouth days. Their house was modest, and there was a pub next door, with "rowdy . . . customers" who threw "newspapers, and empty bottles" over the wall.[12] Early on Patty may have had great expectations about her place in life; her disappointments were equally large.

The middle-aged "Aunt Patty" struck her nephew Stephen as "not clever, . . . narrow in her views." Like her sharp-toothed little dog, Patty had a soft exterior that veiled the strong feelings underneath. She could be "censorious" and sharply cutting when she allowed herself the freedom, and she did allow it—expressing stinging views of "Napoleon III, or Mr. Gladstone, or [her sister-in-law] . . . Clara" Paget.[13] Disappointment had taken its toll on both personality and temperament.

Katherine (Kate), the youngest child of the family, seemed very different from Patty. A shy young girl when the family money crisis began, she confronted the loss of prospects early in life. She steeled herself for the ordeal of the auction, concerned only that her frail old father survive the trial with dignity. During the sale she saw friends fingering the family's goods, eager for bargains. After the dissolution of the family's Yarmouth life, Kate faced some serious choices in her life. She might have married a Shrewsbury schoolmaster, and the family always said that "Mr. Fisher worshipped her." She chose spinsterhood instead, perhaps out of loyalty to her older sister. Kate had an "ardent" and "aggressive" family chauvinism, and her "strength of will and loyalty" were focused more especially on her successful brothers, George and James. The result was sometimes less than happy: for example, no woman, not even her sister-in-law Lydia, was good enough for her beloved James. The strain between the two women was often visible.[14]

As an adult Kate was "tall" and "had a 'beautiful figure.'" She "moved . . . grandly, like the great lady she was." Handsome rather than beautiful, her face was "Sharp-cut, thin, strong-featured. A big aquiline nose, high cheekbones, mouth rather hard and thin-lipped . . . eyes grey, steely." Her hair was "black, smooth, and tight-drawn." She was always "well-dressed," for she loved "beautiful clothes." Kate's dissatisfaction with her own life was sublimated in "her passionate love of all the success and the honours" that came to her brothers. "She approved or disapproved of the rest of us," an

undistinguished relative ruefully recalled, "by our nearness to" her successful favorites.[15]

Kate was more independent than Patty, and Kate's very autonomy made
suburban life intolerable for her. She seemed "discontented, imprisoned in
the dull enclosed suburb . . . of Woodridings." In the mid–1870s Kate (then
aged fifty) traveled to the continent with her nephews Frank and Stephen
(aged twenty-four and twenty). Otherwise she stayed home. Kate liked the
sensuous roar of high-speed trains: she shared with her nephew the excitement of "the 'Flying Dutchman,' which tore through Pinner Station every
night, on its way to Scotland: it was a sensational sight even for grown-ups,"
her nephew recalled, and she "took me to [see] it, as much to please herself,
I think as to please me." If Patty was a terrier, Kate was a "great eagle in
a cage intended for a parrot." She "beat her wings against the bars of it,
and often hurt herself." She longed for a "fling" (Stephen said), longed for
London, Oxford, and Paris, longed for "money and wide influence." She
wanted success and power; she had to make do with proximity to it. In old
age Kate developed breast cancer. She bore the pain in silence and told no
one for many months. When she finally consulted a surgeon, it was too late
to operate.[16]

Patty and Kate bore the weight of limited means for the rest of their lives.
Even with the growing prosperity of their brothers, they lived on the margins of social life. Perhaps their financial dependency limited them, perhaps
the memory of the Yarmouth troubles paralyzed them. Certainly the memories of prosperity now lost made them cling to the glories of Yarmouth. Although these women may have been depressed by the dislocations of their
lives, they were not resigned and accepting. Their responses were angry
and aggressive.

Three of Patty and Kate's brothers married, and through them five women
entered the family. Frederick Paget married, successively, Elizabeth Ann
Rogers (d. 1832) of Great Yarmouth, Hester Maria King (d. 1849), daughter
of a clergyman and mother of all nine of Fred's children, and Sarah
Shoubridge (d. 1880). All were, apparently, the daughters of gentlemen.
Frederick left his father's faltering brewing business, only to fail on his own.
He tried inventing and engineering, and, in search of a new start, he and
Sarah moved the family to Le Havre and then to Vienna in the early 1850s,
where they remained outside the English family circle until Elise, the only
surviving daughter of Hester and Frederick, returned to England in the
1860s.[17]

At the center of the Paget women's circle were Betsey's other two
daughters-in-law, Lydia North Paget and Clara Fardell Paget. Lydia North

(1815–95) (one of four daughters of a London cleric and schoolmaster, the Reverend Henry North) married Betsey's son James in 1844. The couple established a household near St. Bartholomew's Hospital in London, where James was a struggling young surgeon. Important hospital and medical school posts and his appointment as surgeon to Queen Victoria in 1858 marked his rise to professional success. His prestigious and lucrative consulting practice made possible a move to London's West End, the lease of a large house in Harewood Place, a growing staff of domestic servants, and, like most of the families to be examined here, ready access to all the "paraphernalia of gentility."[18]

To all appearances Lydia was the embodiment of the clinging, dependent, reliant daughter and wife: "the spare flat chest, the sloping shoulders, the large forehead and nose, the rather weak tired-looking eyes, and the soft indecipherable mouth . . . [were] very feminine, very dutiful, very gentle." "She was," one of her sons insisted with more candor than kindness, "not handsome nor fashionable nor witty nor learned nor well-dressed nor 'clever' nor 'up to date.'" Her virtue was in her character, he thought, "one of the most beautiful lives that I have ever known. . . . a simple little white soul."[19] But the children of the Victorians were not always reliable witnesses to the characters of their parents, and Stephen, powerful observer though he often was, saw his mother through his own lenses.

Pious—many women earned this epithet, and it is surely the word to describe Lydia North. In contrast to Betsey's Laodicean coldness about matters religious, young Lydia's Christianity infused her life and relationships. She prayed for spiritual growth for James and for herself. May "He," she wrote to James in 1840, "give us grace *successfully* to war against the world the flesh & the devil." She sought humility and rejected any credit for virtue: "flattery from indifferent persons is not without its dangers," she told her fiancé, "but from one so dear to me as you are . . . oh! my dear James, . . . the expression of your good opinion is most injurious, most calculated to foster that self esteem which indeed darling it is your duty & your interest to endeavour to root out of me. . . . Pray for me but *never never* praise me." Praise, she said, led to pride and pride to sin. She considered James her spiritual guide and invited him to criticize her: "*dearest*, I pray you tell me *frankly* of all my *faults*."[20] She yearned for greater spirituality, and she prayed for grace in order to do good.

But if piety means the realization of Christian submission and selflessness, then Lydia did not deserve to be called pious. Her strivings for spirituality mirror her human foibles, and her deeply held Christianity must not disguise from us her complex and sometimes unchristian character. She was often sarcastic or bad-tempered. Tempted to engage in undisciplined criticism of those around her, she gave way. She found fault with clergymen: one of the Reverend Robins's sermons she dismissed as "a purely Robinnial effusion . . . the worst sermon we ever heard from him." She tried, she said self-righteously, "to learn something from his sermon, but *that* was no easy matter." She criticized her family, and she damned others with the faintest of praise.[21] In Lydia, piety did not denote the absence of sin; it reflected her struggle for virtue, not its achievement. This Victorian woman's piety did not preclude strong feelings, moral failings, or even a sense of humor.

Lydia North was also passionate and intense. That strength of feeling was apparent early, in the tensions of her adolescence and young adulthood. These arose at least in part from conflicts with parents and reflected themselves in her emotional life and moods: she was fascinated with fierce storms, turbulent seas, and death. One winter night in 1837, when her father was recuperating from a dangerous illness, Lydia had a violent fantasy: after the family had retired for the night, she began to fear that "perchance I *had* let one spark fall on the carpet, & a fire was to be the consequence, & Papa in his state had to make his escape out of doors, what should I think of my carelessness."[22] Her fears, she found, were groundless, but her anxious fantasy suggests guilt and ambivalence about her silent, commanding, and—in his illness—especially demanding father.

Truthfulness and obedience were part of daughterly Christian duty. Lydia was usually an obedient daughter to her father, the stern, severe Reverend North, but she occasionally fell short of the mark. In the summer of 1836, Lydia and James announced their plans to marry. Her parents acquiesced but his father questioned the prudence of the match. Sam insisted on "the inexpediency, & indeed the impropriety" of "an engagement which cannot be fulfilled perhaps for half a dozen years." Lydia and James seemed to bow to Sam's objections, but in fact they made no change in their plans except to hide them from Betsey and Sam. Their engagement lasted for eight years, and Lydia colluded with James in deceiving his family. She visited Yarmouth frequently and saw his family there: "I was but too happy to make [delivering] your letter," she told James, "an excuse to go & call at your [parents'] house."[23] She designed her encounters so as to give the impression that her relationship with James was merely friendly.

Lydia's theories about human nature reveal what are probably the essentials of her own character: "Generally, I believe, it is almost inherent, in all human beings, to strive for power, *independence*, self-exaltation, & sometimes the proportionate humiliation of others." Only in her relationship to James were "these desires . . . strangely rooted out of me." She did not, in fact, submit even to his judgment "in *every point*," she said. She often forgot his express wishes, put pressure on him to do as she wanted, and showed "pain or temper" when he implied any criticism of her.[24]

The rhetoric of female obedience was a form of bonding. Only you, Lydia told her fiancé, are "superior . . . to myself." He stood "quite alone" as the one source of "joy" for her on earth. In her relationship with James, she experienced "the sweetness of . . . dependance [sic] and leaning on you." In her other relationships Lydia abandoned even the appearance of submissiveness. When her brother Isaac married and went to live in the Isles of Scilly, Lydia visited him there. She observed him closely and began to worry about his health. She "induced him to write" to her surgeon-fiancé for medical advice, and, she confided to James, "You would have smiled to see me managing him."[25] She became even more authoritative with age, and her firmness occasionally erupted into open conflict. When Lydia's children found insects in their bedroom in Harewood Place, Lydia loudly blamed their nanny, Mrs. Vinton. "My mother and Nanny had a scene over it," Stephen remembered.[26] Lydia may have appeared demure, pliable, even timid. In truth she could be critical, deceitful, manipulative, assertive, and ill-tempered. Lydia strove for power and, as she said, "*in*dependence."

Lydia Paget's sister-in-law, Clara Fardell Paget (*c*. 1825–99), daughter of an Ely clerical family, entered the Paget family in 1851 as the wife of Betsey's son George (1809–92), a physician and teacher of medicine at Cambridge University. Clara's open assertiveness stands in stark contrast to Lydia's superficial dependency. Perhaps Clara modeled herself, however unconsciously, on her own mother, Emma Clara Anne Fardell (d. 1874), whose brusque style is visible even in the pages of her last will and testament.[27] Imperious was the word for Clara. She ruled her household in an entirely unsentimental, often abrupt, way. When she wanted to communicate with her daughters, for example, she simply tore off a half-sheet of paper and, in a sprawling, hurried hand, put her wishes on paper. She wasted no time on the niceties but got immediately down to the business of housekeeping and the multiple errands her daughters Rose and Maud had to do for her. "Get me please," she wrote to Rose, "13 Candlesticks for the bedrooms at 1s/ or 1s/4d if you can & send them in the baskets carefully packed." On another occasion she instructed Rose about the laundering of the Pagets' servants' clothes: "I must have the servants clean. I said so before." And, of another housekeeping matter, she demanded, "please send me the P.O. Order at once." Her peremptory orders always ended with "Best love to your Papa & to you. Your affectionate mother, Clara Paget."[28] One of her daughters objected to her terse style and the apparent one-sidedness of their relationship. Clara responded: "My dear Rose, Thank you much for your letters, & please go on & write, but I am much engaged in Antiquarian as well as domestic work & really cannot write much." Indifferent at times, Clara could also appear harsh. When one of the lower servants attempted suicide, Clara fired him.[29]

Perhaps there was a sensitive heart behind Clara's brusque exterior. She was certainly sensitive to her own treatment at the hands of others. When her daughter Rose wrote some poetry, Clara "seemed hurt" that Rose had not read the poems to her. But Clara never made it easy for her daughters to share their achievements with her. Maud had to admit to Rose that "your feelings in reading poetry to M[ama] cannot be much otherwise to mine in showing drawings & singing songs neither of which may be understood."[30]

Like her mother-in-law, Clara liked to manage those around her, men as well as women, sons as well as daughters. She had views about her son Charles's future, which she communicated to him through his sister. This second-hand attention suggests a woman too busy to bother, but at other times Clara could be tender with her family. When away from her little boys, she sent messages to them: "I hope and trust that Meiric [sic] & Owen will both be good Boys," she told Rose. "I long to kiss them both again, I miss them so very much, tell them how I long to see them."[31] (Despite her fondness, she never brought herself to spell Meyrick's name consistently.)

Clara's fond feelings for her husband may be inferred from the way she looked after his interests, even at long distance. From north Wales she saw to it that George should "have some of the apples . . . if he likes them." When she worried about his health, she instructed her daughter to give him fish and chicken "if he feels tired."[32] She oversaw the workings of her Cambridge household by mail, with the help of her daughters. Her concern aside, Clara acted first in pursuit of her own interests, even when they took her away to Wales for many months of the year. She liked Wales and her Welsh friends, she enjoyed the outdoor life and antiquarian studies that she could pursue there, and nothing kept her from this self-indulgence.

The Paget women of the third generation include the daughters and daughters-in-law of Lydia and Clara, together with Frederick and Hester's daughter Elise. Lydia's eldest daughter, Catharine (1846–1937), grew up in the glittering social world of mid-Victorian London. When she was thirty-one she married a clergyman and Oxford don, Henry Lewis Thompson (1848–1905) of Christ Church, and they had three sons. They spent their early married life in Iron Acton (near Bristol), where Thompson was a parish priest. In 1888 Thompson became headmaster of Radley School. Both were happy to return to Oxford in 1897 when Henry became vicar of the university church, St. Mary the Virgin.[33]

While she was single, London was Catharine's world, and she met it full of self-assurance. Very little daunted her. She praised "a grand sermon of

Mr. Liddon's" at St. Paul's Cathedral as "original & eloquent." She was equally ready to dismiss sermons that were not up to standard. When one Mr. Edgington preached at St. James's Church, Picadilly, she labeled his sermon "rather . . . horrifying."[34] Her self-confidence was also evident in her relations with her brother Francis (Frank) (1851–1911), five years her junior. She took the lead in their relationship, acting as Frank's "counsellor" and "sister-confessor." Frank went away to Shrewsbury and then, in 1869, to Christ Church, Oxford, where he met, socialized with, and argued with many of the future leaders of the nation. The issues of the time, and ritualism in particular, were also discussed at the Paget breakfast table in Harewood Place. There were, their brother Stephen recalled, "lengthy family arguments," in which "home-life at Harewood Place, so far as the sons and daughters were concerned began to be . . . deeply committed to disputes on these lines." Catharine participated fully in these debates. One night after a dinner party, "Papa, Frank & I sat up till 20 minutes to 2 arguing." In spite of the arguments (or perhaps because of them), Catharine's relations with Frank were close throughout their adult lives.[35]

Although less inclined to guilt and introspection than her mother, Catharine acknowledged her capacity for ill temper: "I wonder," she asked herself soon after arriving in Wales for the summer, "why I always languish & feel cross & stupid, the first day in a new place." Catharine also had a sense of humor, even in relation to her social duties: "I spent the morning seeing poor people, the afternoon calling on rich ones." A wholesome sense of the ludicrous in "society," perhaps a bit of cruelty as well, led her to a mischievous social prank. Catharine and her brothers all agreed that at Twining dinner parties "nobody could have much fun." The bane of any party was Uncle Richard, an upright but "depressing" man, with his "dull voice and bleak petrified grey eyes." On one occasion when Catharine dined there, she "set herself to say nothing all through dinner, to be as dull as the rest of the company," and she "achieved this end without anybody finding her out!"[36] Afterward she and her brothers laughed at the shortcomings of their seniors.

Helen Church (1858–1900), daughter of Helen Frances Bennett and Richard William Church (1815–90), dean of St. Paul's Cathedral, married Catharine's brother Frank, also a clergyman and Oxford don. They lived in Oxford, where he was Regius Professor of Pastoral Theology, dean of Christ Church, and bishop of Oxford. After Helen's death at the age of forty-two, her unmarried sister Mary moved to Oxford and took over the care and upbringing of Helen and Frank's children.[37] Catharine's sister-in-law Elma Katie Hoare (d. 1958) came from a Norfolk banking family, and her father had been a member of Parliament. She entered the Paget circle through her marriage to the Reverend Henry Luke Paget (1853–1937) in 1892. She accompanied him to a central London parish and then to the East End, when he was named bishop suffragan of Stepney in 1909; he became bishop of Chester after the First World War.[38]

Lydia North Paget's other two daughters-in-law were Julia Norrie Moke (1864–1926) and Eleanor Mary Burd (1854–1933). Moke, an American-born heiress with English and Dutch connections, lost her father at the age of ten. In 1883 she married the Pagets' eldest son, barrister John R. Paget (1848–1938), and the couple had five children. Moke brought a large fortune to the marriage, but not the self-assurance to withstand the force of John's adamantine personality. Eleanor Burd was the daughter of Dr. Edward Burd, a Shrewsbury medical practitioner. She married the Pagets' youngest son, Stephen (1855–1926), who left a surgical career for writing and medical politics. The youngest of James and Lydia's offspring, Mary Maud (1860–1945), remained a spinster, living at home with her parents until both died. When she was forty years old, she established her own home in London. Her parents left her well supported financially, and she had a busy spinsterhood. Blindness limited her activities only marginally, and she remained active until her death.[39]

Clara Fardell Paget's daughters multiplied the family's links to the Cambridge scientific community. Her eldest surviving daughter, Clara Maud (usually called Maud) (1857–1949), married Hans Gadow (1855–1928), a German vertebrate paleontologist who had moved to England in 1880. After four years on the staff of the British Museum, he joined the paleontology faculty of Cambridge University. They married in 1899 and settled at Cleramendi, their house just outside of Cambridge.[40]

Robust, assertive women were a Paget tradition in Cambridge as well as London. In her youth Maud was the champion of common sense among her sisters, brushing past pretension with blunt rebukes. As an adult, she continued to be a commanding force, intrepid, some would have said opinionated. She loved birds, and as a consequence hated cats. She adopted, by the interwar years, an open prejudice against those she called "people of Oriental heritage." Perhaps she reflected biases common in English society; perhaps she had adopted her German husband's views.[41]

Rose (1860–1951), the second daughter of Clara and George Paget, carried on the robust tradition. Well-behaved and dutiful, she was also eager, personally intense, and assertive. In her mid-teens she took an equal interest in poetry and in newspaper accounts of violence: the "Ashantee war," a Welsh miners' strike, typhus, railway accidents, gunpowder explosions, and cyclones in India. Morbid events in the family also intrigued her—her Grandmother Fardell's sudden death of a stroke, the incarceration of her former governess in a German madhouse, a servant's suicide attempt. Rose enjoyed the *frisson* of fear she felt on seeing the spot called "Devil's Ditch," where her father and his coachman were accosted by three men intent on "robbery & perhaps murder." Her fascination with violence and death suggests hidden passions, perhaps hostilities. At the same time, her experience indicates that girls and women were not protected from the facts of violence, crime, and death. Indeed, squeamishness or excessive decorum in a young woman earned censure from her close associates. When Rose seemed to be overreacting or taking herself too seriously, her sister scolded her for being "missish." The epithet itself suggests that truly well-reared Victorian girls understood that swooning, helplessness, and sentimentality deserved ridicule, not admiration. At age thirty, Rose married J. J. Thomson, a physicist at the Cavendish Laboratory in Cambridge. He eventually became master of Trinity College.[42]

Violet (1860–1924), Rose's twin, had an emotionally difficult adolescence. She overcame these troubles and in 1887 brought another Cambridge scientist, the brilliant young Charles Smart Roy, into the family. After his untimely death in 1897, she had a brief sojourn as a single woman and then married J. H. Batty (d. 1946), a wealthy businessman involved in African mining and trading ventures. Her preferences and his economic interests took Violet permanently away from quiet Cambridge. In succeeding years, Violet, the fashionable sophisticate, always seemed at ease in the international set to which she and her husband belonged. All of Clara's daughters were at least comfortable economically. All traveled more widely than their parents had. Only one, Rose, had children.[43]

Clara's sons were less uniformly prosperous than her daughters. Three of Clara's daughters-in-law, Ethel Brandreth Pilkington (m. 1890), Hilda Ashley Cooper (m. 1896), and Christobel Mary Barrow (m. 1895), entered the family through their marriages to sons who were medical men. Charles and Ethel lived in the north of England, where he was the medical officer of health in Salford; Hilda and Owen Paget moved with their family to western Australia. Alfred Meyrick Paget and his wife, Mary, also migrated there, after a period of medical missionary work in Tanganyika. These three women remain largely hidden from historical view.[44]

Clara's fourth daughter-in-law, Stella Salomons (d. 1939), was the daughter of Phillip Salomons and niece of Sir David Salomons, Bt., banker, barrister, and a leader of the London Jewish community. Both her parents died when she was young. In 1877 Stella married Clara's son (George) Edmund (1852–1929), who left medical training to become a stockbroker. This marriage formally linked the Pagets to the Anglo-Jewish elite, but it was an exceptional match and one that met with disapproval from both families.[45] Stella and Edmund lived in London, getting on adequately but never at the level of economic comfort that their respective families enjoyed.

Stella Salomons Paget had been, perhaps, courageous, perhaps foolhardy, to marry out of her faith, against the wishes of her guardian and in defiance of the obstacles placed in the young couple's path—most clearly her family's obstructionism in the negotiations over the marriage settlement. After the wedding she tried to circumvent her mother-in-law's hostility by writing charming letters to her new sisters-in-law—family news, communicated in violet ink, on flowered paper. The birth of her first child, Arthur, in the autumn of 1878, brought other reasons for firm character. Sister-in-law Rose wanted to visit in December, but Stella was cautious: "I shall be very glad to see you, provided you are quite well. You will think I am very particular," she continued, "but I will not let baby run any risk & erysipelas [from which Rose's little brother was suffering] is so very catching." She entirely disallowed a visit from Rose when her budget was too tight to allow for the hospitality of even a weekend visit.[46]

In London, where Catharine Paget was reigning queen, her cousin Elise Paget (c. 1844–89) was a lowly subject. Elise returned to England from Vienna in 1861 and lived with her maiden aunts in Pinner. Elise was a "poor relation" to her six cousins in Harewood Place. She lived quietly, pursuing her artistic interests. Her cousin Stephen thought she kept a "steady hold over herself." Behind the reserve she was "quick tempered, and sometimes showed it, flushing and speaking sharply." With age, she began to express herself more boldly, wearing more assertive clothing and exercising greater personal freedom. She rented a flat in London and traveled to the continent with friends.[47]

The Paget family's circle of associations began in Yarmouth but extended to London, Oxford, Cambridge, and other Victorian cities and towns. The family's associations encompassed diverse occupations, from businessmen and naturalists to physicians and surgeons, lawyers, university dons, parish priests, and bishops of the Church of England, as well as the worlds of art and music. To acquaint ourselves with the women's circles requires, perforce, some attention to the occupations and socioeconomic circumstances of the men in their families.

BUSINESS AND COMMERCIAL TIES

Yarmouth's elites were local professionals and businessmen—the shipowners, merchants, shipbuilders, brewers, bankers—who stood at the center of Yarmouth's economic life. The ranking family of the town was that of

Sir Edward Lacon, Bt., but the Lacons and their sort, with ties to Parliament, belonged to a regional and national elite. Betsey and Sam Paget had occasional contact with the Lacons but found their peers among the local notables of Yarmouth. Chief among these were the Turners, bankers in the town. Mary Palgrave (d. 1850) came from a Norfolk family and settled in Yarmouth at the time of her marriage to Dawson Turner (1775–1858) in 1796. Turner was a partner in Gurney's Bank and Sam's partner in the brewing business. He was also an art patron and a noted naturalist. Unlike Betsey Paget, Mary Turner was "a woman of genuine piety," as well as being "vivacious and intelligent." Mrs. Turner was a cosmopolitan woman, at home with Yarmouth folk and with visitors from London and the continent. Callers found her home a calm, well-organized place, with children attending to their appointed tasks. Mary worked hard, and she expected her family to do so too.[48]

Mary and Dawson had six daughters—Maria (1797–1872), Elizabeth (1799–1852), Mary Anne (1803–74), Harriet (1806–69), Hannah Sarah (1808–82), and Eleanor Jane (1811–95)—and two surviving sons. Spinster Mary Anne was remembered in her family as a charitable woman, dutiful, industrious, interested in local history and lore. The next generation praised "dear aunt Mary" (with more symmetry than illumination) for "counsels in which a natural love of wisdom was guided by the wisdom of love." Such praise signals Aunt Mary's affectionate relations with her nieces and nephews.[49]

Hannah Sarah Turner maintained her family's ties to business when she married Thomas Brightwen, the Yarmouth banker. She and Thomas remained in Norfolk all their married life. When Hannah died, the family "felt we had lost a very dear and bright life, for she eminently preserved her youthful brightness to the age of all but seventy-four." Hannah was noted for her bubbling enthusiasm.[50]

Another commercial link in the second generation came through Lydia North's eldest sister, Hannah. Hannah, a "thin and quiet and gentle and unselfish" sober young woman, had the potential for enjoying "love and interests and ventures . . . and freedom and laughter." But she married Richard Twining III, the London tea merchant. They lived in London with their daughters and sons, in comfortable economic circumstances. Richard was a sour, humorless man and, it seems, a domestic tyrant. Hannah bent under his harsh will and, in the end, seemed drained of life and any will of her own. Far more than Lydia, Hannah Twining displayed the passivity, dependency, and oppression that has been the presumed hallmark of Victorian ladies' personalities. But her passivity seems more the result of a battle lost than mere conformity to ladylike submission.[51]

Although prosperous business laid the foundations of the Paget family's life and many of their social connections, their associations in the second and third generations increasingly centered on science and religion, the professions, especially medicine, the church, and the universities.

NATURALIST, MEDICAL, AND SCIENTIFIC CIRCLES

In the course of the Victorian period, natural history became more formally identified with the sciences of anatomy, biology, and zoology, and with the profession of medicine. Through the Turners, the Paget men and women had a century-long link with natural history, and then with the biological sciences and medicine in England. Mary and Dawson Turner's eldest daughter, Maria Sarah, established the first link in the chain in 1815 when she married naturalist William Jackson Hooker (1785–1865). After a brief stay in Suffolk and twenty years in Glasgow, the Hookers moved to Kew in 1841, and he took up the post of the director of the Botanical Gardens there.[52]

The Pagets continued to be linked to the Hookers and to natural history through Maria's son, Sir Joseph Dalton Hooker (1817–1911), who succeeded his father at Kew in 1865. Joseph's first wife, Frances Harriet (d. 1874), was the daughter of another noted naturalist, the Reverend John Stevens Henslow. Also associated with the Hookers was Marianne North (1830–90), daughter of Frederick North, M.P. She shared their enthusiasm for natural history, and she traveled widely in pursuit of her interest in flowers and plants.[53]

Through the Hookers and others in the intricate medico-scientific network of the day, the Paget circle also included the Ormerods. Susan Mary (d. 1896), Georgiana (d. 1896), and Eleanor Ormerod (1828–1901) came from a Somersetshire family. An uncle and two brothers had studied at St. Bartholomew's (Bart's) Hospital, London, where James Paget also worked. The Ormerods' friendship with the Hookers led Eleanor and Georgiana to live near Kew from 1876 on and to enjoy the social and scientific companionship of Sir Joseph, Lady Hooker, and their circle. Family money allowed the two sisters to live comfortably in Kew and, after 1887, in a large house in St. Alban's. Susan Mary, who also remained single all her life, lived in Exeter amid the usual comforts of men and women of her class—silver, furniture, jewelry, good wines, and art work, as well as the financial security her family had accorded her.[54]

Georgiana seems to have been a shy woman. One acquaintance called her "a most lovable person. . . . the quiet support of her youngest sister," Eleanor. As a girl Eleanor was a prankster, "embarking," for example, "to navigate the horse pond" in a tub. As an adult she continued to be "the licensed jester to the family circle." Eleanor never lost her capacity for good humor. Her friends found her "witty" and "cheerful." In her seventies she continued to greet friends with bouncing step and ringing laughter. But she was not all joviality; she could also be "quietly determined," and she met difficulties with "coolness and power of action," in dealing, for example, with a rabid dog, or removing a crochet hook from her sister's hand, or uncovering a case of plagiarism and pursuing it.[55]

St. Bartholomew's Hospital was the link in another chain of connection, that to the Busk family. In 1843 Ellen Busk (b. 1816) married her first cousin George Busk (1807–86), a Bart's man, a practicing surgeon, and an acquaintance of James Paget. Busk wrote about biology, medicine, and anthropology and distinguished himself as a naturalist. He was elected fellow of the Royal Society in 1850. The Busks had four daughters, Jane (b. 1844), Ellen Martha (1846–89), Elinor (b. 1847), and Frances (b. 1849), and no sons. Their extended family included Rachel Harriette Busk (1831–1907) and Julia Clara Busk (1819–94), cousins of Ellen and George. Julia married William Pitt Byrne, a barrister and newspaper editor, first of the *Morning Post* and then of *The Times*. The Busks lived in London, and in the 1870s the Busks and the Pagets, both senior and junior generations, met socially in Harewood Place and at the many parties, musical evenings, and balls that shaped their leisure calendars.[56]

The Lubbocks represent another of the Paget family's links to natural history. Sir John Lubbock (1834–1913) was a banker, naturalist, archeologist, and member of Parliament. Lubbock's first wife was Ellen Frances Hordern (m. 1856, d. 1879), a well-connected clergyman's daughter. The Lubbocks had three sons and three daughters. The girls, Amy (1857–1929), Constance (Connie) (d. 1892), and Gertrude (d. 1934) often entertained Catharine and Mary Maud when the Pagets visited the Lubbocks at High Elms, in Kent. Lady Lubbock died when her daughters were young, and in 1884 Sir John married for a second time. His new bride was Alice Lane (d. 1947), daughter of Lt. Gen. Augustus Henry Lane Fox Pitt-Rivers; these two had five children. Alice's sister Agnes (d. 1926) married Sir George Grove, Bt., M.P.[57]

Connie was an expressive young woman, affectionate, generous, and given at times to hyperbole. When her widower father remarried, Connie told him that "I nearly rampaged down" to London "to see you." She surely defused the potential tension between a new wife and her grown stepdaughters when she said that "it is very dear of her [the new Lady Lubbock] to like me." Connie married Sydney Charles Buxton (1853–1934), sometime M.P. and civil servant (later the first Earl Buxton), in 1882. The couple had two sons and one daughter before Connie's short life ended in 1892, when she was in her early thirties.[58]

The relations between natural history, the biological sciences, and medicine were close. Medicine was the one profession easily open to men interested in natural history and lacking the independent means necessary to support science as a second, unpaid vocation.[59] Five of the Paget men practiced medicine, and thus many scientists as well as medical men were part of the family's circle. The marriages of Paget daughters to scientists reflect that propinquity. The major English centers of medicine and science were London, Oxford, and Cambridge, but the medico-scientific community was a national community at its highest levels, and the Pagets' associates were scattered everywhere.

One of the oldest of the Pagets' medical ties was that to the Acland family. It was a bond forged in the 1830s at St. Bartholomew's Hospital between James Paget and Henry Wentworth Acland (1815–1900). The association came to include their families and lasted into the twentieth century. Henry Wentworth (later Sir Henry) Acland was one of seven sons of Sir Thomas Acland (1787–1871), of an old gentry family, and Lady Acland (the former Lydia Elizabeth Hoare) (d. 1856). The family had ties to commercial life through Lydia's father, Henry Hoare (1787–1871), a banker and early Victorian evangelical. Henry's oldest brother, Sir Thomas Dyke Acland (1809–98), heir to the Acland estates, interested himself in agricultural chemistry and politics. He married the "deeply pious" Mary Mordaunt in 1841, and they had seven children. After Mary's death in 1851, her cousin Mary Erskine (d. 1892) cared for the children, and in 1856 she became the second Lady Acland. Mary Erskine Acland was also pious, but "not given to extremes" either of High Church or evangelical religion. Although she had been nearly an invalid in early life, her marriage to T. D. Acland at mid-life brought her new spirit and vigor. Thereafter she had energy to spare: she helped rear the children, managed the household, and helped her widower father-in-law manage his household as well.[60]

Henry Acland and James Paget met as students and continued to be colleagues and friends all their lives. Acland became Oxford's Regius Professor of Medicine in 1858 and practiced medicine in Oxford. Sarah Cotton (d. 1878), a clergyman's daughter, and Henry Acland married in 1846. They had seven sons and one daughter, Sarah Angelina (Angie) Acland (1849–1930). Angie never married and lived with her parents her whole life. After her mother's death, she played the role of hostess for her father in their house in Broad Street, Oxford, for the remainder of his life, while also pursuing interests of her own.[61]

The character of Sarah Cotton, Lady Acland, expressed itself most clearly in her relations with her family. Her husband, often ill, needed much of her attention, and the result tended to be Sarah's brusque indifference to-

why should we care?

ward her daughter Angie. Perhaps predictably, Angie as a girl seemed dependent and excessively interested in her parents' approval. She apparently suffered from weak health, a cause of much worry to her father. But her ill health itself required a certain independence in that she had to travel on her own to warmer climates; in the process she became more self-sufficient. However much she longed for parental approbation, she was nevertheless tough enough to accept criticism, even of her art work. She valued her friends and family and was sensitive to their feelings and personalities. Her religiosity, later in life, took the form of a childlike hope for "God's forgiveness for all my sins."[62]

The next generation of Aclands maintained their links with the landed gentry. Two of Angie's brothers married sisters, daughters of the Rt. Hon. W. H. Smith and his wife. Emily Anna Smith (d. 1942) married the eldest, William Alison Dyke Acland, in 1877, two years after her sister, Beatrice Danvers Smith, had wed Angie's youngest brother, Alfred. Eleanor Margaret Cropper (d. 1933), daughter of Charles James Cropper (1852–1924) of Ellergreen, Westmoreland, and the Hon. Edith Emily Holland, entered the growing Acland clan by her marriage in 1905 to Angie's cousin Sir Francis Dyke Acland (1874–1939). This couple had one daughter and three sons by 1914. As a little girl, Eleanor Cropper suffered fits of jealousy, especially at the arrival of a new baby in the family. In adulthood, friends saw her as a "splendid woman . . . radiating cheerful vigour and love of life, humorous, fearless, strong, [and] tender." Her energy and enthusiasm hid a darker set of views and feelings, especially her anger and bitterness at the child rearing that she had at the hands of a cruel nanny. She blamed her parents for the hurt, and she never forgot.[63]

Another of Angie's brothers linked the Acland family to London medical life and to another part of the Paget circle. In 1888 Theodore Dyke Acland, himself a physician, married Caroline (Carrie) Cameron Gull (d. 1929), daughter of Susan Anne, Lady Gull (d. 1894), and Sir William Withey Gull (1816–90), one of Queen Victoria's physicians and a colleague of James Paget. Carrie Gull was, from her girlhood, a friend of the Paget women in London. In all, the Acland connection glittered, graced as it was by many of the greater lights of Victorian artistic and intellectual society—Henry George Liddell, John Ruskin, George Richmond, and many other Oxford luminaries. At the same time, the Acland-Paget connection was one place where the old country gentry and the new urban gentry met and mixed. Other Oxford scientific associations include George John Romanes (1848–94), the zoologist, and his wife, the former Ethel Duncan (m. 1879, d. 1927) of Liverpool. The Romanes had three children.[64]

The Cambridge scientific network included Mary Humphry and her husband George Murray Humphry (1820–96), surgeon and professor of anatomy in the university, and the large and busy Stokes family. George Gabriel Stokes (1819–1903), mathematician and physicist, had migrated to Cambridge from Ireland, and the Stokeses and the Pagets socialized together in the 1870s and after. Margaret M'Nair Stokes (1832–1900), a cousin of the Cambridge Stokes and friend of the Aclands, interested herself in archeology. She was a tenderhearted woman but she could be sharp-tongued when provoked. Annoyed at the loquacity of some of her acquaintances, she criticized them and the prime minister at one blow by expressing the hope that they "not get Gladstonian and veil all truth in a fog of words."[65]

The Pagets' London orbit encompassed Eliza Parbury (d. 1879), who was a regular member of their social set, and Thomas Smith (1833–1909), a student and surgical assistant of James Paget at St. Bartholomew's Hospital. Smith, a frequent guest at the Paget lunch table, crossed paths with the Parbury family and their unmarried daughter at the parties and balls that were part of the London social season for these professional families. In 1862 Eliza married Tom (later Sir Thomas) Smith. The medical man John Marshall and his wife, the former Ellen Williams (1831–1919), had two daughters, Ellen Jeannette (1855–1935) and Ada Blanche (1856–1936), and two sons. Professional ties brought the two families together, but competition often marred their social relations.[66]

The long reach of scientific connections linked London and Glasgow in the persons of the Thomson family. Margaret Crum (d. 1870) was the daughter of a Glasgow manufacturer, and she married her second cousin, William Thomson (1824–1907), in 1852. He was the fourth of seven children, the offspring of Margaret Gardner and James Thomson, professor of mathematics at Glasgow University. Two notable women of Thomson's family were his eldest sister Elizabeth (b. 1818), who married cleric David King, and Thomson's maternal aunt Agnes Gardner Gall, who became housekeeper to the Thomson family after William's mother's death in 1830. William Thomson held the post of professor of natural history at Glasgow from 1846 to 1899 and earned distinction as a physicist. He won a baronetcy and in 1892 a peerage (as Lord Kelvin), but Margaret died before that date. Thomson's second wife was Frances (Fanny) Blandy (m. 1874).[67]

Many of the Pagets' scientific and medical associates need little introduction—the geologists Lyell and Prestwich and their families, the Listers, Joseph and Agnes (d. 1893) (she the daughter of the illustrious surgeon James Syme of Edinburgh), and Henrietta (Netty) and T. H. Huxley. Other families of the medical and surgical elite in the Pagets' circle were the William Lawrences, Sir George and Lady Burrows (she a godmother to one of Lydia's sons) and their daughter Rose Burrows, who married medical man Alfred Willett.[68]

THE CHURCH OF ENGLAND "CONNEXION"

Throughout the century, from Yarmouth to Oxford and Canterbury, the Pagets had extensive ties to the Church of England. Those in the first and second generations were mainly modest ones. The Penrice family were Yarmouth gentlefolk with several clerical sons. In another Yarmouth family, two of Mary and Dawson Turner's daughters married clergymen: Harriet wed the Reverend John Gunn (d. 1890), rector of Smallborough-cum-Irstead, Norfolk, and Eleanor (Ellen) married the Reverend William Jacobson (1803–84), vice principal of Magdalen Hall, Oxford, and eventually bishop of Chester.[69]

Betsey's daughter-in-law Lydia North Paget brought ties to clergymen in London. Her father, the Reverend Henry North, was a schoolmaster and domestic chaplain to the duke of Kent. Two of Lydia's brothers, Isaac and Jacob, were also clergymen of modest achievements. Both were married, Isaac first to Eliza Bourchier in 1842 and later to "Aunt Leila." Jacob and his wife, Harriet, lived in Brighton. Both couples had children.[70]

Lydia North's piety may mark her as a cleric's daughter. Another of the Reverend North's daughters, Sarah, is less obviously the offspring of a sober religious household. Sarah North enjoyed flirting with James, her sister's suitor, later husband. Sarah aged into dowdy spinsterhood and made her home in the seaside town of Dawlish, Devonshire. She lived frugally in an apartment above a shop, presumably supported by an inheritance from her parents. She visited James and Lydia in London frequently and, perhaps because of the deprivations of life on a small budget in a small town, ate greedily and consumed, equally hungrily, the pleasures of London social life in Harewood Place. The flirtatiousness of her youth survived into her middle years.[71]

The other North sister, Mary, offers an even more striking example of departure from the traditional idea of the clergyman's daughter. The wife of the sculptor John Graham Lough (1806–76), Mary was a full-blooded woman, enjoying what life had to offer including "lots of diamond rings" on her fingers and a taste for wine at dinner that went beyond what her (perhaps priggish) young nephew thought proper for a woman of fifty. Young Stephen found her "selfish, vulgar, ill-tempered, fat, and quite strangely ugly. She . . . looked as if she drank: and she certainly seemed to enjoy dinner and wine rather too evidently." She had, he said, "shaky, fat, unrefined hands,"

and "she talked either dull commonplaces or angry gossip: she had griev-
ances." She often complained "that 'Johnnie's' genius was neglected and not
appreciated." But Stephen insisted that "the plain fact is that she spoiled
his prospects by her quarrelsome, gossiping tongue."[72] Perhaps this assess-
ment of Aunt Mary is overdrawn, sharpened in Stephen's mind by contrast
with what he thought (mistakenly) to be his mother's delicacy and meekness
of personality. Stripped of Stephen's palpable dislike for his aunt, the description presents us with a woman of the flesh, of indulgence, as well as
of sharp tongue and open anger—a most un-Victorian Victorian woman.

Lydia North's family friends included some who, although not clergymen,
were active in Church of England affairs, in particular the Woods—Emily
Charlotte (1840–1904) and her brother Charles Lindley Wood, the second
viscount Halifax (1839–1934). According to J. G. Lockhart, her brother's colleague and biographer, Emily was "clever" and "capable," but "spoilt" as
a child by her father. As a result she could, under stress, be "difficult, exact-
ing and even dictatorial in her dealings with strangers." At the same time
she was also competent and courageous. In 1863 she married Hugo Francis
Meynell Ingram (1820–71), from an old gentry family. He died only eight
years later.[73]

James Paget's tie to St. Bartholomew's Hospital in the 1830s may have
been the source of another clerical link, that to Francis Thomas McDougall
(1817–86), also a medical student, and Harriette Bunyon (d. 1886), his future
wife. By the 1840s Frank McDougall and James Paget were both betrothed
and planning to marry. In her youth Harriette Bunyon earned no more than
the standard epithets reserved for women of her rank: "A pretty fair-haired
creature, . . . a picture of refinement." She was also known for her "vivacity," her "singularly amiable temper," and "her sweetness of disposition."
In old age she continued to be known for her "cheerful kindliness" to all
she met. With Harriette's full support, McDougall opted for a missionary
career so that, while Lydia and James stayed in London for the rest of their
lives, the McDougalls ventured far afield to Borneo. Harriette's life as a
missionary's wife called forth her "courage and character." And maturity
made Harriette "a person who formed independent opinions on intellectual
and religious subjects, sometimes arriving," her biographer reported tact-
fully, "at different conclusions even from her husband." When that happened, the couple "agreed to differ."[74] Harriette was, despite appearances,
no shy violet.

Henrietta Rowland (1851–1936) and her husband, Canon Samuel Barnett,
belonged to the Paget circle in the third generation by their involvement,
like many men and women of the day, in work among the poor of East London in the 1860s and after. Mrs. Barnett's social background stood in marked

contrast to the environment of her work among the poor. She was brought up in "a luxurious home," and she enjoyed "hunting and gardening and out-door life."[75]

Henrietta Rowland was also a serious, socially committed Christian, but she was not meek. She shared the same sort of forthrightness that we have seen in all three generations of these women. She worked with social re-former Octavia Hill and admired her immensely, calling her "the heroine of my life." But Rowland's no-nonsense approach left little room for senti-mentality. When Miss Hill died, Henrietta was "annoyed" by the obituaries that "credited her with the commonplace virtues of kindness and unselfish-ness and gentleness." Rowland praised Hill in other terms: "She was strong-willed . . . but the strong will was never used for self. She was . . . often dictatorial in manner but humble . . . before those she loved. . . . She had little sense of her own humour, and none at all of other people's."[76] Rowland rejected conventional praise in favor of stronger truths about her friend; she also revealed her own character in the process.

Henrietta Rowland's outspoken candor was not reserved for women friends. When the Reverend Samuel Barnett proposed marriage to her, she was not enthusiastic. At twenty-seven, he had "a bald head, and shaggy beard," she observed, "far removed from a girlish idea of a lover." Worse yet, "he dressed very badly." His hat didn't fit, his gloves were too large, and he wore a flannel shirt buttoned to a white collar and "a black silk ready-made tie." Her critique did not stop there. His personality also gave her pause: he was "both shy and aggressive, defects which he covered by a fre-quent nervous laugh." He often appeared "servile," and, with respect to money, he was "punctilious almost to parsimony." Henrietta Rowland man-aged to find an admirable man behind Samuel Barnett's unfortunate facade, and she married him, but she never lost her ability to tell the truth as bluntly as she saw it.[77]

Other members of the Anglican establishment in the Paget circle included the Tait family. Catharine Spooner (1819–78) came from a Warwickshire clerical family. In 1843 she married Archibald Campbell Tait (1811–82), a clergyman who held appointments as headmaster of Rugby School, dean of Carlisle, bishop of London, and archbishop of Canterbury. Catharine Tait's friends described her in conventional Victorian-lady phrases. She had "sweet looks," they said, a "buoyant, cheerful nature," "tact," adaptability, a love of home, and a deep Christian faith. But the more Victorian observers say, the more they reveal. Catharine Tait had a "warm intelligence," the "enthusiasm of a school-boy," "perseverance," and an "indomitable will."[78]

The Taits had four children who survived to adulthood: Lucy (b. 1856), Edith (1859–1936), Agnes (1860–88), and Craufurd (1849–78). Edith often spent time with Catharine Paget in London, and she visited the Cambridge Pagets at their summer house in North Wales. Both Agnes and Edith were at ease in their elite world, playing games, for example, with the choristers at Windsor Castle. Agnes was known for her "Christian common sense" and her "warmth of sympathy." She died suddenly at age twenty-eight, two months after the birth of her first child. Friends were left with the glowing memory of her as "vivacious, brilliant, beautiful, sparkling, in quite indescribable ways."[79]

Perhaps feeling incapable of such beauty and brilliance, Edith sought to be warmhearted and good. Her fiancé, Randall Davidson, her father's domestic chaplain, admired her for her virtue: "she is . . . so absolutely ready to do what is . . . *right*." But he saw the possible difficulties of such goodness. "I positively *dread* her unselfishness after our marriage. One will need," he told a friend, "to be very watchful to prevent her from giving way over-much." Davidson was a sound psychological observer, aware that excessive self-sacrifice could lead to domestic unhappiness. Perhaps Edith's compliance was a way of winning the attention of a busy young clergyman, one whom she found "cool and Scotch and right and always to the point." By contrast, Edith seemed vulnerable, in need of special "cherishing." Edith married Randall Davidson in 1878, had a long married life with him, and watched him fulfill his early promise of ecclesiastical success. She eventually could claim close relations to two archbishops of Canterbury, for her husband achieved that position in 1903.[80]

With age Edith grew in self-assurance. Associates found the Davidson home a "welcoming one." Bishop Francis Paget considered it not only the "busiest" but the "kindest of homes"—filled with work and full of sympathy for others, but also marked by a willingness to see the "pleasant and humorous" side of life. Edith was known for her egalitarian kindness to everyone around her, "be it duchess or curate's wife, or the youngest kitchen maid."[81]

Among the many other episcopal families in the Pagets' circle by the end of the century were the Bensons, the Creightons, the Talbots, and the Hensons. The Creightons and the Bensons (originally of Birmingham) had had a nineteenth-century pattern of occupational mobility similar to that of the Pagets—from business into the ranks of the Church of England and the universities. Mandell Creighton (1843–1901) came from Carlisle, where his father was a businessman. Louise von Glehn (1850–1930) came from a merchant's family as well. The two married in 1871 and had four daughters and three sons. The Paget and Benson families had a common tie of friendship with Charles Kingsley, but otherwise their associations were primarily professional. The Benson women included Archbishop Benson's sister Ada (1840–82) and his wife, Mary Sidgwick Benson (m. 1859), daughter of the late Reverend William Sidgwick and Mary Sidgwick. Mary's brother was Henry Sidgwick (1838–1900), a Cambridge philosopher and husband of Eleanor Mildred Balfour (1845–1936). The Bensons' daughters, Mary Eleanor (Nelly) (1863–90) and Margaret (Maggie) (1865–1916), also form part of the larger circle in which the Paget women moved. Both daughters were intelligent, but their personalities differed markedly. Nelly was "a quick, active, resourceful and adventurous girl, fond of games, sociable, naturally inclined to take the lead." Her younger sister Maggie was by contrast usually "serene" and "amiable," a person "who took her own time about everything." But she could also be "remorseful," even if she had done no wrong.[82]

The Reverend E. S. Talbot (1844–1934) was warden of Keble College, later a parish priest in Leeds, and eventually bishop of Winchester; his well-born and lively wife was the hon. Lavinia Lyttelton. Even with the serious business of being a clergyman's wife, Lavinia found room for laughter and sometimes "a charming spice of *diablerie.*" When the women in their Leeds parish gave her a gift of a set of diamonds, she responded mischievously: "O diamonds, diamonds," she exclaimed. "I think I could sell my soul for diamonds." Mrs. Talbot teased the sober ladies who had presented her with such a gift. The Talbots had two sons and two daughters. Another cleric's wife of this generation was Mrs. Herbert Hensley Henson, born Isabella Dennistoun, of an old Scottish family. She married the controversial Reverend Henson in 1902 when he was a missioner in the East End of London. He went from there to the deanship of Durham Cathedral and then to the bishopric of Hereford.[83]

Mary Sumner (1828–1921), daughter of the Manchester banker Thomas Heywood, married George Sumner (1824–1909) in 1848. He came from a distinguished clerical family that included an archbishop of Canterbury and a bishop of Winchester, and he was himself suffragan to the bishop of Winchester from 1888 until 1908. Through the marriage of one of the Sumner children, the family was associated with the Benson family, too. The James Frasers of Manchester, he the bishop from 1870 to 1885, also form part of the ecclesiastical circle.[84]

THEOLOGY AND SCHOLARSHIP

The clergymen discussed thus far include those who worked at the parish level, many of whom rose to church administration at the highest ranks. It is useful to distinguish parish work and church administration from the other direction that a clergyman's career could take, the one that led to university teaching and scholarship. Early in the century, when holy orders were a requirement for university posts, dons were clergymen as well as scholars;

they taught Biblical as well as classical languages, and theology as well as mathematics. Later, with the abandonment of the rule that university dons be clerics and with the growth of scholarship, laymen began to hold posts in classics and the sciences, and the university cleric more often specialized in theology or biblical scholarship.[85]

Clara Fardell Paget, as the daughter and granddaughter of Ely clergymen and wife of a Cambridge don, had associations with the Church of England centered in the Cambridge community. Among them was the Reverend Edward Harold Browne (1811–91). Browne's career illustrates the way clerical careers took a man into the school and the university, as well as the parish and the diocese: he was vice principal of St. David's College, Lampeter, and Norrisian Professor of Theology in Cambridge. But before that he had been a parish priest and afterward he became bishop of Ely. Browne married Elizabeth Carlyon, she the daughter of a Truro physician, in 1840. He and George Paget were teaching at Cambridge in the 1850s. By 1860 the families were well enough acquainted that Clara and George could ask Elizabeth Browne to serve as godmother to their newborn daughter Rose. Such a commitment tied the two families firmly together, and the next generation of Brownes and Pagets visited in Cambridge, London, Ely, and later at Farnham Castle, after Elizabeth's husband moved from Ely to the see of Winchester.[86]

Clara and George Paget were also on close terms with the Kingsleys, another family that demonstrates that clergymen were often something other than parish priests or theologians. The Reverend Charles Kingsley (1819–75), sometime rector of Eversley, was also professor of modern history at Cambridge, and a novelist besides. He married Frances (Fannie) Eliza Grenfell in 1844. Charles and Fannie often visited the Pagets' summer home in North Wales. The Kingsleys had four children, two sons and two daughters—Rose Georgina and Mary St. Leger (1852–1931). In 1897 Mary wed a clergyman, the Reverend William Harrison, rector of Clovelly, and they lived in that parish for the rest of their lives.[87]

Charles Kingsley's brother, George Henry Kingsley (1827–92), was a physician, traveler, and writer. His wife, the former Mary Bailey, was an innkeeper's daughter—the only woman of this study whose origins were plebeian. The couple had one daughter and one son. In 1884 the Kingsleys moved to Cambridge and their daughter Mary Henrietta (1862–1900) became a special friend of Violet Paget. A father much given to traveling and ill-tempered when at home and a mother often ill—both parents disrupted Mary's life. Perhaps as a reaction, Mary was prone to childhood mischief; as an adult, she became a witty conversationalist and correspondent, occasionally with an "acid" edge.[88]

Clara Paget's circle included many other wives of clergymen-dons. Fanny Dyson Holland Hort (1828–1925), her husband Fenton John Anthony Hort (1828–92), and their children moved to St. Peter's Terrace, Cambridge, in 1872 and became Clara Paget's near neighbors. Hort was a theologian, scholar, and university don. The Westcotts lived only "a few yards away" from the Horts and the Pagets. Mrs. Westcott, formerly Sarah Louisa Mary Whithard (d. 1901), was a Bristol girl who had met Brooke Foss Westcott through her brother, a schoolmate of Westcott's. The Westcotts had three daughters and seven sons, of whom six were clergymen. Hort and Westcott collaborated on an edition of the text of the New Testament which they published in 1881.[89]

Clara and her daughters had neighborly relations with members of the Phillips-Pilkington connection. Emily Frances Pilkington, a descendant of the Anglo-Irish gentry, became the wife of the Reverend George Phillips, a mathematical and biblical scholar who, by the 1870s, was the president of Queen's College, Cambridge. Mrs. Phillips's brother was a barrister in Dublin, and her nieces, Charity Mary (1859–1911) and Emily Georgina Catharine (1861–1954) Pilkington (known familiarly as Cherrie and Emmie), often came from their home in Tore, Co. Westmeath, to visit their aunt in Cambridge. Their brother Henry matriculated in 1876, and they had yet another reason to visit the university town. While in Cambridge they made friends with Clara's adolescent daughters, particularly Rose and Violet, and the girls shared walks, lectures, and confidences, and they made playful puns on their friends' names. Rose became "Bud" and was only later admitted to be a "full-blown Rose." In 1894 Cherrie married Harry Reichel (d. 1931), later the principal of the University College of North Wales, and lived thereafter in Wales. Eight years later Emmie married the Reverend Henry Nathaniel Joly, rector of Athlone. Neither couple had children.[90]

The Pagets' associations with members of Oxford theological and ecclesiastical circles were fixed most firmly by Francis (Frank) Paget, Christ Church don, professor, college dean, and bishop. His marriage to Helen Church, daughter of the dean of St. Paul's, London, linked Oxford and London church elites. As both Francis and his brother Henry Luke Paget moved toward high university and ecclesiastical preferment, bishops and theologians as well as professors and dons continued to be common features of the Pagets' social landscape.

College heads and professors aside, Oxbridge dons were forbidden to marry for much of the century. Bachelor clergymen-tutors (like Charles Dodgson at Christ Church) were the norm for most of the century, and the mothers, sisters, and female cousins of these men (rather than wives) formed most of the female society in university towns. William Forbes Skene (b.

1809), for example, was a Christ Church don, and his sister Felicia Mary Frances (1821–99) spent her life in the environs of the university and the town of Oxford. She was a deeply religious woman, thoughtful about theology and personal piety. Known to her friends as "Fifie," she was not above a certain archness of style with her friends; to one, for example, whose manuscript she was reading, she called herself "your humble Editor." She could also be blunt and contemptuous. The "Editor of a Periodical which occupies itself with the welfare of the human race," she observed with sarcasm, "has sent me letters & papers to comment upon;" she found these papers "full of the most glaring fallacies & rather trying to [my] temper."[91] The married couples in the Christ Church circle included Professor and Mrs. E. B. Pusey and Dean Henry George Liddell and his wife. In the late 1870s and early 1880s, when dons were permitted to marry, the social face of Oxford began to change as brides and wives and children became a more important part of the Oxford scene.[92]

Among Frank and Helen Paget's Oxford associates in those last decades of the nineteenth century were the Moberlys. Robert Campbell Moberly (1845–1903) was the son of George Moberly (1803–85), bishop of Salisbury. Robert Moberly and Frank Paget both contributed to *Lux Mundi* in 1889, and Robert succeeded Frank as Regius Professor of Pastoral Theology in 1892. Moberly's wife, the former Alice Sidney Hamilton (d. 1939), was related to another bishop of Salisbury, Walter Kerr Hamilton. The wider Moberly clan included Robert's sister Charlotte Anne Elizabeth (1846–1937), who spent much of her adult life in Oxford, and their cousin Lucy Gertrude Moberly (1860–1931). Lucy's parents were Henry Moberly (1822–1907), a cleric and schoolmaster, and Lucy Chase (m. 1860), the daughter of an officer in the Indian Army.[93]

Mary Evans Moule (b. 1801), the daughter of a city merchant, was an active woman, one of "decided character." Her son, the Reverend H. C. G. Moule (1841–1920), took a special interest in the women's charity activities that Elma Paget and others were fostering. He and his wife, Harriot Mary Elliott Moule (1844–1915), a clergyman's daughter, had two daughters of their own. They spent their lives first in Cambridge, where he was the head of Ridley Hall, and then in Durham, where he was bishop.[94]

A MISCELLANY OF CONNEXIONS

The Lewin-Grote connection bridged the worlds of business, *belles lettres*, and academe in the course of the nineteenth century. Harriet Lewin's father was in the Indian civil service, and her mother was a descendant of a military and gentry family. Harriet (1792–1878) married George Grote (1794–1871) in 1819, thereby allying herself with a family of merchants and bankers. George Grote's early life in the family banking firm gave way to studies of political economy and history and led eventually to Parliament and the vice-chancellorship of London University, which he had helped to create.[95]

Harriet's mother-in-law, Selina Packwell Grote, was the daughter of a cleric, and her religiosity, far from making the Grote household a haven, cast a pall on the family. Her "extreme Calvinistic tenets indisposed her to receive visitors . . . except such as reflected her own strong religious sentiments." She expressed "such repugnance" toward her husband's guests that he found it almost impossible to entertain at home. The result, predictably enough, was alienation between husband and wife. Harriet Grote's reaction to her mother-in-law reveals her own capacity for censoriousness: "dulness and vapidity" ruled the Grote house, she thought, and the atmosphere was "so positively disheartening" as to "quench every spark of mental activity and ambition."[96] The rigidity of the mother-in-law found an answer in the hostility of the daughter-in-law.

Harriet was no more generous when assessing her own mother. Mary Hale Lewin had married very young, and the result, in Harriet's view, was a "totally undeveloped character . . . to whom as with most 'fond mothers,' her younger babes were dolls to play with, but her growing children never companions to take interest in." Harriet described herself in this environment as a child "full of capacity and talents, and of a loving, gay temperament, which rose above all suffering." I "cheered my comrades to mirth and enterprize." Harriet kept this temperament into young adulthood; she continued to be "high-spirited, . . . beautiful and enthusiastic, . . . 'up to everything'—playing, singing, dancing . . . —no less than joking, quizzing, mimicking." By middle life she was a formidable woman, a friend recalled. She had "a grand and haughty manner, tinctured with formality. . . . a calm and proud certainty of power, and sense of self-dependence." At the same time she had "a heart of the warmest and largest sympathies." Indeed, people of all sorts came to trust her and "hearts were bared before her, with the certainty of being kindly understood and wisely counselled. . . . You feared her," a friend said, "till you loved her."[97]

The Pagets' academic circle late in the century began to include more of those who, like Grote, were neither clerics nor theologians—the new brand of university don whose academic specialty might be astronomy, or Greek, or history. Arthur Lionel Smith (1850–1924) and his wife, Mary Florence Baird (b. c. 1855, m. 1879), represent this new sort of career. She came from minor landed gentry. They settled in Oxford where he taught history and, after the First World War, became master of Balliol. Other Oxford academic couples included Mr. and Mrs. J. R. Green, friends, too, of the Creightons and Mary Kingsley. Alice Stopford Green (1848–1929), daughter of the arch-deacon of Meath, married John Richard Green (1837–83) in 1877. He was the son of an Oxford tailor. Green took holy orders but left the clerical life to devote full time to writing history.[98]

The Pagets and their friends had also planted themselves in another major Victorian profession—the law. The eldest of Dawson and Mary Turner's daughters, Elizabeth, married a young barrister, Francis Palgrave (1788–1861). Elizabeth was a woman of "remarkable culture and brilliancy of mind," the most talented of the Turner daughters. She expressed her sense of superiority in her tendency to be "quick and imperious and some-times arrogant" in her dealings with both friends and family. She "frequently complained," for example, of her son's "childishness and love of play." Per-haps this came of the "high standard to which, as an exceptionally gifted and clever woman, she expected her children to attain." The Palgraves were "eminently pious," and their religiosity was "brought forward . . . to bear upon the occupations and amusements of their children." Elizabeth Turner Palgrave has all the appearance of a domineering, imperious, demanding, and humorless woman. She and Francis made their lives in London, where he became deputy keeper of the Public Record Office, earned a knighthood, and distinguished himself as a scholar.[99]

Lydia and James Paget counted among their associates Arthur Cohen (1830–1914), Q.C. and privy counsellor, a well-connected Jewish barrister, his wife, Emmeline Micholls (formerly of Manchester) (d. 1888), and their daughter Lucy (b. 1861). The Cohens' circle included others of the Pagets' friends—Constance and Sydney Buxton, Elma Katie Hoare's parents, and the Pagets' eldest son, John. John Paget, the only barrister in the Paget fam-ily, admired Arthur Cohen, particularly on account of his legal scholarship, and he dedicated his book on banking law to Cohen. John married Julia Norrie Moke (1864–1926), whose brother George E. Moke was also a barris-ter. The house in Harewood Place received visits from other legal families: Hugh Pollock (1859–1944), whose father was the eminent surgeon George David Pollock, Sir Richard (1805–82) and Lady Malins, and Sir William (1814–73) and Lady Bovill (she the former Maria Bolton of Blackheath). Clara Paget's barrister brother Sir (Thomas) George Fardell (1833–1917) married Letitia Oldfield (d. 1905), daughter of an Indian civil service family, and practiced law, first in the north of England and then in London. The Fardells had four children.[100]

Only rarely did the men of this upper-middle-class circle take up school teaching. The exceptions are Lydia's father, the Reverend Henry North, the bachelor cleric Alfred Tolver Paget, who taught mathematics at Shrewsbury School, and Dawson William Turner (1815–85). Turner had his own school in Liverpool, and he and his wife (formerly Ophelia Dixon, m. 1846, d. 1896) visited frequently in Harewood Place: the ties to Great Yarmouth survived to the twentieth century.[101]

The Victorian art world may often have partaken of the bohemian rather than the respectable or the genteel. Nevertheless, some members of the Paget circle did involve themselves in the world of the visual and literary arts, whether as creators, collectors, or critics. In the first generation we find the most self-conscious patrons of the arts in Great Yarmouth, in the persons of Dawson Turner and Samuel Paget. In both families, wives and children were also involved in the arts. Among the creative artists were novelists Charles Kingsley and Henry Kingsley, and Elizabeth and Francis Palgrave's son Francis Turner Palgrave (1824–97), who was a poet and art critic. F. T. Palgrave was married to Cecil Milnes Gaskell (d. 1890), the daughter of J. Milnes Gaskell, M. P., and they had four daughters and one son. Lydia North's sister Mary was married to the sculptor John Lough. His best known works were the lions in Trafalgar Square. Sir John Stainer (1840–1901), composer and organist of St. Paul's Cathedral, his wife, and their daughter Eliza Cecilia Stainer (d. 1937) were also a part of the Pagets' London circle in the latter half of the century. Among critics of the arts was Sir George Grove (1820–1900), editor of *Macmillan's Magazine* and *The Dictionary of Music and Musicians*. Lady Grove was the former Harriet Bradley, daughter of a clergyman; the couple married in 1851.[102]

To summarize this socioeconomic and personal profile of the women of this study and their male relatives: the first generation of Pagets and their friends belonged to the commercial elite of Great Yarmouth. They associated with the families of naturalists and clergymen. Some sons of the second and most of the third generation were educated in public schools and Oxbridge and then entered the Victorian professions—medicine, the Church, law, the university. They did not aspire to join the ranks of county society; they belonged to the urban upper-middle class, or what might better be called the "new urban gentry," metropolitan professionals who became the new gentlefolk of industrial society. Their material circumstances varied, from the relative narrowness of a Dawlish spinster's resources to the prosperity of a successful medical man or the comfort of inherited wealth. They all had servants—some had only two or three, others had reasonably large household staffs. Their specific wealth matters less than their shared culture as gentlefolk.[103]

Some of the women came from families that had experienced social mobility, particularly from the ranks of business into the professions. At the other extreme, the line separating the professional classes and the aristocracy was not always a clean one. Few among the Pagets' friends belonged to the landed gentry, but marriages and other sorts of alliances between the gentry and the urban professional classes were not uncommon. Along with individual mobility, some families benefited from the growing wealth and national visibility of, for example, medicine, law, and (for much of the century) the Church of England. There were very few military men, bureaucrats, government officials, or politicians in this circle before 1914.

The social world these women occupied varied somewhat from country to city, but there were some common features that all three generations shared. Theirs was the world of high culture, partaking in every generation of the visual, musical, and literary arts of their time. It was, finally, an actively sociable world—with teas, parties, dinners, balls, and other forums for entertainment and connection.

The Paget women and their friends were in every way conventional ladies and, in their very ordinariness, seem typical of the Victorian upper-middle class. Most of them married and bore children, but whether married or single, none had what we today would call a career. Very few had any connection with female suffrage campaigns or women's rights. Most were Anglican and their religious activities ranged from the occasional to the extensive. Their interests and pursuits were normal activities for nineteenth-century ladies of their status—painting, sketching, needlework, and morning calls. They engaged in charitable activities but few carried social reform into the political arena. Some wrote and published, but the subjects were always those suitable for a lady's pen. They were, in short, the entirely predictable wives and daughters of the new urban gentry.

When looking at the Victorian lady's personality and temperament, we might have expected to find a religious woman, a peacemaker, a comforter, and a submissive woman—submissive to father, perhaps to brothers, certainly to husband. Some of these women certainly had such characteristics. They conformed to the norms of admirable female behavior when propriety demanded, and they won praise for their warmth, sympathy, kindness, and piety. But the personalities of the Victorian women discussed here show that there is no single reality of what a lady was. They displayed a wide variety of personalities and characters.

Integral to any notion of Victorian ladyhood is the idea of piety. For some Victorian women this merely meant regular religious observance. For others it meant Christian devotion and character. For still others piety involved a recognition of sinfulness and a continuing (often losing) struggle against it. That would scarcely be new in the annals of Christianity, but it puts Victorian ladies in the human struggle rather than above it. Many of us continue to think of piety as a form of priggishness or a sign that Victorian women were "taking themselves too seriously." Certainly Victorian girls (like young people of any era) were capable of sober self-absorption, but they were also capable of pleasure, pranks, and play. Their religion was not an alternative to lightheartedness. Christianity and the Church of England offered, instead, an ordering principle of life, a guide to the boundaries of good behavior in both sacred and secular terms—a guide to doing and being good.

What also emerges from an exploration of this circle of women is the women's development as they matured. Without the experience of boarding school to hasten the process of breaking away from parents and finding some independence, many did not develop the gloss of self-assurance and independence that school boys affected, at least, by the age of eighteen or nineteen. But by their mid-twenties, these gentlewomen often had wide social experience. They were meeting dignitaries of church and state, Oxford and Cambridge professors and dons, illustrious writers, and a host of other Victorian luminaries. They learned to meet these men and women with calm self-assurance, a feature notable by the time they married and began their families. By middle age many were commanding figures, managing households and involving themselves in their communities. Sometimes that command was wielded gracefully, sometimes not, and angry looks and remarks could follow the woman who trod on the toes of her associates in the process of getting things done. But many kept on treading on toes.

Some Victorian ladies were modest and shy, others robust, extroverted, even aggressive, some self-assured, some uncertain, some warm and loving, some hostile and angry. Diversity—not uniform submissiveness—is the hallmark of the Victorian upper-middle-class women of this study. More strikingly, the varieties of women's personalities, their strengths, their assertiveness, even their nastiness, requires that we relegate the myth of the demure Victorian gentlewoman to the ash-heap. In the end the learning, the life experiences, and the work of this circle of gentlewomen—the subjects of the rest of this book—all show that ladies were eager participants, not observers on the sidelines, in the life and achievements of the Victorian age.

contradicting claims

CHAPTER TWO

Ladies Learning: The Education of Victorian Gentlewomen

In George Gissing's bitter novel of love, marriage, and money, *In the Year of Jubilee,* he describes young Nancy Lord: she "deemed herself a highly educated young woman,—'cultured' was the word she would have used." But Nancy knew little French, no German, no classical languages, and little geography. She was badly read and pretended to higher culture than she really possessed. Her education is the very model of what we have long thought of as "middle-class female education" in Victorian England. But Nancy was no gentlewoman. Her father had "a small business in Camberwell." He was "a dealer in pianos . . . , a respectable business," but one that left Nancy "haunted by an uneasy sense of doubtfulness as to her social position." She "dressed and talked rather above her station," one young gentleman judged, "but so, now-a-days, did every daughter of petty tradesfolk." In fact, Nancy Lord represents "a type": "a sample of the pretentious half-educated class" who were "only just above [the rank of] wage-earners."[1] Such examples as this have, even as fiction, reinforced the long-held notion that the education of "middle-class" girls and women was typically trivial, shallow, superficial—designed to impress the bachelor in search of a wife, but fundamentally without content and without value.[2]

It is, of course, possible to find Victorian gentlewomen with education apparently little better than Nancy Lord's. Mary Baird's education was of a patchwork nature, with an inattentive mother, a variety of governesses, and a smattering of school. Only worse was her own attitude toward education: she was happy to throw her "lessons . . . to the winds" when the alternative was caring for a new baby sister. But Baird candidly (and repeatedly) admitted that she was "never an industrious pupil." She considered the gaps in her education "deficiencies" and acknowledged the superior and more conventional education of her sisters. They wanted to be "educated" and worked hard at their studies.[3] Mary Baird's very apologies and explanations point to the norm of education for girls of her class: it was regular, it was serious, and it mattered.

Fenton John Anthony Hort, professor of divinity at Cambridge from 1878, and father of two daughters, offers a perspective on women's education more representative of the upper-middle class. Hort, who considered himself a "stiffish Tory," confided to a female acquaintance the essence of his ideas on women's education: "My own impression is that the helpless charmer theory [of female education and character] finds favour with very few men except the supremely silly." Hort thought that some men, to avoid criticism, said in public what they thought other men wanted to hear. But "I doubt," he added, "whether even *Saturday Reviewers* believe a quarter of their own rubbish" about women's education. In fact, Hort insisted, "men with the least stuff in them almost invariably hate" merely "decoratively prepared" women.[4] While showy and shallow education may have been the fate of the daughters of upwardly mobile tradesmen, it was not the standard of the upper-middle class. The education of the Paget women and their friends suggests that a fine education, whether formally or informally obtained, was part of the cultural equipage of the new urban gentry of both sexes.

The Victorian period is famous for the rise of schooling: the reform of boys' public schools, the introduction of public education for the masses, and the appearance of a greater number and variety of educational institutions for girls and young women, from boarding school to university. Few of these catered to upper-middle-class girls. Most were schools for daughters of the new middle class, the arrivistes of the booming Victorian economy. The women of the aristocracy and of the landed gentry continued to receive their education at home. The daughters of the new urban gentry followed, in large measure, this model. This chapter will explore the nature of that education and assess, where possible, its quality.

THE LOCATION AND PERSONNEL OF LADIES' EDUCATION

The locus of Victorian upper-middle-class female education was the home. There the Paget women and their friends learned the basics of reading, writing, and arithmetic. Specific details are often lacking. For the first generation, for example, we know only that Betsey was "well-educated" and "very accomplished"; there is no clue about how or where. We have glimpses of her daughter Kate in Great Yarmouth in 1839 having lessons at home, and, four decades later, Betsey's ten-year-old granddaughter Mary in the schoolroom upstairs in the big London house in Harewood Place. Mary Florence Baird's family moved about a great deal, back and forth between England and the continent, but wherever home was, she had her education there.

In the 1860s Jeannette and Ada Marshall had their lessons in the schoolroom of their Savile Row, London, home.[5]

Mothers, of course, headed the army of teachers. Some mothers had a gift for teaching, others did not. The Turner girls in Yarmouth had a talented teacher in their mother, Elizabeth. Mary Baird's mother taught her and her sisters "dancing and . . . exercises," and she gave them all their religious instruction. Mrs. Baird was "painstaking but not patient," and her daughters thought lessons with her a "penance." Other daughters had happier experiences. During her girlhood in the 1830s, Mary Mordaunt did much "serious reading" with her mother.[6] In the rural reaches of West Gloucestershire in the same decade, the three Ormerod girls and their seven brothers studied at home with their mother. In both basic education and "more advanced work," Eleanor recalled, "my mother's own great store of solid information, and her gift for imparting it, enabled her to keep us steadily progressing." Mother and children worked together in the morning; the girls and boys worked on their own in the afternoon, preparing the lessons for the next day independently. They followed this schedule throughout the year, with only occasional days or half-days off. The Ormerod curriculum included all the subjects: "biblical knowledge and moral precepts," French, geography, and "the higher branches requisite for preparation for Public School work"— presumably mathematics, Latin, and Greek. Mrs. Ormerod won praise from Thomas Arnold, headmaster of Rugby School, who taught her sons afterward, for "the sound foundation [she] had . . . laid." Lydia North Paget taught her daughters (and her sons, too) the rudiments: one of her children remembers the schoolroom in the late 1850s and early 1860s and "lessons with my Mother." The lessons "began with reading a Psalm aloud." The little children learned to spell by working with "letters printed on little strips of cardboard." They learned to write with copybooks: "my Mother set copies in a very beautiful Italian style." They studied arithmetic but never used the abacus provided for the purpose. Their readings included the catechism, English history, Bible history, geography, and fiction—such works as Charlotte Mary Yonge's *The Little Duke* (1854). "[S]he also grounded . . . some of us in Latin Grammar."[7]

Other females also participated in girls' education. Older sisters helped educate younger girls. When Mary Paget was ten and eleven years old, she had school lessons from her older sister Catharine, then in her mid-twenties and living at home. Those lessons came on a regular schedule: Monday, Wednesday, and Saturday mornings involved "Mary's lessons" unless exceptional circumstances interfered. Family friends sometimes played a less formal role in education. Lydia North, on occasional visits to Yarmouth, gave piano lessons to young Kate Paget.[8]

For girls and young women of this social rank, governesses sometimes provided instruction. A governess freed a mother's time for other activities, and she brought expertise not available in the family. Mrs. Ormerod, for example, felt she had no musical abilities, and she left the music lessons to a paid teacher. Three governesses supervised the Marshall girls' education: a young Scots woman, Jane Chessar, an even younger but capable Esther Greatbatch, and a Swiss woman, Mme Noel. The Cambridge Paget girls had an unnamed "Fräulein" as their teacher, presumably of German language and literature. Mary Heywood had foreign governesses for her language studies. With limited patience for teaching, Mrs. Baird employed governesses to teach her children reading, music, and poetry.[9]

Although women may have provided most of the girls' education, men frequently participated, and they sometimes played a major role. For Helen Church, her "father was her teacher." Rachel Harriette Busk, too, was "well educated by her father." Lydia North's father, a silent, withdrawn, and unsociable man, did not (as far as we know) educate her, but he played an important part in Lydia's educational life. It was he who made sure that she had music lessons, and he encouraged her development as a musician. After Sir Thomas Dyke Acland's wife died in 1851, he withdrew from society and devoted himself to family life, including the education of his two daughters and three sons. "He taught them himself from time to time, and kept most careful records in notebooks of their progress." Even after he married again, he continued his work as instructor to the children.[10]

Fathers sometimes taught their daughters one favorite subject; sometimes they ranged across a variety of topics. T. D. Acland taught his children botany, a subject of special interest to him, while F. J. A. Hort, as a cleric and biblical scholar, took on the task of teaching his daughters religion. Handley C. G. Moule taught his daughters swimming and rowing as well as astronomy, literature, and some history. Fathers' methods varied as much as the subjects they took up. In the 1870s Sir George Paget wrote regularly to his daughters during the summers, when they were at the family's country house in North Wales and he was at work in Cambridge. He used his letters as instruments of pedagogy, to communicate information to his children on subjects as they arose out of current events or the family's activities. He informed young Rose about cannons, warships, the history of shipbuilding, portrait painters, and Indian jewel-work. He treated her to a brief biography of that other Paget family, the Marquises of Anglesea. Mandell Creighton and his wife shared teaching duties, he regularly teaching the girls and boys Greek and Latin. His eldest daughter remembered that "At a very early age, six I think, he began to teach me Greek. . . . It was delightful when all went well, particularly when we gaily left grammar behind and . . . I plunged into

Homer and Euripides." When Louise was out of town, Mandell took all the lessons on himself.[11]

Fenton Hort, the Pagets' neighbor in St. Peter's Terrace, was a more subtle commingler of domesticity and education. When his daughter Ellen was eight years old and he was away on a short business trip, he sent her a note asking her to gather a bouquet of flowers for him to take to his friend B. F. Westcott in Cambridge: "I should like a few nice pieces of *Deutzia*, either open or in bud, three or four pieces of the bright red *Lychnis Flos-Jovis*, . . . and two or three *small* but bright pieces of the Lupine, with a few Lupine leaves." Ellen may, at eight, have been familiar with the scientific names of the plants he wanted. More likely, her father's letter was one of a series of steps designed to teach her the names of the plants, while she gathered the bouquet. On other occasions Hort used letters to inform his eldest daughter about European geography and medieval history.[12]

George Paget kept a minatory eye on his daughters' study habits and progress. When Rose was in Wales for the summer, he exhorted her to "learn all you can. Now is your time for learning, now you are young. If you do not make a good start now, you will run the risk of being behind-hand all your life." He attended even to the details of writing and arithmetic, and he could be severe. "You require some practice in letter-writing," he told Rose. "Your English is not always grammatical, and your spelling & stops not such as Rose Paget's should be. You have spelt pieces thus *peices*." He urged her to "Write to me every week. . . . [T]he practice in writing will be useful to you, for 'practice makes perfect.'" The fourteen-year-old girl's arithmetic lessons also got his attention. "I am glad you are . . . doing sums. I just looked at the last sums you sent. They were not properly set down. . . . The mistake seemed to be in your not being clearly aware that the sign = means *equal to,* and must never be put between two quantities unless they be really *equal to* one another." Behind his criticism was genuine, affectionate interest in his daughter and her education: "If you have any difficulty with your Algebra, write to me about it—indeed write every week, whether you have any difficulty or not." As he admitted to his daughter, "I like to hear how you are going on & what you are doing." In a similar way Professor Hort attended both to the details of his daughter's spelling and the general oversight of her education.[13]

George Paget advised his daughters, as they grew older, on the subjects they might study. "I hope you are learning to *speak* Welsh. You have a grand opportunity with Miss Ellis [in Wales]." He suggested that Rose follow the lead of one of the family's neighbors: "If Miss West is studying Botany, you might study it also." The family's library in Wales had books suitable for learning "how to distinguish plants and learn their names." But if she wanted "to study the *Physiology* of plants," he would send her appropriate texts from Cambridge. When Paget took his children on a trip to the Low Countries in 1878, he prepared them in advance for the tour: "An acquaintance with . . . [Belgium's and Holland's] history will greatly add to the interest of seeing them," he told Rose. And he went to the University Library to get J. L. Motley's volumes on *The Rise of the Dutch Republic* (1855) and sent them to Wales for Rose to read.[14]

In every generation men other than their fathers were also involved in the education of these girls. When Betsey Paget, as a young wife and mother thirty years of age, wanted to study painting in Great Yarmouth, a man came from Norwich to give her instruction. Mary Turner and her daughters also had male teachers of painting in Yarmouth, and the Ormerod girls and Charles Kingsley's daughter Mary all studied art with men.[15] Lydia North's music teachers included men as well as women. Lydia's daughter Catharine studied music in London in the 1870s with male teachers, and Rose, Violet, and Maud took their various art, music, and language lessons in Cambridge from Messrs. Amps, Wiles, Archer-Hind, Boguet, and Steinhilper.[16] In London Helen Church took music lessons and learned to play the pipe organ from a male associate of her father's.[17] Sex segregation and "separate spheres" did not characterize these girls' education. Instead, gentlewomen's families took care to employ the best teachers that they could afford, whether male or female, in the search for superior instruction for their daughters.

Although much education took place at home, daughters were by no means housebound, and many families supplemented their daughters' home education with opportunities outside. The Acland family arranged to share a governess's services with relatives down the road, so that Eleanor and her siblings went to what amounted to a private school at their cousins' house. Very few families went so far as to send the daughters to day schools, let alone boarding schools. The two Hort girls were exceptions: Ellen went to boarding school at the Cheltenham Ladies' College, and Mary was a day pupil at the new Perse School for Girls in Cambridge, which her father had helped to found. Mary Baird's education was unusual in that she had more governesses than most and, when she was in Germany, she went to a day school in Stuttgart.[18] Similarly, almost none of these women enrolled in the universities when women's colleges opened at Oxford and Cambridge.

Nevertheless, girls and women did find the classroom an appropriate place for learning special subjects outside the home. Lydia North, an adolescent in London in the 1820s, had the standard education at home, but she went to "botannical lectures" from time to time. Lydia's clergyman father took advantage of the newly founded Royal Academy of Music as a source of superior musical instruction for her. Old Rev. North loved music, hated idleness and frivolity, and enrolled Lydia at the RAM to give some direction to what he recognized as her musical talent. During the second decade of the nineteenth century J. R. Macculloch (1789–1864), the statistician and political economist, gave lectures in London on political economy, which were attended by "many ladies" as well as "the studious of the male sex," George Grote among them. Families living in London, university towns like Oxford and Cambridge, and the growing provincial metropolitan centers found it relatively easy to provide their daughters with the benefits of excellent lecturers.[19]

Lecture halls continued to be the site of women's informal education throughout the century. In 1870, for example, Catharine Paget went to lectures at the Royal Institution in London. There on March 25 she heard Professor George Rolleston speak on "Anglo-Saxons," and on April 5 he spoke on "The Nervous System." In June she heard Friedrich Max Müller, the great philologist, deliver an address there on "The Migration of Fable." At this same period Clara Paget, her adolescent daughters, and other Cambridge girls and women attended the art history lectures of Sidney Colvin, the new Slade Professor of Fine Art. Art history was a new subject in the Cambridge curriculum, and Colvin was glad for the opportunity to influence "the taste of the rising generation," and women took full advantage of the lectures. Colvin's Cambridge audiences consisted for the most part of "adult residents of the place, the wives and daughters of professors, a lot of junior dons, girls from Newnham and Girton, and a sprinkling of high-brow undergraduates. It was rather a large audience, two or three hundred in number." Similarly at Oxford in the 1870s, John Ruskin drew large crowds on Tuesdays, Wednesdays, and Saturdays at 2:00 p.m. for his lectures on art history. Some four to five hundred people attended, "about one third ladies."[20]

Science, anthropology, art, and even economics were among the subjects that these women pursued in the lecture halls, and lecture series were available to women outside of the educational centers of Oxford, Cambridge, and London. In Glasgow James Thomson, professor of mathematics, "announced an afternoon course of lectures for ladies, on geography and astronomy [in 1833]. . . . Such a thing had never been heard of before in the University, and it was extremely popular." Thomson's classroom was full of "fashionably-dressed ladies, everyone looking intent, and many taking notes. All the belles of Glasgow were among the students." From Tore, Co. Meath, in the winter of 1877 the Pilkington girls reported happily to their friend Rose that they had enrolled in a class in political economy. Some classes were smaller and less formal than those offered at a university or scientific society, and they depended more on the initiative of the women themselves. When several daughters of Cambridge faculty wanted to study language, they organized a class themselves.[21]

This education outside the home continued into adulthood. Rose Paget, at the age of twenty-seven, pursued her interests in science by going around to the Cavendish Laboratory in the 1880s to work. Rose was one of the few women in this study who linked herself in any way to the formal system of education for women; she took the Higher Local Examination and attended classes at Newnham. Charlotte Moberly and Eleanor Balfour (later Sidgwick) also enrolled in the newly opened Oxbridge colleges for women. During the 1870s Eleanor Burd and Mary St. Leger Kingsley studied at the Slade School of Fine Art in London.[22]

An important avenue of Victorian education was self-education, particularly through reading. The Paget nursery in Harewood Place in the 1860s contained books for both girls and boys to read: Johann David Wyss's *Swiss Family Robinson* (first published in English in 1814), Mrs. Margaret Gatty's *Parables from Nature* (1855–71, with new editions appearing up to 1883), Thomas Day's *The History of Sandford and Merton*, a vastly popular children's book first published in 1783 in three volumes, and *Philosophy in Sport, Made Science in Earnest* (1827), by physician John Ayrton Paris. The children had *Aunt Judy's Magazine*, founded and edited by Mrs. Gatty, and there were the sex-specific *Boys' Own Annual* and *Girls' Own Book*, and a subscription to *Chatterbox* for Mary Paget. One of Mary's books at this period was *The Adventures of Baron Munchausen* (1819) with illustrations by Gustave Doré, but when it frightened her, her parents took it away.[23]

Children's independent reading was, for both sexes, an important complement to parental and hired tutoring. As children grew older, self-education continued. This style of learning was, and is, easily open to attack. Mary Kingsley, looking back on her girlhood, considered her self-education chaotic. She feared that freedom to pursue her own interests had led only to crippling false starts and confusion. Kingsley's dissatisfaction with her education may, however, reflect more on her insecure home life than on the quality of her knowledge, skills, and achievements.[24] The fact was that male as well as female education, for much of the century, often partook of the disorder that Mary Kingsley found so disheartening. For both sexes Victorian education seems disordered when compared with the regimentation of the twentieth-century school. Nevertheless, Kingsley and all the other women of the Paget circle achieved a high standard of learning and skill in those areas that they marked off for themselves. Self-education at its worst might lead to continued ignorance or dilettantism; at best it left room for freedom and variety in the female curriculum, and the women of this study pursued widely diverse educational paths.

As the Paget girls and their friends grew into womanhood, their reading contributed much to their culture as educated adults. In Great Yarmouth, Kate's favorite books included volumes by Scott and Byron, the *Arabian Nights*, and a shelf of Shakespeare's works. Marianne North had a similar pattern of reading. Lydia read a range of materials, from religious works to geology. Mary Sidgwick, even as a little girl, read "a great deal." At seven she had "learnt a Lay of Macaulay's for pleasure, and [knew] both Bible History and English History well."[25] Eleanor Ormerod, in an unusual variation on the country lady's interests, educated herself in entomology, and particularly the entomology of agriculture, from the age of twenty-four. She continued her studies of insects all her life. Catharine Spooner's "daily routine" as a young woman included "reading some interesting book of history, philosophy, or theology all morning." In the 1830s Elizabeth Thomson was reading Locke's writings on education. In the process of self-education through reading, the girls and young women served as models and guides to one another; sometimes competition spurred their efforts. The Pilkington girls read Thomas Carlyle when Emmie was sixteen and Cherrie eighteen years old, and Cherrie recommended his work to Rose Paget with enthusiasm—and perhaps a bit of boasting.[26]

Among the women studied here, the fullest record of private reading is Catharine Paget's. In 1870 and 1871 (when she was twenty-four to twenty-five years old) her reading included history. She selected Pierre Lanfrey's works, presumably the early volumes of his *Histoire de Napoléon I*[er.] published in five volumes between 1867 and 1875, J. A. Froude's *History of England from the Fall of Wolsey to the Death of Elizabeth*, which was published in twelve volumes between 1856 and 1870, and Carlyle's *French Revolution*. She read biography—G. H. Lewes's *Life of Goethe* (1855)—and a work she identified only as "Mr. Robertson's Life." She read religious books (the Oxford Lenten Sermons for 1869), as well as the latest in folklore, *Vikram and the Vampire; or, Tales of Hindu Devilry*. She may have read George Sand's *François le Champi* (1847–48) out of sheer interest or out of a desire to keep up her skills in French. Later she read one of George Eliot's novels and Henry Knollys's *From Sedan to Saarbruch, via Verdun, Gravelotte, and Metz* (1870). In Cambridge, Catharine's cousins followed a similar regimen. In 1880 Maud was reading William Gresley's *Siege of Lichfield* (1840), *Some Elements of Religion*, and *Eternal Hope*.[27]

Friends and family often guided a girl's reading. Winnie Talbot had the special interest of one of her father's colleagues, the bishop of Winchester.

The bishop and the young girl read aloud to each other, and the shared study meant a great deal to her: "I remember best Lindsay's *History of the Reformation*, which occasioned many an argument. . . . We also read Macaulay's History." Mary Kingsley's reading had some features in common with those of her Victorian cohort. She read Richard Burton's *Two Trips to Gorilla Land* (1876) and the travel writings of Paul Belloni Du Chaillu and Pierre Savorgnan de Brazza. She made forays into her father's scientific library, where she found materials in medicine, physics, chemistry, and mathematics. She read Sir Joseph Norman Lockyer's *Contributions to Solar Physics* (1874) as well as the writings of Charles Darwin, T. H. Huxley, and E. B. Tylor, the ethnographer. Critic Frederick York Powell's *Corpus Poeticum Boreale* (2 vols., 1881) and the works of Bigfusson also made their way into Mary Kingsley's informal syllabus.[28]

Not all their reading led women to the highest intellectual and spiritual planes. In 1870 Catharine Paget read Bulwer Lytton's *Harold* (1848), Florence Wilford's *Nigel Bartram's Ideal* (1869), and Willkie Collins's *Man and Wife* (1870). No empty-headed consumer of romance, she offered critical assessments even of the entertainments: "I read [the] 1st vol. [of Disraeli's novel] Lothair," she recorded in her diary on May 12, "such *false* stupid stuff it seems to me." She read the Kingsley brothers' fictional works— Charles Kingsley's *Hypatia* (1853) and Henry Kingsley's *Ravenshoe* (1862)—as well as Margaret Oliphant's three-volume novel *The Minister's Wife* (1869), all during 1871. Mary Kingsley read the novels of Jane Austen, Charles Dickens, and George Eliot, as well as those of her uncle and father.[29]

This piecemeal style of learning suggests that female education in the Victorian period was singularly haphazard. Perhaps so. What is equally striking is its flexibility, its adaptability to the predilections and needs of both girls and their parents. Moreover, one of the by-products of this independent style of education was the fact that it did not end when a woman reached eighteen or twenty-one. The habit of self-education, begun early, was powerful, and women continued to read, some of them widely, others deeply, all their lives.

Engagement and marriage could bring women new interests and new avenues to learning. Harriet Lewin followed the guidance of her fiancé, George Grote, in what may appear a Pygmalion-like relationship: "He set her themes on various subjects, and gave her books to read, on which he required her to send him a digest." George "commenced that discipline of her mind . . . to which she owed that depth and fullness of intellectual life, which, far from quenching her natural vivacity, gave it new and worthier materials. Her rare intelligence," an admiring friend said, "required only a gentle hand to guide it in paths seldom followed by a young woman, and

still seldomer traced by an ardent lover." He helped her extend her education in directions that her parents had not taken. Together they read, among
others, the writings of Plato, Aristotle, Kant, Bentham, James Mill; they
studied poetry, painting, and music, as well as logic, philosophy, and political economy. And, while the initiative originally came from him, "Each gave
and took an education." She sent him digests: he sent her his digests of
books, too. "He endowed her mind with a more solid basis, she fashioned,
mounted, framed and glazed him." She taught him not to be narrow and
prejudiced and, in the end, friends thought her contribution to their educational enterprise to be more significant than his. Mandell Creighton and
Louise von Glehn established a less formidable curriculum. After their engagement in 1871, Louise recalled, "He began to teach me Italian, and I
was able to help him with German."[30] Men who tutored their future wives
may appear to have been establishing some sort of intellectual hegemony
over them. Perhaps so, but their behavior bears witness to their expectation
that wives were to be intellectual companions, partners of the mind as well
as of the sentiments and the body. And in the Grotes' and Creightons' cases,
each learned from the other.

After their marriage the Grote household became the meeting-place of
"a choice society of logicians" including the Austins (husband and wife),
David Ricardo, and other political economists and theorists. Harriet "made
herself mistress of the leading principles of the science" of logic, and both
she and Sarah Austin participated in the group's discussions.[31]

As the bride-to-be of an Oxford don in the late 1870s, Mary Baird felt a
need to prepare for her move into university life: she read the early volumes
of *Ancient Classics for English Readers* (edited by Rev. W. Lucas Collins),
a series that had begun to appear in 1870; she read S. H. Butcher and Andrew Lang's translation of *The Odyssey, The Earthly Paradise* (presumably
William Morris's poem of 1868–70), and an antislavery tract by W. J.
Grayson, *Friends in Council*. After their marriage she and her husband read
together every day, sometimes "'improving' books" like Justin M'Carthy's
multi-volume *History of Our Own Times from the Accession of Queen Victoria to the Berlin Congress* (1879–80), sometimes lighter literature, like Robert Louis Stevenson's *Treasure Island* (1882).[32] A woman of more serious intellectual commitments, Catharine Tait "studied Dr. Schmitz's volumes of
Niebuhr's Lectures with . . . zest" in her early thirties. Fenton Hort put the
matter of intellectual development clearly to his daughter just as she was
finishing her formal schooling: "Foolish people will, I daresay, talk about
your education being finished. You know better than that. . . . It is a bad
state of things when education does not go on all through life."[33] In this social
stratum learning was the norm, and a girl's childhood and adolescent educa-

tion was the beginning ~~of a woman's life-long~~ relationship to reading, study, and intellectual growth.

Educational accomplishment for Victorian females can be measured in two ways: first, by the subjects they studied, and second, by the depth of knowledge or the level of skill they achieved. It should be clear from what has already been said about girls' and women's education that, beyond reading, writing, arithmetic, and religion, there were few subjects that *every* female studied. Many studied history, botany, literature, art, and music. At least a few had instruction in astronomy, and the possibilities in foreign languages and literatures were varied and nearly endless. School curricula can be identified, but as so few girls in this study attended schools, they are of limited use for knowing what upper-middle-class women learned (even assuming that published offerings matched what was really taught in a school). Where it exists, private correspondence gives some help. Fenton Hort's letters to his wife, for example, allow us to infer something of her level of education. His vocabulary shows that he assumed Fanny's knowledge of French, of botany, of architecture, and of politics. And letters between Hort and his daughters indicate that the Hort girls were studying history, literature (including poetry), and art history.[34]

It is one thing to explore (however partially and superficially) what these women studied. It is another matter entirely to assess the quality of their education and the level of their achievement. For many Victorian women we have only the general, and perhaps doubtful, effusions of family members. A. F. Hort, for example, insisted that his grandmother, Anne Collett Hort, "had been extremely well educated." But he qualified his praise: she was "well educated, so far as the opportunities of that day [the 1820s] allowed."[35] But let us begin with the fundamentals.

The Paget women and their friends—even including the dissatisfied Mary Kingsley—were all literate and numerate women. Letters survive from every generation that testify to these women's ability to write clearly and effectively. Occasional financial records demonstrate their ability to manage numbers logically. Such skills were, of course, a part of the standard preparation for a Victorian lady's duties as household manager. Betsey Paget, even with servants in the Yarmouth house, "took the close charge and guidance of . . . all [her children]: she managed household affairs and, after the manner of the time and place, did all the marketing and shopping, directed the cookery." In the second and third generations the gentlewoman's close attention to household chores may have been attenuated by social mobility, the demands of urban life, and changing domestic mores. But occasional cookery, light sewing, and shopping, as well as flower arranging, continued to be part of these women's lives. In Cambridge the girls were specifically taught such household tasks as ironing, and from early adolescence they helped entertain guests and manage servants.[36] But the interests and skills acquired by these upper-middle-class women went far beyond the household. So far we know what they studied, and where, but the question of quality remains to be examined.

The Arts

The arts were traditionally an arena of Victorian female "accomplishment." But "accomplishment" has implied (at least in the context of women's education) the leisurely mastery of the trivial. The women of this study achieved much more. In fact, women who studied art did so seriously. When the Turner women were in the process of changing art teachers, the new drawing master sent the women "a few pencil drawings to copy." This was a standard learning exercise, put forward in this case "in order that they may not lose time."[37] Such action suggests that teacher and pupils alike considered women's time and their artistic studies important. It is worthwhile to assess women's accomplishment as far as that can be done. Two rough measures of their levels of accomplishment are, first, the quality of their teachers and, second, the time spent on, and the complexity of, the work these women did.

Seventeen children born in the space of twenty-five years might reasonably be expected to have filled Betsey Paget's life, and her responsibilities as the wife of a community leader also took time. She wanted to paint, however, and paint she did. Her teacher, John Crome (1768–1821), was a leading regional painter of the period, better known as "Old Crome" of Norfolk, and, under his direction, whatever her talents as a painter, she did master the technique of working in oils. Other women in Yarmouth also had fine artistic training. Betsey's neighbor, Mary Turner, studied with Crome for a time, but in 1812 she and her daughters began to work with another noted Norfolk artist, John Sell Cotman (1782–1842). He "gave a drawing lesson every Saturday morning to the Miss Turners in the [Gurney] bank drawing-room." His association with the family lasted for twelve years. Mary Turner also studied etching with James Sowerby, the younger (1787–1871), and drafting with William Camden Edwards (1777–1855), both well-established artists of the time. In the first decade of the century Cotman had charged the Turners 10s.6d. a lesson. The expense of their lessons in the 1820s ranged from 31s.6d. for three months (for group lessons for beginners) to twelve guineas a quarter for advanced private lessons.[38] The expense, as well as the choice of teachers, suggests that the family considered the women's acquisition of artistic skill an important investment.

Mary Turner's distinguished art education resulted in a life-long involvement in artistic work. She did portraits, among them an "etching in profile" of her distinguished son-in-law, botanist William Jackson Hooker. And, when the French biologist Alphonse de Candolle visited her husband at Yarmouth, he noted that this "mère de famille trés distinguée" was engaged in both drawing and etching; she engraved his portrait while he was there. Art critic Henry Crabb Robinson, too, visited the Turners in Yarmouth, and Mary offered him any of her etchings that he might like to carry away. He took a half dozen. Harriette Bunyon (later McDougall) had an art education similar to that of Mary Turner. She studied with Cornelius Varley (1781–1873) and Henry Gastineau (1791–1876), both London painters of note in the first third of the nineteenth century. According to her brother, she was "a good amateur artist, painting in watercolours with considerable skill."[39]

Susan Mary, Eleanor, and Georgiana Ormerod, living in the west country, did not have ready access to the well-known artists of the metropolis throughout the year. But the family culture demanded artistic education for its daughters; Mrs. Ormerod had studied oil painting in her youth, encouraged by John Flaxman (1755–1826), the famous sculptor and a family friend. The Ormerods' eldest daughter, Susan Mary, studied with Copley Fielding (1787–1855), an "elegant and original" watercolor painter. In addition, once a year the daughters and their father came to London from Sedbury Park, and, while he was off studying at the British Museum, they took lessons from William Hunt (1790–1864), a well-known painter in watercolor and oils. Georgiana and Eleanor became skillful artists, having "learnt from [Hunt] how to combine birds' nests and objects of still life with fruits and flowers into very lovely pictures."[40]

Marianne North studied "flower painting" in London with "a Dutch lady, Miss van Fowinkel," when she was nineteen or twenty years old. The next year she had "a few lessons in water-colour flower-painting" from Valentine Bartholomew (1799–1879). She longed to study with William Hunt, but he was no longer teaching. Later she had lessons in oil painting from Robert Hawker Dowling (1827–86), the Australian artist, and she knew she had found her medium—"oil painting being a vice like dram-drinking, almost impossible to leave off," she said, "once it gets possession of one." The details of Ellen Busk's art education are not available, but she developed skill enough to paint her father's portrait in oils, and the portrait subsequently hung in the Linnean Society's rooms in Burlington House. Between 1873 and 1889 she exhibited thirteen portraits at the Royal Academy.[41]

Elise Paget worked both with oils and with watercolors. As part of her training she copied paintings in the National Gallery, and she traveled to France to study works in Paris galleries. Recognition for the quality of her work came in 1878 and again in 1888 when her paintings won places in exhibitions at the Royal Academy of Art. She also exhibited ten works at the Royal Society of British Artists, Suffolk Street. In all, Elise exhibited twenty-one of her paintings in major London exhibitions between 1877 and 1888. Henrietta Huxley exhibited at the Royal Academy in 1887 and 1888.[42] Maud Paget began her art studies while living at home in Cambridge. In the 1870s she and her sisters studied with Henry Wiles, the Cambridge sculptor who exhibited regularly at the Royal Academy. In 1878 Maud traveled to Dresden, where she lived for most of the academic year and studied sculpture, painting, and drawing from life. There were other English girls in Dresden that year, including Edith Tait. The following year Rose's sister Violet made her way to Dresden for the same studies. Maud continued to paint after her return from Germany. While in Wales in the summer of 1880, she did landscapes and portraits of friends. The Stainer sisters both spent time in Germany in the 1890s, "working at music and polishing up their German talk."[43]

At the Slade School of Fine Art in London, Charles Kingsley's daughter Mary St. Leger Kingsley studied with Sir Edward Poynter (1836–1919), painter and Slade Professor of Fine Art at University College, London. She contemplated a career in art but gave up that idea when she married in 1876. Eleanor Burd had, as a girl, taken up sketching; later, she, too, attended the Slade School, where in 1885 she "won the first prize for drawing from life." Marriage that year (to Stephen Paget) did not stop her from sketching and painting. Indeed, her father-in-law provided the funds to build a studio for her at the back of her house in fashionable Wimpole Street.[44]

A new medium in the visual arts emerging in the nineteenth century was photography. In Oxford Angelina Acland had developed fine skills as a painter, with the assistance and encouragement of her family's friend John Ruskin. She had exhibited her work at the Royal Academy and the Society of Water Colour Artists. But she found photography more to her liking and did extensive work in that medium, with particular interest in portrait photography. She associated herself with the Royal Photographic Society and pursued various features of photographic art and technique all her life.[45]

Music

Music, too, was part of the Victorian lady's repertoire of accomplishments. Among the Yarmouth women, the visual arts seem to have taken first place, but some of them also studied music. Betsey Paget kept a music notebook in which she transcribed the music of Handel and other composers; her notebook was her private record of her work at the task of mastering music.[46] Beyond this manuscript there is no clue as to the level of musical skill Betsey achieved.

To assess the level of women's proficiency one must look to their teachers. Once again, the quality of women's teachers offers strong support for the high caliber of their achievements. At the Royal Academy of Music in the 1820s and 1830s, Lydia North studied not only with Domenico Crivelli (1793–1851), the son of a famous Italian tenor, but also with Mrs. Lucy (Philpot) Anderson (1790–1878), a renowned concert pianist. Her most important teacher was Dr. William Crotch (1775–1847). Dr. Crotch had been professor of music at Oxford and was the first principal of the Royal Academy of Music from 1822 until 1832. He was, moreover, "one of the most distinguished English musicians of his day." Lydia's daughter Catharine studied music in London a generation later and her instructors, too, were notable members of the English music scene. Ciro Pinsuti (1829–88), an Italian composer and teacher of voice, had been, from 1856, a member of the staff of the Royal Academy of Music. Henry Leslie (1822–96), a choral conductor and composer of note, led the prize-winning Henry Leslie Choir from 1855 to 1880 and served briefly as principal of the National College of Music. Catharine also studied with Mme Charlotte Sainton-Dolby (1821–85), a singer, composer, and teacher, who was a former student of the Royal Academy of Music, a favorite of Mendelssohn, and head of her own Vocal Academy after 1872. Catharine's voice teachers reflected Lydia's musical sophistication and Catharine's abilities as well.[47]

Helen Church, perhaps benefiting from her father's position as dean of St. Paul's, had instruction at the organ keyboard from Sir John Stainer, composer and organist at the cathedral. She was advanced enough in her skills to play the organ there. Harriot Elliott (later Mrs. Handley Moule) studied with W. Sterndale Bennett (1816–75), the composer and pianist, as did Cecil Grenville Milnes, later Mrs. F. T. Palgrave. Sterndale Bennett had studied with Crotch at the Royal Academy of Music, was professor of music at Cambridge, and then returned to the RAM as its principal. He has been judged "the most distinguished English composer of the Romantic school." The Cambridge Paget girls' musical tutor, William Amps (1824–1910), was a composer and organist for three Cambridge colleges, and conductor of the Cambridge University Musical Society.[48] That upper-middle-class women had teachers of distinction was, apparently, common. Even the famous Sir Charles Hallé took lady pupils. Some had admittedly little talent, only enrolling in his music classes "to make the requisite number," but Hallé enjoyed teaching them because of their "goodwill and perseverance." Others had a "real disposition and love for music." The Paget women, their friends, and their families chose illustrious teachers because they had high aspirations for the level of skill they wanted to achieve. The willingness of leading musicians to take these girls and women as their pupils also reflects their high levels of ability and skill.[49]

Other measures of their achievements can be found in the students' dedication and in public recognition of their success. In these respects Lydia North shone, for she was both talented and serious. As a girl of twelve or thirteen she won silver and bronze medals in the piano competitions at the Royal Academy of Music. Although some of the Academy's students earned "severe censure" in the 1820s and 1830s for their poor performance, Lydia's teachers judged her among those "most highly satisfactory in all their studies" in 1830. And when Lydia was seventeen years old the school records showed that "Miss North has composed a Quartett for Piano, Violin, Tenor and Violoncello, which reflects the highest Credit upon her." She also learned how to "read a full orchestral score at sight." In her late teens Lydia was apparently invited to begin a concert career. She refused, for she did not like the prospect of "publicity." But she did not give up music. As pianist and singer, she entertained family and guests, gave music lessons, and continued composing. She wrote glees (four-part unaccompanied songs) for performance in the family, and she and James played duets for piano and flute. One of her later compositions—"a little French dance"—made its way into the hands of the Princess of Wales, and another seems to have been prepared for use at the Birmingham Oratory, for her friend Cardinal Newman.[50]

No other women in the Paget family achieved Lydia's level of musical skill, but her daughter Catharine's musical education reflected a similar seriousness of purpose and commitment, in the time devoted to her studies as well as in the quality of her teachers. Catharine had ear-training, sight-singing, music theory, and composition—enough training to be able to write down with ease the songs her little brother composed. The Cambridge daughters had musical instruction that, while not from famous teachers, had substance and depth. The predictable voice and piano lessons were only part of a systematic schedule of musical training that included harmony and composition. Eleanor Ormerod's musical education had similar dimensions. We do not know of its nature, but its results are some clue. She "sang and played the piano very well" throughout her adult life. She also "composed music with great facility," so that friends thought she might have superior musical talent. But nature interested her more than music. Harriette Bunyon's musical education included voice and harp lessons, and she and her sisters played piano-harp duets, including the works of Mozart and Beethoven.[51]

Music constituted an important part of these women's lives. Concerts, operas, and private musical evenings made for a rich musical environment, and these women took an active part in it. Music was a part of life and entertainment at home throughout the century. At Harewood Place from the 1860s on the family enjoyed Sunday evenings together with "hymn singing, and . . . when the boys had got grown up voices, . . . quartets and choruses." Guests brought music too: when laryngologist Sir Felix Semon and his wife came to dine, there was music afterward, "Lady Semon singing, and her husband accompanying." Scientist Rokitansky "played dance tunes" on the Pagets' piano on a Sunday and shocked the children. Professional musicians like Miss Janotha and Mme Haas were only the most expert in a continuum of musical performers in Victorian upper-middle-class homes.[52]

The women who heard Charles Hallé's concerts in the 1840s were the first to put their stamp of musical approval on the Beethoven sonatas he dared to play at public concerts. When these ladies liked what they heard, they "arranged afternoon parties in order to hear it once more." Women's training helped them appreciate the performances of professional musicians, such as Alfredo Carlo Piatti, Sir Charles Santley, Adelina Patti, Joseph Joachim, Sims Reeves, Zelia Trebelli, and the others they heard in the private musical evenings and public concerts of Victorian London. Catharine did not hesitate to say that "Mme Reboux sang *dreadfully*" at a musical afternoon. When she and her cousin Elise heard "Flauto Magico" with "Titiens, Lesso Gardoni, Cotogni &c." she thought, "lovely music but such a ludicrous story." On another occasion she went to "Mme Sainton's Concert" where "the performers were Miss Zimmerman, Piatti, [and] Miss Angela Edith Wynne, who sang charmingly." As a result of their musical education these women became the tastemakers of the music scene in their generation. As trained amateurs, women also contributed their talents in public performance. Typical was the St. Cecilia Society, founded in Manchester in 1840, under the direction of Charles Hallé, where some fifty "ladies and gentlemen of the best society . . . met weekly for the study of choral works." In London Mary Maud Paget sang in the Bach Choir in the 1880s. The ensemble, founded in 1875, had a role in the Bach revival that took place in England in the late nineteenth century.[53] Such activities made their own contribution to the cultural life of Victorian England, in drawing rooms and concert halls alike.

The musical and artistic accomplishments of these women reveal the high standards of artistic culture they and their families enjoyed. What later generations found exclusively in the concert and recital halls of a commercialized musical culture, these women were producing in their homes and those of their friends. The most powerful sign that musical culture and a high level of skill in both composition and performance were common among upper-middle-class women was the founding, in 1911, of the Society of Women Musicians, for the purpose of representing "the interests of women in music and to give concerts, especially of works by women."[54] Only extensive and deep musical culture and education among women could have produced, so early, an organized effort to bring women composers and performers into the mainstream of English musical life.

Language and Science

While the ambitious lower-middle-class woman might have thought that a smattering of *s'il vous plaît* and *comme il faut* might make her marriageable, gentlewomen had both the resources for, and the traditions of, a more integrated and thorough-going approach to learning. Their experience in language and science, as much as in the arts, reveals the depth of Victorian upper-middle-class female education. Of course, women's knowledge of modern western European languages can be understood entirely within the confines of ladylike learning: for reading, for travel, and for their study of music, Italian, French, and German were entirely appropriate. But in fact they did more than chat, sing, and read novels in the languages they learned.

Language training for these women was extensive. Normally they learned French, usually well enough to read French literature, often well enough to converse with continental visitors. German studies took the same form, but most women went beyond the two major continental languages, opting for those that best suited their needs and interests. A look at individual cases will indicate the depth of their knowledge and, in some cases, the determinants of language study.

In the first nineteenth-century generation little information survives regarding the linguistic training and skills of Betsey Paget. Nor do we know about her two daughters, Patty and Kate, although the latter's travels to the continent suggest some knowledge of French and possibly Italian. As for their neighbor, Mary Turner, the record of her relationships with European visitors indicates that she knew at least French and German. Information about Mrs. Turner's daughters is also sparse. Elizabeth Turner's language education certainly included Italian: her journal was full of Italian phrases, and, when her son was old enough, she read Dante with him. While Lydia North's fiancé spent a term studying in Paris in the 1830s, she was learning French at home. She often despaired of keeping up with him, and rightly—he lived with the daily pressure to use the language.[55] Her reasons for these French studies are not clear: she may have looked forward to travel in

France, she may have wanted to keep up with his language proficiency, or she may simply have used the occasion of his French travels to extend the culture that was the standard of her social rank.

Travel and residence abroad brought some young women knowledge of continental languages. Elizabeth Thomson and her brothers all studied German before making their first trip to Germany in 1840. In the 1860s and 1870s Mary Baird's family traveled abroad often. As a result Mary learned French and German fluently, in spite of the fact that Mary was not, in other respects, a diligent student. At about the same time, Harriot Elliott went to school at Coblenz and Geneva and then lived in Italy for some time with her parents. Thus she gained proficiency in French, German, and Italian. She did not neglect these skills when she returned to England; rather, she kept them up all her life.[56]

The Cambridge girls in the 1870s took lessons in French three times a week. They also studied German. Maud and Violet extended their knowledge of German by living in Dresden for a year, their goal—a firm mastery of the language. The Stainer girls went to Berlin for the same purpose. Carrie Gull and Catharine Paget took Italian lessons together. Catharine's command of French was good enough to allow her to write letters in French. Her German may have been even better. She translated scientific and philosophical materials from German to English. Her brother Frank, while a Christ Church don, sought her help as a tutor: "I wonder whether you would read some German with me . . . this autumn. If so, would you mind our trying Neander's *Church History*? I'm afraid I shall only read it very slowly, but I think it's the best way to begin on a reasonable book." Catharine's linguistic learning also served her musical interests. She translated German *Lieder* into English, and her studies of Italian also complemented her musical studies. Catharine's sister Mary studied Italian, "plough[ing] through Dante" with their brother Stephen.[57] Helen Church studied Italian and German, the latter well enough to read a four-volume biography of Bach in that language. Adolescent Mary Kingsley had German lessons. As a girl Mary Heywood Sumner studied French, German, and Italian. The Acland women, like the others we have studied, had a wide linguistic repertoire. Mary Erskine, the second Lady (Thomas) Acland, had mastered (her stepson thought) three or four "continental languages." Like her aunt, Angie Acland also had an extensive list of languages to her credit: "She mastered French, German, Italian, and even Portuguese, and had some acquaintance with Russian." Eleanor Ormerod specially studied foreign languages, the better to pursue her natural history interests. In her old age she reported, "I can read serviceably French, Italian, and Spanish, and also Latin for what I need;

likewise, of course, German; Russian I could read once but not so readily now; and with the dictionary I can make something of Dutch and Norwegian."[58]

Modern languages had practical (although leisured) uses: their utility in music, literature, and travel make clear why they might have been attractive to the "decorative" female. The place of the classical and esoteric languages in women's self-defined curriculum is not so obvious. Charlotte Mary Yonge's *The Daisy Chain* (1856) depicts the daughter of a provincial doctor studying Latin alongside her brother—indeed they competed with each other over their grasp of the language and their ability to write Latin verse. The experience of the Paget women and their circle suggests that Yonge's heroine may have been typical of her class. Most of the women studied here had some knowledge of classical languages. For the women of the first nineteenth-century generation, the record is least clear: it is impossible to know whether Betsey Paget knew any of them, but indirect evidence suggests that Mary Turner knew Latin and Greek. Selina Grote taught her little boy George the "rudiments of Latin" before he was six years old. And it is certain that the Turners' daughters were learning Latin and possibly Greek. In the next generation Elizabeth Turner Palgrave put her Latin to use teaching her children to read and write that language. In the years 1814–17 Lydia Elizabeth Hoare (the banker's daughter who married into the Acland clan) taught her son Latin before he went to school at age eight. Mary Sidgwick at the age of seven could "pass a good examination . . . in Latin Grammar, to the end of the Pronouns" at the hands of a young Oxford man who was visiting her family at the time. Lydia and Clara both knew Latin well enough to teach it to their sons and daughters. Lydia's son Stephen recalled that she "grounded us . . . in Latin grammar." W. G. Rutherford recognized the erudition of Lydia's youngest daughter, Mary, by calling her a "Latinist," and Sir Alfred Milner sent her long quotations in Greek. She was invited to judge in a schoolboys' Latin competition. All the Creighton girls studied Latin and Greek.[59]

The daughters of Cambridge University faculty organized their own class in Greek in the mid–1870s, and a Mr. Lewis of Corpus Christi taught them. Among the pupils were Rose Paget and Elizabeth Cookson, the daughter of Henry W. Cookson (1810–76), master of Peterhouse. In the winter of 1880 Emmie and Cherrie Pilkington were both doing Greek (whether in a class or at home is not clear). Alice Stopford taught herself Greek. Like young men of the time, the Paget women and their friends displayed their classical learning by peppering their letters with Greek phrases. When at home, Frank tutored Catharine in Greek, and, when away, he advised her by letter. "I am sorry you have begun with the New Testament in your Greek studies:

for the English translation is a thousand times more charming than the original. I will bring you the *Phaedo* of Plato when I come home, which, with the aid of a translation, you will read quite as easily as the New Testament, and I think with far more pleasure." "Don't you think it would be well," he asked, "if you always wrote to me in Greek, I to you in French? whereby we should mutually improve."[60] Frank, a traditionalist in many ways, nevertheless positively encouraged his sister's study of classical Greek and treated her as a peer in their shared efforts at language-learning.

It is only a short leap from the classical languages to the truly unusual languages that Victorian women knew. The record is nearly silent as to whether many women knew Hebrew. Lady Acland did. George Eliot's matter-of-fact introduction of Hebrew in the list of Dorothea Casaubon's potential studies in *Middlemarch* suggests, at least, that such knowledge was within the range of ordinary gentlewomen's studies. Mary Kingsley had taught herself Latin, and then, while attending her mother in a two-year illness, she carried out a program of "strenuous, demanding study" that included more Latin, plus Arabic and Syrian.[61] Most women left no clue as to their reasons for studying Latin, Greek, or other languages. One can speculate that they saw such studies as part of their equipage as cultured gentlewomen, a culture they shared with friends, brothers, and husbands.

The mathematics and science curriculum of Victorian female education was less consistent than the linguistic training. It was also more subject to a young woman's interests and the family's traditions. Daughters of medical and scientific families were more likely to study science than were girls from other sorts of families. Most of the girls in all these families studied arithmetic, algebra, basic science, and geography. Beyond the basics they followed individual intellectual paths and read extensively in subjects of interest. Jeannette Marshall studied algebra, first with a governess and then on her own, for several years. Rose Paget enjoyed geology and botany, but her sister found them unpalatable. As Maud told her, "I have finished your odious little book on Botany & never was so confused in my life!" Maud did better with more abstract subjects: "Your book of logic is very good," she told Rose in June of 1880. "I feel my mind much enlarged already by its perusal." By the end of the month she had read four books on logic. Mary Kingsley studied mathematics, physics, chemistry, and medicine on her own, drawing on the resources of her family's library.[62]

Like Rose and Maud Paget and Mary Kingsley, most Victorian gentlewomen who studied science did so at home. In the 1840s and after, Eleanor Ormerod gave way to the "naturalist element" in her character by studying "bird, plant, and insect life, to say nothing of reptiles." She preserved snake skeletons and, with the help of her brothers' microscope, she prepared "sections of teeth and other objects for the microscope as beautifully as any professional microscopist."[63] Until late in the nineteenth century, women and men alike usually pursued their scientific interests outside the framework of formal institutions of learning.

Women's educational opportunities were institutionalized with the foundation of schools and especially the colleges for women in Cambridge and Oxford after 1868. With these developments came the formal opportunity to study science in a university context. Even independent of women's colleges, some women made use of the universities' laboratories and scientific facilities.[64] Most of the women of the present study avoided institutionalized education and the examinations and career orientation that went with them. The exceptions at the university level include Rose Paget and Eleanor Balfour Sidgwick.

Rose Paget's interest in science led her first to mathematics and then into the laboratory. Physicist Lord Rayleigh described her experience: "feeling the need of intellectual food more satisfying than French and German she gained a fair acquaintance with elementary mathematics." She began attending lectures and demonstrations at the Cavendish Laboratory in 1887, and in 1888 she moved on to the advanced demonstrations presented by J. J. Thomson, professor of physics. On October 15, 1888, Thomson wrote to Paget to tell her, "I think I have found a subject which you could work at with advantage," and Rose began research in the Cavendish Laboratory, studying "the stationary vibrations of soap films at audible frequencies." Thomson explained the project to her, provided her with the necessary laboratory apparatus, and lent her reading materials. Rose studied physics for over two years. When Eleanor Balfour Sidgwick was a girl, her mother was her tutor and the source of her early interest in mathematics and science. She continued her studies after her marriage, doing research in physics at the Cavendish Laboratory for several years.[65]

For all that one may say about the lack of structure, indeed the anarchy, of the education of these girls and women, it is also clear that they had access to all the subjects in the Victorian curriculum. It is also true that they based their learning upon their own interests, their initiative to read, their families' support, and their local circumstances. In the end, many had the finest education the times and family resources could offer.

Some gentlewomen may have suffered from the haphazard quality their parents tolerated in their education, but they also enjoyed a great diversity of options. They could study what they wanted, and most were highly educated. They show that female education could be thorough. In this respect they differed very little from the leisured gentlemen who pursued a liberal education in philosophy or biology with no need to make a profession or career of such interests.

The education of gentlewomen in the Victorian period was useful and relevant in much the same way that a gentleman's was so—incidentally rather than systematically, in broad cultural terms more than in merely practical ways. It was liberal, not narrowly functional. Of course they taught their children what they had learned, Latin and Greek and some knowledge of the world around them, and they may have adorned their drawing rooms with their paintings and their music. Education and custom were, alike, the foundations of their culture as English gentlewomen in the Victorian age.

They studied widely, often deeply, and their education, although usually not formal, institutional, and tidy, was rich and strong. Unlike *Middlemarch*'s Rosamond Vincy, whose education may have been schooled and orderly, but was shallow and showy, the Paget women and their circle went far beyond the basics of reading, writing, and arithmetic. They learned geography and history and foreign languages—sometimes many modern and classical languages. They found arenas of learning that they enjoyed, and they pursued them to some depth. Their education did not end at age seventeen. For most, reading and learning went on for a lifetime. Like George Eliot's Dorothea, who married and expected to continue learning, the Victorian women of this circle began habits early that led, for most, to their continuing development as literate and cultured women.

Victorian gentlewomen's education was not market-oriented. Nor was it oriented to the marriage market in the usual sense of that phrase. Typically the education of women is dismissed as "man-catching" in the sense that a Victorian husband would only be attracted by drawing-room skills, by abilities that made a woman seem decorative, but that were essentially trivial. But if Fenton Hort was correct, gentlemen were attracted by a woman of achievements and intellectual seriousness, not by a frivolously got-up female. In that sense, an education of quality was an education most likely to attract a gentleman. It also led to the best sort of Victorian marriage—but more of that in later chapters.

The Paget women and their friends were not the reformers and the avantgarde, not the path-breakers for new opportunities for women. They were the most conventional of Victorian women, oriented toward the status quo, toward married life and the ordinary experiences of their class and time. For that very reason, their serious involvement in language, art, and science seems to indicate a pattern of intellectual life common to Victorian gentlewomen. Their education was the first measure of their culture as gentlewomen; the second was the use to which their learning was put.

CHAPTER THREE

Sex, Friendship, and Love: Gentlewomen's Physical and Emotional Lives

Jeannette Marshall, daughter of a London surgeon, entertained her fiancé in her family's house in Savile Row. The couple spent their time alone together in kissing and cuddling, mainly at his initiative. When he "wants to kiss me madly," Jeannette confided to her diary, "he does." He wanted her to sit on his lap and, she said, "I consented for a minute or two, tho' I warned him I was very heavy. He exclaimed 'Heavy! I cd. nurse you all day!' He kissed me, & declared I had the most beautiful figure, & whispered a fair amount of nonsense."[1] Her maidenly reluctance gave way, first to a willingness to listen to her eager lover, then to gratification in his attentive "nonsense." Her acceptance and enjoyment of his embraces make her an unusual, even un-Victorian, lady. Perhaps.

This chapter will examine women's so-called "private" lives—their bodies, physical activities, and health, their sexual knowledge as well as their sexual relations and their emotional relationships with men—to try to establish what ladies' lives in these domains were really like. Avoiding the theorizing of Victorian doctors and sexologists, this chapter will examine what the record can tell us of women's day-to-day life. Implicit in the discussion presented here is the understanding that the personal is political, that gentlewomen's physical freedom (or lack thereof), their sexual knowledge, and their various relations with men are all indices of women's power.

WOMEN, BODIES, AND SEX

The subject believed to be most fraught with tension, secrecy, and denial in the Victorian code of morals and mores was sex. Steven Marcus, in his influential volume, *The Other Victorians*, argued that Victorians were "alienated" from their own physical existence. If this was true of Victorians generally, it was considered particularly true of the Victorian lady. On this point Marcus, and many since, quoted Dr. William Acton, who claimed that "the majority of women (happily for society) are not very much troubled with sexual feelings of any kind." Peter Gay has challenged this image of sexless Victorian bourgeois womanhood in Europe and America, but he draws most of his cases from Germany and the United States. Recently Edward Shorter concentrated on the problems of women's health—what women suffered in the lifelong trial of being female—and another scholar has repeated the received wisdom that there was a "high incidence of female invalidism."[2] But to look only at sexual function or at female disease is not enough; Victorian women's sexuality needs to be seen as part of a larger discussion of their physical lives and their attitudes toward their bodies, their knowledge of and attitudes toward sex, and their relationships, both physical and emotional, with men.

To begin with, most of the females of this study were physically energetic and active—as children, as adolescents, and as adults, both before and after childbirth. Even the most cursory examination of *Punch* and other Victorian illustrated periodicals reveals women depicted in a variety of energetic physical activities: riding, skating, cycling, and other sports. But only the records of women's real lives can tell us whether the magazines represented their lives accurately. Harriet Lewin Grote took pride in having had "from earliest childhood . . . a remarkably energetic disposition." She took "most pleasure in active exercises requiring bodily agility, nerve, and invention, and involving skill, and even some personal danger." In the first decade of the nineteenth century, when she was in her teens, she rode horses "bare backed," flew kites, and "of course she was . . . proficient in climbing trees" whether in the country or in London's Green Park.[3]

Walking was a basic form of exercise, sport, or entertainment in every generation. Lydia North went for walks in London, along the quayside in Great Yarmouth, and around St. Mary's on her holiday in the Isles of Scilly in the 1830s and 1840s. When Emmie and Cherrie Pilkington visited Cambridge they arranged walks several times a week with their friends. The Cambridge women also took long walks on their vacations in Wales. Maud walked the six miles from Penmaenmawr to Conway and back one autumn day in 1879. Catharine Paget was aware that physical activity could be an antidote to the tensions generated by family problems or bad moods. In July of 1870 she had "A vexatious wasted sort of day, all indecision about [our] summer holiday." Her therapy: "I went at 5 o'clock for a little walk to get reasonable." In August, when she was feeling ill-humored, she said, "I walked myself a little out of my stupidity." Sometimes she walked many miles because of the demands of her day: after morning charity work, Catharine and her brother saw to some picture-framing and after that "walked . . . up to Hampstead which tired me immensely." They then made some social calls and went home.[4]

Hiking and climbing were natural extensions of women's walking. In the summer of 1870 James and Lydia took a house in Wales, and Catharine spent much of her summer there. She and her companions had more than one "splendid scrambling walk" in the hilly Welsh countryside. On another occasion they climbed Mt. Snowdon all the way to the top, some 3,500 feet. On August 25, 1870, the Pagets made a long day of their outing. Together with the Gull and Rowden families, they left Penmaenmawr for Llanberis at 8:30 a.m., arriving at 10:30. There they joined forces with Sir Richard and Lady Malins and a Miss Cary and "all went up Snowdon a long cavalcade & many walkers. I," Catharine reported, "walked all the way up & down. It was very windy at the top but *perfectly* clear & a grand view." The party "had a capital dinner at the Royal Victoria Hotel & got home by our favourite 7.26 [train]."[5]

A decade later Catharine's cousin Maud was in Penmaenmawr with her guest, Edith Tait, the daughter of Archbishop and Mrs. Tait. Both were climbers. Maud judged that Edith was "quite equal to me in energy, &c." Maud and her party hiked up Mt. Snowdon in less than two hours in the rain. Other women went further afield, finding Alpine climbing to their taste. For example, Maggie, Nellie, and A. C. Benson (all in their twenties) went to the Swiss Alps for climbing in the 1880s. Climbing was not reserved for the young. On her frequent trips to Wales, Clara (now Lady Paget, and forty-five to fifty years of age) took pleasure in hours-long hikes in the mountainous regions of North Wales. Visitors of both sexes, including one Miss Challis and Anna Maria Perowne (nearly fifty years old, too) joined her on these vigorous expeditions.[6]

Summer activities also included riding, tennis, swimming, and other outdoor sports. Young Lydia North went horseback-riding with her sister Sarah during their holiday in the Isles of Scilly. Sarah was not fond of riding, and Lydia paced herself to her sister's lower level of skill. Usually she rode with more vigor, and her brother labeled her "Minshi [sic] the Son of Jehu." Lydia reported all this to her fiancé with pride: "so you see dear, what a very Amazonian young lady I am become." Victorian magazines depicted women driving carts and carriages, sometimes with male passengers. Lydia North drove a pony chaise; her brother thought she drove too fast. Lady Prestwich, wife of the geologist, was also known for her hard riding. The Pilkington girls rode horseback in the late 1870s, and in Oxford Felicia Skene was "devoted to riding." Maggie Benson was an "excellent horsewoman," and Catharine Tait was never happier than when she was "galloping by . . . [her husband's] side in the green lanes and over the meadows." Tennis was a standard summer sport; the Pilkington girls played regularly. Rose Paget had many games of "Lawn Tennis" during her visit with them in Ireland. She played with Mr. Apjohn, too.[7]

In 1870 Catharine Paget, her younger sister Mary, and their friend Carrie Gull enjoyed a "capital bathe in a good rough sea." Catharine and Mary's mother Lydia, aged fifty-five, also went swimming that summer. When the sea was rough, swimming posed minor dangers. The sea was "frightfully rough" in late August and Catharine's "mamma cut her hand & legs" while bathing. Rose and Maud learned to swim during their summers in Wales.[8]

Croquet is the stereotypical Victorian ladies' game, but I have found no evidence that any girls or women of the Paget circle ever played croquet. Cricket, however, was the summer favorite among the young women as well as the young men. One Wednesday in that summer of 1870, church services, swimming, and music practice took up the morning hours. A game of cricket followed after lunch. Catharine noted that "I played a brilliant innings with a stick at cricket." A few days later the Paget holiday-makers and their friends—"we *all 20 in number*"—had their pictures taken in front of the Pagets' house in Penmaenmawr. After the picture session "we turned to playing cricket & had a grand double wicket match." When the Gull family visited the Paget family in North Wales in 1870, they had a picnic on the "heather covered high ground behind Moel Lys," and afterward the eager party of young men and women "played cricket with a will and shouted more than was prudent," given the singing scheduled for the evening. A decade or two later, young women in Oxford played cricket for their colleges. In addition to being an "excellent lawn-tennis player," Nellie Benson was a "member of the ladies' cricket eleven" at Oxford in the early 1880s.[9]

In the winter, skating attracted the young people, and sedate decorum was not the order of the day on the ice, any more than on horseback or the cricket pitch. At age twenty-four, Catharine learned to ice skate: "I had lots of tumbles but enjoyed it all." Mary Baird, on the other hand, felt herself a "coward" because she did not enjoy spills on the ice. Another sport requiring energy and skill was hockey.[10]

With the invention and perfecting of the bicycle, women and men found a new means of locomotion, and the Paget women were among those who enjoyed its benefits. Mary Maud Paget took a trip to the continent in July of 1899 with several friends, including Daisy DuCane. "We rode 40 miles yesterday [on bicycles] in heat," she told her father. She admitted that she found it strenuous, but at that point she was almost thirty-nine years old. Only regular habits of exercise could have made such a trip possible for "MMP." Other sorts of outdoor activities also revealed women's physical energy and freedom of movement. Margaret Benson was thought to have "weak" health, a circumstance that "necessitated her spending much time in foreign travel, especially in Egypt." But a reputation for fragility did not mean helplessness or inaction: Margaret and her friend Janet Gourlay used the opportunity of being in Egypt to carry out some archeological work; they "excavated a temple precinct near Luxor."[11]

Maud Paget Gadow engaged in some of the most sustained physical activity to be seen among the women studied here. She and her husband took five trips to the Spanish-speaking world, two to Spain in the 1890s and three to southern Mexico in the summers of 1906 to 1908. Even in the wild, Maud did not abandon her ladylike style. She had "the strongest possible objection to appearing singular by a want of attention to the suitability of dress," so she found "a strong good tweed suit," good travel wear, she thought, even in the summer. But she also took along "a thin silk skirt, with a couple of thin pretty blouses" to wear when in town, meeting academics and local dignitaries. Maud's concern for propriety should not mislead us. The Gadows' travels were demanding ventures, calling for much energy and physical prowess. Their routes covered hundreds of miles, and Maud and Hans traveled on foot and on horse- and donkey-back as well as by train and carriage. They encountered some demanding terrain. In Spain, climbing to see a cave, they found that "The last bit, near the peaky cliffs, was arduous, and we had to make use of the rope, hauling each other up and crawling along an uncomfortable ledge, just before we reached the entrance of the cave." When the couple traveled on horseback in Spain, Maud used a "lady's saddle," her husband said, "a sort of gaily caparisoned armchair with a footboard, which looks very comfortable, but," he admitted, "is not." On horses or donkeys they forded rivers, crossed plains, and climbed to about 4,600 feet altitude in Spain's Los Picos de Europa.[12]

Hans and Maud's Mexican travels, for a total of eight months in the summers of 1902 and 1904 (when Maud was in her mid-forties), took them "off the few tourist-tracks, through some rather wild and little-known districts" in southern Mexico. On horseback they rode into the mountains, to heights of 14,400 feet, where they camped in a tent and stored their gear in a roughly-built shed. The summer's heat in the lowlands, the cold of the high mountains, the "fine, gritty dust which [crept] into everything," the rain, hunger, rattlesnakes—all these were part of the physical rigors of travel Maud encountered.[13]

The high point (literally) of their Mexican journey was the climb up Mt. Popocatepetl. In September of 1904, having seen the mountain from Mexico City and Cuernavaca, they vowed to climb to the top. They approached the mountain by train and then on horseback. At 14,500 feet they had to leave the horses behind and go the rest of the way on foot, because "the loose lava and ashes, into which the horses sink, and the steeper slope make progress very difficult." Once they reached the snow, the "ascent," Hans recalled, "was easy. . . . The snow was in excellent condition, firm, with a thin hard crust." Hans "kicked step after step into the snow" for Maud to follow. He found "this step-kicking, continued for hours, became very exhausting work." Whenever they paused in their ascent, they had to dig their poles into the snow and hold on to them to keep from slipping.[14]

The climbers began to experience "some difficulty breathing" when they neared an altitude of 17,000 feet. At that point the light was "fierce," the air was freezing cold—and thin. They began to feel tired and experienced "a curious lassitude, with slight nausea." Progress became more difficult: "It required some force of will to make fifty steps without stopping. Then these were reduced to thirty, twenty, and at last five." They were "panting and gasping for air" and suffered the other marks of oxygen shortage, "throbbing in the temples, . . . giddiness and a nauseous sinking feeling." After climbing steadily for four and one-half hours, with less than half an hour in all of short rests, they reached the "rim of the crater," at an altitude of some 17,500 feet. They rested and enjoyed the spectacular scenery, "dazzling sun, . . . pillars of ice, . . . bright yellow patches of sulphur." They descended, using a straw mat as a sort of toboggan, with a stick serving as a crude brake. Hans, Maud, and their guide all sat on a single mat and slid at increasing speed down the mountain side, barely missing rocks along the way. The snow, meanwhile, became too soft to support them and for a half-hour they "floundered about, breaking through [the snow] . . . up to the armpits." Fierce weather and nightfall overtook them, making the last hours of their return both frightening and dangerous. Hans came away from the climb with a severe sunburn, but Maud, having worn a hat and veil, came out unscathed.[15]

Maud's physically demanding travels were not unique. George Kingsley's daughter Mary traveled extensively in Africa. She "travelled rough," and she learned to navigate and to climb a rope ladder. Marianne North went to Syria and Egypt with her father and traveled all around the world by herself after he died. Many of the women of this study traveled in Britain and on the continent, taking time to walk and climb, for anthropological or aesthetic purposes.[16] Physical vigor exercised with apparent freedom in a wide range of environments was a norm of gentlewomen's lives.

Their physical activities and generally high level of energy point to excellent health and very little sign of "female invalidism." Most often Victorian observers took that for granted; only occasionally was a woman's "wonderfully good health" a matter of mention. Such health was interrupted by occasional illnesses. Predictably, given the limited record and Victorian reticence about sexual matters, little evidence exists that these problems were sex-specific, except in the case of pregnancies and childbirth. Rather, it is clear that the Paget women and their friends suffered, aside from the problems accompanying pregnancy, from sex-neutral diseases and discomforts that might appear in the health histories of either sex, but not evidently from the major gynecological disorders that could limit women's lives and pleasures. In July of 1870, Catharine suffered from a "face sore and stiff," which was "not very bad." A month later she had an "unlucky toothache," probably the source of the difficulties in July. At other times she was out, about, active. The McDougalls both suffered from "Labuan fever" in Borneo and, after they returned to England, from recurrent attacks of bronchitis; Harriette also suffered from pleurisy. Mrs. Gull was "unluckily laid up" briefly in 1870 with a "sprained foot." Maud also "managed to twist her foot" while learning to play tennis on a summer holiday in Ireland, but it was "nothing very serious." Netty Huxley had bouts of unnamed illnesses in her adult life but there is no clue to their nature. Catharine Paget's experience seems typical of the Paget women and their circle. Apart from common ailments—a cold, a toothache, an inflamed eye—their health was generally good.[17]

The reproductive histories of these women follow the pattern of what is known about Victorian demography. Most before 1870 had large families, although none as large as Betsey's seventeen. After 1870 family size declined among these women—as in the middle classes generally—presumably with the use of contraception. A few of the women of this circle died as young married women; we can guess that these deaths came in childbirth or complications resulting from it. For example, Frederick Paget's first and second wives, Elizabeth Rogers and Hester King, probably both died as a result of complications in childbirth. Agnes Tait Ellison died two months after the birth of her first child, and Mary Louise Moberly died one year after her marriage to George Ridding. A few died in mid-life: Connie Buxton died in her early thirties, Helen Paget in her early forties (of meningitis), and Ellen Hordern Lubbock in her late forties or fifties.[18]

There is little evidence that specifically female diseases were a source of trouble for these women. Menstruation was an evident problem for at least one woman. Rose Paget suffered some discomfort, she consulted her father, a physician, and he advised her. "During your 'poorly' times," he said, "*rest yourself*—lying, if convenient on a couch. At other times, when you are *not* poorly, you can take exercise and will be the better for it." Lydia North had intermittent difficulties with ill temper and depression that suggest a cyclical problem related to ovulation and menstruation. Catharine Paget, too, may have suffered a bit from her menstrual cycle. She found herself at intervals feeling "dull" or low—perhaps describing what is now known as premenstrual syndrome—but she never explicitly linked her blue moods to her physiology.[19]

In middle life and after, the women continued to suffer from disorders common to both sexes. Some were serious, even life-threatening. Betsey, for example, seems to have suffered from a series of minor strokes late in life. Eleanor Ormerod had occasional migraine headaches in mid-life, from overwork, her friends thought. In 1882, when she was fifty-four, she had an accident: she was hit by a carriage. She did not take proper care of her injury and as a result she was lame for the rest of her life. She had to live quietly after the accident, "in marked contrast," she observed, "to the extremely active life I had led in my early years." Despite this disclaimer, her life continued to be a busy one. A decade later her health worsened and she had to curtail her activities further. This new development may have been the first sign of the cancer that took her life in 1901.[20]

Only a few women in this study suffered chronic ill health. From the beginning of their married life Harriet and George Grote lived with his parents in cramped and unpleasant circumstances. Harriet ailed often and seemed fated for a life of illness. Her health improved as soon as they moved into their own quarters, suggesting that the origins of her illness were psychosocial. Henrietta Barnett had "uncertain health" all her life, including bouts of "nerve failure" and "pneumonia" in middle age, but she lived to the age of eighty-five. Angie Acland seemed to be ailing all her life. As with many illnesses of both men and women, it is difficult to assess the seriousness of Angie's health problems. She suffered from minor ailments like boils or wens, and she was lame. She also had occasional depression, perhaps brought on by her parents' severity with her and their demands for her conduct. Advised to avoid severe climate in winter, she sometimes spent the winter in Torquay, or in Madeira or on the Riviera. No illness was, however, serious enough to send her to bed or to disable her permanently, and she lived to the ripe age of eighty-one. The senior Mrs. Moule was an invalid from mid-life, and Fanny Hort's mother-in-law, Anne Hort, reportedly suffered long ill health before her death in 1865 at the age of sixty-four.[21]

Mental illness, whether depression or more severe disorders, appears to have occurred only rarely. Among the women whose lives displayed exceptions to this norm of good mental health were Elise Paget and Maggie Benson. Elise, the reader will recall, left her family in Austria to spend her life from age eighteen to her mid-forties in England, living with two maiden aunts in Pinner. Never entirely at home in England, separated from her (by now) very Austrian family, she suffered an anomic existence, belonging nowhere. After her two aunts died, her life showed signs of some greater degree of freedom—a London flat, travel with friends, but never, perhaps, the stability and security she might have wished. In 1889 she made a will and soon thereafter left for the continent. On this "little holiday . . . , she died: she died suddenly, and mysteriously," her cousin Stephen recalled, and Stephen's father "went out [to France], and came back and would say nothing to us. There was something which we must not talk of."[22] Suicide is just below the surface of Stephen's account.

Maggie Benson's life had a less obscure, though no less tragic, finale. Maggie had from childhood been overly sensitive, too capable of remorse, intensely emotional. She never married, and she spent her life productively, in ways to be discussed later. But in her forties she was subject to increasingly frequent bouts of depression that made her fear for her sanity. Her depression was accompanied by the certainty that family and friends were plotting against her. Finally, hospitalized with a "breakdown," she began to struggle to recover the mind she had lost. The mental illness from which she suffered may have been paranoid schizophrenia. She recovered, apparently spontaneously. But (whether from medication or from genetic heritage) her heart was weak. She died of heart disease at the age of fifty-one.[23] Anomie, depression, breakdown, and possible suicide were rare among the upper-middle-class women studied here; their rarity was, in any case, a far cry from the endemic physical and mental illness that is thought to have been a Victorian female norm.

Physical and mental health are the larger frame within which to examine the vexing question of Victorian women's sexuality. In this specific matter of sexual relations, the search for evidence becomes difficult. The Pagets and their friends are typical in their relative silence about this, and one might argue that such silence provides irrefutable evidence that the Victorian middle classes were repressed and hypocritical. But a careful examination of the record reveals, first of all, that these women knew about sex and had levels of tolerance about sexual matters and sexual misbehavior that belie the Victorians' reputation for prudery. At one level we can observe the casual physical intimacy of home life, for example, in the Tait family in the 1840s. Catharine Tait was very close to her little boy, Craufurd, and when one of his "little sisters . . . came into the world, he was found watching, stretched on the mat at his mother's door" during the delivery.[24] Less casual, but no less intimate, was Mary Baird's awareness, early on, of the sexual and emotional tensions in her parents' lives. "My mother," Mary said, "*was* extravagant and she did like new clothes and to look nice, and when this meant—as it inevitably did—attracting moth-like men friends, there was trouble, and the worst was I always knew it!"[25]

As adults, these women knew about the sordid versions of sexuality. Nellie Benson, for example, heard accusations of father-daughter incest from one of the poor women in her district. Edith Davidson discussed child prostitution and W. T. Stead's campaign against it with her husband. Charitable work took women into the homes not only of respectable poor families in their districts but also into the homes of the disreputable and "immoral." Elma Paget, one of the many who worked among the poor, made it clear that women did not (and should not) blind themselves to the evils, sexual and otherwise, they saw in their work: "you have to learn about some of the sorrow in the world, and then it is very tempting to say I *won't* know, and to stop your ears and run away." Instead, women recognized the existence of "intemperance" and "lust." Effective charitable work required that women understand the temptations and dangers confronting poor families. These women workers were fully aware, for example, of "the sale from house to house of indecent literature, the advertisement and sale of illicit drugs or appliances, [and] the exhibition of impure postcards," as well as "street betting" and "bad houses." There were "signs of vice" everywhere.[26]

Victorian ladies knew about sex, sexual vice, prostitution, and pornography. And men did not try to protect them from that knowledge or from meeting the problems face to face. Henrietta Rowland, in her work among the poor of London's East End, became acquainted with a young woman identified only as "Lucy T——." One day Lucy left her home and went "to live with a disreputable companion," and Henrietta asked her fiancé, Samuel Barnett, to go with her to look for Lucy. Barnett refused: it is "neither brave nor kind," he said, "to shield one we love from what might be unpleasant." Henrietta went alone to look for Lucy in "those haunts of vice." Henrietta Rowland also faced vice when she dealt with the problems of the "feeble-minded" girls she worked with. They had no work and nowhere to go. If they went into the workhouse, "they had the right to take their discharge, and often did so," Rowland observed, "with women fiends"—brothel-keepers "who offered to 'take care' of them." Whorehouses and prostitution awaited these helpless creatures, and Henrietta and her co-worker Miss Jennings did what they could to help; Jennings agreed to live with twelve of the girls and tried to teach them the beginnings of "character" and "self-respect."[27]

Neither age nor marital status kept women away from the rescue work that brought them in touch with the sexual underworld. Spinster Felicia Skene began her rescue work in Oxford when she was young and continued it throughout her life. Mary Baird Smith began working in Oxford as a young married woman. She dealt often with "fallen women," not prostitutes, but women who had been engaging in illicit sex with a lover. Smith found more fault with women who were "cruel, or even unkind," than those guilty of sexual sins. Women who had "fallen," she said, had done so out of love. Even in her sympathy Smith was fully aware of their sexual acts.[28]

Whatever we may think of their attitude toward pornography or prostitution, it is not possible to charge these women with prudery or blindness or denial of the facts of sex in the world they inhabited. Ignorance of sexual exploitation and prostitution would have served no charitable or Christian purpose, and the women workers in the poor neighborhoods of Victorian cities and towns did not disguise the truth from themselves. Their candor about the sexual dangers confronting poor women was not often matched— at least in the written record—by such frankness about their own sexual feelings. But there are hints, and more than hints, that these women were sexually active and responsive and recognized sexual responsiveness in others. As in the matter of bodies and sexuality, a narrow focus on female-male sexual relations is less useful than a look at the largest possible picture of women's relations with men.

VICTORIAN LADIES' RELATIONS WITH MEN

The classic dinner scene of upper-middle-class society—men together after dinner with port and cigars, women retiring to a separate social space—may stand as a metaphor for the presumed segregation of men and women in the Victorian era. We have already seen how, within families and among a family's friends, such segregation did not hold: fathers and daughters, mothers and sons, sisters and brothers, and women and men in groups participated together in educational and social activities—from Latin lessons to cricket games. But one-to-one relations between the sexes, we have assumed, must only have taken place between suitor and courted, or between husband and wife. On the contrary, among the networks examined here, friendships and close associations between women and men were common, but up to now these relationships have had almost no attention.

George Eliot's heroine in *Middlemarch* illustrates the point very well. Seventeen-year-old Dorothea Brooke and her neighbor and friend, Sir James Chettham, joined forces to draw up plans for improved cottages for agricultural laborers. Her plans and his money together were to make a difference in the lives of the poor.[29] Their shared activities suggest something of the possibilities for social relations between women and men. The historical record reveals two distinguishable sorts of relationships: friendship between age peers, and mentorship—often between older men and younger women, sometimes between an older woman and a younger man.

In Great Yarmouth Betsey Paget's sisters, Maria Jane and Frances, "did not understand" her and they "were vexed sometimes at her reserve and her indifference to their sentiments," but both of them enjoyed the "gaiety and swiftness" of the house on the quay and they "greatly admired Samuel." A similar set of relations existed in London in the next generation. During their engagement Lydia and James often had the company of her sisters. Sarah North in particular found James a congenial companion, and her notes and letters to him carry friendly, sometimes flirtatious, messages. Her coy apologies for writing to him "unsolicited, and uncalled for by a previous communication from you," gave way to the more straightforward admission that "I miss you very much [on] Sundays."[30] Sarah's affection for James was a quasi-familial one. More striking are those outside the domestic circle.

The friendship between Louise von Glehn and J. R. Green began in the family circle, for he was a friend of her parents and her sister Olga as well. The difference in age between young Louise and the historian was twelve or thirteen years, but parity rather than inequality marked their relations. She supported him as much as he helped her, and they shared ideas about many things. The test came in 1871, when Louise told him of her plans to marry Mandell Creighton. He congratulated her but added candidly, "there is always a shadow of dread about a friend's marriage, and I have too few real friends to care to lose *one*." Louise had reassured him on this point: "such a frank, warm-hearted note as yours dispels all dread. I feel that our friendship will remain just as warm and true as ever, although you will have some one else now to treat you to 'wise conversation.'" As a bachelor in his mid-thirties, Lydia Paget's son Frank had close female friends, in particular Miss Lawrence (daughter of a London surgeon) and Miss Lightfoot. Miss Lightfoot ran a London nursing home in the 1880s, and she and Frank exchanged letters on theological matters. Sometimes a will provides the only surviving evidence of a woman's friendships. Clara Fardell Paget named Austen Leigh one of her executors. He was not a solicitor and, in the absence of any other clues to his ties to the family, one must guess he had this role because of their friendship. Angie Acland called her medical attendant Hugh Robinson "my friend." Hannah Brightwen made a clear distinction between those who were "my dear Husbands [sic] and my friends" and those who were hers alone. Among the latter were several men: "my valued friend William Barber," "my valued friend The Venerable Archdeacon Henry Ralph Nevill," and "my kind friend and helper William Jackson."[31]

Felicia Mary Skene counted Sir Henry Acland among her close Oxford friends. The thirteen-year difference in their ages may have mattered in the early years of their association, but it was insignificant in the 1890s, when she was in her seventies and he over eighty. They shared professional, religious, and family confidences. For example, Acland asked Skene to read one of his lectures, an address on medical missions, to be sure that his religious views were clear. She reassured him on the point, made suggestions about the lecture's content, and insisted on the suitability of the piece for publication. In the next year she gave him prepublication comments and suggestions on another pamphlet he was working on, all the while assuring him that she found his work "admirable." Skene also advised Acland on religious matters. When he asked her "what book of private prayer to use," she refused to offer any recommendation, explaining that her idea of intimacy with God precluded such props. She relented, however, and two months later sent Acland "a small litany" she had put together, made up of "some of Christ's words." Felicia Skene acted as an intermediary in Acland's relations with his daughter Angie. When relations between Angie and her ailing father were strained, Skene tried to reassure her, reporting Acland's opinion that she was "perfect." He thought you were "an angel," Skene told her, "in the way you did everything for him" during his illness. She tried to convince the distressed daughter that her father's "loving trust" was more important than "the vague fancies & mistaken ideas his weakness produces."[32]

Other friendships took place between women and men of disparate ages; commonly the man was older and the woman younger. In 1827 Harriet Grote, then a married woman in her thirties, began a long correspondence with the French political economist Jean Baptiste Say (1767–1832), a man many years her senior. From 1844 she provided both hospitality and a quiet haven to her friend, the German composer Felix Mendelssohn (1809–1847), a man much younger than she. In these friendships both parties benefited. Grote's biographer also suggests mentorship or patronage in Harriet's relationships with English politicians, but the hints are tantalizingly vague: she noted only that Harriet Grote was "a recognized authority" on some matters of international and domestic policy and that, as a result, she was the source of "inspirations" to "many a leading man" in public life. Eleanor Ormerod found male friendships important in her intellectual pursuits. Her father rather disapproved of her interest in natural history, but he nevertheless introduced her to an Oxford entomologist, Professor J. O. Westwood (1805–93), in whom she found a mentor. He was twenty-three years older than she, and a man of experience and connections. From the earliest days of her interest in entomology, he helped her. He read her writings and made unhesitating suggestions for their improvement. A mark of their friendship was his habit of taking "the privilege of knocking her work about" and her delight in the fact. Later in life she was on close friendly terms with the Scots entomologist Robert Wallace, she in her sixties, he in his thirties. She was also mentor and friend to naturalist C. V. Riley (1843–92), fifteen years her junior.[33]

Handley Moule kept up an affectionate correspondence with his great-niece, Joyce Barton. Amy, Lord Houghton's daughter, and F. T. Palgrave wrote to each other often, and the father was grateful for Palgrave's interest: Houghton found Palgrave's letters to Amy "charming" and "an education in themselves." Catharine Paget and T. H. Huxley met through her father's association with him, but the relationship between the twenty-five-year-old single woman and the forty-five-year-old man had a dimension of its own. They shared linguistic interests and collaborated on some translations. Meanwhile Netty Huxley kept up a friendly correspondence with Charles Darwin.[34]

Angie Acland remained single all her life, but she developed a wide and long-standing set of relationships with men. She met many through her distinguished father, and "his friends were her friends." She and Sir James Paget exchanged greetings through her father in the early days, but Angie's friendship with this man who was thirty-five years her senior developed independently. They grew very fond of each other, their affection clear in the course of mundane communications. When, for example, Angie asked Mary Paget to ask her father's advice about wines, James Paget wrote back: "I love [my daughter] very much but I shall not give her the pleasure of writing to you when I may myself justly have it." In the 1880s Angie took Sir James's photograph. When Lady Paget complained that Sir James looked sad in the photo, he comforted Angie with the assurance that "this is my fault, not yours." The old Sir James and the middle-aged Angie continued their correspondence and fond relationship for the rest of his life, and he was always grateful to his "Dear Angie" for her "affectionate" letters and "loving wishes."[35]

John Ruskin (1819–1900), thirty years older than Angie, was another of her fond friends. He came to the Acland home frequently in the 1870s and after. Catharine Paget, visiting the Aclands in the summer of 1871, saw Ruskin there "almost every day." "Nothing could be simpler or more charming," she thought, "than his ways with Angie." The two had luncheons and teas and drove together. He "comforted" and "scolded" her. Ruskin took particular interest in Angie's painting, and he came to have an influence on her artistic work. George Richmond (1809–96), the artist, and W. H. Smith (1825–91), M.P. and heir to the newsagent W. H. Smith, were also Angie's friends. Smith addressed her as "My dear Angie" and asked her advice on parish personnel matters.[36]

Margaret Stokes's father, William, was a medical colleague of Angie's father, and after Dr. Stokes's death in 1878, Margaret (then aged forty-six) found a "dear friend" in Sir Henry Acland (aged sixty-four). She looked to him for advice and support. When thinking of writing a memoir of her father, for example, she asked Acland to recommend the "life of a remarkable medical man which you would advise me to look at as a pattern." In a similar vein Harriette Bunyon looked to F. D. Maurice as her "honoured friend and teacher."[37]

Winnie Talbot, the daughter of Bishop E. S. Talbot, had a close friendship with Bishop (later Archbishop) Randall Davidson that began when she was sixteen and he was fifty. Her early shyness in their acquaintance disappeared as she saw Davidson and his wife frequently at Lambeth Palace in the late 1890s. From the earliest days of their acquaintance, Davidson took an interest in her religious life. On one occasion, he and Miss Talbot "said Evensong together in his room." On another occasion he asked her, she said, "searching questions about my Bible reading. I remember trying to hedge," she later recalled, but Davidson "pierced at once" through her evasions. The two established the habit of reading together. While reading a book on the Reformation, she reported, he expressed "shock . . . at my abysmal ignorance." They went on from church history to the national debt, he quizzing her, "and when [she] . . . had to cry ignorance," Davidson mock-scolded her: "'You old donkey, don't you know *that?*'"[38] His outrageous language speaks to an intimacy between them that precluded insult.

It is hard to know just what to make of these associations. (Indeed, the question itself suggests that the problem may belong to our century and not to the nineteenth, for the Victorians apparently took them for granted.) It is tempting to see these relationships as Pygmalion-like arrangements, with an older man involved in a relationship with a younger woman to whom he was a teacher to a developing personality, but the Pygmalion story is a cross-class one, whose focus is the distance between the Cockney world and the upper-middle class. Moreover, in some cases Victorian gentlewomen were the senior partners in these friendships. These relationships suggest that Victorian men (and women) at mid-life may have found some gratification in admiration from, and affectionate closeness to, a younger person. And these relationships might have served young people as an apprenticeship for marriage. Certainly these associations shaped women's and men's relationships, especially if they came early in life. Specifically, young people learned to get along with each other outside the context of courtship: they learned that they could be friends. The friendship and the intimacy of these relationships are remarkable, and they may explain the nature of Victorian marriages. Finally, these friendships enriched the lives of women and men, young and old alike. In the end, they teach us that in friendship, as in many other features of these women's lives, sex segregation and "separate spheres" were not a rule of life.

ROMANCE, DESIRE, LOVE, AND MARRIAGE

The fact of friendship between men and women provides a new framework for understanding romantic and sexual relationships between the sexes. In the first place, the girls and women of the Paget circle repeatedly expressed their awareness of, and interest in, males in sensual terms. Attraction and physical contact between the sexes might begin at an early age: flirtations were common among the teenaged students at the Royal Academy of Music in the 1830s, when Lydia North was a pupil there. A generation later an unnamed girl had a surreptitious kiss from Lydia's boy Stephen "behind the schoolroom blind . . . at a little children's party." Stephen was "only 11 or 12 at the time." During their engagement, Lydia got into a debate with James over the relative evils of card-playing and dancing. Lydia argued for the lesser wickedness of dancing, but, she admitted, "I fear I rather like dancing." She believed her taste for it was "in *some degree* innocent as it would give me equal pleasure to dance *alone* to good music, as to dance with the ordinary run of strangers one meets."[39] She was aware that paired dancing, with its physical contact, might be a source of physical pleasure as well as an opportunity for merely social flirtation.

When Maud Paget (aged twenty-one) spotted a Mr. Bower at church, she "nearly jumped." "Do you remember," she asked her sister, the man "who used to play divinely on the fiddle at the Wed[nesday] Pops.'Twas he—'twas! he & no mistake." In the summer of 1880, Maud "went in the morning to look at the cricket for a couple of hours which was very pleasant; a certain person," male, surely, "came there and bowed & smiled," she told her sister. They found some men attractive, and one sister teased the other when a particular young man caught her fancy. In London Catharine's social life brought her into contact with many attractive men—and she noticed them. H. P. Liddon, canon of St. Paul's Cathedral, especially fascinated her. One service at St. Paul's included "A grand anthem . . . 'Lift up your heads' then a grand sermon the last alas! of Mr. Liddon's for the present. He preached on the rules of force, law, and love . . . pressing home the solemn responsibilities of man for man, the glorious duties of Love. Where," she asked herself, "shall I hear his earnest voice again."[40] Religious passion and earthly attractions were melded in Catharine's enthusiastic response to the handsome Canon Liddon.

In one rare instance a Victorian gentlewoman testified to sexual desire without a romantic object. Mary Smith's sympathy with the "fallen women" who were objects of her rescue work was accompanied by another reaction to their sexual activity. Speaking in the third person, she described the effects of working with the sexually fallen: "I have seen its harmful effect on young women, and how it may become as a 'craze' like anything else, with a spicy flavour all its own." When Felicia Skene told stories of her experience in rescue work, they "used to thrill me," Mary Smith admitted, "with horror."[41] Desire is not far below the surface of Smith's testimony of spice and thrills.

Flirtation and more serious sexual interaction were an acknowledged part of the byplay between two engaged people. Victorian biographers described the engagement as a time for the couple to be together, to have "opportunity for sweet communings in the interval between engagement and marriage." The intimacy could be playful. The Westcotts' romance, for example, partook of youthful courtship rituals: he addressed her by the Greek letter that stood for "Dearest," making it his secret sign of affection for her. Lydia North used scolding as a disguise for expressing her affection. "*How can you*," she asked James, "*be so cruel* as to endeavour to aggravate that miserable feeling of jealousy which you know is already so predominant in my disposition? . . . really I am quite shocked!!!" Beneath the teasing, she acknowledged herself to be both affectionate and ardent. She admitted to "a love so intense for an earthly object that I *dare* not indulge it but with some reference to the mercy of God." A generation later Caroline Gull confessed to similar feelings of the divine origins of Theodore Acland's love for her: "I wonder most that the great gift of his Love should have been given to me—to crown and perfect my life . . . a great wonder; to be explained only by GOD's Goodness."[42] The notion that one might love the beloved so much as to be sinful recurs in Victorian love letters. At the same time, religious observance could be the locus of emotional intimacy for a couple. Early in their courtship Lydia and James shared a hymnal during Sunday service, both a metaphorical and a physical drawing-together of the young man and woman. After they were engaged to marry and were separated for three months, they agreed to read the same chapter of the Bible at the same time each night, she in London and he in Paris. Perhaps sharing intimacy in a religious setting served to sanctify love and desire, to enfold sexuality in the Divine will.[43]

Lydia and James's discussions about matters sexual contain nothing of the blunt and bald style of late twentieth-century sexual discourse; nor were they coy or foolishly circuitous. James, for example, found Paris shockingly irreligious. And he told his fiancée of "the most indecent sights in the open streets in broad day." He admitted that his views of "female delicacy" were considered "rather ultra" but insisted that the sort of "degradation" he saw in Paris only confirmed his views. Protesting that decent women should be protected from such sights, he nevertheless went on to tell Lydia about the French women whose appearance he found "almost disgusting," particularly because of "the rather loose mode of dress wh. they adopt, and wh. as I believe you know is singularly offensive in my eyes."[44] His reticence and propriety did not prevent him from sharing his most striking experiences of "indecency" with the woman he most loved and trusted, a part of an increasingly intimate relationship.

Beyond talk, flirtation, and even deep emotion, evidence of the physical relations between Victorian gentlewomen and their fiancés and husbands is rare, but it does exist. There are hints of activity beyond what has normally been thought of as the Victorians' limits. During their long engagement in the 1830s, Lydia and James developed a close—and physical—relationship. When the two were apart, long letters carried their passionate feelings across the English Channel. James felt, he told her one evening in May of 1839, "buoyant delight in thinking of you, and in remembering the enjoyment of those sweet privileges of love." He imagined, as he wrote, that they were together: "Kiss me, dearest," he wrote her, "and I will go on [with my letter]." Her answer?—"accept my ready and fervent compliance . . . now." They watched other couples and (not without some self-congratulation) noted that not all observed the same social decorum in matters of affection. James told Lydia what he had seen among friends at a party: "H. D. [Henrietta Dowson] quite astonished me by her daring. Entre nous Lydia do not be induced by any praises you may hear of her to imitate her. . . . [T]hat extreme and ardour of affection when openly exhibited is as displeasing to me as, when privately shown, it is delightful."[45] What the young couple disapproved of in public, they indulged in and enjoyed when they were alone together.

In the next generation there continued to be those who displayed their affection in public. Lydia's daughter Catharine observed her cousin Agnes with her beau, one Mr. Donaldson, at the Twinings' one evening in 1871—"he on show & she supporting him. They looked," Catharine thought, "intensely happy." A month later she saw them at a "musical party at the Samuel Twinings," and noted that "Agnes and Mr. Donaldson [were] very demonstrative."[46]

A rare exception to Victorian reticence about sexual activity is the Reverend Charles Kingsley. Thanks to his candor we know what at least one Victorian engaged couple was doing. Charles and Frances (Fanny) Grenfell met in 1839, and the two felt deep physical and emotional attraction to one another, but family disapproval led to a long courtship. In the autumn of 1843 they spent a few days together in Dorset at the home of Fanny's sister and brother-in-law. They had periods alone together for what were delicately

termed the "quotation of tender affections, etc." They took full advantage
of their freedom in their walks through the countryside. In the weeks that
followed, Charles reminded Fanny of what they had experienced together:
"my hands are perfumed," he told her, with your "delicious limbs, and I
cannot wash off the scent, and every moment the thought comes across me
of those mysterious recesses of beauty where my hands have been wander-
ing, and my heart sinks with a sweet faintness and my blood tingles through
every limb." He tried to regain "self-control" and discipline over "the happy
body, to which God has permitted of late such exceeding liberty and bliss."
Fanny and Charles were engaging in extensive sexual exploration, and their
activities were an expression of her desire as well as his.[47]

During their courtship and marriage, Charles Kingsley represented his
feelings about their sexual relations in drawings that blend the sensual and
the religious. One recent biographer has found his drawings repellant and
has suggested that they reveal Kingsley's sexual repression, in that he could
"only accept the idea of carnal relations with his wife once he had convinced
himself that the body was holy and . . . sex a kind of sacrament." In this
view, Kingsley considered sex indecent, only redeemed by a gloss of religion.[48] Perhaps. But there is an alternative view.

It may be a feature of human culture that significant arenas of our experience stand as metaphors, analogs, or images, for other similarly significant
aspects of life. Perhaps the Victorian linkage of sex and religion was the natural outcome of their deep religiosity, analogous to the twentieth-century
linkage of sexuality and health. If so, there is an integrity in Kingsley's approach to sexuality as a part of his and Fanny's emotional and spiritual lives.[49]
For our purposes here, Fanny and Charles Kingsley demonstrate two things:
one, that some respectable Victorians engaged in extensive physical intimacy before marriage, and two, that they could do so in ways that were con-
sonant with their religious principles. Indeed, perhaps the linkages of sexual
and spiritual intensified the experience of the ecstatic in both arenas of life.

The evidence does not warrant the following speculations to be anything
more than that. But I want to suggest that extensive physical intimacy was
a respectable and acceptable part of Victorian engagement. Indeed, such intimacy may have been thought of as moral (as well as normal). If the Victorians expected engaged couples to be physically intimate, in preparation for
the intimacies of married life, such a mind-set would go far to explain why
broken engagements were so shocking among the Victorian middle classes.
If engagement meant, ipso facto, intimacy just short of intercourse, then a
broken engagement was an abandonment (by one party or the other) of a
relationship that had taken many steps toward the consummation of the wedding night. Perhaps the most telling evidence about the Victorians' accept-

ance of physical intimacy comes not from their seriousness, but from their ability to laugh, especially about intimacy. A *Punch* magazine of 1871 carries a cartoon depicting a young couple, seated on a chaise at a distance from each other. A third party enters and finds the two "sitting respectably apart from each other." "But how," the cartoonist asks, "comes it that he has an earring hanging from his beard?"[50] The Victorians' willingness to laugh at the near-discovery of a couple's embraces may show us just how thoroughly the Victorians accepted the private displays of love.

What began in the engagement continued into the marriage. The women studied here seem, at least as far as the record shows, to have had enjoyable physical relations after marriage. It must be emphasized: the record is limited. We cannot extrapolate, for example, from Betsey's nearly perpetual pregnancy for the first twenty years of marriage. She may have been a delighted partner, or Sam, her husband, may have been a sexual tyrant. The smallest verbal clues that he was not come from Betsey's style of addressing him: even after fifteen years of marriage (and a dozen children) she could address him as "My beloved Paget."[51]

Evidence about other married women does survive, some general, some specifically about sexual life. A woman might be very attuned to sensual experience. Harriette McDougall had, for example, a physical sense of her children. In 1850 she described her little boy Harry: he is, she said, "tall and fairly stout, with pretty curling golden hair and great black eyes." He is reasonably well-behaved, she could say, and he is "as fond of kissing as his mother." In describing him she revealed as much about her own sensual capacities as she did about the nature of her little boy. Sometimes negative evidence also informs us of Victorian expectations. Mary Benson, wife of the cleric and eventually archbishop Edward White Benson, regretted throughout her life her lack of sexual satisfaction with her husband. In her grief, she felt sorrow for not feeling "what women ought to feel."[52]

Within the family, Lydia Paget displayed a relaxed sensuality. Her son Stephen remembered a delicious scene from his childhood: in 1860, when Lydia was forty-five years old and pregnant with her sixth child, and Stephen was five years old, "my mother used to lie . . . [on the schoolroom sofa] and I used to 'tickle her foot.'. . . I believe my Mother really enjoyed it: and I was a most expert tickler: the forefinger of the left hand . . . lightly tracing away up and down and across foot and ankle, rarely and very lightly touching the sole: mostly the arch and the inner aspect of the stockinged foot. Sometimes I tickled her hand: but usually her foot." As a married couple Lydia and James shared a bedroom and a four-poster bed, even when their prosperity allowed them more distance and individual privacy, and they knelt together at the bedside for prayer before retiring. They chose an upstairs bedroom that did not adjoin the sleeping quarters of any of the children, giving them added privacy as a couple. It was not the nicest room upstairs, and their son Stephen never understood their choice. Lydia's capacity for sensuous self-indulgence may explain part of why James could call her, after twenty years of married life, "My darling, my life, my comfort woman."[53]

Women's athletic activities, their stamina, their knowledge of sex, and their sexual activities all point to the conclusion that gentlewomen were physically and sexually at home in, and not alienated from, their bodies. They may have been relatively silent or reticent about speaking or writing about the body and sexuality. Equally possibly, we have ignored the many hints and clues that tell us of the integrity of their spiritual and physical lives and the pleasure they found in sex and marriage.

THE OTHER RELATIONS OF MARRIED LIFE

The emotional characteristics of Victorian marriage may be as difficult to uncover as the sexual. In marriage, one might guess, even the most assertive and independent Victorian ladies would have begun to give way. Dependent, they would defer; materially powerless, they would have acknowledged the primacy of husbands; and, unused to responsibility, they might have avoided even those possibilities of authority that came with having households and children of their own. Lawrence Stone has suggested that the nineteenth-century family moved away from the companionate model of the eighteenth century toward a structure he describes as "repressive," and there seems widespread agreement that paternalism and male authority were characteristic of Victorian marriage.[54] But the marital experiences of the Paget women and their friends suggest another conclusion: that the oppressive potential of the institution of marriage, as outlined by such reformers as John Stuart Mill, did not in fact work out that way in most upper-middle-class households.

Some Victorian marriages were patently unhappy. A clear example is that of Betsey Tolver Paget's sister. Frances Tolver married Charles Bagnall around 1800. Bagnall was no marital tyrant or villain in the usual sense. At the time he seemed merely "quite unable to appreciate the Tolver atmosphere of respectability." The family arranged an informal separation between Frances and Charles by shipping him off to Jamaica in 1805, expenses paid, on one of Sam Paget's ships. The maneuver did not work. Bagnall returned from Jamaica as a common sailor and continued to plague his wife and her family in Yarmouth for a decade, turning up, causing an uproar, and so frightening Frances that she often chose to hide herself "from scenes of possible passion." Bagnall was given to begging and stealing (possibly out of poverty, perhaps compulsively), and the family feared he would go to prison. Perhaps he drank to excess. He was surely improvident and went to the workhouse more than once. It is possible he was mentally ill. Despite Frances's fear and embarrassment, she agreed to live with this pathologically unreliable husband again in the 1830s, after her nephew James removed him from a London workhouse. Uncomfortable outside of institutions, Bagnall returned to the workhouse not long after James had rescued him, and there he eventually died, releasing Frances from more than thirty years of marital misery.[55]

Few marriages were so scandalously unsettled as the Bagnalls'. Others did, in more quiet ways, bring unhappiness to one or both partners. The Twining marriage was one such: he selfish, harsh, and mean-spirited, and she depressed and resigned. Hannah's husband was not patently and positively unkind to her, but he was "A cold, sparkless, business-bound man" with a "dull voice and fishy eyes," and "nobody could have much fun, with him there." Hannah was "a dear, good, little lady through and through . . . very dutiful, very gentle." And, her nephew said, "Aunt Hannah rather withered in the Cromwell Road." He believed death was her way of escaping from Twining.[56]

The situation was somewhat different in the Lough marriage. Sculptor John Lough, some thought, was a "dear, simple, philosophical old boy" whose life was made miserable by the selfish and nasty character of his wife, Mary. His early career was marked by poverty, and, in her way, Mary Lough stood by him. But she undermined her own efforts and "his prospects by her quarrelsome, gossiping tongue." She was ill-tempered, full of resentment and perpetual grievance. She expressed her anger publicly over her relations with her husband: "Influence I may have," she pronounced bitterly, "authority I have none." Mary's brother Jacob seems to have found a similar wife, pushing in her ambition and leaving him little peace. Jacob and Harriet North lived in Brighton, where he was a parish priest, but Brighton apparently "tempted Harriet to think too much of social shining. . . . Poor . . . Harriet: for they had no money to shine with." This marriage would have been worse had it not been for Jacob's ability to make "the best of things as he found them." In short, he submitted to her ways. Most often Victorians drew the cloak of silence over at least the worst of the unhappy unions of their time. Only chance—or the rare separation or divorce—allows glimpses into others. Agnes Gardner Gall left her husband and went to stay with her sister and brother-in-law Margaret and William Thomson. When her sister died, "Aunt Agnes" made the arrangement permanent by becoming "housekeeper to the family" for the rest of her life.[57]

There was another sort of Victorian marriage as well. Perhaps the word "detachment" best characterizes the marriage of Lydia's sister-in-law, Clara Fardell Paget, to George Paget. An enthusiast of things Welsh, Clara convinced George that they should have a country house in Wales and, once acquired, she spent much of the year there. Clara left for Penmaenmawr in early April and did not return until October. She took the preschool boys with her and left daughter Rose to manage the house and to play hostess for the busy Cambridge don. Each year George took a short vacation in Wales, and he managed an occasional weekend there, when he needed the rest. But he spent most of his time in Cambridge attending to his medical practice and his many duties as regius professor. Clara apparently did not bother to write to George but sent numberless messages to him through her daughter. These varied from requests for his opinion to pro forma expressions of affection.[58]

Clara may have removed herself physically from Cambridge and from George, but her attitude toward him was never one of overt hostility. She often expressed care about his comfort and concern about his well-being. One summer she sent apples to Cambridge and told Rose, "Let your Papa have some of the apples I send if he likes them." When George was returning from a trip she told Rose to "Have all comfortable for your Papa & Maud on their return." In the summer of 1880 she was worried about his health and she instructed Rose, "Whenever your Papa feels tired let him have some Fish, & a Chicken." And, when there was a chance George might go to Wales, even for a weekend, Clara urged Rose, "Do all you can to help & persuade your Papa to start by the 2 o'clock train . . . & come down to Wales," and, she had to add, "mind he brings warm clothing." She watched over his health and urged that he take a holiday when he was overworked and tired.[59] It may have been easy for Clara to be benign when she was in her beloved Wales. If, on her account or his, the marriage was less than satisfactory, then the house in Wales was a source of liberation for both of them—a separation, without the legalities or the stigma, an amicable solution to the problem of a tense marriage. If it was not a troubled marriage, it was surely one in which domestic convention took second place to the individual wishes of the partners. These upper-middle-class Victorian marriages reflect the possibility of various solutions to the question of how married couples lived together in relative peace.

When Victorian marriages worked well, they often partook of an admirable mutuality. Perhaps one beginning of that parity was the apparent similarity of age among these couples. Few of the women married men very much older or younger than they. And when a man or woman embarked on a second marriage, that age pattern tended to continue. Frederick Paget, for example, married three times. His first wives, whom he married when he was in his twenties, were nearly the same age. When he married again in his late forties, he married a woman of similar age. Congruity of age, along with affection, the chemistry of personalities, or perhaps the very habits of life together, tended to maintain the companionship that many couples experienced. Partnership seems to have characterized, for example, Betsey's relations with Sam. Their shared concern for their children meant that when Sam went to London to see to James's interests at St. Bartholomew's Hospital, he wrote back to her to report on all he had heard and tried to do. When he was away on business, she wrote "Sunday letters," reporting on all the news of the family and the community, and asking about the state of his work. On one occasion she had a chance to send him a second letter on the same day, and she was bemused by the level of intimacy it bespoke: "twice in a day would I think create a laugh in most circles of the present day," she observed, "particularly after a marriage of fifteen years. But I think I cannot spend a leisure hour better than in writing a few lines to you." She expressed fears for his safety and for life without him: "I do not much like your risquing your life upon the sea, without I am with you." When he had to stay away from home for many days more and when she heard that he was exhausted, her first impulse was to go directly to him, to be at his side and support him. Two generations later Eleanor Burd contributed to Stephen Paget's growth as an independent man. His perspective on their marriage, and indeed on his life, was "our life in Harley Street," "our love for the children, and their love for us," "our holidays abroad with the children or by ourselves."[60] Sharing, partnership, mutuality, these constituted one kind of marriage in the upper-middle-class experience.

However much Lydia Paget might have appeared to be "a simple little white soul," her marital relations with James were not built on his dominance and her submission. Late in life James described their marriage as one "blest with constancy of perfect mutual love not once disturbed." This might seem too beatific, were it not that snatches of evidence from various points in their married life support his memory of marital devotion and mutuality. In 1855 their older children had scarlet fever and, to advance their convalescence, Lydia took them to the country, leaving James in London with four-year-old Frank and baby Stephen. The boys provided James with company, but, he wrote her, "It would be hard to tell how much and often I have wished for you all to-day." The fright caused by his children's serious illness made James specially sensitive to divine mercy and to his wife's role in his life. She was his "sweet one." He treasured her for "mak[ing] all my enjoyment of mercies more deep and true." She was "in joy, and in fear, and in sorrow . . . alike the true and good help" who had only grown more excellent in eleven years of married life and "more than twenty years of love." Almost a decade later, when Lydia was forty-eight years old and James nearly fifty, the couple again spent time apart. "My dearest Lydia," he wrote, "I miss you more on Sunday evenings than at any other time." After dealing with mundane matters, he returned again to his feelings: "Oh! how I wish you were here."[61]

The symmetry of their relationship revealed itself in small homely ways as well as in these moments of emotional disclosure. In the haste of packing for a trip with the children, Lydia forgot a favorite shawl; she asked him to find it and mail it to her, and he complied. While Lydia was away, James oversaw the household but looked to her for guidance: "You must tell me, dearest," he said, "if there be any thing that you wish done before your return. I am so accustomed to leave all home affairs to you (and so happy in the custom) that I have no eyes for the needs or proprieties of the house or household:—so pray instruct me for this time, & your teaching shall be obeyed."[62] She once promised to obey him; now he offered similar obedience.

Cecil and F. T. Palgrave's daughter Gwen described her parents' marriage, surely with some hyperbole, as "twenty-seven years' perfect happiness." The details are more telling: the couple regularly read books together and shared their private ideas with each other. Warm marital affection could even appear in the chilly context of a legal document: in his will, William Jackson Hooker named his wife his executor, but he could not resist abandoning strict legal formulaics to refer to her as "my dear wife dame Maria Hooker."[63]

At some points and in some marriages neither female dependency nor egalitarian sharing were the rule: some couples' marriages were characterized by female strength and male dependency. James Paget's reliance on Lydia for support began during their engagement and lasted all their lives. He first confided in her about his spiritual struggles and his efforts to resist temptation and added: "Lydia, you know I have never before had one to whom I could write this." He confessed his weakness and fears and labeled them the "sign of a diseased spirit." He looked to her for help: "Regard yourself Lydia as my spiritual nurse. . . . [Y]ou are of all the world the one to whom I can most safely look for support." Fenton John Anthony Hort, who married in 1857, had similar feelings: "it was a necessity to his nature to have one nearest to him with whom to share every thought. This . . . was the natural outcome of his reserve," and he was "reserved and sensitive . . . to the highest degree."[64] Only with his wife did he let his guard down.

Other Victorian marriages were, quite simply, amiable and relaxed relationships. T. H. Huxley's happy fondness and liking for his wife creeps out even in his (feigned) complaints about her: "My wife," Huxley told Ethel Romanes, "is 'larking'—I am sorry to use such a word, but what she is pleased to tell me of her doings leaves me no alternative—in London, whither I go on Monday to fetch her back—in chains, if necessary." The Westcotts were warm friends from youth, sharing their painting and musical pleasures. As adults, they continued to share their private life in a way that indicates their genuine liking for each other.[65]

The line between this sort of fondness and the great intimacy that some couples shared is difficult to draw. Clearly, however, many Victorian couples enjoyed the emotional satisfaction of intense closeness. The multivolumed lives and letters of Victorian professional men contain few love letters, per se, but the letters men wrote to their wives often half-fill the volumes. The letters are full of sharing, of confidence, of reflection, of trust. Bishop Moule's colleagues praised him for being "the lover and knight to the last" in his marriage. The ideal of marriage that the Moules embodied was one of "boundless intimacy, and . . . profound underlying mutual respect." As George Gabriel Stokes put it, "there is nothing so fatal to fulness of love as reserve." Stokes's ideal, like the Moules', was "deep mutual confidence and love."[66]

Frank and Harriette McDougall offer a similar picture. Perhaps because they were thrown on their own mutual resources in Borneo, this couple shared much, and they offered each other a great deal emotionally. Such support is clear in Harriette's report to her sister on the puerperal fever she had suffered in the wake of childbirth in 1849. Her husband, a physician as well as a missionary, took care of her, but it was more than mere medical attendance. He watched over her hour by hour, and she noted the special quality of his attention: "To be so nursed and tended by Frank would compensate for any pain, and while the memory of that [pain] has already passed away, the delightful conviction of his love will make all the rest of my life happier." When Harriette died, her husband was inconsolable. He wrote to a friend soon after her death in May of 1886, "My life is broken now—it is but a feeble one, and all the brightness centred in her is gone, until the day in which the shadows flee away, and we shall join our souls' darlings in the presence of Him whose name is Love." Ethel Romanes suffered similar grief at her husband's death but did not rely on God for comfort: "I ought to bear this much better than I do," she told her friend William Gladstone, "but it's terribly hard. We loved each other so."[67]

Sometimes there was a price to be paid for the intensity of married love: Mary Baird recalled that her parents were very close. They spent a great deal of time together, making the rounds of their favorite continental resorts and enjoying a life that was little more than an extended European holiday.

They were "much to each other," she concluded. The results of such closeness between husband and wife were not all beneficial. Mary's parents "lacked . . . real understanding . . . of any of their children." Perhaps, Mary thought later, "in spite of superficial differences and even quarrels, they were really too much to each other to leave room for much [else], certainly much maternal affection."[68] In such marriages, children had to take second place to the spouses' affection for each other.

These women had a fascinating variety of relationships with their husbands. For some, the sexual was one feature of a strong marriage bond. For others there was no bond but the legal. For still others the bonds of marriage were those of friendship, partnership, or shared experience. Some marriages included dependency relations—a dependent wife, or, equally possible, a dependent husband. Romance, mutuality, and friendship were more often the patterns that emerged.

Vigorous physical lives, reticence but not repression in matters sexual, the possibility that sexual love might bring pleasure to women—these were among the Victorian facts of gentlewomen's lives. The tendency for husbands and wives to be of like age, hints that they enjoyed satisfactory sexual unions, the clear evidence of their companionship as well as romance, their shared culture and interests—all these point to a high degree of marital satisfaction among the Victorian upper-middle-class people studied here. If the Victorian couples of this study are at all typical, then one must at least consider the possibility that "companionate marriage" was at its full flowering in the Victorian period; such a speculation then raises the question of what has happened to companionate marriage in the twentieth century. Chapter six will pursue the nature of Victorian companionate marriage into the workaday world.

Not all women enjoyed the potential empowerment that came to upper-middle-class women from sport, from the liberty to move, from good health, and from their access to knowledge about the body and sexuality. It is tempting to speculate that women of lower ranks lived under different rules with regard to men—rules that left women more exclusively relegated to a separate sphere. The private was surely political, and gentlewomen's experience of the (relative) freedom of their rank was, in their view, only their due as members of the "upper orders" of society. Their sense of hierarchy and their due left them indifferent to the severe constraints under which women less fortunate than they had to live. Gentlewomen shared the political empowerment of their rank; lesser rank meant lesser power, they knew, for women and men alike. That was the way of the Victorian world.

Sarah Elizabeth (Tolver) Paget, as a young woman. (Courtesy of Dr. Oliver Paget, Vienna.)

Sarah Elizabeth (Tolver) Paget, in middle age. From a painting by her granddaughter, Elise Paget. (Courtesy of the late Mrs. J. M. Thompson.)

Lydia North, later Paget, as a young woman. (Courtesy of the late Mrs. J. M. Thompson.)

Lydia (North) Paget. (Courtesy of the late Mrs. J. M. Thompson.)

Catharine (Paget) Thompson, 1879, with her infant son James. (Courtesy of the late Mrs. J. M. Thompson.)

Lydia Paget's daughters-in-law, the former Elma Katie Hoare, Helen Church, Eleanor Burd, and Julia Norrie Moke. (Courtesy of the late Mrs. J. M. Thompson.)

Mary Maud Paget as a girl. (Courtesy of the late Mrs. J. M. Thompson.)

Mary Maud Paget in middle age. (Courtesy of the late Mrs. J. M. Thompson.)

Rose and Violet Paget, as little girls. (Courtesy of the late Mrs. J. M. Thompson.)

Rose and Violet Paget, as adolescents. (Courtesy of the late Mrs. J. M. Thompson.)

Some of the Paget family at Penmaenmawr. *Left to right, front:* Mary Maud Paget, Catharine (Paget) Thompson, Eleanor (Burd) Paget, Stephen Paget, Eleanor (Paget) Howarth, Stephen Howarth. *Rear:* Mrs. Howarth, Dorothea Mary Paget, Rev. James M. Thompson, Mrs. Horton, O. J. R. Howarth. (Courtesy of the late Mrs. J. M. Thompson.)

Eleanor Ormerod in academic garb, 1900. Artist unknown. (Courtesy of University of Edinburgh.)

Georgiana Ormerod. (From E. Ormerod, *Eleanor Ormerod* [London, 1904], p. 281.)

Henrietta (Rowland) Barnett, with her ward. (From Barnett, *Canon Barnett* [London, 1921], facing p. 534.)

Catharine (Spooner) Tait. (From Benham, ed., *Catharine and Craufurd Tait* [London, 1880], frontispiece.)

Edith (Tait) Davidson. (From *The Times* [London], June 27, 1936, p. 16.)

Eleanor (Nellie) and Margaret (Maggie) Benson in 1876. (From Benson, *Maggie Benson* [London, 1918], facing p. 22.)

Maggie Benson in 1893. (From Benson, *Maggie Benson*, facing p. 150.)

Mary St. Leger (Kingsley) Harrison. (From William Archer, *Real Conversations* [London: Heinemann, 1904], facing p. 216.)

ATTRACTIVE ATHLETICS.

oys and Girls must have their little games. Athletics are as necessary to the health of the softer sex as the harder, besides being useful aids to innocent flirtation.

Lawn-Tennis has superseded Croquet; but probably to be sooner or later discarded in its turn. Still, lawns will remain, and there are other games besides Tennis for which a lawn could serve as an arena. Among these may be suggested Lawn Cricket —with the due distinction from the masculine game as played at Lord's; Lawn Football, adapted for the softer sex and weather, under modifications of the Rugby Rules; Lawn Prisoners' Bars, or Prisoners' Base; Lawn Rounders; Lawn Stag - out ; Lawn Hockey; Lawn Tipcat; Lawn Hopscotch. Duly developed to suit the lawn, Hopscotch might be rendered a very elegant game, so as to afford much the same facilities for graceful display as dancing. Lawn Marbles, perhaps, would hardly be quite compatible with " tie-backs ; " neither would Lawn High Cockalorum-jig and Lawn Leapfrog, at least without the 'adoption of those reforms of costume which may be expected speedily to supervene on recognition of the Rights of Woman.

"Attractive Athletics." (From *Punch* [London], July 28, 1877, p. 36.)

(Clara) Maud Gadow at a campsite, at 12,500 feet in the mountains of southern Mexico. (From Gadow, *Through Southern Mexico* [London, 1908], p. 60.)

(Clara) Maud Gadow fording a swamp on horseback, with two Mexican guides. (From Gadow, *Through Southern Mexico*, p. 447.)

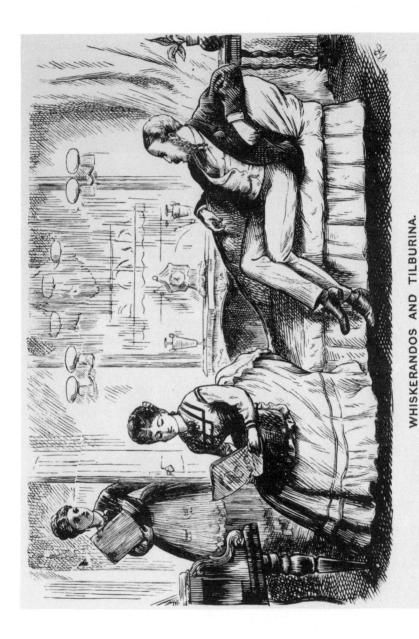

WHISKERANDOS AND TILBURINA.

COUSIN GUY AND MARY ARE LOOKING VERY INNOCENT, AND SITTING VERY FAR APART, WHEN EMILY COMES INTO THE ROOM. BUT
HOW COMES GUY TO HAVE AN EAR-RING HANGING TO HIS WHISKER ?"

Intimacy between a Victorian lady and gentleman, as depicted in *Punch*, August 19, 1871, p. 67.

"A Tennis Party," 1885, by Sir John Lavery. (Courtesy of the Aberdeen Art Gallery and Museums.)

"A Summer Shower," 1883, by Edith Hayllar. (Courtesy of the FORBES Magazine Collection.)

Sarah Elizabeth (Tolver) Paget, still life. (Courtesy of Mrs. Joan Charnock, Cambridge.)

Marianne North, at her easel in South Africa, 1882. (Courtesy of the Royal Botanic Gardens, Kew.)

White gum trees, Australia, an example of Marianne North's work. (Courtesy of the Royal Botanic Gardens, Kew.)

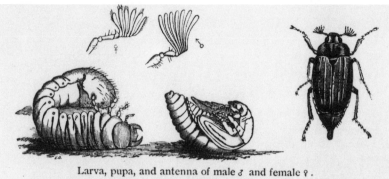

Larva, pupa, and antenna of male ♂ and female ♀.

FIG. 58.—COCKCHAFER, *MELOLONTHA VULGARIS*, FAB.

An example of Eleanor Ormerod's entomological drawings. (From Ormerod, *Eleanor Ormerod*, p. 233.)

(Clara) Maud Gadow, drawing of the Pass of Deva, Spain. (From Gadow, *In Northern Spain* [London, 1897], p. 8.)

CHAPTER FOUR

Other Facts of Family Life

"It makes one in love with death," Harriette McDougall told a friend in 1854, "to lose so many sweet ones, and most of all our first born and dearest boy."[1] This poignant statement points to one of the common but little studied experiences of mothers of all ranks before the twentieth century, the death of a child. High infant mortality was a fact of Victorian life, demographers and historians know, but women's individual experience of this phenomenon deserves attention. McDougall's confession, at the same time, raises a question about women's ideas of motherhood, expressing (as she did) favoritism for one child over others.

Another powerful fact of Victorian women's lives was the state of health of the men in their lives. Much has been made of the frailty of women in the Victorian age; much less is known of the health of men and its effects on family life. From girlhood onward, women had to face these problems of family sickness and death, but accounts of women as oppressed wives and repressed women have tended to crowd out knowledge about other powerful features of women's experience.

A third neglected area of women's lives is the matter of money and women's relationship to it. Peter Cominos saw an analogy between the "spermatic economy" and the material economy: women were excluded from sexual knowledge and pleasure; they also had no relation to money.[2] The Victorian gentlewoman's relationship to money goes beyond earning; her possession and control of wealth is an important issue in understanding women's power. It is the task of this chapter to begin the exploration of these neglected matters.

THE VICTORIAN LADY AND HER CHILDREN

The upper ranks of Victorian society suffer from two contradictory reputations. On the one hand, they are notorious for their willingness to leave their children's upbringing in the hands of nurses and governesses. On the other hand, Victorian middle-class women's domain was the private sphere: home and children must have been the ideal woman's primary activity. The historiography of this practice has focused on the neglected child and cruel servants. Wifehood perhaps, motherhood certainly, had to be the central focus of her life.[3]

The Paget women and their circle do not conform to either of these extremes. Many among the upper-middle-class families examined here had nannies and governesses, but mothers and fathers also involved themselves directly and frequently in their children's lives. At the same time these women show no evident commitment to the theoretical notion of the primacy of motherhood, nor do their day-to-day activities support the view that the relationship between the Victorian mother and her children was the central focus of a woman's life.

Lydia North and Mary Florence Smith illustrate Victorian ladies' ideas about motherhood. Lydia was a devoted wife, but she had less enthusiastic feelings about children. As a young single woman, she and her sister went to visit their brother and his new wife, who were expecting their first child. For the sake of family peace and social grace, Lydia felt it necessary to disguise her own attitudes. But she admitted privately to her fiancé, James, "I have assumed an interest very foreign to me concerning small children." A generation later Mary Smith found herself in the growing society of Oxford dons and their brides, many newly wed after the end of the ban on marriage for fellows. When she found out that she was pregnant, her husband "solemnly warned me 'not to let myself become a mere mother like Mrs. ———.'" "It shows the change in public opinion," she later remarked. "In these days [the 1920s] maternity is perhaps unduly exalted, but it was very different then." In fact, Mary Smith enjoyed children very much, felt she had "a knack" with infants, and became something of an expert on child-rearing among young Oxford mothers in her day. But she considered herself an exception, not the norm of Victorian mothers of her social rank.[4] Most of the women of the Paget circle had rather more differentiated feelings about their children than Mary Smith. They got on well with some and not with others, and never, apparently, attached any special mystique to "motherhood."

If there was no mystique of motherhood in the nineteenth-century upper-middle-class home, there was surely one way in which many Victorians saw their offspring: they were the bearers of family traditions, they brought earthly continuity, immortality in the world to their parents and their forebears. Such a role for offspring, such hopes, are revealed in the Victorian habits of naming children, which we can see in every nineteenth-century generation. Sarah Elizabeth (Betsey) and Sam named one of their daughters

Elizabeth Sarah, and three of their infant sons were christened Samuel. Two of the babies were named after Betsey's father, Tom Tolver: one Thomas, the other Henry Thomas. Mary and Dawson Turner, too, saw their children as bearers of names: three sons received the name Dawson. Lydia and James named no children for themselves, but James's dead brother Frank lived on in their son Francis. Clara and George Edward Paget gave their children versions of their names: daughters Georgina and Clara Maud, and son George Edmund. And the much-loved Arthur Paget was remembered in George and Clara's grandson's name. Sarah Angelina Acland bore her mother Sarah's name.[5] The children at birth had no identity and hence could be vested with family names and family continuity.

Once offspring survived infancy and began to develop as individuals, parents began the process of differentiation that brought them to favor some children over others. Harriette McDougall considered her eldest son her "dearest," and she was prepared to say so even in the wake of the deaths of several of her children. Betsey had a special affection for her second son, Arthur, he of the shining whiskers, the "damask-rose cheek," and the flair for extravagance. Her special favor was visible to the other children: son Alfred noted her "affection" and Arthur's "confident boasting of it as his own." But her favor was not merely a matter of sentiment. She "would hoard money for him, sovereigns, savings from her pocket money or her marketing." And when he wanted something from his father, he would ask his mother, telling her, "I know where to come for an advocate whose pleading . . . [is] more effective than the eloquence of all the barristers of England." Catharine Tait acknowledged her eldest daughter and namesake Catharine, whom she called Catty, as her favorite.[6]

Clara, Betsey's daughter-in-law, had specially tender feelings for her little boys: "I long to kiss them both again," she told Rose. "I miss them so very very much, tell them how I long to see them." Although Clara coddled these little boys, she was impatient and domineering with her older children. She sent brusque missives full of orders from Wales home to her adolescent daughters in the long summers while she was away. And when advising her son Charles on his career, she didn't bother to write to him but sent messages via her daughter Rose.[7] Clara vacillated between indifference and the desire to control, and her children easily saw her attitudes. As a result, relations between Clara and her adult offspring were often strained.

Clara's relations with her eldest son, Edmund, offer one example of that tension. Clara disapproved of his choice of Stella Salomons as his bride. Perhaps she objected to the religious differences, even though Clara's own religiosity was limited to Sunday church-going. After long negotiations over the marriage settlement, the ceremony finally took place in a London registry office in August of 1877. Clara did not go to the wedding, and the conflict went on unresolved. At the end of the year Clara's husband wanted to invite the newlyweds to Cambridge for Christmas, but "Mama did not like it," their daughter Rose observed, "so it was not done." This marriage produced Clara's first grandchild, Arthur Paget, in September 1878. The new father, perhaps hoping that the arrival of the new generation would provide the occasion for reconciliation, asked his sister, "When is Mama likely to come to see him?" Later Stella sent a message to Clara via Rose: "Please give my love to your Mother, and tell her I hope she will *soon* name a day to come & lunch here to see Arthur, he is now in short clothes & looks very pretty in them." It was many months before Clara visited this first grandchild.[8] Clara adopted a mystique of grandmotherhood no more readily than she did one of motherhood.

Most remarkable of all Clara's conduct as a mother was her relationship with her daughter Violet. In the 1870s, when Violet was a teenager, some crisis arose between the two of them. Scattered clues point to some health problem for Violet; but it is equally clear that a conflict of personalities between mother and daughter was central to the problem. The crisis was so serious that Clara and George agreed to send Violet away. She went first to her Aunts Kate and Patty in Woodridings, then to a clergyman and his wife—the Howards—in Hampshire, and finally to her cousin Catharine Thompson in Iron Acton. For several years the family colluded in domestic arrangements to ensure that Mama and Violet should never be in the same town (let alone the same house) at the same time. Violet behaved badly. Family members watched for signs of improvement: when Edmund saw her, he thought she was "making many changes for the better, and was really nice." But Louisa Howard told Rose that Vi "does embroidery by the hour 'pour passer le temps' she says. It comes out generally at table before meals are finished. . . . [T]his continual stitch-stitch seemed such a waste of time." (But it was a wonderful use of "feminine" activity as a tool of her rebellion.) Violet showed no interest in any of the other activities of the household and, Mrs. Howard reported, "she resists 'interference' as she thinks it, of any kind." Vi's physical and emotional symptoms (especially her struggle for power) suggest a Victorian case of anorexia nervosa. Whether anorexia or hysteria, both of which upset and angered Victorian parents, the years-long alienation and silence of mother and daughter present a form of motherly behavior not tied to some abstract ideal of motherhood.[9] Clara, as the parent, must surely carry a heavy responsibility for the alienation and for the extreme solutions that the family adopted. Clara's responses suggest that her own comfort and peace were more important to her than her daughter's well-being.[10]

Similar results (from different causes) came in the relations of Alice Smith and her son, A. L. Smith. Mrs. Smith became a widow at a young age and—perhaps from grief, perhaps out of indifference or financial necessity—took measures that divided her family. She sent her six-year-old boy to live all year around at his school, Christ's Hospital, while she lived abroad, first in Italy and then in the United States. She left him at school for twelve years, visiting only rarely. He left only when he went into residence at Oxford. Similarly, Mary Benson, by 1872 the mother of six children, left all of them, including an infant teething and not yet walking, to try to recover her health. She stayed away from children and husband for at least six months, perhaps as long as two years.[11]

Eleanor Cropper Acland lived through her childhood in the late 1870s and early 1880s. On the classic upper-class model, Eleanor's parents left basic care, discipline, and rudimentary schooling in the hands of her nanny, Barley. Nurse Barley used slaps and "humiliation" to control the small children of the family. For solace and "pure inexhaustible love" Eleanor and her siblings turned to their mother. She (and their father, as well) spent time with the children only during social and leisure time; neither parent cared for them on an hour-by-hour basis. Later Eleanor asked the inevitable question: why did mother not notice Barley's cruelty? Eleanor's only answer was that her mother simply did not see it. Mrs. Cropper could avoid seeing the physical abuse of her children by putting herself at some distance from them, by considering such treatment normal, or by not considering herself responsible for the nurse's actions. Acland's experience may be extreme, or her memory of her upbringing may be distorted. But memories of abuse, neglect, or indifference may also be part of the impetus that drove her, and women like her, to redefine motherhood and mothering, to elevate its importance, and perhaps to develop the mystique of motherhood, in the post-Victorian era.[12]

Earlier I argued that Victorian women often had intensely satisfying emotional relationships with their husbands: they were companions, friends, lovers, each the first person in the other's life. When that happened, perhaps *because* that happened, women's relationships to their children were secondary. This is not to say that they did not love their children (or some of their children) deeply. They were not conforming to a model of idealized mother-child relations; a mystique of mother-love did not evolve until the interwar years. I suspect that these women were not so concerned about an ideal of motherhood and mother-child relations as about individual relations with the people who happened to be their children. When they loved their children, they were responding to them as individuals.

CHILDREN'S ILLNESS AND DEATH

So far this study has dealt almost exclusively with the accomplishments, the vigor, the awareness of Victorian girls and ladies. So far it has been a story of well-being, freedom, and optimism. It is certainly true that upper-middle-class women lived privileged lives, but privilege provided no protection against pain, sickness, and death. A major fact of gentlewomen's lives was the vulnerability of their families to sickness and death—that fact served as a constant reminder of the limits of prosperity and privilege.

Every family had to face the routine sicknesses of childhood—so routine that they often disappear from the historical record. Toothaches, catarrh, erysipelas, the occasional broken bone were all part of children's and parents' experience. Clara Paget's little boy Owen had a case of ringworm that had to be watched and treated, and her daughter had an ankle injury. Other disorders were more dangerous. Edith Tait's children had measles before the oldest was ten years old, but all survived.[13]

Some illnesses were serious. Lydia Paget's little children had scarlet fever, a disease of great virulence in the first three-quarters of the nineteenth century. She took them to the country to recuperate. Some children's health problems could reshape their families' lives. In 1841 Elizabeth and E. H. Browne brought their first child into the world, a daughter, Alice. She was an invalid from birth, the result (it was thought) of prenatal injury during a train ride. She had no control over her muscles. Because of Alice's condition, her mother curtailed the amount of time she spent traveling with her clerical husband in his duties. The child's helpless condition also meant that she could not be moved. As a result, when her father accepted a new position at Cambridge, the family had to be divided, with mother and children staying in Kenwyn while father, accompanied by his sister, moved to his new post.[14]

The death of infants and children under the age of five was also a common feature of family life across social classes. With limited medical knowledge, with even more limited medical power (without—in short—antibiotics), and with many dangers to infant life, death was an ever present possibility in every family. The question of how infant mortality affected family affections has generated much controversy. The experience of the women of this study sheds little light on those debates, since it all postdates the rise of the so-called "affective family."[15] But their experience is worth examining because it allows us to see individual families rather than abstract mortality rates and because their experiences suggest some of the features of death in the family. Sometimes only traces of evidence exist, giving us only hints about the feelings, attitudes, and involvements of families in the death of children.

The record is littered with the names of infants born and named and dead within the year. Mary Turner's daughter Harriet Gunn had little Katherine only nine months before she died in 1811; she also had a son who died in infancy. Cecil and F. T. Palgrave's little boy Arthur Frederick was born July 14, 1840, but it was soon clear that the infant was ill. His father knew "as this sweet patient little Arthur lay on Cecil's lap [that] every hope was clearly over." The child died two weeks and three days later, and they "buried him in the quiet country ground at Barnes." In 1848 Harriette McDougall "had the disappointment of the arrival of a baby which only lived a few hours." Carrie Gull Acland lost one child in infancy in the 1890s, and Eleanor Burd Paget lost twins in 1885.[16] The list could go on and on.

Betsey and Sam Paget lost two sons in early infancy—little Samuel died in 1801 at seven weeks, and Thomas died in 1803 at five weeks. The ninth year of their married life, when they were both thirty, was "the dreadful year 1808." In April of that year they had five surviving children and another child was expected in early summer. Samuel (b. 1802, the second son so named), age six, Henry Thomas (b. 1804), age four, Elizabeth Sarah (b. 1807), age one, Patty (b. 1800), age eight, and Frederick (b. 1805), age three, all contracted measles or whooping cough. (The exact details are lost.) The six-year-old, the four-year-old, and the one-year-old (Samuel, Henry, and Elizabeth) all died within a few weeks. The other two, Patty and Fred, were whisked off to Norwich, presumably to remove them from the vicinity of the disease. By June this crisis was past, and the pregnant Betsey gave birth to Arthur, thought to be the "most brilliant of the sons" but at the same time a "delicate" child. Between 1800 and 1807 seven children were born; by 1808 five of them were dead. The Pagets' neighbors, the Turners, had analogous experiences: they had eleven children between 1797 and 1815, of whom eight survived; three died in infancy and early childhood.[17]

These Yarmouth families were typical. Throughout the nineteenth century parents saw their infants and little children die. Anne Collett Hort gave birth to five children between 1828 and 1838. In late 1841 her three-year-old Josephine, the youngest of the children, died. Only five months later her eleven-year-old boy Arthur died "from the after-effects of measles." Soon after, Anne Hort entered a period of ill health and periods of "often painful depression." Clara and George Paget's thirteen-month-old child, Georgina, died in Cambridge in August of 1857, only nineteen months after the death of their two-year-old Hester. George's colleague, George Gabriel Stokes, mentioned the infant's death to his fiancée: "Dr. and Mrs. Paget, who have recently lost their second (by age) child, hav[e] now out of three only the eldest left." Siblings remembered the death of an infant brother or sister: Rose noted in her diary: "today is the anniversary of my baby sister's death." Rose had not been born at the time of her sister's death and her memorial reflects the family's collective memory of the event.[18]

Catharine and H. L. Thompson were both well over thirty when they married in 1877, and three sons and then a daughter were born to them in the next seven years. Alexandra was "a delicate and beautiful child" who brought her parents great happiness. "Then sorrow came at last: for she died of diphtheria, on November 3, 1886, after two days' illness." Catharine thought that the loss of this child "was the most poignant grief of Henry Thompson's life."[19] She did not mention her own.

Like the Pagets and the Turners, many families had multiple losses of children in the first five years, the most dangerous years of life. Elizabeth and Harold Browne had to bear not only the lifetime invalid condition of their daughter Alice but also the deaths of several other children. Of the eight other children born to them in the 1840s and 1850s, a total of three died in infancy, one of scarlet fever, the others of unknown causes. Among the sacrifices made by the McDougalls to pursue their missionary work was the increased risk to their health and the health of their children. And those risks were realized. Between 1845 and 1852 seven children were born to them. The eldest son was left behind at school in England, and the rest went to or were born in Borneo. Of those six, five were dead by the end of 1853. The causes varied. One died of diphtheria, some were thought to have died of "the climate," but Harriette's brother thought several had been born with weak hearts. Three of the children died in a period of fifteen months, between late 1848 and early 1850, the last being their darling boy Harry. Harriette wrote home to report on the family's condition: "do not think of us as grieving without hope; . . . every day, I think, raises our heads from our child's grave to his bright and happy home."[20]

One of the great killers of children before about 1870 was scarlet fever. Lydia Paget's children contracted it but survived. Many families saw it take a child away quickly. The T. D. Aclands lost one child to the disease and another to some other cause.[21] Perhaps nothing illustrates more strikingly the dangers of scarlet fever than the Taits' experience. Their story brings close to view the trial and grief a child's death brought to parents.

The Tait family had moved to Carlisle from Rugby after Archibald Campbell Tait's appointment as dean of the cathedral there in 1849. In early March of 1856 Catharine was thirty-six years old and the mother of six girls and one boy, ranging in age from ten years to three weeks.[22] The deanery was noisy with the laughter and bubbling voices of seven children. Catharine was recovering from the birth of her youngest child, little Lucy, and especially enjoying the good-natured and loving attention of all her children.

One Monday in early March, Catharine noticed five-year-old Charlotte (Chatty) looking pale and tired. The next morning one of the servants told Catharine that "May [aged eight] had a bad cold" and was staying in bed, and that Chatty continued to be sick and had taken some medicine. By late afternoon Chatty seemed "weak and hot" when her mother checked on her, and, Catharine recalled, "a look about her eyes gave me a feeling of anxiety." Chatty seemed worse in the evening and so, instead of returning to the nursery, she slept in a bed in her mother's room. The child slept fitfully, and, toward morning, she sat up in bed and said her evening prayer: "O my God, teach me to love Thee. O my God, teach me to pray. O my God, keep me from sin. Pray God to bless me, make me a good and holy child, and keep me to Thy heavenly kingdom. Forgive me all my sin. Teach me to know and love my Saviour Jesus Christ. . . . Bless my dear little baby [sister], for Jesus Christ's sake. Amen." She followed this prayer with the Lord's prayer and then with a poem she had been learning the day before. Her mother was alarmed and, when she heard her husband in his dressing room, she called him to her and asked him to send for the doctor. Meanwhile Chatty awoke and said her prayers again, this time her mother praying with her.[23]

The doctor arrived and saw the child's rash; he asked if the child had had measles. When the answer was yes, he said, "Then most likely she is going to have the scarlet fever; separate the other children." His instructions were followed immediately, except that the newborn baby remained with her mother. The listless five-year-old stayed in bed, suffered spasms and "strange, wild" looks, apparently delirious. Soon after, she had convulsions, which were treated, on medical advice, by a bath and the cutting of her hair. She recovered somewhat and, with the housekeeper in attendance, the doctor calling in frequently, and other family members helping in the watch throughout the day, she struggled with her illness. She had bouts of vomiting and was only conscious enough to say, "Sick again."[24]

Late in the evening, urged for the sake of her family to get some rest, and pressed by her own post-partum weakness, Catharine agreed to go to bed. But "before leaving her," she later recalled, "I knelt down beside her to seek for strength to give up this darling, should this be her call home." Catharine's husband, too, had begun to believe that Chatty was dying, and Catharine saw that "his dear heart was torn with bitter grief." Suddenly the housekeeper called both parents back into Chatty's room. They all knelt and Catharine's husband "read the prayer commending her spirit to Him who had but lent it to us, and who now had come to take her to Himself." At "one o'clock in the morning . . . this precious one left us."[25]

In the face of Chatty's death and fears for their remaining children, the Taits decided not to leave the infant Lucy's baptism to the scheduled date, a week away. Instead, they had a private service immediately in the drawing room at the deanery, with only the family and servants present. The Monday morning of Chatty's funeral Susan, the nineteen-month-old, was ill. It was scarlet fever again. The children were once more segregated from the sick one and also from the nursery staff. Plans were laid to send the healthy children away with their governess. Given Susan's pattern of symptoms, the doctor was optimistic, but convulsions followed by late Monday evening. Her nurse and then her mother held the stiff, twitching body of the child all through the night. She seemed close to death by Tuesday morning but lingered on until early afternoon "when our darling little Susan left our poor home on earth."[26]

Meanwhile, the other children had been taken out of the deanery to the house opposite to protect them from disease. The doctor prescribed port wine twice a day "to strengthen them." Catharine and Archibald suffered at the thought of the anxiety and fear that the children had to bear without any comfort from their parents. On Wednesday, two days after Chatty's funeral, Susan was buried. The remaining children (except the infant) stayed in the neighbors' house, and the parents visited them through the glass of the front window. At the same time the deanery rooms were given many days of thorough airing "to prevent infection."[27]

Catharine watched her children closely for any signs of illness, but none appeared. On the next Saturday, as Catharine looked forward to the prospect of a church service for the first time since her confinement four weeks before, the news came from across the street that four-year-old Frances was ill. Again it was scarlet fever, the third case, and clear evidence that the isolation of the children had not helped. Over the next two days, three medical men, in addition to the family's own doctor, saw the little girl. They all agreed on the diagnosis and treatment and expressed optimism for a good outcome. Vomiting and delirium, as in the other children, characterized the course of the illness. As Catharine looked at her sleeping child on the Tuesday night, she wondered whether she should ask God "for the life of this sweet child . . . at any cost." But "No!" she decided. Instead "I knelt and asked Him who could see all that was before her and us, to do as he saw fit with this our blessed child." The doctor thought Frances was better on Wednesday morning, but the day saw her worsen. She could not swallow the port wine that the doctor prescribed. Parents and servants watched through the evening and into the night. Catharine's husband read a service and prayers, and Frances died soon after 1 a.m. on Thursday. The Taits decided that the remaining three children (still with neighbors) should be taken away from Carlisle in the morning.[28]

Now Catharine began to be haunted by fears for her surviving children. In the night she imagined that she heard the piano and their voices in the nursery below. In the morning news came that the planned move of the children was too late. Catharine Tait's firstborn and namesake, ten-year-old Catharine Anna (Catty), had been vomiting and feeling faint. With a dose of champagne and water from the doctor she seemed somewhat improved. It was Maundy Thursday and she asked her governess to read some of the Easter Week service to her; her father came and prayed with her. The elder Catharine gathered her strength. She prayed for "calmness of spirit to enable me to take my watch beside my first-born." The doctor was encouraging; he thought her age was a point in her favor and that the disease might now be in a "milder form." While Catty lay sick on Good Friday, Frances was buried and Catharine made her first visit to church since the birth of her baby. She thanked God for her own "deliverance" and for the birth of her little girl, but she could not help saying to her husband, later that day, "Oh, surely God is not going to take from us all our children!" "O no," he replied. "I feel almost sure God will spare us the rest."[29]

Catharine could not face the death of another child. She could not say "Thy will be done." Instead, she prayed that God would spare her eldest daughter. Her husband, too, was praying for their children; he asked all those he met to pray with him for Catty. And he sent to all the churches in Carlisle asking for their prayers for her. Saturday came and went and Easter Sunday dawned. And with it the fact of yet another illness: the eight-year-old Mary Susan, known to the family as May, recognized her own symptoms and gave instructions to the servants to keep her seven-year-old brother Craufurd away from her. The parents sent the boy to nearby Stanwix to stay with a cousin.[30]

Parents and servants watched over the two sick girls. They kept their spirits up when with them, "only leaving . . . to find some vent for our suffering, and to pray with a very agony of prayer, that, if possible, the bitter cup put in our hands might be taken from us." More doctors were brought in. On Easter Monday Catty was worse, her throat swelling with the disease. Catharine was so distraught that at first she could not even go to her child, but "At length God heard my cry for help, and gave me calmness and a little strength. I went over to her then." Catharine and her husband stayed at Catty's bedside, prayed with her, and watched her suffering and her dying. Even as they watched over Catty they knew that May "lay very ill in the third day of her fever." Alternating hope and despair took their toll on

Catharine and her husband as they watched Catty and May slip down and then revive. "At length the agony was too much for me," Catharine recalled, and she left her darling Catty in the care of husband and servants. "I could not stay." She slept, and when she woke she heard the news that Catty had died in the night.[31]

May lingered for two more weeks, at times unable to speak, in pain from abscesses, sometimes delirious, and when wakeful asking for her sisters or for Scripture or a hymn. As the end neared Catharine quoted a hymn that the eight-year-old had asked for: "Away, thou dying saint, away, / Flee to the mansions of the blest." The mother resigned herself to May's death. "I turned my anguish into prayer,—prayer that God would comfort us in our extreme desolation, and strengthen us to bear and suffer all His will." And May died.[32]

In five weeks five of the Taits' seven children were dead. Only their son Craufurd and the infant Lucy had survived. The Taits left Carlisle and the deanery and vowed not to return, convinced that the house itself carried disease and death.[33]

Few families had such massive blows dealt them in the course of family life as did the Taits, but almost all of the upper-middle-class families of this study had to face the trials of infant death and the grief that invariably followed. The Taits' story seems extreme in the family's staggering losses. In fact, it is only unusual in two respects; one, that the loss of so many came so rapidly, and two, that the record of their experience of disease is so complete. But almost all of the families studied here lost children, many more than one.

Even more devastating than the deaths of little children were the deaths of offspring who had survived the dangers of infancy and early childhood and who seemed well on their way to a full term of life. Such loss hit every nineteenth-century generation and indeed was a predictable risk for adult daughters in pregnancy and childbirth. But sons died too. The McDougalls' eldest son, presumably safe at school in Ipswich while they were in Borneo, was hit by a cricket ball, took a chill on the playing field, and died of "inflammation of the lungs" in June of 1854. He was nine years old. It was then that Harriette began to think of herself as "in love with death," when she thought of all the children that waited for her in death's arms. Arthur, the darling of Betsey Paget's heart, came down with consumption in November of 1833 when he was a law student in London. By December he was too weak to go to the country, as his family had planned, but instead went home to Yarmouth where his mother and brother nursed him. On Christmas day he left his bed to join the family's dinner and holiday rituals; the next morning he was gone, dead of galloping consumption at the age of twenty-five.

Betsey was not with him when he died, but James was haunted by her reaction to the news, "one of the most fearful scenes I ever saw." Elizabeth Browne's helpless daughter Alice died at the age of seventeen, and two of Connie and Sydney Buxton's children died, one in childhood and one as an adult.[34]

Catharine Tait survived the deaths of her five daughters and went on to have two more children and a productive life. By 1877 her son Craufurd was twenty-eight, recently ordained, and newly engaged to marry. He set off on a three-month trip to the United States for a change of scene and a round of visits with churchmen in North America. He returned in October suffering from fever and pain. He did not tell his parents the extent of his suffering but went ahead with plans for taking up new parish work. He consulted Sir William Gull, and the physician's judgment was serious. The "insidious deterioration of the blood" that the doctor thought he detected was incurable. Craufurd carried on until February of 1878, when he collapsed. Three months of "the most intense anxiety" for Catharine and her husband ended when Craufurd died in early June of 1878. Catharine lived on for six months more before she, too, died, at the age of fifty-nine. It seems reasonable to believe that Craufurd's dying was a factor in Catharine's own death. Her family believed that she never recovered from this last loss of a much-loved son. The Moberlys, too, lost adult children. It is not difficult to imagine the desolation that Mary Ann and George Moberly felt when their son Arthur, aged eighteen, died in 1858 and then, in 1859, daughter Mary Louise died at age twenty-one, probably in childbirth. Twelve years later their son Selwyn died at the age of seventeen. Henry George Liddell and his wife called for the best medical attention in the land when their adult daughter Edith became ill, but there was no help to be had, and she died two days later, at the age of twenty-two.[35]

The deaths of offspring reveal the occasions of private, unsharable, grief in the lives of Victorian gentlewomen, but they also show how husband and wife coped together with the crises they faced. Faith, hope, and the loving support of husband or wife helped parents of both sexes to cope with the pain. A woman's response (and indeed that of her husband) was mediated by her belief that in her turn, death would come and take her to heaven where she would be reunited with the lost children. Perhaps the real transformation in parent-child relations came not when infant mortality declined, but when belief in that heavenly reunion faded, when a mother or father could no longer say, my child is in a better place. Parents' response to infant death may be a function of religiosity rather than a measure of the existence of the "affective family" or of the confidence parents could have in the infant's survival.

HUSBANDS SUFFER

Much attention has been devoted to women's health issues, both by feminist historians of medicine studying the relationship between women's status and their treatment at the hands of doctors, and by those who would see medicine as the foundation for the modern liberation of women. Aside from the pioneering work of Peter Stearns, *Be A Man!*, scarcely anyone has taken up the question of men's health.[36] An examination of the experience of men's health may give some new perspectives on the lives of the women in their families.

Ordinary ill health among these men, as among women, included accidents and contagious diseases. Fenton Hort had scarlet fever as a child, Harold Browne fell and hurt his back in 1848, when he was thirty-seven years old, and Charles Kingsley had "great sufferings from neuralgia" for a month in 1852. Catharine Thompson's husband suffered from asthma for much of his life, but his only life-threatening illness was an attack of peritonitis that occurred while he was traveling in Switzerland. Fortunately for Thompson, his traveling companion was a medical man, his father-in-law Sir James Paget, and that probably saved his life. Infectious disease, like the McDougalls' "Labuan fever," also struck at men's well-being. Eleanor Ormerod's brother Arthur took a "bad chill" in the winter of 1884 that resulted in an "inflammation of the lower part of the right lung." He died in a few weeks.[37]

Occupational health hazards were an issue for professional men, as they were for the miner or the mill-hand. The clearest cases are those related to science and the practice of medicine. James Paget had three major bouts with disease in his adult life—two bouts of septicemia, and one of typhus, all arising from his work in the hospital and the pathology laboratory. The ills that flesh is heir to—and in Britain that included bronchitis and "dyspepsia arising from gout"—took their toll on the husbands and fathers studied here. Some disorders cannot be identified at this distance, but their severity is nonetheless clear. Marianne North's father had worked hard in Parliament during the struggles over the Reform Bill of 1832. Afterward "his health broke down, and he had to give up Parliament for a while." North did not return to political life until 1854.[38] All these illnesses caused grave worry for the women of a family. Servants and hired nurses made the physical burdens of care easier than they would have been for those with fewer resources, but the worry remained.

There is one disorder that appeared frequently among the professional men studied here. As an Oxford undergraduate, Randall Davidson was "nervous and unhappy." As examinations drew nearer, his health became "very poor" and he came "very near a break-down." In his advanced years

Davidson continued to be of "nervous constitution." B. F. Westcott, as a young bachelor, considered himself "melancholy." He often found himself "distracted," and he "resolved to dispel all excessive anxiety."[39] Fenton Hort's early scarlet fever and Harold Browne's back injury were blamed, rightly or wrongly, for their life-long ill health, including recurrent depression. Browne's bad back, together with "hard work," led to several months in bed in 1850. Browne, his friends knew, had always been "rather delicate." Moreover, he did not "by nature take a . . . rose-coloured view of things." Browne's emotional style was, in fact, pessimistic and depressive. Fenton Hort had a similar psychological profile. From the age of twenty-four he had health problems of unknown origin, and over the years he experienced repeated health crises. In 1859 and 1860 his problem was "exhausted powers," leading to a "breakdown in health." In 1862 he suffered a complete collapse; on his doctor's advice, he did not return to work for three years. No organic disease was found, but Hort suffered from "a thorough enfeeblement of brain and spine, from which came other secondary disorders connected with circulation." Hort's health was a subject of constant attention for thirty years. J. R. Green was "frail" as a child, and his health continued to be precarious in adulthood. He had a severe attack of "pleurisy" and bouts of other illness that he attributed to "the stress of work" and "overwork." Green was also subject to depression, perhaps a by-product of his low health, perhaps independent of it. When he and Alice had to postpone their marriage, for example, he suffered yet again a bout of low spirits: "I felt," he said, "the old feeling of the disappointment of life waking up again, and carrying me back into the old grey dead hopelessness which has vanished of late."[40]

Other professional men exhibited signs of depression without its being related to any somatic disorder. Henry Wentworth Acland was an unhappy child, and his whole life had periods of unhappiness and "despondency," sometimes accompanied by vague references to illness. At age seventeen he had a severe breakdown of his health, perhaps physical, perhaps tied to his conflict with parents over his career, perhaps linked to earlier bouts of guilt over an accident. More crises in his mental health occurred in 1839, the year his mother died, and 1840 was a year of "mental storm and stress." He was then twenty-five. Acland married in 1846, and his wife, Sarah Cotton, provided a "calm, cheerful, serene" complement to his rather more turbulent character. After their marriage, his health continued frail but "he was cheered and supported throughout," his biographer rather elliptically reported, "by a devotion worthy of its object." Acland's friend James Paget also had a depressive personality; he found a lifetime of support in his marriage to Lydia. Their son Frank tended toward depression as well. In his young adulthood he was given to fasting, and that worried his parents. James asked Henry Acland to keep an eye on the young bachelor cleric who, at the age of twenty-nine, continued to have symptoms of mental disturbance: Paget attributed two bouts of fainting to the fact that Frank "works too hard; sits up too late; fasts (I suspect) rather too much; is too emotional. . . . [H]e is timid about his health & rather over-watchful of unmeaning symptoms." Paget thought "good counsel" from Dr. Acland would do much to correct Frank's problem. Edward White Benson was one of a number of other clergymen in the Pagets' circle who suffered from bouts of depression.[41]

Novelist George Gissing said that depression was the "intellectual disease of the time." It is not obviously an "occupational" disease, but it was often the disease suffered by professional men, including clergymen. Perhaps both clergymen and doctors felt less than adequate to the demands of their professions, powerless to help those who came to them for aid. In the families under study here, very few women had documentable instances of anything resembling melancholy or depression, other than specific instances of grief over a death in the family. What is striking is that men suffered so often from depression, and descriptions of their illnesses sound very much like those usually attributed to Victorian women.[42]

Men's health problems had clear effects on women's lives. The practical arrangements for the care of the sick man—nursing, special diets, medical attendance—were part of a wife's duty as manager of the household. Most important, illness (especially depressive illness) demanded attention, concern, support, stability, and strength in the partner. The wives of Victorian professional men often provided that kind of care to their husbands. The best documented case here is that of James Paget.

On February 6, 1870, James Paget (aged fifty-five) showed signs of illness, a result of "poisoning his hand" at the hospital. His daughter Catharine was worried enough to pray, "May it please GOD to keep from us, in HIS mercy, greater anxiety." Her prayers were not to be answered. Paget suffered what his son called "the worst of all his illnesses—a terrible attack of blood-poisoning from infection at a *post-mortem* examination." He was moved to a hotel at Norwood (in the London suburbs) "that he might have the benefit of fresh air in his fight for his life." His condition fluctuated between apparent improvement and deterioration, and at one point he seemed so near death that his children were called in to say their goodbyes. Paget's three-and-one-half-month illness unsettled the family in many ways, not the least being their grief at his pain and depression and their worry as to his survival.[43]

For the adult men and women of the family his illness had additional effects, in the disruption of life and the practical demands it placed on them. Doctors, one or several, visited daily, sometimes more than once, and the family heard their reports. Attention to and worry for the sick one meant less time and mental energy for other matters, like ten-year-old Mary's lessons, which often were curtailed during the long illness. When Paget was moved to the suburban hotel, sons and daughters traveled back and forth between Norwood and Harewood Place by carriage or train, sometimes for brief visits, sometimes spending a twenty-four-hour period with James and the hired nurse, before returning to London. The travel alone was a time-consuming addition to their burdens. Other duties and social obligations were often dispensed with, in view of the worry and the demands of patient care. Dinner parties were postponed, and fewer social calls made. Only church-going continued at a relatively regular pace. Once the sick one was moved out of town, some social life was fitted into the space between visits to Norwood.[44]

Other social obligations arose. Many of Paget's friends and associates called at the house or sent notes inquiring about his progress and expressing their good wishes for his recovery. One day early in the siege Catharine replied with "22 letters & notes" to inquirers. (She tried to answer all the mail daily.) Later, when the news of Paget's recovery was released, she and others in the family sent out six hundred notes of thanks to well-wishers.[45]

Even with servants and nurses, the family had much to do to care for the sick one. Paget's wife and adult children who were at home sat with him day and night. On February 8, for example, "John sat up till 4, then called me," Catharine reported, "to sit up the rest of the night & keep in papa's fire so that Mamma got better rest." To cheer—or perhaps merely to distract—the sick one, family members read to him (poetry, Psalms, or portions of the Anglican service) or conversed with one another in his presence. Frank came from Oxford often to see his father and to help care for him. Lydia was at his side almost constantly, watching over him, seeing to his diet, consulting the doctors, and seeing to the material arrangements for his care and comfort. Paget's illness required two rounds of minor surgery, done at the hotel with family members present. Catharine was there when the doctors opened the "abscess on Papa's shoulder." "It was a sad miserable morning," she recalled, for "Papa did not take the chloroform well & it left miserable effects of sickness. . . . It was all so wretched."[46]

And over it all was the worry. Day after day without any improvement meant "monotonous days" broken only by anxiety. Some days the news was dreadful: on February 12 the family heard "A formidable account of dear papa: threatenings of two abscesses forming, which must alas mean a long illness whether they disperse or no." Catharine's only consolation was that "the future is graciously & blessedly hidden: may GOD keep & help us all day by day in the present." Again on March 11 his condition seemed worse and Catharine, surely exhausted from the demands of the past five weeks, "got such anxious thoughts" and "had a most wretched evening and night." Her world was filled with "hopeless bitter misery." James was not a very good patient; he knew too much about his illness and its possible outcome, and he was visibly worried: "Dear Papa's anxiety about himself & incessant pulse feeling are very painful." The disease and the worry often made him restless and irritable.[47]

On Thursday March 23 "things were as bad as they could be. Very little hope was left us." Despite the nourishment (in twelve hours) of "10 glasses of wine, brandy *twice* & plenty of soup, milk, essence of meat, & eggs beaten up, all seemed to have no effect," and Paget's "strength only failed the more." On the 24th he "seemed so much worse, humanly speaking we had no hope, but I do believe GOD's special Mercy help us still to hope in HIM." All Paget's children were summoned by telegram to come, because the end might be near. But in the course of that day he seemed to improve. He rested quietly, and his pulse (which at its worst had been 120 or 130) was down to 100 and later in the day down to 92. "He could hardly believe it then, nor we—but it was so, and one could only humbly & wonderingly thank GOD, Who had so helped & heard us."[48]

Paget stayed in Norwood until April 14, at which point the doctors thought him well enough to return home for the rest of his recuperation. A week later he was getting up for meals, and on April 25 he "drove out," accompanied by his daughter.[49] The Paget story epitomizes the realities of *men's* health problems and the burdens such problems posed for women. There could be no fainting ladies here; these Victorian gentlewomen attended and nursed, for weeks, months, or even years, these suffering Victorian husbands. Women did not have exclusive claims to poor health and helplessness.

Nor—to address another cliché—did men have exclusive control of family money.

LADIES AND MONEY

Victorian ladies, it is said, did not earn; such activity was beneath a lady's dignity. Earning, indeed, declassed her.[50] It is certainly true that a woman's earning a living usually put her outside the pale of genteel society, but this was not because of some mystical relationship between money and genteel womanhood or femininity. There were solid practical grounds for such an attitude. A gentlewoman earning her own living fell outside the circle of social activities that would keep her in touch with her own kind. A ball that lasted until 3 a.m., for example, was not conducive to alert employment the following day. More important, the very fact of having to earn a living demonstrated to the world, and to prospective suitors in particular, that a woman had no effective, economically viable family. A good match was one in which each partner brought to the marriage social and economic resources and safeguards (above and beyond the dowry itself) that would sustain the new family being created. The social message of earning a living was the fact of an economically crippled family. In addition, a lady's working would rob of employment those who needed it—those whom it was her social responsibility to aid.

Such strictures about earning a living, however, do not reveal the whole of Victorian gentlewomen's experiences with money. Victorian ladies did not, in fact, reject the idea of earning. Novelist Charlotte Mary Yonge depicted her heroine, Ethel May, imagining working for pay. Ethel May saw poverty around her and dreamt of being paid for "writing poetry, romance, history—gaining fifties and hundreds. . . . She would compose, publish, earn money," not to support herself but to contribute to the welfare of the poor. It is true that not one woman among the Paget circle had to earn her own living. All were supported by an inheritance or by the earnings of a father, husband, or brother. The two spinster daughters of Samuel and Betsey Paget were worst off because of their father's financial collapse. But even they did not have to earn a living. They survived with the support of their brothers Alfred, George, and James.[51]

Still, there is ample evidence that Victorian ladies earned money and that they were not declassed by the experience. Lydia North and her sisters grew up in a prosperous family. In the 1830s family friends invited the musical Lydia to give piano lessons to their children, and they insisted on paying her. She accepted their offers to teach as an excuse for a day out of town for the sake of her health, but the work itself soon became a source of pleasure as well as income. She enjoyed the work enormously. "[T]he esteem, the parental affection . . . combined with . . . respect" from her employers brought her "almost uninterrupted enjoyment." She also enjoyed the money. On her way out to a lesson "she used to buy a twopenny apple of the old woman who kept an apple stall near the house" and "munch it in the streets." She carried on her teaching for several years. Later in the century Lydia's spinster sister Sarah North settled in Dawlish, on the Devonshire coast. She established a boys' school there, perhaps to give her something to do, possibly to supplement the income she had from her family inheritance.[52]

Catharine, Lydia's daughter, had experiences in the mid-Victorian years analogous to those of her mother. Her father gave her an allowance of some £3 a quarter while she was single and living at home in the 1870s, in part, perhaps, as compensation for the responsibility of her sister Mary's lessons. In addition, Catharine received a quarterly sum of £10 or £11 from an unnamed source (perhaps stocks in her name). In all she had some £50 or £60 a year to spend as she wished. She did not seem to consider such income earned. Only payment from outside the family, for work she had done, qualified as true earnings. She submitted articles to George Grove, the editor of *Macmillan's Magazine*, they were accepted, and in due course fees came her way. One day in March, 1870, she was exultant: "I came home to the *delight* of finding a cheque for £4 from Macmillan. The first money I have ever *earned!*" Even her accounting sheets reflect her excitement; there, too, she reported the £4 *"Earned."* She did not need this money for the necessities of life but used it for church offerings, ribbons, shoes, and gifts. In the process she learned how to keep financial accounts and enjoyed the recognition that came with work for pay. Eleanor Ormerod, well established with family money, nevertheless (like Lydia and Catharine) accepted money for her services. Information about her earnings is extremely limited, but there is at least a clue. She was invited to lecture on insects before the Royal Society of Agriculture in the 1880s; the stipend was £10.[53]

Social reaction to girls' and women's earning was somewhat mixed. Lydia's earnings from music lessons had her clergyman-father's approval; "dearest papa," she said, "ever considered it much for the happiness of young people that they should be actively employed." Her father's approval of her teaching implies, *ipso facto*, his toleration of her earning. Lydia's mother and sisters did not object to her earning either. Only her brother-in-law, the tea merchant and banker Richard Twining, was somewhat censorious in the matter. But Twining was "a hard, dry, inexorable laughterless man," and he found much to disapprove of in all around him. Lydia did not lose status by earning. Indeed, her employers continued to receive her socially throughout her life.[54] Perhaps most important was the reaction of Lydia's future husband. When she and James Paget decided to marry, she began to worry about what he might think about her musical work and earnings. When she confessed to him that she had done something "regarded by the world as lowering," James's response was so free of any hint of censure that she came to see her anxiety as "absurd." Later in their engagement, when Lydia saw the heavy financial burden James was carrying, she regretted that she was no longer earning so that she might "in some measure lighten . . . the constant & laborious duties you have to perform." Sarah North, although probably earning, was received in her sister's fashionable London home among the Pagets' guests, whenever she chose.[55] If there was any negative reaction to Catharine Paget's earning, it is nowhere recorded. Her father surely approved: she worked closely with him on his writing, and he had to know of and support her literary activities. Eleanor Ormerod suffered no social penalties because she earned money. Indeed, her colleague Robert Wallace reacted very specifically to her £10 lecture fee: he thought it shameful that it was so very small. Other ladies who earned money for their work included a friend of Mary Kingsley, Emily Maud Bowdler-Sharpe, who was paid for her entomological work, mounting butterflies and other insects for her clients.[56] Gentlewomen in the mid-Victorian years may not have earned money regularly, but when they did, such earning caused them no loss of status.

The Paget women and their friends also had power over money, for they were involved in decisions about money, their own and their family's, throughout their adult lives. As a single woman Catharine managed her own money, keeping accounting records of income and expenditure. Perhaps such action was rehearsal for the household management of married life. And single women certainly had to manage their own financial affairs. Spinsters Georgiana and Eleanor Ormerod each inherited £9,000 from their father in 1873. Invested at three percent, such a sum would have provided an annual income of £270 to each of them. Such a sum was not grand, but together they had a combined income of £540 a year, and the two sisters managed quite well. They had other monies from their family and were able to buy real property, first a house near Kew and then one in St. Alban's, where they lived comfortably for the remainder of their lives. Another single woman, Marianne North, had plentiful resources. When she died, her estate was valued at £39,329.[57]

Marriage and a husband, far from putting women outside the realm of decision making, often widened their realm of financial power. For women of the upper-middle class, marriage settlements provided at least a measure of financial freedom. A rare surviving marriage settlement reveals how a woman's money and her control of it were guarded in this way. An agreement arranged at the time of Harriet Grenville's marriage to James Morier in 1820 created, out of property from father and husband-to-be, a fund to provide her with "pin money" income of £200 a year. The new husband was enjoined from "meddling" in these fiscal arrangements, and his debts were not chargeable to the account. Moreover, the settlement guaranteed that no changes in the trust could be made without the approval of both husband and wife.[58] This marriage settlement suggests that, even before the married women's property acts began to lead to women's increased power over their money, such powers were the subject of private contract.

Testamentary documents show that many women in the Pagets' circle had power over money, whether by marriage settlement or will, or both. A. C. Tait arranged that his three daughters, for example, should each receive

£10,000 plus an interest in his residuary estate. When one daughter married before his death, her inheritance became her marriage portion, subject to the same terms as the bequests. His will declared that "each of these my daughters shall have entire control of her own income." Under his will the women could "appoint that all or any part of the annual income of her legacy and share in the Residuary Trust Fund shall . . . after her death be paid to her husband for his life or for any less period," but such a legacy should be made "upon such conditions and with such restrictions as she shall think fit." Sir William Gull was equally clear about his intentions: his daughter, "during any couverture" (that is, if married), would have her legacy "for her separate use." These arrangements for daughters could reach over generations. Sir George and Lady Burrows arranged their daughter Rose's marriage settlement out of their own: "under a power in our marriage settlement [we] appointed one fourth share of all the trust funds subject to our Settlement to my daughter." Only after Lady Burrows's death and by the express stipulation of the original settlement could Sir George exercise further power over the settlement monies; he did so in the interest of his daughter.[59]

In all these cases, wills and marriage settlements gave women exclusive power over marriage portions and legacies. Such monies gave women a separate financial sphere. She was not subject to a husband's control in these matters, but neither did she, by these arrangements, have any direct influence over him or the family's finances. It is important to look to the "family purse" for a measure of women's role in money matters. Women's roles in family financial management included both the mundane household matters that were a standard part of middle-class women's lives and major responsibilities related to family finance. In Great Yarmouth in the first third of the nineteenth century, Betsey Paget "took part," her son James said, "even a leading and decisive part, in all grave business-questions."[60] In a family that faced, by the 1830s, a decade of serious financial strain, the issue was important.

Information about other aspects of women's relationship to family money is scarce for the first generation of this study. Much richer detail is available about the generations from 1830 onward, the fullest being the case of Lydia North and James Paget. The two lovers discussed money matters from the very beginning of their relationship, and their financial affairs were characterized by candor and equality. Financially the pair was mismatched—the Norths were prosperous while the Pagets had severe financial problems. The discrepancy might have been a source of tension, but it was not. James, the impoverished medical student, was punctilious about money, but not hypersensitive. In the winter of 1837 the couple wrote long letters to each other between London and Paris (where James was studying). When minor money problems arose, like postage due on his letters to her, James suggested that Lydia "put it [the postage] down to my account with you, in which you have already two or three items against me. . . . [I]t is but fair that we should enjoy our pleasure at equal expence." He went on to note that "there will be a considerable amount of expenditure of this kind before we can have a common purse, and till then let our business be fairly transacted—after that we can make some mutual arrangement."[61]

After their marriage, Lydia handled ordinary family accounts. For this purpose James made regular disbursements "To Lydia" out of his professional income. Their son Stephen recalled, "One morning a week, [my brother] Luke and I used to go with my Mother 'to pay the bills.' The shops were Lidstone's, Holland's, Bradley's, Luckie's—these were the butcher, grocer, greengrocer, and poulterer: and a fishmonger's in Marylebone Lane."[62] When her elder daughter was old enough, Lydia turned some of these accounts and duties over to her.

Clara Paget managed domestic money matters, whether in Cambridge or at long distance. From Wales she called on her daughters Maud and Rose to act as her agents in family money matters. One particularly vexing June in the late 1870s or early 1880s Maud complained to her sister about the difficulties of family finance: "Oh, deary me! this horrible housekeeping, here's Papa haranguing on the 'Tea Bill' again & a nice little lump is to be paid at Church's next week." Some bills needed explaining and she urged Rose, "Pray enlighten me quick before we are reduced to £ a week [*sic*]." From the beginning of her marriage, Catharine Spooner Tait was the family financial manager. She was not only the record-keeper but an active participant in decisions about spending. Mary Smith, too, managed the family money—she called herself the "Domestic Bursar." So firmly were the financial reins in her hands that her husband had to refer to her when considering any expenditure. She believed that he missed learning important lessons about money management by leaving family finances so much to her.[63]

These scattered bits of information hint at women's involvement in family money matters and suggest that women were not isolated from money and the facts of financial life. The most systematic evidence comes from wills, the documents that show husbands and wives, fathers and mothers, planning for the disposition of their resources. These documents reveal that gentlewomen were not simply the beneficiaries of men's wills. Victorian men and women alike had clear expectations about women's proximity to, and ability with money—and more besides.

In the first place, women were often named executors of men's wills. Some men excluded women from the management of their estates, and their reasons were not always obvious. In the 1840s Betsey Paget's bachelor son

Charles named his father and business partner, Samuel, as his executor. When making his will Charles also had a choice of several competent brothers, an ailing mother, and two spinster sisters, one over forty, the other not yet eighteen. His choice of his father may reflect no more than their existing business partnership; it does not necessarily imply his rejection of female competence in money matters. James Paget also chose males over females. When he wrote his will in the late 1890s, his wife Lydia was dead, and his younger daughter Mary may already have been losing her sight. His elder daughter Catharine might have been a suitable choice as executor, but he passed over both daughters to name his eldest son, John (a barrister), his son-in-law, the Reverend H. L. Thompson, and his former student and professional associate Sir Thomas Smith, to administer his £74,861 estate. Like Sir James Paget, Archibald Campbell Tait was a widower when he made his will in 1883. He left the management of his £77,773 personalty in the hands of his son-in-law and a clerical friend. Sir Henry Wentworth Acland, also a widower, named his three sons and a male friend as executors. Other men who left the execution of their wills in the hands of men, while excluding female relatives from the process, include the Ormerod men (Edward, Arthur, and George), J. S. Henslow, Lord Halifax, and T. H. Huxley.[64] The logic of these decisions is not always clear.

Sometimes passing over the wife as executor may have signalled strained relations between husband and wife or between the husband and the wife's family. Tensions with in-laws may account for Edmund Paget's choice of his solicitor to administer his estate. Sir George Paget's decision in 1892 to leave the management of his £21,939 estate to his sons, but to leave in his wife Clara's hands the power to appoint new trustees, is difficult to assess. Perhaps he wanted to leave the day-to-day details to the younger members of the family, while leaving major power in the hands of his sixty-six-year-old wife. But he did exclude all his daughters from involvement in the administration of his estate. Lydia's son John, the barrister, and an expert on banking law, left his affairs in the hands of a bank. His wife had predeceased him, but he left two adult sons as well as two adult daughters without responsibility in his affairs. Perhaps his will reflects his confidence in bankers; perhaps it reveals his relations with his children.[65]

These few cases aside, upper-middle-class women figure largely in the management of fathers', brothers', or husbands' estates. Indeed, when it was possible to do so, men in this study almost always designated women to administer their estates. Such choice of executor did not depend on the size of the estate the man left. The Reverend Isaac William North made his wife, Elizabeth, the sole executor of his £1,256 estate, and his brother the Reverend Jacob North did likewise with his small estate of £2,222. Henry Luke

Paget, the bishop of Chester, named his wife, Elma, and son Paul executors of the small personalty of £497 he left in 1937. In 1862 the Rev. Alfred Paget left his £1,500 estate in the hands of his thirty-seven-year-old spinster sister, Katherine, this despite the fact that Alfred had several responsible brothers he might have appointed. Widower Francis Paget, bishop of Oxford, named his sister-in-law Mary Church the executor of his small estate. Miss Church had taken over the care of his children after Helen Church Paget's death in 1901. Soon after Catharine Paget married the Rev. H. L. Thompson in 1877, he named her executor of his estate. He died in 1905, leaving an estate valued at £4,164. Catharine's youngest brother, Stephen, called on his wife, Eleanor, for this task; he died in 1926 and left an estate valued at £6,660.[66]

Testators with large estates also left them to be administered by women. Rose Paget's husband, J. J. Thomson, in 1940, named their daughter Joan and their son George executors of his £82,601 estate. (By this time Rose was eighty years old.) Many other men with sizable estates left their wives in full or partial control: Sir William Jackson Hooker in 1865 placed his estate (valued at £40,000) in the hands of his wife, together with their son and his brother-in-law. George Busk chose his wife, Ellen, and his two brothers to administer his estate (valued at £46,933 in 1886). The Reverend R. W. Church left his wife, Helen, his sole executor in 1891, in charge of an estate valued at £32,021. In Cambridge George Murray Humphry relied on his widow and his son to administer his £80,199 estate in 1896. Sir William Withey Gull, one of the wealthiest members of this network, left a personal estate valued at £344,023; his son, two friends, and his wife, Lady Susan Anne Gull, were his executors. The Reverend William Jacobson's estate, valued at £65,850 in 1896, was left in the care of his wife, his son, and two other males. In 1913 Alfred Willett left his widow, Rose, and three male relatives in control of his £21,463 estate.[67] The sum of these men's wills suggests their confidence in the financial abilities of the women of the family to take on—most probably to continue to carry out—family financial affairs.

Executorship involved the distribution of money and possessions. A woman's appointment as executor testified to her responsibility, but it says nothing about women's ability or autonomy in money matters. Inheritance, on the other hand, brought money and possessions directly into a woman's own hands. Occasionally a husband and wife planned a widow's financial management of her inheritance in advance of his death. Such plans are evident in Hannah Turner Brightwen's will. She reported that "My dear husband by his Will devised and bequeathed all his estate real and personal to myself absolutely. He entertained desires respecting the application of his property at my death and these desires I wish fully to carry out and have done so by this my will." Her husband, Thomas, a Yarmouth banker, had left an estate valued at under £40,000 at his death in 1870. Twelve years later Hannah Brightwen's estate was valued at £50,309, and her will reflects her husband's wishes and her own as well.[68]

Emily Wood Meynell Ingram had more than the executorship when her husband died in 1871. Much to his own family's unhappiness, Hugo Meynell Ingram left "the whole of his property [a personalty worth nearly £180,000] to his wife absolutely." The estate was sizable, but the family need not have worried: Emily had "a good head for managing the properties which had come to her." Acting with due regard for her husband's memory, she built a church in their village, the estate of Hoar Cross near Leeds, to honor him. She also used her money to provide "major support" for Pusey House in Oxford. In 1889 she gave £500 for the maintenance of the house.[69]

George Grote, James Paget's predecessor as vice chancellor of London University, left a similarly large fortune in the hands of his wife, Harriet, when he died in 1871: she was the sole executor of his £120,000 estate. Grote set up a trust to oversee certain aspects of his estate. Mrs. Grote was his major heir; she received a lump sum of £20,000, annual income from some of his properties, and a life interest in others. As a result of such inheritances from husbands or parents, women came to have assets and estates of their own to dispose of. Eleanor Ormerod left a large estate, one whose net value was assessed at £51,583. Edith Tait, Lady Davidson, had a small estate, valued at just over £6,700. She named her cousin and companion, spinster Mary Catherine Mills, and a clergyman as her executors.[70] Nearly all these women had some money to manage and, in time, to bequeath to others.

Men first looked to the well-being and support of their wives, but they were also alert to the needs of other women in the family. The professional men studied here showed special concern for their spinster daughters, and their wills reveal the sometimes extensive financial resources left to these women. Alfred Willett, for example, provided for his wife Rose's financial support after his death, but he also knew that she might become her father's residuary legatee. In that case, with his wife provided for, Willett arranged that the monies set aside for Rose for her lifetime should instead go directly to their unmarried daughter Eliza Maud. In a similar case, Angie Acland's father and grandfather had insured that she would have at least half of the income from the family's lands in Somerset. Angie's father also left her two houses in Oxford, with £400 set aside annually for their upkeep, one-fourth of the income from his and her late mother's marriage settlement, and the proceeds of £16,000 of investments. When Angie died in 1931, she left a personal estate valued at £12,049.[71]

Fathers made it clear that their daughters were to control their own inheritances. When Hans Busk left one-fifth of the income of his estate to his daughter Sophia Emilia Crawford, he declared (in language entirely typical of such a bequest) that it was for her "natural life for her own sole and inalienable use free from the debts engagements control or intermeddling of her present or any future husband that she may have or marry." Fathers sometimes reached very far into their daughters' financial affairs, even after they married. Caroline Cameron Gull's father settled £26,000 on her when she married Theodore Acland, and the settlement included provision for her children, should there be any. In his will, he made provision for the disposal of the money, in case she had no children: "I do hereby in that event empower her by Will or Codicil notwithstanding coverture to appoint and dispose of in any manner she may think fit any sum or sums of money" up to £10,000 of the legacy. In other words, Sir William Gull used his will to circumvent even his married daughter's legal status in order to give her greater freedom over her money than the law conventionally allowed. Gull's actions are typical. A. C. Tait set up trusts for his wife, his daughters, and their children, but he also provided that "it shall be lawful for each of my said daughters when married by Will or Codicil to appoint that all or any part of the annual income of her legacy . . . shall from and after her death be paid to her husband . . . upon such conditions and with such restrictions as she shall think fit."[72] Men's wills were, in other words, instruments by which laws of property ownership, coverture, and the wills themselves could be bent to the wishes of wives and daughters.

Another—and revealing—feature of many upper-middle-class Victorian husbands' and fathers' wills was the trust. Funds generated by the sale of stocks and real and personal property were placed in a trust, and the trustees were charged with the investment and oversight of the resources, the proceeds to be distributed according to the will, to wife and daughters as well as other heirs. Such fiduciary arrangements appear, on their face, to be a form of male control over women—attempts to control investment and expenditure, presumably because of women's inexperience and their need for protection after a father's or husband's death. The facts of trusts created by the men of the Pagets' circle suggest that another interpretation is more appropriate.

In the first place, most husbands named their wives and daughters among the trustees they appointed. Maria Hooker, Eleanor Jacobson, and Rose Willett were named trustees in their husbands' wills; widower Hans Busk named his daughters Julia Byrne and Rachel Busk trustees. Moreover, wives had the power, usually sole power, to appoint new trustees, when those appointed by their deceased husbands died, went abroad, or otherwise became unavailable for such service. Harriet Grote, one of her husband's trustees, had sole responsibility for appointing new trustees. Neither Edith Tait nor

Clara Paget was a trustee of her husband's estate, but both had the sole right to name new trustees.[73]

Finally, the role of the trustees was the oversight of investment, and no more. Dawson Turner called on a relative and a friend from Yarmouth, John Brightwen and William Worship, to be his trustees, and it was their job to sell off his personal and real property to create Turner's trust. When all legacies, settlements, and bonds were taken care of, the remainder was to be paid to Turner's second wife, Matilda, in the form of an annuity of £700 a year "for her sole and separate use and benefit for and during the time of her natural life . . . she shall so long continue my widow." On Matilda's death or remarriage, the whole estate and trust monies were to go to Turner's spinster daughter, Mary Ann. Like other fathers of single daughters, Turner made special provision for her support. A husband's or father's will never gave guidelines for or set limits on his wife's or daughter's spending, and it never gave trustees such powers over his female heirs. Most often the will explicitly declared that "the receipt alone of my said [wife or daughter] and hers alone notwithstanding her present or any future coverture shall be a good and sufficient acquittance and discharge" to the executors. In other words, she had only to sign a receipt—she did not have to account for her use of the monies she received.[74] Men who established trusts for their wives and daughters (especially spinster daughters) created them to maximize the income from the estate.[75] The trustees were charged with the responsibility for sound investment, but they were not called upon to put limits on women's use of the proceeds of those trusts. Trustees were not there to protect "foolish widows" or innocent daughters but to multiply their financial resources. Victorian women were not controlled by their late fathers' or husbands' trusts; rather, they were empowered by them and were at liberty to use inherited monies as they chose.

Money, its ownership, and its management were a fact of these gentlewomen's lives. Members of the Paget family's circle, men and women alike, expected the women of these families to be involved in financial affairs throughout their adult lives. Money was power and it is clear that some gentlewomen had the influence that wealth bestowed. Some did not seem to have exercised it. Others used their money actively to build a church or endow a library. As executors, women had legal responsibility for the administration of a will, including the management of money. When they inherited, they also had full responsibility for its management and disposition. Across the century men's estates, whether large or small, went to sisters, wives, or daughters when the male relative died. Money may have been "filthy lucre," but that did not mean gentlewomen did not touch it, control it, and use it for their own purposes.

The neglected features of Victorian ladies' lives include their relations to children, their encounters with sickness and death, and their relationship to money. Without a mystique of motherhood, Victorian families were a problematic fact of life. Children were surely a fact, but they were not always a pleasure, not automatically the objects of love. Children took second place to a woman's husband or even to herself. Some mothers were affectionate and devoted, others cool, distant, or preoccupied by other matters than motherhood. Some were unkind, others incompetent. The point is that Victorian gentlewomen did not fit a single mold of motherly devotion.

Illness was commonplace, and nearly every family had to accept the death of infants; little children were vulnerable to a host of fatal dangers. But adulthood was not safe either, and many women, after seeing their offspring to maturity, lost males and females alike, whether to disease or the risks of childbearing. Marriage, too, could be fraught with psychic danger, with a husband liable to be ill, whether from the ordinary processes of disease or accident, or from his work, its dangers and stresses, and the resulting potential for physical or mental injury. A woman's life could be significantly shaped by a husband's acute health problems or his chronic mental or physical illness. The Victorian gentlewoman had all the benefits of superior education and family resources, but no family's money stood against the power of disease and death in her life.

She may have been powerless over disease and death. She may even have been legally without control over money or property. But in the upper-middle-class family a gentlewoman was usually empowered by the private legal creations of marriage settlements, wills, and trusts. As a consequence, the Victorian gentlewoman had a sphere of power, a realm of autonomous existence, based on the financial resources inherited from parents, settled on her at marriage, and made available to her as a widow. The world of money (like the world of sexuality) was not forbidden to gentlewomen. And while men and women alike had no power over disease and death, gentlewomen, like their brothers, fathers, and husbands, were empowered by their access to, and control over, wealth.

CHAPTER FIVE

Gentlewomen at Work

"The condition of being female is somehow associated [in Victorian fiction and Victorian life] with a degree of incompetence, inadequacy, and ineffectuality." So wrote one Victorian literary critic. More recently another writer has asserted, with respect to gentlewomen's lives, that "any serious outside interest was incompatible with the rituals of 'calling' and . . . the 'sacred rite of dinner.'" These writers and other scholars see Victorian ladies' lives as ineffectual and trivial—lives defined by decorative leisure, the demands of sociability, and the "tyranny of the card case."[1]

Recently Martha Vicinus examined the experiences of Victorian single women. She rightly recognized the Victorians' belief in "the morally redeeming power of work" but singled out "paid public work" as the sole "source of dignity and independence" for these women. The alternatives were "unremitting idleness," or acts of charity, "meeting trivial responsibilities," and family and "private" duties that included "teaching in the local church school."[2] Vicinus studied those exceptional single women who rejected the Victorian status quo and whose actions brought about changes in opportunities for unmarried women in the period between 1850 and 1930. By contrast, the women studied here are those who stayed at home, and, whether married or single, made useful lives for themselves without abandoning the conventional upper-middle-class women's sphere.

The women of this study were typical of their class in that none needed to earn a living. Fathers, brothers, and husbands provided for their material needs. Nor did any seem to feel the need for a career. But leisured does not mean idle. They spent part of their time, as we all know, in a whirl of social activities: visits, parties, dances, balls, trips to theaters or to art galleries or to Regent Street shops. They taught their children and supervised the household, but when they had superior servants, they had no onerous domestic duties. They did needlework, and they collected shells, old china, and the autographs and photographs of eminent Victorians. Child-rearing aside, these all seem trivial pursuits. But socializing and shell collecting do not represent the limits of their lives. This chapter will explore the sorts of work gentlewomen—single or married—did on their own. The record, as always, is patchy. Sometimes all we know is that a woman worked. In Cambridge, for example, Mrs. F. J. A. Hort (we are told) engaged in "various educational and philanthropic works."[3] The details of her activities, and those of many other gentlewomen, are lost to historical scholarship. What remains, however, tells us of gentlewomen's involvement in charity, teaching, and some unusual alternative choices.

THE WORK OF CHARITY

The publication of Andrew Mearns's *The Bitter Cry of Outcast London* brought "revelations of the condition of the poor to comfortable people in the seventies and eighties" that carried with them the "shock of novelty."[4] The awakening of the Church of England to "the social question" led to a rush of men, young and old, to the slums of London and other cities to bring both the Gospel and social amelioration. Gentlewomen worked in these new missions, too. The settlement house movement may have brought women into the lives of the poor in new ways, but women had been visiting the poor and helping the disadvantaged of their neighborhoods and parishes for more than two generations. The movement merely brought a new style of organization to work women had been doing all along. Whether early or late in the century, nearly all gentlewomen engaged in some kind of charity.

Visiting the poor was one of the commonest forms of charity throughout the Victorian period. The practice was widespread among the women studied here. Even when we know only the barest facts about a woman's charitable work, we know that she visited the poor. As a young woman in London, Mary Erskine (later Lady Acland) did some visiting. The North sisters went regularly to visit the poor of their London district in the 1830s.[5]

Some gentlewomen visited jails, workhouses, or schools, where they inspected the management of the institutions as well as helping the inmates. Catharine Paget visited her district workhouse in London, and Felicia Mary Skene visited the Oxford jail and prison regularly for more than fifty years. Visits to private homes also involved helping the poor. Such aid might take the form of simple moral support. If there was illness or some other suffering, a visitor offered the consolation of religion, by reading a passage of Scripture or a sermon. Sometimes the family needed material aid, and the visitor brought food or blankets or clothing. Catharine Spooner went regularly to "visit the cottagers [of Elmdon] and help them in their difficulties." Even in the absence of illness or hunger, the visitor might bring a gift—a basket of food or a tract—to those in her care.[6] The visitor's goals were Christian service and the improved material and spiritual lives of poor and suffering people.

Visiting was common enough to inspire entrepreneurial ventures in the publication of handbooks so that visitors could keep records of their charitable work. Such books also carried instructions to visitors. Appearing as early as 1835, they offer clues to the visitor's specific purposes in visiting the poor. These goals included, predictably enough, the promotion of church going and the education of children. Visitors were also expected to assess the literacy of members of the family, foster prudence in money matters, and see that charitable aid did not go to "the idle, drunken, and profligate." The handbook provided space for the visitor to record the name of each family, occupation, status with respect to parish relief, habits of domestic prayer and church attendance, tracts and books lent, and records of savings and interest.[7]

Fiction offers illustrations of these relations between charitable women and the poor they visited. Charlotte Mary Yonge's *The Daisy Chain* (1856) describes village philanthropy: visitors brought food and clothing, and they consulted with parents about such matters as children's education and the employment of an adolescent daughter. Mrs. Humphry Ward's heroine in *Marcella* (1894) brought apples and more substantial help to the poor of her neighborhood. Marcella's most important "gift" to her people was news of employment opportunity in the district.[8]

By midcentury women were increasingly conducting their parish work in cooperation with local clergy. In the early 1850s, for example, the Reverend E. H. Browne, then vicar of Kenwyn-cum-Kea (Cornwall), called on his parish visitors for information about "the condition of his people." The women gathered data on a variety of matters. Demographic data included family and household size, occupation, and the ages of family members. They investigated such religious questions as church affiliation, the baptism of children, and whether or not adults in the household were communicants. Finally, they tried to find out about educational matters: whether the children of a family went to school and what the level of literacy in a household was. These latter matters, although secular, had a direct bearing on what sorts of services the church might provide in the parish. Clergymen in the mid-Victorian years were fully ready to recognize what Browne described as the "great reserves of strength and work" that women contributed to the church.[9] In organized visiting, women became the earliest social surveyors, the precursors of Booth and Mayhew.

Nearly forty years after her mother's parish work, Catharine Paget was taking time from her busy social life to visit the poor in her district—St. James's parish, Picadilly—every week. Her work was not the one-time venture into a poor neighborhood that could fairly be called "slumming." Nor was it haphazard. Rev. and Mrs. Browne and others like them had helped to make the work of visiting much more formal and organized than it had been for Catharine's mother's generation. Catharine went regularly, usually on Tuesday and Friday mornings, to visit two or three poor people. Each trip took an hour, sometimes two. Mrs. Kempe, the wife of the parish clergyman, and other women in the parish, coordinated the work. They held visitors' meetings regularly at the parish church, where they offered instruction for visiting, help with problems, and lectures on the most effective approaches to poor families, together with such fundamental matters as organization and record keeping.[10]

These Victorian Christian women provided other sorts of help to the poor, sometimes in response to a specific crisis. The cholera epidemic of 1853–54, for example, brought many women out of their houses and into the homes of the poor. When cholera broke out in Oxford, Felicia Skene organized nurses to care for the sick poor in the town. During the same period Edith Davidson and other clergymen's wives went to work to help cholera victims in London.[11]

Other forms of charity sprang from a woman's own beliefs about what good she could do for others. In the 1830s, when Georgiana Ormerod was sixteen years old, she began a book-lending club in her Gloucestershire neighborhood. Its purpose: to distribute "useful healthy literature" to the poor. She spent her own money on the project and continued the work all her life. Constance Buxton found herself temporarily in the rural environment of Belmullett, Co. Mayo, in the 1880s. She took up work for the needy there. Without the elaborate organization of London charity, she set up her own "little fund" to help the poor, and she was grateful for her father's £10 contribution to her campaign. She planned her charitable spending with care, so that the fund would foster peasant independence. She thought the purchase of seeds for poor farmers would serve this end.[12] In London Mary Maud Paget used her brother Luke's appointment as vicar of St. Pancras Church in 1887 as an entrée to work in the parish. In the next two decades she worked with the Girls' Club, which, under her leadership, "grew from cheerful rowdyism to a more ordered company." The purpose of the club was to transform the girls into "faithful Communicants." Along the way, Mary, well trained in music, taught them to "sing and appreciate the best music." Mary Maud also gave her name, time, and money to the work of the Factory Girls' Country Holiday Fund. Such charities sent working-class youngsters to the country for a few days, and sometimes for as long as a week or two. They lived with village families and had close "contact with Nature." The holidays were meant to improve children's health, to give them "new experiences of the meaning of family life," and to "bring them nearer to God." In the early decades of the twentieth century, Harriot Moule's work in the Durham diocese included "ardent efforts" on behalf of the Girls' Friendly Society.[13]

Christian socialism and the settlement house movement led some of the late Victorian generation of Paget women and their friends, like the men of their social class, out of their own neighborhoods and into mission work in London's East End. In the 1880s, Catharine Paget's spinster aunt Kate, by then in her late fifties, brought "wisdom and devotion" to her work in the Poplar district of east London, where her nephew Luke headed Christ Church's mission. Three decades later Catharine Paget Thompson, a widow in her sixties, worked among the poor under the auspices of the Magdalene College mission in east London; her son James also worked there. Violet Paget Roy served as lady superintendent of St. Saviour's Homes, established by the National Association for Promoting the Welfare of the Feeble Minded. There she dealt with those whom Henrietta Barnett had described as "deficient in the qualities necessary for the battle of life" who, without such a refuge, had to live in the streets, liable to be the butts of "cruel merriment" and torment at the hands of their neighbors.[14]

Later in the century the rescue of "fallen" girls and women took an increasing portion of women's charitable efforts. Spinster Felicia Skene added work among Oxford's "fallen" women to her prison visiting, both of which she carried on for many decades. Harriot Moule helped establish St. Monica's Rescue Home in 1908, an institution created to save the lives and souls of Durham's "fallen" women. The home owed its existence "largely . . . to her strong and loving initiative." She was also instrumental in the formation of the Preventive and Rescue Association in Durham in 1909, and she headed the ladies' committee there.[15]

Work among the poor could be unpleasant and the rewards were never material. Questions have therefore been raised about the motives of women who involved themselves in philanthropy. *Punch* presented graphic critiques of women's motives, showing ladies bountiful as ladies slumming. Historian Frank Prochaska implied a biological imperative when he suggested that charity activities grew out of women's "mothering and family instincts." Alternatively, he offered boredom as a motive. Martha Westwater, too, pointed to the "dryness of boredom" as well as "sentimentality" and "obligation" as motives for charity. Vicinus put forward a multiplicity of motives, including women's "traditional role," escape from boredom, the possibilities of "adventure," and the "satisfaction" of "service to a higher good."[16] Perhaps some individual cases will offer a test of these hypotheses.

Lydia North felt deeply ambivalent about her work among the poor: "I always go with such reluctance to visit the poor people under our care; . . . on setting out I feel inclined to bend my steps in any other direction rather than the right." She thought her "aversion" to these good works sprang from her sinfulness, and it is not now clear what specifically repelled her. Nevertheless, she carried on her work among the poor because it was "good," perhaps because it was her Christian duty as a pious and prosperous woman. And her negative feelings did not last: "when I once get amongst them," she admitted, "I quite enjoy myself." Her positive satisfaction in the work does not bespeak a morbid interest in the poor. She found pleasure in the people she saw, and perhaps joy in the self-discipline of doing "His service." What is clearest in Lydia North's discussion of her charity was her close identification with the task: she called the people "*our* poor people," and when some of the old people suffered from severe winter weather in 1836, she said "*we* have had several deaths . . . lately."[17] Deeper than her feeling of sinful reluctance was her belief that the poor of her district belonged to her, and responsibility flowed from that belief.

A generation later women seemed less introspective about their charity. Lydia's daughter Catharine left a day-by-day account of her service, but her motives are never apparent. Indeed, she seems to have taken her charity efforts for granted: "visited today . . . visited some poor people today . . . visited in the district," were her laconic reports of her work. She offered an indirect clue to her motives in March of 1870, when she was referred to Mrs. Kempe, the wife of her parish priest, for "work to do." She promptly followed up on this lead and on Tuesday, March 15, 1870, "I went to see Mrs. Kempe who was very kind & directed me to a Miss Howlett . . . who will put me in the way of work." She found such work on the very next Thursday when she "went to Miss Howlett at 3, she was very pleasant & introduced me to a poor woman to visit." Visiting was, in short, Catharine's work. Her ironic report that "I spent the morning seeing poor people, the afternoon calling on rich ones" suggests her awareness of the contrast between the two sorts of calls she made. Her casual style veils only thinly her satisfaction in finding useful work to do. Catharine's cousin Maud involved herself in the less personal activities of charity fund-raising during summer holidays in Wales and spoke with annoyance of the antimacassars she was making for a "horrid bazaar at Beddgelert." Maud considered bazaars and needlework tiresome duties, but she did them nonetheless. By contrast Mary Baird took on her charity work with "intense delight." She did it "not from any self-sacrifice on my part but because I loved it."[18]

Henrietta Barnett had rather more clearly articulated and more complex reasons for her work with the poor and the unfortunate. Of her work among the "feeble-minded" in the 1880s, for example, she said: "It was heart-breaking to hear the uncontrolled laughter of the mentally deficient as they wandered aimlessly in the streets. . . . How," she asked, "could one leave one's crippled sisters in the midst of the battlefield to the tender mercy of the devils?"[19] Her responses were emotional and empathetic: Barnett felt a kinship with, and a compassion for, those in need. Where Lydia saw a test of her own character, Henrietta Barnett saw sin and suffering, and her role was to do battle against both.

Mary Smith illustrates the compassion and courage of philanthropic gentlewomen. As an Oxford proctor, her husband was responsible for undergraduates' morals, and she became involved as well. While he tried to help the sinning undergraduate male, she tried to rescue the "fallen" female. "I remember going," she reported, "with the courage born of ignorance and innocence, into the purlieus of St. Ebbe's to hunt up a girl of fifteen in a 'bad house.'" In the brothel she confronted the madam and some of the prostitutes: she stared into "the eyes of the hardened woman who kept the house. I trembled . . . and pleaded my cause, or rather Annie's, very feebly, to their evident amusement, and got no further." Despite her inexperience, Smith did not find Annie's sexual involvement with the Oxford undergraduate shocking: "it seemed to me as if it could not be like other sins because, to my mind, it was based on love." She could "more easily forgive the woman who sins in that way than the woman who is just cruel, or even unkind."[20] Feminine delicacy was not blind to the emotional needs of the poor nor to the sexual realities of slum life.

The search for excitement or the mere impulse to conform to upper-middle-class norms could not, in themselves, sustain women in the demanding and sometimes harrowing work of charity. Christian commitment, an abiding compassion for their fellow creatures, and the need to lead useful lives were the sustaining motives in women's charity work. Adolescent girls and spinsters of sixty, young brides and middle-aged matrons—they all took a share in caring for the poor. They gave of their resources but they also gave their time to this work. Charity was not a snug little duty, carried out at home or in the safety of the parish hall. Gentlewomen went out into the streets of the East End, into the squalid homes of the very poorest, and into the jails and brothels of every city and town. In all their work gentlewomen had to confront the bitter facts of life for the poor—the "verminous" condition of factory girls, the sexual temptations of working-class life, and the hopeless cruelties of slum streets.[21]

The Victorian Lady as Teacher

Historians have long known of women's role in the primary instruction of their own little children in the basics of reading, writing, and religion at home. We also know that teaching was a major form of "middle-class" female employment: women in Victorian England were governesses, they taught in dame schools, and some were proprietors of the growing number of day and boarding schools for middle-class girls. Education was also the subject of women's reformist action, especially in the expansion of secondary and university education for middle-class girls and women.[22]

The history of education touches this collective biography of Victorian women at several points. A very few of these gentlewomen taught for pay; a few had formal ties to the new women's colleges in Oxford and Cambridge. Lydia North taught piano for pay but certainly had no need for the income. Decades later Sarah North, Lydia's spinster sister, established a boys' school in Dawlish, Devons., possibly to supplement her income, perhaps only to occupy her time. Eleanor Balfour Sidgwick helped to establish Newnham College for women at Cambridge and then worked in the college's administration in the 1880s and after. Charlotte Anne Elizabeth Moberly headed St. Hugh's College, Oxford, from 1886 to 1915.[23]

Although we know a fair amount about governesses and even more about women's work in schools and colleges, we know virtually nothing about the other sorts of teaching most Victorian gentlewomen did. The role of upper-middle-class women in voluntary educational work outside the home has disappeared from historians' sight, perhaps because the history of charity education itself has fallen between two stools. Historians of popular education, interested in organized, state-supervised public instruction and the rise of a paid corps of professional teachers, have largely ignored the roots of universal education in the charity education of the nineteenth century.[24] Meanwhile, students of philanthropy and social work have readily acknowledged women's work as district visitors, as the vehicles by which material benefits passed from donors into the hands and homes of the poor, but they have left women's teaching out of the account. All this is understandable; education is an odd hybrid, seeming not quite to fit the mainstream of Victorian charity, and education outside the framework of record-keeping institutions is extremely difficult to trace. But education was an integral part of Victorian social action. Charity teaching provided something to the poor without charge which they might otherwise have to purchase in the open market or do without. It was (like other charity activities) designed to help the recipients help themselves.[25] Educational work took gentlewomen into churches and other institutions to carry out an important social and public service. Whether in the family or as charity, teaching was, arguably, the most important work gentlewomen did. In exploring the teaching roles of gentlewomen in the Victorian age, the major issues are whom did they teach, and where, and to what end.

Despite our familiarity with women teaching at home, that activity deserves a bit more scrutiny here. We know women taught young children the basics of reading and writing; we know that they taught their daughters domestic skills and much of what else they learned, aside from those tasks left to the governess who specialized in music or art. What is perhaps less obvious is the extended role women played in the education of their sons. Mothers were the first to introduce sons (as well as daughters) to the rudiments of the classical languages. Latin and sometimes Greek were first transmitted from parents, through mother more often than father, John Stuart Mill's experience notwithstanding. The work of teaching in the home went beyond a woman's own offspring; some gentlewomen took on part of the education of their servants. Mrs. Tait had, as the wife of Rugby School's headmaster, a large household with many servants. She trained them in domestic work, and she also prepared the younger servants for their confirmation. She seems to have given the housemaids some general education as well.[26]

Victorian Sunday schools, a second major sphere of women's educational work, were more than a setting for the telling of Bible stories to little children: they offered working-class children four to six hours of education that included "reading, writing, religion, and occasionally other subjects." Thomas Laqueur tells us that working-class children were instructed "largely by teachers of their own class." Marion Johnson, historian of Derbyshire education, agrees that teachers of the poor in the Sunday schools came from the "lower orders." But he also found evidence of the "influence of the clergy and their families" in the evolution of Derbyshire education in the nineteenth century. He credits the educational progress achieved in Edensor up to 1841 to "the pains and skill of the wife of the clergyman." In the town of Buxton, progress was the result of "the talent and energy of the clergyman's lady."[27] Johnson makes nothing of these clues about women's work, but the experience of the Paget women and their circle suggests that women made a major educational contribution through their work in Sunday school teaching.

Nearly all the women of our study taught in the Sunday schools of nineteenth-century London and the countryside. For many years H. C. G. Moule's mother "superintended the Girls' Sunday School" in Durham and worked with her husband's pupils as well. Lydia North and her sisters regularly supplemented their weekday visiting in the 1830s with Sunday school teaching in their London parish. This teaching could occasionally be a family affair, with females and males alike taking part. Lydia recruited her fiancé James Paget to work in her parish Sunday school. Even in the worst of the winter Lydia "braved the weather" to get to the Sunday school. A female friend of Mary Baird's founded a Sunday school, and Mary began teaching a "regular class" there when she was seventeen. "I taught for nine years, and regularly, too, in spite of other distractions." It was hard work, for teachers had to appear at 9:45 a.m. for Sunday school; the church service followed. They returned for teaching at 2:30 in the afternoon and the Children's Service came after that.[28]

While some women did their teaching on Sundays, others carried out analogous work during the week. Catharine Spooner began her charity teaching work as a young single woman in the village of Elmdon in the 1830s. Teaching became part of her "daily routine," and she continued teaching when she moved to Rugby as a young bride in the 1840s. Her husband recalled that "she established a little school of girls," and for the six years that they lived in Rugby, "it was her pleasure to teach" there "almost every day." It is a remarkable record of work. Ann Twining lived a busy life in Bitteswell, Luttersworth, in the 1840s. Her time was taken up with walks and gardening and also with the "*day school* established by Miss P[onells, her niece] . . . which we attend pretty constantly." Lydia Paget's daughter, like her mother before her, taught the poor in London. In the 1870s, under the auspices of her parish church (St. James's, Piccadilly), Catharine became a volunteer teacher at the Burlington School, a charity school for girls. It was work she particularly enjoyed. The official records of the school indicate that the charity pupils learned needlework and apparently little else, presumably to prepare them for work as servants or needlewomen. In fact, Catharine taught these girls basic academic subjects, much as they might have found in the schools attended by their social betters. She taught geography and arithmetic as well as religion.[29]

Even in the foreign mission setting, teaching was a specifically (although not exclusively) female role. Harriette McDougall, the clergyman-missionary's wife, confessed that she disliked teaching, but even her dislike reflects her sense that teaching was a role she was expected to fulfill. Despite her aversion to it, she took on the responsibility of teaching women and children in Borneo. With the help of other missionary women, Mrs. McDougall played a leading part in establishing a school for children, and she helped to introduce adult education there as well.[30]

The work of teaching went beyond the home, beyond the Sunday school, even beyond tidy little classrooms with well-behaved (if ill-dressed and poor)

little girls specially selected for charity schools. Victorian gentlewomen went
into the poor districts to bring education to young people and adults on their
own ground. Even very young, unmarried women served as charity teachers
and thus came into contact with the problems slum life presented.

As a young woman of eighteen, Henrietta Rowland began working with
Octavia Hill in Marylebone. Rowland took charge of children aged thirteen
to fifteen and taught these youngsters three evenings a week. At the girls'
night school she found filth and lice and labeled the students her "dear dirty
girls." The problems of teaching the poor often included the struggle for discipline in the school, church hall, or settlement house. Henrietta Rowland's
adolescent female charges used foul language and engaged in the physical
abuse of their peers. Incidents of arson and violence were also common in
the night school. "The people were very rough, and many fights and quarrels
took place," she recalled, and she sometimes had to act "as umpire." But
this committed worker was fond of her students; she found "their hearts . . .
good, full of tenderness."[31] As with visiting, teaching brought women face
to face with desperate poverty and its consequences, with the humanity and
neediness of the poor.

Teaching the poor was not a sex-segregated job, with men teaching boys,
women teaching girls. Few laymen, aside from the socially committed Oxford and Cambridge men of the late Victorian period, had the time or the
inclination to give their services to the task. The vast majority of charity
teachers were women, and they found themselves teaching classes of boys
as well as classes of girls. A family friend remembers the Pitt-Rivers women
"working night after night in teaching big rustic boys." The boys were, of
course, as unruly as the girls. A volunteer teacher and colleague of Henrietta
Barnett's, Mrs. Nassau Senior, was confronted with a crowd of shouting, fist-
throwing, fighting boys; she broke up the melee by singing a hymn at the
top of her voice.[32]

The women of this study also taught adults. Predictably, they taught poor
women, and the curriculum was as diverse as these women's needs. Frances
Henslow Hooker was a tutor in the adult literacy classes for young women
in Hitcham starting in 1849. These classes continued for at least a decade.
From mid-century on, Anglican women were holding meetings in their parishes to educate poor mothers in how to care for their children, how to plan
healthful meals, how to cook, and, of course, how to bring up a Christian
family. Often, but not always, it was the clergyman's wife who saw the educational needs of poor women and took action to meet those needs. A Mrs.
Bayley was credited with founding the first of what became known as "Mothers' Meetings," held "among the pigsties and brickfields in the Kensington
Potteries in the year 1853." Mary Heywood Sumner, wife of a cleric in the

Winchester diocese, was, at age forty-nine, looking for some useful work of her own to do. She began having meetings in the rectory to help mothers do their domestic duties more effectively. These classes went on for nine years.[33]

Classes for mothers went beyond purely parental issues to take up other family matters: "public morals or family ethics" and home life, and particularly the matter of "how to deal with drunken husbands." Some mothers' groups had a "newspaper class," where poor women learned about current events. Religious and theological subjects were always part of the informal curriculum of mothers' education. Clergymen sometimes addressed the women on religious subjects, but often the lady-organizers carried the responsibility for theological teaching as well. Henrietta Rowland Barnett worked with the St. Jude's Mothers' Meeting, which was established early in the 1870s. There, women heard lectures on child care and the problems of adolescence and how mothers could deal with them. Elma Katie Hoare Paget, whose husband was suffragan bishop of Stepney before the First World War, also had first-hand experience teaching London's poor.[34]

Poor men as well as poor women were students in classes taught by gentlewomen. Mary Church worked alongside her husband, R. W. Church, the rector of Whatley in the 1850s, in the night school he organized for the winter. There "the men and elder lads of the place" were gathered "for instruction on two or three evenings a week," and presumably both wife and husband taught them. Taking their cue from her classes for mothers, the men in Mary Sumner's parish began calling for meetings for fathers as well. Mrs. Sumner agreed to teach them, and some thirty to forty men came on Sunday evenings for Bible study and also for the discussion of paternal responsibilities in child-rearing. Mrs. Sumner also discussed marital relations in her meetings, encouraging the men to treat their wives with affection: with gifts and love and courtesy. Mary Eleanor Benson taught girls at Lambeth and had "a class of country boys and men at Addington."[35] Gentlewomen were teaching their adult charity pupils history and geography as well as basic literacy, public affairs as well as household management, theology as well as cookery and diet.

Mothers' Meetings spread. To share what they had learned about organizing classes for the poor, many of the lady-teachers published pamphlets, articles, and books based on their experiences. Elma Katie Hoare Paget edited three collections of articles of advice, sermons, and guidelines, addressed to women who were organizing the work of teaching mothers in their parish or neighborhood. One of the more prolific authors of this sort of material was Jane M. King, who published five books about Mothers' Meetings between 1898 and 1916. Two of them, *A Happy Mothers' Meeting* and *A Letter for You,* were sufficiently popular to warrant new editions in 1912. The needs of the growing Mothers' Union provoked Mary Sumner to write books and pamphlets to disseminate help to union workers. Her titles include four books as well as pamphlets on *Home Life* (1895), *To Mothers of the Higher Classes* (1888), and *Nursery Training* (1892).[36]

As women's involvement in religious teaching became more widespread (or perhaps only more visible), the clergy offered ways to improve the quality of their theological teaching. In 1905 the archbishop of Canterbury established a program of instruction to lead to a License in Theology for Women. The program involved a course of study and a test that would assess their systematic study of theology, their proficiency in New Testament Greek at university honors level, and their teaching. In 1906 the first five women received the archbishop's Diploma in Theology, certifying their academic knowledge, and six months later their teaching skills were certified by the archbishop's License and Authority to teach sacred Theology.[37]

Victorian lady-teachers went far beyond the ABCs (or even the alpha-beta-gamma) of their own children's education. They stepped out of the private sphere of the nursery and schoolroom into the public light of the church hall, the settlement house, and whatever other classrooms contained boys and girls and men and women who needed or wanted instruction. Their work fell somewhere between the working class's own self-help initiatives and proprietary educational ventures on the one hand, and the growth of state-funded, paid professional teaching on the other hand. At this stage there is no way to measure the magnitude of their service. But gentlewomen's contribution to mass education must certainly be taken into account in our assessments of the supply and demand of Victorian popular education.[38] Pauper education was an important theme of social theory, Anglican missionary activity at home, and Victorian social policy. In the East End of London and the slums of industrial towns, the fruits of philosophical discourse on the subject of poverty were the settlement houses staffed by Oxford undergraduates eager to serve the nation, to serve the poor, and to serve their God. Side by side with them were Victorian ladies of all ages.

Charity was one of the given features of gentlewomen's lives. Like it or not, committed or not, ready or not, charity was part of their duty in society. The poor may not always have welcomed their attentions. But if class enmity was exacerbated by ladies' philanthropy, it was not because these women could be fairly accused of meddlesome trifling in the lives of the poor. Resentment and class hostility came, more tragically, because wanting to do good is no guarantee that one does good—nor do one's motives always matter to the recipients of one's dutiful but unwelcome actions. Gentlewomen wanted to help, to be useful. They may not always have accomplished that goal, but they surely did more than treat the poor as exotica to enliven a boring afternoon. And some, at least, of the poor welcomed their help. In this way these leisured ladies contributed their labor to the general good.

THE UNUSUAL CAREERS OF A FEW

Some women in the Pagets' circle went beyond charity visiting, rescue work, and teaching to take up less typical vocations and avocations. These women demonstrate that it was possible to take an independent and self-defined path to useful and satisfactory lives without breaking away from their social circle or the norms of gentlewomen's lives. These women are important because their achievements place women like Harriet Martineau, Florence Nightingale, and George Eliot in a new context—a *tradition* of achieving women.

From at least the eighteenth century, English women were interested in natural history. Women were involved in the Botanical Society of London from its founding in 1836, their membership in the society ranging from 6 to 10 percent in the years before 1900. Such involvement constitutes a mark of women's sustained interest in this science.[39] In some cases science was a sideline in a woman's life rather than a central feature of her activities. Such was the case with Mary Kingsley, whose primary interests were in ethnography and exploration but who provided Sir Joseph and Lady Hooker at Kew with botanical samples "quite new to us." Marianne North's primary interest in plants was artistic, but her botanical knowledge was extensive. She brought unusual samples back from her travels for A. R. Wallace and her friends the Allmans, among others. Mary Kingsley's circle included other women naturalists, in particular a Mrs. Duggans and Miss Emily Maud Bowdler-Sharpe, daughter of ornithologist Richard Bowdler-Sharpe. Mary Kingsley employed Miss Bowdler-Sharpe to mount insects she had collected.[40]

Eleanor Ormerod chose a subject of study entirely suitable to the daughter of a Gloucestershire landed gentleman—the study of insects. She had learned how to use a microscope at home while in her early twenties, in the process of helping her brother William, a young medical man, to prepare botanical specimens. She began studying insects casually in 1852, with the observation of an unusual locust. Her father sent the insect to Professor C. G. B. Daubeny at Oxford, who verified the rarity of its appearance as far west as the Ormerod estate. With newly kindled interest, she bought her first book on entomology and began by studying the book and dissecting beetles. She extended her reading and observation of insects, enlisting agricultural laborers on her father's farm to gather specimens for her.[41]

Ormerod linked herself to the larger world of natural history by volunteering her services for a Royal Horticultural Society exhibition in 1869. Increasingly her interests centered on applied entomology, specifically the role of insects in agriculture. Ormerod continued her studies independently in Gloucestershire until 1873, when her father died and left her with independent means. She and her sister Georgiana moved to Isleworth—close to London and to the intellectual stimulation and encouragement provided by naturalist Sir Joseph and Lady Hooker at Kew Gardens. In 1884 her brother Arthur died; he left his brothers £300 each, and he made his sisters his residuary legatees. Eleanor was gratified by the legacy for it allowed her greater freedom than she had known before, and she no longer needed "such very strict economy as I have had to exercise to carry out my work."[42] From Isleworth and later St. Alban's, Eleanor Ormerod carried on her career in entomology.

Ormerod used all the resources within her reach. She had social rank, she had funds, she had a name, "good address," and the connections that went with it—access, in short, to the best help in the kingdom. Her relations with Professor J. O. Westwood of Oxford University may have begun because Westwood knew her family, but they continued because he recognized her abilities and knowledge. He encouraged her in her interests and supported her studies and activities in the pursuit of expertise in the area of agricultural entomology.[43]

After gathering information on the helpful and harmful insects of the British Isles, Ormerod prepared a pamphlet presenting her findings, and she asked two scientific friends, Messrs. Preston and Fitch, to lend their names as "referees" for her first report, which was published in 1877. She did this, she said, because her name was unknown. The result of her careful research and her publication strategy was a report that was widely read and respected. After 1877 Ormerod published subsequent reports under her name alone. In all, she published twenty-four volumes of her *Annual Reports on Injurious Insects* between 1877 and 1900. She paid for the cost of publishing the reports and mailed them initially to those she thought might be interested. Thereafter they went to those who requested a copy. Her mailing list was international, including readers in North America, Europe, and Africa. In addition to her annual reports, Ormerod produced three substantial books on applied entomology. Her *Textbook of Agricultural Entomology* first appeared in 1881, with a second edition in 1890; it remained in print until at least 1904.[44]

These studies and their distribution in Britain and abroad resulted in

Ormerod's growing reputation in agricultural matters and an increasing demand for consultations. Individual gardeners, florists, and farmers wrote to her for help. She judged that her correspondence amounted to some 1,500 letters a year. Managers of large estates also called on her for aid—the duke of Bedford's staff being the most notable example. Organizations and societies also sought her advice. She was consulting entomologist to the Royal Agricultural Society from 1882 on and examiner in agricultural entomology at Edinburgh University from 1896. She served on advisory committees for local authorities in connection with their museums, and she gave expert evidence in lawsuits involving insect damage. When Ormerod was invited to serve on a committee of the Council of Education, she claimed that "It made me so anxious to think of sitting with such scientific *men* that I wrote . . . asking them to excuse me." She was finally persuaded to serve, and she found her fears abating: "The work is," she admitted, "in my own special line." Indeed, her reticence may have been a bit feigned. When appointed honorary consulting entomologist to the Royal Agricultural Society (honorary because she refused a salary), she arranged to have a paid deputy who went to some of the agricultural sites and reported back to her. And she enjoyed it all: "I like the work very much," she confided to her brother; she was glad to have "a definite authorized appointment and it has met with very strong approval from the agricultural press." She cared little for money, but she wanted work and she wanted recognition from her peers.[45]

Publication and consulting work naturally led to lecturing. She gave courses in agricultural entomology at the Royal Agricultural College, Cirencester, at the Institute of Agriculture, South Kensington, and at the Farmer's Club, all in the 1880s. The lecturing carried a fee—not always, a colleague thought, as large as she deserved.[46] No questions, it should be noted, were ever raised about the propriety of her speaking in public or of the fact that she was addressing men.

With her public connections and her growing fame, Eleanor Ormerod had the opportunity to be a mentor herself, and she exercised patronage in behalf of men. When the death of her friend and mentor J. O. Westwood left the Hope Professorship of Zoology vacant, Ormerod worked hard for the election of an American entomologist and colleague of hers, the distinguished Professor Charles Valentine Riley (1843–95). She was unsuccessful. Her efforts were more successful outside Oxbridge, in placing entomologists in posts in Kenya, in Edinburgh, and elsewhere. Another recipient of her favor was naturalist Robert Wallace (1853–1939) of Edinburgh. They consulted together from early on in his career, she gave him professional help, and he later served as her literary executor and the editor of her *Life and Letters*. While Wallace was still at Edinburgh, Ormerod introduced him to the Oxford academic establishment. Ormerod also tried to use her influence and wealth to advance the status of economic entomology, first (unsuccessfully) in Oxford and then (with effect) in Edinburgh. The crowning recognition of Ormerod's life came when she was awarded the honorary degree of LL. D. from the University of Edinburgh in 1900.[47]

Ormerod had a full-fledged career as an agricultural entomologist. Like gentleman-naturalists before her, she did not follow her career to earn a living; indeed, her work cost her more than she ever earned from it. Her inherited means gave her the liberty to attempt to establish herself in the science that interested her, but the work she did stood on its own merits. In the end she found, in entomology, useful work to do. Ormerod's interest in agriculture was not unique among Victorian women. The founding in 1899 of the Women's Agricultural and Horticultural International Union in London suggests the strength of female interest in farming and botany as well as gardening. The founding of Lady Warwick College by gentlewomen after the turn of the century to train women to be farmers offers further evidence of women's interests in agriculture.[48]

In other respects, too, Ormerod was not so very different from many of the women in this study. Prosperity bought many of them the leisure for philanthropy; Ormerod's financial resources brought large projects within reach. Like many of the women here, ties to the establishment gave her access to a network of support from men that would not have been available to women (or men) without "connexion." Ormerod's interest in entomology is also part of the larger picture of women's interest in the sciences.

Although few women distinguished themselves as public figures in the world of science (for reasons that may become clearer in chapter six), many had an introduction to science early in life and then did advanced studies in science on their own. Sir Charles Lyell's secretary, Arabella Burton Buckley, learned about science in her work with him, and she went on to become a science writer herself. We can presume that Rose Paget had, as a physician's daughter, her first introduction to the sciences at home in Cambridge. After studying mathematics and physics on her own, she began working at the Cavendish Laboratory in 1887. She consulted the head of the laboratory, physicist J. J. Thomson, and, at his suggestion, began research on "the stationary vibrations of soap films at audible frequencies." In all she worked at the Cavendish Laboratory for three years. She ended her research when she married and turned her attention to her family, professional, and social life in Cambridge academic circles. Rose Paget was one of fifteen women (6.3 percent) whom the Cavendish claims in its list of 240 scientific workers between 1871 and 1910. Eleanor Balfour Sidgwick was another of the physics researchers at the Cavendish in the 1880s. She collaborated with Lord Rayleigh on research on electrical measurement and other subjects, and they published their results in the *Philosophical Transactions*.[49]

At the same time that Rose Paget and Eleanor Sidgwick were studying physics in Cambridge, many other women were also studying science. From the 1880s on, women undergraduates at Cambridge participated in increasing numbers in the Natural Sciences Tripos. They were also reading mathematics in these years. Historians McLeod and Moseley have suggested that with scientific education "women could 'ornament' scientific gatherings." More likely, women attached themselves to the Botanical Society of London in the 1830s or the Cavendish Laboratory in the 1880s because of their serious interest in science.[50] These women's scientific studies were not a new phenomenon but an extension of what women had been doing throughout the century.

In addition to being the story of a scientist, Eleanor Ormerod's scientific consulting career is also the story of a manager. The administration of what became an agricultural information service was a major feature of Eleanor Ormerod's work. Catharine Tait displayed similar skills. After the cholera epidemic of 1866 she took the responsibility for making some provision for girls orphaned by the disease. She had plenty of space on the grounds of Fulham Palace, and, with her own money, she built an orphanage there. Later she persuaded her husband to buy land at Broadstairs, in the Isle of Wight, where she planned to build a larger home, one that housed eighty to one hundred girls together with a staff. The new project involved fundraising, the planning and construction of the building, the establishment of the home's management and clerical assistance, and finally the provision of medical care and education for the orphaned girls. To bring the children into closer association with interested adults, Catharine Tait organized a plan of "Children's Associates"—a one-to-one pairing of a child and a donor who supported her in the orphanage and served as "a friend and adviser" in after life.[51] Mrs. Tait's organizational abilities earned her nothing except praise for her concern for the needy and suffering.

Mary Sumner exercised similar administrative skills, far from science, in the world of women's work in the Church of England. She had been teaching mothers in her own parish, and others had adopted her methods in other towns. At a church congress in 1885 Mrs. Sumner and an "old friend," Ernest Wilberforce, now the bishop of Newcastle, launched a "Mothers' Union" whose goal was "rais[ing] the national character" by raising the "moral and religious tone in . . . family life." Mrs. Sumner presented a plan for the Mother's Union to E. H. Browne, bishop of Winchester, and she traveled around the diocese with her husband, by now archdeacon of Winchester, working for the union. It became a national organization, and by 1895 the Mothers' Union had a branch in nearly every diocese, 13,000 subscribers to its organ, the *Mothers' Union Journal*, 70,000 members, and an increasingly complex administrative structure. Mary Sumner retired from her work with the Mothers' Union in 1914. The union's official history says Sumner considered the growth of the Mothers' Union "a widening of her family circle."[52] This drape of domesticity should not hide from us the remarkable administrative and organizational skills that went into the creation and establishment of what became an international organization.

As the wife of the bishop of Winchester, later the archbishop of Canterbury, Edith Davidson had many opportunities to see issues of charity in national and structural terms, and she used her position to create and sustain organizations for Christian work among the poor. In 1908 she proposed the organization of a group (eventually called the Central Council of Women's Church Work) which brought together representatives of all the dioceses of the Church of England to discuss women's contributions to Anglican social and religious projects. She was also instrumental in the creation of the Church of England's board to advise "rescue and prevention workers," afterward called the Church of England Advisory Board for Moral Welfare. Harriot Moule, Elma Paget, and others engaged in similar organizational and administrative work at the diocesan level. Others carried on the work of organizing charity without any institutional base: after the turn of the century Eleanor Burd Paget's daughter established St. Francis House in Notting Hill, a club for "working girls and boys." Eleanor left a bequest of £1,000 to help maintain the venture.[53]

Like natural history, art was frequently a component of the education of upper-middle-class girls and women, and it is not surprising, given the quality of that education, that some should have made unusual careers in the world of art. Marianne North combined the interests of the naturalist with those of the artist. North had traveled extensively with her father during his lifetime, and, after his death, she determined "to devote myself to painting from nature, and try to learn from the lovely world . . . how to make that work henceforth the master of my life." She had no idea of making money from her art; rather, she looked to her work as an organizing principle of her life. She worked under the beneficent influence of Sir Joseph and Lady Hooker at Kew and used her artistic skills to record the beauty of exotic flowers and plants. She traveled all over the world—Egypt, Syria, Australia, New Zealand, the Caribbean, and North and South America—painting the flora of foreign environments. In all she completed over eight hundred paintings of "no less than 727 genera" and almost one thousand species. Late in life she decided to give her paintings to Kew Gardens. She provided a building to house the collection, later named the North Gallery in her honor.[54]

The Ormerod story has another facet, one that pertains to Eleanor's sister Georgiana. In the way that some Victorian women helped brothers or fathers, Georgiana was a helpmeet in Eleanor's entomological enterprise. With a good art education behind her, Georgiana contributed to her sister's work by preparing the visual aids for her sister's museum exhibits. Occasionally scientists outside her family had the benefit of Georgiana Ormerod's artistic skill. When Sir Joseph Hooker needed "some drawings for the *Botanical Magazine* . . . she offered her services and drew three or four very beautifully." Eleanor acknowledged that "she helped me enormously in very many ways (by pencil & paintbrush, and the correctness of her eye)." Others of her illustrations found their way into Edinburgh University's entomological collections in the Museum of Science and Art, where they were used for the teaching of entomology.[55]

Elise Paget's story is also a modest version of a life in art. The level of her productivity was lower than that of North or Ormerod, but her life was given over to her painting. She studied in London and Paris art galleries, and she exhibited at the Royal Academy, the Society of Water Colour Artists, and perhaps elsewhere. In addition, she published at least one article on art history. Elise's artistic work ordered her life and perhaps her identity. One Miss Henslow (her given name now lost) had a similarly quiet life path. She had artistic training from teachers now unknown, and she spent much of her life providing advice about signs and illustrations for a local museum and preparing botanical illustrations for the published work of a brother. We know almost as little about Miss Henslow as we do of the sculptor "Miss S. Durant," whose "marble profile in high relief" of George Grote was displayed at University College, London, after his death.[56]

Illustration offered an opportunity in art that many Victorian women took up. Lillian Chitty, one of Mary Hort Chitty's daughters, served as an illustrator for some of the novels of the pseudonymous "Ismay Thorn" (in life Caroline Pollock), who published thirty novels between 1878 and 1903. Pollock's other illustrator was Clara Creed, who worked under the pseudonym "T. Pym." Miss Mary Edith Durham (1863–1944) illustrated Hans Gadow's scientific work on amphibia and reptiles. The daughter of a surgeon, she trained at the Royal Academy of Arts, and she exhibited there and at other major galleries. She prepared illustrations for the reptile volumes of the Cambridge Natural History. She went on from illustration to writing, and published eight books on the Balkans. Given the relative anonymity of illustrators' work in much Victorian publication, it would not be surprising if these women's work represents a mere fraction of that of a host of women artists and illustrators whose work and lives will never be known.[57] The women of the Paget circle epitomize the possibility of artistic activities and sometimes careers among gentlewomen, not as a bohemian alternative to respectability, nor out of the need to earn a living, but as an integral part of upper-middle-class life.

Sarah Angelina (Angie) Acland's career had something of both art and science in it. Angie had, as the daughter of an Oxford professor, associations with distinguished professional men and landed gentry, in the midst of a society where both learning and leisured dabbling were possible. She did not marry, and, given her family's wealth, she had no need to earn a living. Although serving as hostess for her widowed father, she did not neglect her own interests: she was a talented painter and exhibited her work at the Royal Academy and the Society of Water Colour Artists. She found greater interest in the relatively new art and technology of photography. Angie worked at photography for many years. She did portraits of her fathers' friends and associates, some of the more famous men of the late Victorian period. Her work was well regarded and some of her photographs were displayed in the Bodleian Museum after the First World War. Her photographic work included experiments in color photography as well.[58]

More remarkable, and less traceable, was her work with photographic technology. Like other Victorian women who worked in science, Angie came from a medical family, where chemistry would not have been alien, and neither chemistry nor photographic technology intimidated her. The Times reported at the time of her death that Angie Acland had worked with E. Sanger-Shepherd (probably in the period between 1890 and 1910) to develop new chemical processes in color photography "that now bear his name." The process for making color transparencies involved "printing on to celluloid coated with bichromated gelatine containing a little silver bromide." The Times report of her role leads to the speculation that Sanger-Shepherd took credit for an invention in photographic chemistry that Angie Acland ought to have shared. Acland put some of her research on photography into print in her book, The Spectrum Plate—Theory; Practice; Result, which appeared in 1900.[59]

As a member of the Oxford Camera Club, Acland gave a lecture there in 1899. G. W. Norton, the honorary secretary of the club, told her afterward that "it was the most valuable contribution we have ever had from our members." Angie Acland's male and female friends alike commended her for her "wonderful lecture," "perfect in both matter and manner." Acland was elected a fellow of the Royal Photographic Society in 1893 and presented papers at the society which were later published in the British Journal of

Photography. Her friend Margaret Stokes, an archeologist, author, and lecturer, congratulated Acland on her public speaking and spoke of "lecture work" as "one of the highest of all enjoyments." Mary Maud Paget's musical interests brought her into a similar situation. When Cecilia Stainer heard of Paget's scholarly work in music history, she invited her to join the Musical Association and "read us a paper sometimes."[60]

Scientific research, the application of organizational and administrative skills, lifetime artistic productivity, lecturing to communicate knowledge—these were indeed unusual careers. But they were not unique. Rather, they were the extension of pursuits in which Victorian gentlewomen commonly engaged. Whether single or married, these women had the education and the direction to find ways of expressing their talents, commitments, and desire to do meaningful and enjoyable work. And I suspect that the Ormerods and Aclands were only a sampling of the women at work in unusual spheres.

WOMEN WRITING

Writing was not the exclusive province of men, or, among women, the George Eliots and Harriet Martineaus of the age. Writing was also not the province solely of desperate women, writing penny-novels to make a living or support a needy family. Philanthropic women, women teachers, and women doing unusual things—all communicated about their work in published form. They wrote about charity, social questions, and teaching, about insects and art and photography.

The writing discussed so far was practical, task-oriented writing linked to women's active lives. Some of the women wrote outside of this work-related framework. Poetry and fiction represent only one small segment of the writing these women did. At least half of the women studied here published in some form or other. Here we will discuss women's literary activities not integrally related to the other sorts of work they did. Their writings are not easily categorized, for they published on a wide variety of subjects and in various forms.

Elise Paget's article on "Old Crome" was only one of many examples of what Victorian ladies published in the area of the arts. In Great Yarmouth Betsey's neighbor Mary Palgrave Turner participated in the composition and publication of a volume entitled *One Hundred Etchings,* which appeared in 1825. Mary Anne Turner's book on embroidery partook of both the artistic and the domestic. First published in 1877, it went into its fourth printing by the end of that year.[61] Musical subjects also occupied the artistically-oriented daughters of the Victorian urban gentry. Mary Maud Paget, Lydia and James's spinster daughter, took a great interest in music, and in the

1890s she published a series of articles in *Temple Bar* on musicians—Henry Purcell, Henry Lawes, John Bull, and John Arne.[62] Other London women wrote about music, too. Cecilia Stainer's father was the organist at St. Paul's Cathedral. She pursued music in her own research and published *A Dictionary of Violin Makers* in 1896, this in addition to her contributions to *Grove's Dictionary of Music and Musicians*.[63] Stainer was one of the 8 percent or more of contributors to the *Dictionary* who were women.[64]

Creative writing also came from the pens of these productive women. Some produced fiction solely for the entertainment of their readers. Others were self-consciously using the novel as an instrument of social commentary: as one woman novelist put it, "[My] first two [novels], and the most important, were 'Anne Sherwood,' on the governess question . . . and 'The Dean' on parties in the Church." The literary career of Oxford-based Felicia Mary Skene had several faces, but her most visible and arguably most important work was the book, *Hidden Depths*, which she published pseudonymously in 1866 and reprinted in 1886 under her own name. A combination of fiction and social commentary, it drew on her own observations of prison life and prisoners. *The Times* described it as her "most powerful" work.[65]

Marriage seems to have been no hindrance to authorship. Charles Kingsley's daughter, Mary St. Leger Kingsley, married the Reverend William Harrison, rector of Clovelly, in 1876. Under the pseudonym "Lucas Malet," Mary Harrison published nine novels between 1882 and 1914, five of these appearing in more than one edition. During the same time she carried out the normal duties of a parson's wife. Her second novel, *Colonel Enderby's Wife*, was particularly successful and, critics judged, showed her "real originality of mind and intellectual honesty." She was a controversial writer, often taking up "themes and situations which seemed to many critics . . . daring and unpleasant." Mrs. Harrison used the pseudonym not, as one might expect, out of "feminine reticence" and the desire for anonymity but "because she did not want to profit by the literary fame of her own family." Late in the century she began to publish in her own name, and five works of fiction appeared under the name of Mary Harrison. In all she published eighteen novels and two books of stories by the time of her death in 1931. Some since have considered this a "limited output," and they have blamed poor health for the absence of a longer list of titles. Another married writer, Mary Charlotte Mair Senior (Mrs. C. T. Simpson), published two three-volume novels, *Winnie's History* in 1877 and *Geraldine and Her Suitors* in 1881, as well as twelve other books of various sorts.[66]

Between 1880 and 1903 Edith Caroline Pollock, the barrister's daughter who published under the pseudonym "Ismay Thorn," produced thirty books for young people. Mainly fiction, most of them were 100 to 150 pages long.

Some of these appeared in more than one edition. Other writers of fiction in this circle of women included Angie Acland's sister-in-law, Emily Acland, who published two novels, *Love in a Life* in 1893 and *The Lost Key: An International Episode* in 1901. The Moberly women were also productive authors. Anne Elizabeth Moberly (1846–1937) published three works, including one novel. Her cousin Lucy Gertrude Moberly, without the duties of Oxford college administration to burden her, was able to write and publish a total of fifty-seven novels.[67]

The women of this group published poetry only very rarely. Harriet Grote included hers in her *Collected Papers in Prose and Verse, 1842–62*. In Cambridge, the teen-aged Rose Paget tried her hand at poetry. When her brother Edmund looked over her poems, he encouraged her to seek a publisher. In at least one instance she seems to have done so, for a poem entitled "Aber Waterfall" appeared in *Temple Bar* in 1880; its style and its Welsh setting are congruent with Rose's authorship.[68]

While clergymen were busy writing sermons, preaching, and administering the religious life of the parish and diocese, their wives, sisters, daughters, and friends were also busy writing about the Christian life. The expansion of women's publication in religious subjects after 1850 reflects the growth of the publishing industry generally, as well as the revival of religion in Victorian life. Some women's writing, related to their religious work, has been treated above. Other women also wrote about religion, devotional life, and theology. Victorian religion was transcendent as well as practical.

Gentlewomen wrote devotional literature for children, books and booklets designed as first religious readings for boys and girls from infancy to adolescence. Mrs. J. S. Henslow published *A Practical Application of the Five Books of Moses, Adapted to Young Persons* in 1848. Eleanor Acland's mother, Mrs. Cropper, published *A Help to Children's Prayer*, and Elma Paget wrote a child's biography of Bishop Patteson (1907). In a widely published family, Connie Lubbock Buxton was at home with the mechanisms of publication; the large and important publishing house Macmillan's published her children's book, *Side Lights upon Bible History*, in 1892. Mary Elizabeth Sumner published only one book for children, *Walter and His Nurse* (1906), among her many works. Although she had been writing for many years, Mary Hort Chitty only began publishing religious tracts for children after the First World War. *Baby's Own Book: First Words about Jesus* was the first of five that she published.[69]

Home life and its religious dimensions are perhaps the most common topics of women's books and pamphlets. The books of Jane King, Elma Paget, and Mary Sumner in connection with mothers' organizations have already been mentioned. Mary Hort Chitty published on family life, too: her work on the *Ethics of Home Life,* published in 1896, was followed by another guide to parents published after the war. Like clergymen and their sermons, women who were involved in mothers' organizations frequently published the talks and lectures they delivered at meetings. Emily Acland's pamphlet *Marriage as the Foundation of the Home* (1902) had such origins. A second publication, *Plain Words to Mothers: Outline Addresses for Speakers* (1913), was clearly meant as a handbook and help to others planning talks for women's gatherings. Louise Creighton's pamphlets and books have a similar flavor: she produced short works of inspiration and advice on family life, including a book of addresses to girls (1904) and another of talks to mothers (1908).[70]

Some women addressed themselves to the more ecclesiastical and theological side of religion. In the 1830s one of the Turner daughters, Harriet Turner Gunn, published *Conversations on Church Polity* (1833); she identified herself simply as "A Lady." Late in the century Elma Paget, the wife of a bishop and herself an active worker in the church, also addressed issues of church life. In particular there were her pamphlet *In Praise of Virginity,* in which she advocated holy orders for single women as an avenue to God's service, and an essay on medical missions. Like other women writers, Felicia Mary Skene published religious biography and devotional literature. Perhaps the most purely philosophical work was Margaret Benson's book, *The Venture of Rational Faith,* which appeared in 1908.[71]

From the theoretical and philosophical side of religion it was only one step to the policy-oriented questions of social life. For much of the century prisons, workhouses, poverty, and sickness drew the attention of gentlewomen, as they did the minds and pens of male social surveyors, great and small. Julia Busk Byrne published much on social questions, in particular *Undercurrents Overlooked* (1860), a two-volume study of workhouse abuse. She took up an implicitly comparative approach in her examination of Belgian treatment of the insane in *Gheel, the City of the Simple* (1869); in *Beggynhof, or City of the Siege* (1869), she discussed French treatment of the unmarried. In the months before her death, Margaret Benson's sister Mary Eleanor (Nellie) Benson wrote a book about the poor, part memoir, part social survey, but she decided against publishing it for fear of offending her subjects. Later her parents had it privately printed, and the book, *Streets and Lanes of the City,* was circulated among the Bensons' family friends and acquaintances. Nellie wrote the book, her mother told Gladstone, "from a heart which though so young was filled to overflowing with the profoundest pity & love for Christ's poor."[72]

Travel writings (and all the variants thereon), history, and folklore were popular forms of women's (as well as men's) self-expression and authorship.

Julia Byrne's social studies tapped readers' interests in the foreign. Her other writings include *A Glance behind the Grilles of the Religious Houses in France* (1857) and *Flemish Interiors* (1856), and these also drew on foreign settings. In all Julia Byrne published thirteen books between 1855 and 1892, as well as six articles in *Fraser's* and *Macmillan's Magazine*. Harriet Turner Gunn published her *Letters Written during a Four-Days Tour in Holland in the Summer of 1834* in 1834. Mary Baird Smith's mother, in all her European junketing, found time to write and publish a *Guide to the Tyrol,* primarily a botanical handbook, which her husband illustrated.[73] The busy Mrs. Sumner, involved in the organization of the Mothers' Union and in writing for mothers, also produced a travel book, entitled simply *Our Holiday*. Published in 1881, it came out in a second edition in 1882. Catharine Paget published articles on travel in *Macmillan's Magazine* in the 1870s, signing them simply "C.P." Harriette McDougall kept private accounts of her experiences of missionary travel to Borneo, which she later published. The first book, drawn from her letters to her son in England, was *Letters from Sarawak Addressed to a Child*. Published in 1854, the book sold "many thousands of copies." When it went out of print, Mrs. McDougall revised the work, to include the last twenty years of her life in Borneo, and published the new version as *Sketches of Our Life in Sarawak* in 1882.[74]

Historical writing seems to have run in families. Harriet Grote encouraged her husband's history-writing and produced some of her own. She focused primarily on biography, including a study of the philosophical radicals and a life of Ary Scheffer, as well as a study of the hamlet of East Burnham, her former home, published under her initials, "H.G." Louise Creighton, wife of historian and cleric Mandell Creighton, put her own pen to work at history. Her first historical book, the *Life of Edward the Black Prince,* appeared in 1876 (the same year in which her husband's first historical work appeared). She published fifteen other works of history and biography, among them an early work in women's history entitled *Some Famous Women,* which appeared in 1909, the same year that her *Life of Walter Raleigh* came out. She published a *Social History of England* in 1887. The book she called *A First History of England,* nearly four hundred pages long, appeared in four editions between 1881 and 1912. Louise Creighton carried on this extensive historical scholarship while bringing up seven children and carrying out her duties as a busy cleric's wife. Alice Stopford Green had no children to take her away from her writing, but her husband J. R. Green, also a historian, was often ailing and in need of her help. He died in 1878. In the last three decades of the nineteenth century, she published fourteen books and pamphlets, primarily historical. At the invitation of John Morley she wrote a biography of Henry II for his English Statesmen series; it appeared in 1888. She also wrote about Irish political issues, past and present. In addition to her own writings, she produced introductions for a handful of others. In her brief life, Nellie Benson had time to become a historian: she wrote a history of Russia as well as two other works.[75]

Rachel Harriette Busk devoted her literary efforts to folklore, an area of study attracting new interest in the last decades of the nineteenth century. Busk published six volumes of folklore collections between 1871 and 1887. Although she was a clergyman's daughter, Clara Paget cared less about religion than about Welsh antiquities and ancient Britain. She spent many months of the year in north Wales after she and George built a country house there in the early 1870s. During her long stays, and perhaps with the aid of the University Library in Cambridge, she carried out research that led to the private publication of pamphlets on Welsh prehistory, Carnarvonshire forts, and norse mythology.[76]

One of the women of the Paget circle ventured into the realm of modern social issues (as distinct from the traditional Christian approaches to home and family). In her writings on *Health Statistics of Women Students* (c. 1890), *The Human Woman* (1908), *Objections to Woman Suffrage Considered* (n.d.), and her preface to T. W. Berry's *Professions for Girls* (1909), Agnes Geraldine Grove put herself at the forefront of the new directions that some women were taking. Others of her social observations appeared in *The Social Fetich* in 1907 (2d ed. 1909) and *On Fads* in 1910. Margaret Benson's social science was more economic than sociological. She published *Capital, Labour, and Trade, and the Outlook: Plain Papers* in 1891.[77]

Among the women studied here, remarkably few involved themselves in literary criticism. Juliet Creed Pollock was exceptional in that she published many articles on French drama and literature. A friend of Mary Kingsley's, Lucy Toulmin Smith, did research and writing on medieval literature and history. In 1894 she was appointed librarian at Manchester College, Oxford. Connie Lubbock Buxton ventured modestly into print for the first time in 1884 with a letter to the editor of the *Spectator* on Steele and Congreve, and she enjoyed the experience immensely. She asked her father if he had seen the issue where "I had burst out into a letter to the Editor? My initials look most imposing in print," she exulted, "but I cannot get any other human being to take any interest in the cause of my excitement."[78] In an oft-published family a letter to the editor scarcely drew the attention Connie seemed to want. And in a social stratum where women were often publishing, she could not expect one short note to attract much attention.

The multilingual literacy that they acquired in childhood gave women skills that some of them put to use in literary work as translators. Indeed, one would expect to find them publishing translations with some frequency.

The case is difficult to establish because many translations were anonymous. Netty and T. H. Huxley first got acquainted because of their shared interest in German language and literature, and it is very likely that she did translations for him after their marriage. Between 1840 and 1853 Elizabeth Sabine, a friend of Marianne North, published English translations of four German scientific works. In the 1870s Catharine Paget worked with T. H. Huxley on some translations.[79] Frances Henslow Hooker made good use of her "considerable knowledge of botany" as well as her knowledge of French to translate E. LeMaout and J. Ducaisnes's *Traité général de botanique descriptive et analytique* (Paris, 1868); her translation appeared in 1873.[80]

Before Angie Acland got deeply involved in photography, she, together with Mrs. William Barnet and others, translated G. Guerini's *Trenta Novelle* into English and published it in 1874 under the title *Fireside Entertainments*. In 1899 Mary Stokes saw into print the *Indian Fairy Tales* that she had collected and translated. Nassau Senior's daughter, Mary, published her translations of the works of Michelet and Madame H. de Witt in 1875 and 1880.[81] Women may have done a great deal of translating, but when the translator was anonymous or identified by initials only, the gender and achievement of these linguists has been hidden from view. I suspect, moreover, that a search of musical materials, libretti, and the like might turn up further evidence of women's activities in the realm of translation.

Like translation, the work of editing has not been recognized as an area of Victorian female activity. But it surely was. Some Victorian women's ventures into editing were one-time works: Rachel H. Busk edited the third and fourth volumes of her sister's popular *Gossip of the Century* (1894). In 1880 Eleanor Ormerod edited and republished the meteorological and phenological work of Caroline Molesworth. Mary St. Leger Harrison, as Lucas Malet, wrote an introduction to the Waverley Edition of Charles Dickens's works in 1913, and Mary Hort Chitty produced a new edition of Elizabeth Sewell's *Principles of Education* in 1914. Often, however, editorial work was a part of women's on-going literary lives. Mary Senior Simpson edited A. F. Sergent-Marceau's *Reminiscences of a Regicide* (1889) as well as several works by her father. Alice Stopford Green contributed the notes for the Rt. Hon. Sir Arthur Paget's *The Paget Papers* (1896). During the same period Louise Creighton served as editor of the eight-volume series *Highways of History* published between 1884 and 1890.[82]

Edith Caroline Pollock (again using her pseudonym Ismay Thorn) got involved in a similarly long-term project with *Bright Eyes: An Annual for Young Folk*. Subtitled "Stories by Ismay Thorn, Janie Brockman and other well-known authors," the publication appeared yearly from 1893 to 1900. Religious publications were often the place women found editorial work to do. Felicia Mary Skene took time from her own writing and social work to serve as editor of two periodicals. The first was *The Churchman's Companion,* which she ran from 1862 to 1880. The second was *Argosy,* subtitled *A Magazine for the Fireside and the Journey,* which Skene was editing at the time of her death in 1899. B. F. Westcott found that it was a woman editor, a Miss Bunyon, who invited him to contribute to a new periodical, *The Children of the Church.*[83]

In some sense this treatment has been arbitrary, in that it has brought to light what the women of one circle published, and particularly what they published in book form or in the pages of major periodicals of the Victorian period. Wider, more systematic searching would undoubtedly reveal more. The point is only partly quantity, however. The major issues are those of mentality and culture.

Students of women in the nineteenth-century United States have found that women there could justify writing and publishing only when the family's economic survival was at stake.[84] George Gissing's novel *New Grub Street* (1891) is full of English women writers who took up pens to earn money, to help support themselves or a family. They share with the Paget women and their friends an interest in a broad range of subjects and the fact that writing and publishing were commonplaces of their lives. But they wrote to earn. The Paget women and their circle wrote because it was useful, it was pleasant, it was what women of their rank did. Indeed, the record of these gentlewomen suggests that writing and publishing were a specific badge of upper-middle-class culture among women as well as men, a norm for the educated gentlewoman with views, ideas, and a pen to hand.

Involvement, activism, and continuing efforts for the well-being of the society were standards of behavior for gentlewomen long before organized reform movements had appeared. Their systematic work of charity and their teaching reflect the commitment and contribution these women made to their world. Women's literacy allowed them to add their share to the stock of fiction, poetry, history, religion, and guidance for the practical work of social assistance, if not social change. The women of this Victorian network brought their education in languages, science, and religion, and their literate writing to bear on the choices and action of their adult lives.

They were not, however, mere scribblers, isolated from the world, protected from its evils in the drawing rooms and morning rooms of their comfortable residences. They went into the world: into the slums, into the homes of the poor, into the brothels, and into the classrooms and lecture halls, where they could be heard. From the lowliest Sunday school to the

Royal Agricultural or the Royal Photographic Society, ladies were speaking in public on every subject from religion to science.

Money was important in their lives. Women's financial resources gave them great freedom, which they used to further their charitable, social, artistic, and intellectual goals. Women's resources also made "careers" possible for them—not money-making occupations but endeavors by which, in the expenditure of money, they might put their skills and achievements to some use in the world. Mrs. Tait used her wealth in the service of the poor and the orphaned. Marianne North traveled and painted, and the Ormerod sisters used their money to give books to the poor and help to the farmers. The advantages of wealth to women with ambition are visible everywhere— from the small opportunities in Mary Turner's private publication on lithography and Clara Paget's on Welsh antiquity to Marianne North's art gallery at Kew and Eleanor Ormerod's extensive expenditure on her mailing list and her entomological reports.

The Paget women and their friends enjoyed many options in their lives. They could limit their activities to the private circles of family and friends, or they could act in public, whether in charity, the arts, politics, or science. In this respect they differed very little from the leisured gentlemen who pursued a liberal education in philosophy or biology with no need to make a profession or career of such interests. With a source of income provided by family (which every gentleman called an "independence"), the Victorian lady enjoyed the freedom of choice to do much or to do little, to obey the dictates of Victorian social responsibility or not, as her taste and upbringing led her.

Work, of course, serves other human needs than earning and mere survival, and activity has other ends and benefits than entertainment. Through work the women of this study established their social identity, found gratification and sources of self-expression, and often found an avenue by which they could make some useful contribution to their society.

Women's work has often been invisible to historians—partly because of our prejudices about Victorian ladies, partly because their style was not (by and large) the style of men's public action. Edith Tait Davidson may have been typical of busy but hitherto unseen women: "Her own work was usually carried out so quietly that few, except those working intimately with her, were aware of the many causes which owed their inception and their stability to Edith Davidson."[85] Gentlewomen worked; we have now begun to see what they achieved.

CHAPTER SIX

"Two Working Together for a Common End"

George Eliot's heroine Dorothea Brooke believed that if she married Casaubon, she could "help him . . . in his great works." Mrs. Proudie, the bishop's wife in Trollope's Barchester novels, may not have cared about great work, but she certainly thought it her place to intervene in diocesan personnel matters. Such women may impress us as shocking deviations from nineteenth-century norms of wifely behavior. Marriage was woman's work: but her career was household-management-and-pipe-and-slippers. When it came to real work, Victorian wives and husbands led "uncommunicative separate lives." There is reason to suspect, however, that Dorothea Brooke and Mrs. Proudie may not have been exceptional; they may exhibit the normal attitudes and experiences of gentlewomen in the professional and public life of their time.[1] The last chapter explored women's independent work; the task of this chapter is to see how women worked with men.

What immediately springs to mind when we think of the Victorian wife is the Biblical phrase the "help-meet." The phrase contains a world of possible roles, from the most passive to the most active, and it is characteristic of many relationships between men and women, not only that of husband and wife. To begin with the most passive, Victorian women were the confidantes of men—they were sympathetic listeners, providing an audience when a man reflected on his work and problems. From their youth, Emily Charlotte Wood was her brother Charles's confidante. Even after both had married, he continued to share with her the details of his political interests and maneuverings. Catharine Paget shared confidences as well as language lessons with her brother Frank.[2] These relations of assistance between sister and brother foreshadowed the way both women and men would later deal with spouses.

Among the marriages examined in this study, spouses were often confidantes. Lydia's fond interest in her husband, James, meant that she listened readily to his discussion of surgical cases and medical politics. In faraway Borneo the missionary McDougalls devoted little time to their personal lives, because "we have so many business matters to discuss." The Reverend Fenton John Anthony Hort was a reserved man. In marriage he found a confidante for life, someone "nearest to him with whom to share every thought." He shared with his wife, Fanny, the minutiae of his work and social life. Moreover, his unflinching assessments, to Fanny alone, of his own poor public performances and failures suggest the depth of his trust in her. Wives often dealt with their husbands' fears of having failed. Samuel Barnett, as head of Toynbee Hall, was deeply hurt when critics claimed that Toynbee Hall was "not . . . religious." His wife, Henrietta, and he "often talked and agonised over it together." The listener frequently became an advisor. F. T. Palgrave described his wife's role to his friend W. E. Gladstone: "she has been from our marriage-day my guide and counsellor. . . . I do not think that in anything, great or small, I ever acted against her judgment." Similarly Mrs. Westcott was, her husband said, "my unfailing counsellor and stay." And Edith Davidson gave her husband, as bishop and archbishop, advice on major issues of the day. Her "quiet counsel" during the constitutional crisis of 1911, for example, "was a real help" to him.[3]

Women went beyond the roles of confidante and advisor to become active helpers of the men in their lives, but the details have not always survived. In the 1860s and 1870s the deaconesses' movement at Ely and Winchester was actively supported by E. H. Browne and, "almost as much, by Mrs. . . . Browne." Browne's biographer gives no details. Craufurd Tait was curate at Saltwood in the 1870s, and his sisters "from time to time stayed with him for weeks and helped him." Similarly, the Reverend Herbert Hensley Henson, as a young bachelor cleric, had help from his widowed stepmother and his sister in Ilford in the 1890s: "those admirable ladies not only made my home comfortable, but threw themselves into my interests and works," he recalled. They set him "free from the meticulous distractions of domesticity" and "assisted [his] work in many ways."[4] Such generalized praise of women's work may be no more than perfunctory nods of gratitude for their domestic services. There is no denying that women's support at home made a significant contribution to the lives of Victorian professional men. Such words may, on the other hand, point to ladies' significant contributions, outside of the domestic sphere, to the family's professional achievements.

Clues to the nature of upper-middle-class marriage and work appear at the very earliest point in the marital relationship—with the marriage proposal itself. In the 1870s, when the young cleric Samuel Barnett was working in London's East End, he met Henrietta Rowland, a co-worker in the mission. They grew close. One day he proposed marriage. Miss Rowland was reluctant to say yes, both because of her lack of feeling for him and because of her own commitment to work among the poor. But he courted her, partly by showing her how their marriage would lead to a life of service: "Please don't you mistake me by thinking that I by myself can do God's work. I don't think I could alone." His appeals worked. A somewhat less selfish but equally work-oriented tone pervaded the Reverend Edward Stuart Talbot's proposal of marriage to Lavinia Lyttelton on June 15, 1869: he "asked her to come and help him in his great work" as warden of Keble College, Oxford. Archibald Campbell Tait's colleague, the Reverend William Benham, described the Taits' marriage in similar terms: Catharine Spooner "became the happy partner of his life at Rugby, Carlisle, Fulham, Lambeth, sharing all his deepest and truest interests, helping forward for thirty-five years every good work which he was called to promote." Mandell Creighton proposed to Louise von Glehn in 1871: We "have a life before us of much good and use to others. . . . I do so wish we were settled in life, with our duties clearly put before us. . . . I want very much to find a sphere for both you and me."[5] There were no separate spheres, but one sphere for both.

When A. L. Smith and Mary Baird agreed to wed, Mary anticipated the demands of her new life as an Oxford don's wife; marriage was a role for which she needed training: "I ought to have been educating myself for the position and for the society I was going to be launched into." Miss Baird was never studious and, although her fiancé lent her books, she "made little headway in them." In any event, she explained, "my days were too full and life was too interesting."[6] Baird's carefree ways should not disguise the fact that she saw her marriage as a position for which she needed to prepare.

Brooke Foss Westcott had a loving relationship of long standing with Mary Louise Whittard, but marriage had to wait until he was reasonably settled in his clerical career. On the day of his ordination as deacon he wrote to Mary with reverent thoughts: "This morning, my dearest Mary, . . . I was ordained Deacon. In this the great work of my life is begun, and so . . . of your life too." When he was ordained priest he repeated this view: "You too share my work, and so, as I pray for myself, I pray for you." In his excitement over the great changes in their lives, he teetered on the edge of grammatical chaos: "Henceforth I—and you with me, for our lives must be one—are pledged to be, as far as in me lieth, 'a wholesome example to the flock of Christ.'"[7]

Although promises of partnership filled the air on the day of the engagement, such formulations may merely have been the rhetorical effusions of devoted lovers or romantic observers, but not very truthful as descriptions of Victorian married life. Some historians believe that when women married, even the knowledgeable, well-educated ones "disappear[ed] . . . from the masculine world of professions and occupations."[8] Their invisibility may mean that women were not there, that women's genuine knowledge and skills came to nothing. Perhaps, however, their knowledge was put to use in some way other than the pursuit of individual careers.

Victorian marriage proposals spoke of shared tasks, a working partnership in the years ahead. What if they meant what they said? What if such avowals reveal what these men (and the women to whom they spoke) expected of marriage and life together? Perhaps Victorian marriage-as-woman's-vocation was not a hollow phrase but a legitimate description of the lives of married upper-middle-class women in the nineteenth century. These phrases may have been mere rhetoric, but it would seem better to begin with the assumption that the Victorians' words reveal at least some version of their genuine beliefs about, and experience of, marriage.

Victorian generalizations about husband-wife relations and married life reveal this same linkage of marriage and work that marriage proposals contained. In the 1880s Frank Paget described a wife as the woman "who is to share your life & work & to make your home." The Reverend Henry Lewis Thompson, former Christ Church don, married in 1877 and took a country parish soon after. He told a male friend about his new post, made satisfying because he had "his heart in his work, and a wife to help him." His language depicted sharing: "we are never idle." His friend married two years later, and Thompson told him, "I have no doubt you find your married life not only more than twice as happy, but also more than twice as helpful and useful to others as the old life used to be. It is marvellous," he added, "what a power comes from two working together for a common end."[9] Mary Westcott fulfilled her husband's forecast for their lives by sharing her husband's episcopal work: "everyone recognizes," Westcott told his sons after her death, "what she did for the [Durham] diocese." Westcott had feared, early on in their life at Durham, "that the cares of her position would oppress" her. (The fact, of course, was that it was technically *his* position.) But Westcott need not have feared. "She was . . . a perfect Bishop's wife, a mother in God to all whom she touched." The episcopal couple was precisely that: the bishop was father in God, she a mother to their flock. The Reverend Herbert Hensley Henson married Isabella Dennistoun in 1902, and he saw their wedding day as the beginning of "her new vocation" and of his relationship with "the most patient and considerate of colleagues," his wife. Nineteenth-century criticism of marriage also supports this collegial view of marriage. Harriet Grote wrote with scorn of marriage between "a porcelain woman" and "a pinchbeck man." She disapproved of "wives . . . who made 'good adjectives' to their husbands,—or 'good doormats.'"[10] Grote expected parity between the partners.

The details of Victorian married life, and in particular the urban gentry's arrangements of men's and women's work, confirm what marriage proposals and Victorian generalities suggest. Wives were assistants, colleagues, and partners in the work that men did. Their husbands took the public credit for the tasks performed—these were not "dual careers," nor was there any ideology of equality. These were "single-career families," but both husband and wife partook of that single career. And among family, friends, and co-workers the wife's contribution was known and acknowledged. In analogous relationships, bachelors and widowers had working partnerships with mothers, sisters, and daughters. As much as among agricultural and working-class families, there was, in the nineteenth century, a family economy of the upper-middle class.[11]

Victorian gentlewomen shared their fathers', brothers', and husbands' occupations, I would argue, in non-trivial ways. This dual participation of men and women in a single career was ubiquitous in Victorian upper-middle-class life. I would go so far as to say that men's work *was* women's work. The length and type of involvement varied, depending on many considerations, including the degree of a woman's interest in her male relative's work, a woman's other interests and duties, and the idiosyncratic circumstances of the household and the family.[12] The family's work often involved some division of labor between the partners. Women's work could involve decision making, personnel management, and specific skills as well. Women did the sorts of work that today would require a paid staff.

WOMEN'S STRUCTURAL AND SOCIAL ROLES IN PROFESSIONAL LIFE

Victorian women often had a voice in the externalities and structures of men's careers: career choice, job searches, career changes, personnel, social relations with colleagues and clients, public relations, and retirement all might come under a woman's influence. Mothers became involved in the career choices facing their sons. Perhaps the most predictable sort came when a boy was still at home. Betsey Paget, for example, talked long and hard to convince her husband that her views about their son James's desire for a naval career should prevail; she succeeded and James did not go to sea. A half-century later Clara expressed her own firmly held opinions on her son's plans for a career in medicine.[13]

Wives had the longest-standing and most direct influence on their husbands' career decisions. The wives of clergymen had wide influence, not so much in the fact of a man's taking holy orders, but in the subsequent choices of work he might make. Perhaps that was to be expected. A parish clergyman's work did not begin and end in the vestry and the pulpit. His duties required, at the minimum, a wife who could accept a husband who worked on Sundays and at irregular hours during the week. Moreover, his work might require sacrifices from his family. His work-life would be smoother, his responsibilities easier to fulfill, if his wife had a similar faith and values, perhaps even a commitment of her own. But, as we shall see, clerics' wives usually went beyond these minimal standards of cooperation, and they were not alone in their deep involvement in men's careers.

Consultation and cooperation began early in the relationship. Even before their marriage the Reverend E. H. Browne consulted his bride-to-be about his work. He had the offer of a living in Stroud, Gloucestershire, in 1839 or 1840. When he found "that Miss Carlyon was willing to make the venture, he accepted the offer. He married and took up the new work," his biographer records, "bringing with him the best helper . . . he could have chosen, his bride." The Brownes continued to consult together on decisions about his career. In considering a move from Lampeter College to a more desirable post in the parish of Kenwyn, both husband and wife felt that "we must sacrifice wishes to duty. And Lizzy," Harold Browne noted, "never offers one argument for Kenwyn," the post they would both have preferred on personal grounds. On New Year's Day, 1847, B. F. Westcott conducted a similar consultation: he had a "Talk with [Mary, his future wife] about my future course of life. A schoolmaster or a clergyman?"[14]

Women sometimes went far beyond advice and consent in these decisions. Harriette Bunyon, the future Mrs. McDougall, knew very well what her fiancé ought to do when he came to her in the spring of 1847 with news of two appointments offered to him. Frank had a choice of a post at the British Museum or a missionary assignment in Borneo. He had, out of family feeling, accepted the British Museum post, but she believed that he wanted to do missionary work above all. So sure was she of this, that she went on her own to McDougall's superior at the British Museum and asked him to release her fiancé from his employment. He agreed, and she went victoriously home to tell him the good news of his release. He was delighted and hastened to accept the mission work. Such intervention would be unthinkable interference if it were not for the fact that "these two lives," as one observer said, "were, in fact, inseparable."[15] Few women went as far as Miss Bunyon to involve themselves without prior consultation in men's careers, but many had extensive involvements in the structure of work.

Women of the family played practical roles in the process of job-seeking. In 1835 Lydia North's brother Isaac wanted the position of chaplain to St. Bartholomew's Hospital in London. Such appointments were made by the hospital governors, and candidates campaigned for votes before the election. Lydia went about soliciting votes, canvassing the governors to gain support for her brother's appointment. Similarly, Agnes Gall, in her role of aunt and stepmother to William Thomson, helped him to campaign for the professorship of natural philosophy at Glasgow. So engaged was she that she "lay awake counting the votes" before the election. After many years in the Indian Army, Catharine Tait's nephew returned home in 1864 because of his health. His aunt tried to help him get a post at the British Museum. To that end she introduced him to Sir Anthony Panizzi, formerly the principal librarian at the museum, and later she asked the Speaker of the House of Commons, J. E. Denison, to help him to get the appointment.[16]

In the larger world of parliamentary politics, similar involvement, including electioneering, went on. Harriet Grote took an "ardent part . . . with [her husband George] in the politics of the day." She was, for example, deeply involved in his battles over the Reform Bill of 1832. A family friend noted George Grote's good fortune in having "a partner so fitted to share, encourage and even advise; for in this, as in all other interests of life, each was alternately guide and follower." She had worked on his parliamentary campaign in 1832 and saw his victory as their victory. When George grew disappointed with the Liberal Party, Harriet advised him to return to his historical studies and writing.[17]

Connie Buxton called on her father, the very popular Sir John Lubbock, for help in her husband Sydney's campaigns at three parliamentary elections—Peterborough in 1885, Croydon in January of 1886, and Tower Hamlets in July of 1886. She used both flattery and logic to persuade her father to throw his support to Buxton, even though Lubbock had much in common with Buxton's opponent: "I expect that you really agree with Mr. Fitz*wm*'s principles . . . more than with Sydney's. But you can conscientiously say that Sydney is the harder worker of the two, & that is a great point here. Even some of the Conservatives say they won't vote for a 'lazy mon.'" Connie did not find the work of converting her father an easy task, for her father and husband disagreed "on many points of principle." But she urged Sir John to support Sydney even while admitting their differences, by urging him to say "that you disagreed with him on allotments, & . . . the Church, but that you thought a member who had political convictions & acted up to them, who cared abt. politics, & worked hard in the House, would be more credit to the town than one like Mr. Fitz*wm*., who really knows nothing & cares less abt. politics, & who is never hardly in his place in the house." Her arguments suggest an intimate knowledge of Parliament and its politics. She moved from political argument to personal appeal when she reminded Sir John that Sydney's "opponent didn't marry your daughter, & doesn't that," she asked, "make *some* difference?" Despite her efforts Buxton lost in his first two attempts. On his third try, this time for the Poplar division of the Tower Hamlets constituency, Buxton had Lubbock's support and won by a narrow margin.[18]

Constance Buxton's involvement may seem simply her effort on her *husband's* behalf, but Sydney's election was her goal, too. A speech from Sir John Lubbock, she told her father, "would help *us* more than I can tell you." And her remarks after the July 1886 election express her sense of her own place in it all: "Sydney got in by 76 [votes]—not a triumphant majority! However we are thankful to be in at all. We had a dreadful time of it during the counting, for it sometimes looked as if we *must* lose: & that wd. have been really too ignominious." "We had a dreadful time," she added: "we might have lost," but "we are thankful to be in." A few days later she still claimed identity with the winner of the seat: "I think we may be . . . thankful to have scraped in."[19] It was not just that he had won, not just that she had helped him to win. It was that "we" were "in." His career was hers.

Perhaps such wifely identification and job-seeking was common in the political arena. Aristocratic women certainly involved themselves in national politics and in the dispensing of high ecclesiastical preferment. The Cecil women and Mary Gladstone Drew are particularly noteworthy examples. Mrs. Drew, some said, "took a keen, not to say, a dominant interest in such matters." One might argue that Connie Buxton's political activity reflects the mores of the aristocracy (into which she was moving) more than the upper-middle class or the urban gentry. But engagement, in both minor and major ways, at every stage of a career was the wide experience of professional men's wives. Alice Stopford Green gave generously of her support and advice to her historian husband J. R. Green: she "encouraged him to begin his [historical] labours on a still larger and complete scale." Fenton J. A. Hort recognized—indeed made use of—a wife's participation in minor career matters when he urged Mrs. Fraser, the wife of the bishop of Manchester, to exercise "your good offices to support the request of the University authorities" that the bishop preach in Cambridge in October of 1884. In 1862 Archibald Campbell Tait faced a major career choice when he was offered the archbishopric of York: "My wife . . . advised me to decline," he reported, and he did. In a similar way in 1882 Elizabeth Browne, wife of the bishop of Winchester, confronted the necessity of involving herself in a major move in her husband's career. Browne was a leading candidate for the see of Canterbury, but questions arose about Browne's state of health at age seventy-one. Emissaries of Queen Victoria and the prime minister went to Mrs. Browne, and "her opinion [was] asked as to whether she thought he could stand the strain of the new duties and of a change of work considering his age . . . and his state of health." Her reply was "cautious and guarded," and, in the end, Edward White Benson—not Browne—became the next archbishop. Women served as useful sources of information and liaison in these delicate negotiations. Only when women intervened against one's point of view were they damned as meddling "episcopal wives."[20]

Medical men's and scientists' wives, no less than clergymen's wives, were activists when it came to decisions about work and career. When physicist William Thomson was negotiating about an appointment with a London firm in 1867, he showed his wife, Margaret, the letter he planned to send about the post. "Much of your letter is excellent," she told him, "but not all." She then proceeded to offer him four suggestions—rather in the form of stern *obiter dicta*—that included specific revisions of his prose, possible alterations in his approach, recommendations as to the style of negotiation she thought most suitable, and encouragement to seek further advice. She urged him to undertake some "hard bargaining" and reminded him that "You do not *need* to do it for a mere livelihood, like a person whose trade it is." Lady Thomson, although in delicate health, did not lack vigor when it came to the family's professional and financial affairs. In the early 1880s the young medical man Victor Horsley was beginning his career. In October of 1883 he and Eldred Bramwell decided to marry, and, before the year was out, her influence on his career could be seen. Later he explained to a friend that "Eldred wanted me to go in for Surgery and not pure Pathology"—and he agreed with her.[21] Throughout men's careers they looked to their female relatives for sound advice.

The Victorian social call once seemed the apotheosis of ladies' idleness, but Leonore Davidoff has argued for its significance by showing how women's calls and visits contributed to boundary maintenance and thus to the defense of the social order among the Victorian upper classes. She has argued that social visiting was the Victorian lady's (albeit unpaid) occupation and her contribution to the family's social status and interests. Davidoff has been wise in seeing the social-structural importance of this aspect of woman's role. Davidoff's work notwithstanding, some historians continue to see visiting as merely the time-filling activity of the idle. And, trivial or not, social calls are considered the quintessential "woman's work." But social life was not play, and it was not solely the sphere of women. Men, too, made calls and "dropped their cards" on their associates. The visit, for professional purposes, was an encounter between colleagues—a cleric and aspiring academic, for example, calling on his academic colleagues in Oxford or Cambridge.[22] In this respect, women's calls formed part of a larger pattern of family network-building. When women called, they stood in for the family unit as a whole (just as men did), not doing a specially *female* act, but a specifically *social* one. This perspective suggests that visiting was not nearly so sexspecific as Davidoff's analysis seems to suggest.

Social calls and entertaining were arenas in which women could have an influence on the structure of the family career. The Paget women and their circle participated in this sort of socio-professional activity. One, Catharine Paget, as a single adult daughter in the household, kept a daily record of her calls and made note of those visiting at her family's home in Harewood Place, London, in 1870 and 1871. It is impossible to tell how complete or systematic her record was. Catharine did not, for example, keep complete track of the calls her mother, father, or brothers paid. But a cursory glance at the calls she made suggests something of the character of social calling in the mid-Victorian years. She recorded her own visits to ladies: for example, a call on "Mrs. Erle" on May 7, 1870, and on "Lady Cooper" on June 29. At other times she went to see "The Gulls" or "the E. Tylors," indicating that she visited more than one member of the family. The entries imply but do not confirm the presence of husbands and sons as well as wives and daughters during these visits.[23] A surer record of the relative roles of men and women can come from examining the pattern of visitors received in Harewood Place.

In the months of May and June 1870, Catharine Paget recorded a total of forty-seven social calls during the day, that is, luncheon or afternoon calls.[24] Of the forty-seven social visits, sixteen were by relatives (aunts, uncles, and cousins of both sexes). The remaining callers were not solely females "dropping cards" on other females. The visitors included a majority of women, it is true: seventeen of the total of thirty-one visits recorded were women calling alone, and another was a mother calling with her daughter. Another six of the visitors were males visiting on their own. The remaining callers were seven married couples who called on the Pagets together. In short, women's social calls were part of a larger family activity, carried on among social and professional acquaintances of both sexes, for boundary-making, perhaps, but also to foster those networks that sustained professional life.

The social call could have other uses. A clergyman and his wife might use social visiting to create an environment of cooperation and community in the parish. In the mid-Victorian years, when feelings on matters of dogma and ritual often ran high, the promotion of peace was critical to the life of the parish. Elizabeth Browne, according to her husband's biographer, brought "the influence of a model *Home*" to her husband's work in Kenwyn and Kea; "gentleness of tone" in her family set an example, he thought, for the whole parish. In a very different sphere, Rose Thomson's longstanding interest in physics provided the foundation for her similar role at the Cavendish Laboratory, which her husband headed. She became well known to the

Cavendish research students, and "she did her part in making the Cavendish the happy and fruitful place it became." Teamwork and productivity were fostered by Rose Thomson's connection with the Cavendish Laboratory.[25]

The social call must take its place in a much larger pattern of activity that served to foster communication, knowledge, mutual trust, and solidarity, and that led to mutual assistance and advancement in professional circles. Many sorts of entertaining and social life played a direct role in the conduct of professional careers. A bishop's wife, for example, might socialize with the wives of the clergy in the diocese. At Winchester the Bishop and Mrs. Davidson established "Clergy Wives Days" in the 1890s: wives of parish priests came to Farnham Castle to rest and find some "stimulating activity." The hard-working wives got some rest and (in the classic busman's holiday) extended their knowledge of the administration of the diocese, and Mrs. Davidson got to know the women who, with their husbands, worked in individual parishes. Such work was not, however, sex-segregated; a bishop's wife considered it her duty to get to know the clergymen as well. This was not a minor task. In the 1850s when A. C. Tait was bishop of London, his "dear wife devoted herself resolutely . . . to do her part." She met all candidates for ordination and all the London clergy and entertained the latter at London House. When one considers that the ordinands numbered some seven hundred and the London clergy around one thousand, the magnitude of Catharine Tait's task becomes clearer. When Tait became archbishop of Canterbury, she continued in this way, attempting to get acquainted with all the members of Convocation.[26]

The scenes of professional socializing in the Church of England multiplied in the last decades of the century. Added to the diocesan conferences were the Lambeth Conferences that began in 1867. During the 1908 Lambeth Conference Edith Davidson entertained, in groups of six to twelve, all the overseas bishops and their wives, and one may be sure that she used the sociability of the occasion to make the conference more effective. There were, of course, local versions of that sort of socializing.[27]

The Victorian medical profession saw the multiplication of professional societies and organizations. Many of their activities centered on the exchange of medical and scientific information, but the organizations were also designed to foster social bonds and networks. A *conversazione* at the Royal College of Physicians, a hospital charity ball, myriad teas, and exhibitions— all these apparently leisure-time activities provided settings in which professional husbands and wives could nurture the social networks of medical life. On a multinational scale the medical man's analog of the clergymen's Lambeth Conference was the International Medical Congress, the first of which took place in 1881. The Paget house in Harewood Place was one of the centers of medical congress activity in that year and was the meeting-ground of English medical men and a host of important visitors.[28]

Junior colleagues and students on their way into the professions were another group that every professional couple dealt with, both out of doors and at home. In the 1840s, when E. H. Browne was serving as vice principal of Lampeter College, the theological school in Wales, Elizabeth Browne invited the students home for tea, conversation, and theological discussions— socializing in which both the Brownes took part. Later when he took up parish work, she entertained and watched over the bachelor curates serving under her husband. For the wives of schoolmasters, such social life focused on the young people. At Rugby in the 1840s Catharine Tait was a favorite with the boys from the first to the sixth form. She entertained them and listened to their secrets and formed a bond of confidence with them. At Christ Church, Oxford, in the 1890s Helen Church Paget soon earned a reputation for her "great excellence as a hostess." Undergraduates specially interested in clerical careers "were invited to meet . . . [the Dean] and Mrs. Paget in her drawing-room, where they had coffee and talked a little."[29] She not only helped set the tone of Paget's administration there, but she also participated in the nurturing and guidance of the undergraduates.

What happened in these social events? When Randall Davidson accepted the post of dean of Windsor, his wife, Edith, took up the responsibility of entertaining the young choristers of the Free Chapel of St. George's, Windsor. One of the boys later recalled that "Mrs. Davidson and Miss Agnes Tait [her sister] . . . read to us, played games with us, and gave us homey Sunday lessons; and the long room in the Deanery became something of a chorister's paradise."[30] Behind the romance of this boy's memories were serious tasks being performed. A sister, mother, or wife was a professional partner of the schoolmaster, the Oxford don, the parish clergyman, or the newly appointed bishop. She fostered good will, and she provided a second pair of ears and eyes, observing, evaluating, and judging the character and condition of the students, the parish and its residents, or the clerical hierarchy, the better to advise her husband or brother in the work he had to do. Similar watching briefs existed for wives of Oxbridge dons and medical and surgical wives at the *conversaziones* and dinners they attended with their colleagues.

Knowledge was power and led to another form of structural involvement in professional life. A Victorian woman's familiarity with business or professional matters is often the first (or only) clue to her participation in the family business or career. The record of the first nineteenth-century generation is often faded, but we see tantalizing glimpses of women's involvements in the business lives of brothers and husbands. Samuel Paget had, among other business ventures, put up securities for, and made other commitments to, the shipbuilding firm of Stone and Custance. The firm went bankrupt and Sam was the object of a suit in the court of King's Bench in 1810. His sister Mary had material information about Sam's business ventures, and, as a result, the litigants tried to bring her into court to give evidence against him in the affair. But she and her sister-in-law Betsey together contrived to protect the family's financial interests and Sam's legal position in the case. Betsey "silently had the carriage to the door [of the Pagets' house in Yarmouth] and evaded the summons issued to . . . Mary by conveying into another county that undesirable witness in the case." The two women "took lodgings for a week or more at Lowestoft" in order to avoid the process server. When the case was finished they returned to Yarmouth to celebrate Sam's victory.[31] Both Mary and Betsey Paget had knowledge of, and potential involvement in, the family's business ventures.

Wives often played specific roles in professional communications, and in that way they became involved in the politics of organizational relations. Sometimes the issues were small ones. B. F. Westcott wrote to Mrs. F. J. A. Hort, asking her to present her husband with a manuscript, but only at a time when it would not be too troublesome. Perhaps he might, Westcott suggested, "read through the pages at tea-time in half an hour." Sometimes the issues were larger. In early 1870 Archbishop Tait was ill, but Gladstone needed his immediate advice in what he called "my greatest Ecclesiastical difficulty, the discovery of the fittest person . . . to be recommended for the Diocese of St. Asaph." Gladstone turned to Mrs. Tait to confirm third-hand reports of her husband's opinion about one of the candidates. A wife might serve as the channel of communication for feedback on her husband's performance. In 1876, when the secretary of the Winchester Diocesan Conference wanted Bishop Browne to know of reaction to his conduct there, he wrote to Mrs. Browne: "I feel I must tell *you*," he wrote, "what everyone has been saying today about our good Bishop. . . . [M]en of all grades and shades of opinion . . . all agree in saying that his skill in managing the Conference was something marvellous." He went on to add that "[L]ed by such a chief as we have we feel ready to do anything for him or for the diocese."[32] A wife may also have been called upon to carry criticism or news of disaffection from her husband's constituents, clients, or parishioners—but laudatory memoirs of Victorian professional men rarely record such events.

Professional men had their conflicts and squabbles, and their wives played a role there, too—in fostering gossip and crisis, or in calming troubled professional relations. Catharine Tait "assisted . . . [her husband, the archbishop of Canterbury] in entertaining representatives of the whole Anglican Episcopate" during the Lambeth Conference in 1876. But "discussions of a somewhat stormy kind" came up during the meetings, and Archbishop Tait, in particular, had powerful differences with the bishop of Cape Town. At the end of each day, when the participants gathered at Fulham Palace, Mrs. Tait's "gentle influence . . . helped much . . . to calm the differences, which might otherwise have assumed undue proportions." Later a triangle of misunderstanding erupted between Archbishop Temple, Randall Davidson, and Edward White Benson; it was finally sorted out, probably through the "intervention of Mrs. Benson."[33]

Clergy and laity alike understood fully the importance of a wife's personality, character, and social relations. Charm was not enough. When Randall Davidson was being considered for the post of dean of Windsor, the queen observed to the archbishop of Canterbury that "Mrs. Davidson would be of great use at Windsor, which is a place of rather a gossiping nature, requiring tact and judgment." Perhaps the ultimate evidence of a wife's centrality came when her conduct made her husband's professional advancement impossible. A clue to such a possibility turned up in 1870, when the search was on for a new bishop of St. Asaph. One candidate had a wife who had "disgraced herself" thoroughly. He stayed in the running only because his wife had died.[34] The wife's role may have been important for a professional man because many were like Randall Davidson: "his methods were largely personal and . . . private, as he trusted in human contacts and the help of proved counsellors rather than in any formal organization."[35] Many professional men certainly depended on personal connection rather than the workings of organizations, and in so doing brought into play the personality, connections, intelligence, political tact, and sagacity of their wives.

COLLABORATION IN THE WORLD OF LETTERS

In Victorian political life and bureaucracies, secretarial work was, until the advent of the typewriter, man's work. But in professional practice the situation was rather different. Professional work was often done in or from a residence, whether the general practitioner's surgery or the bishop's palace. In those circumstances there was no clear separation of work and home, or of public and private. Women's education and the skills they had learned in the schoolroom prepared them—often very well indeed—for the work that professional life demanded. To begin with the simplest tasks: gentlewomen served as clerks, preparing fair copies of letters and records of professional correspondence; they were secretaries, responsible for other written tasks related to the family profession.[36] The Reverend Isaac North, as an unmarried clergyman, was fortunate to have an able sister to help with his work in Yarmouth in the 1830s: Lydia took on some of the work of registering births and deaths and other record-keeping for the parish. Kate and Patty Paget, the Reverend Alfred Paget's spinster sisters, probably gave that sort of help to the bachelor in his Kirstead (Norfolk) parish. Wives and daughters also gave secretarial assistance. Alice Stopford Green "entered warmly into all . . . [her husband's] pursuits" and "acted as his amanuensis" for the six short years of their married life. B. F. Westcott praised his second daughter, Katie, for the quality of her help: "You have been such an excellent secretary that I must send you one line . . . to thank you for doing your work so well."[37]

Scientists and medical men, too, had such help. Maria Turner Hooker accompanied her husband to Glasgow in 1820 when he took up his post as professor of botany at the university. During their twenty years' tenure there she assisted him with the clerical side of his work as a naturalist. Other help came from their son and from one employee at the university. When the Hookers moved south again, this time to Kew, she continued her work. By the end of their lives she had earned recognition for having served as his "secretary and amanuensis . . . for fifty years."[38] The Hookers' son and daughter-in-law followed the same habits. Sometimes the only historical evidence of this service is the fact that a man has signed a letter, but the text is in his wife's or daughter's hand.[39] In other cases a woman's secretarial role was strikingly visible. Frances Harriet (Henslow) Hooker had a clear role in J. D. Hooker's correspondence. In 1860 for example Frances wrote to the publishers of a biographical account of her husband: "Mrs. Hooker," she stated formally, "begs to enclose a correct sketch of Dr. Hooker's life: as there were many errors in that sent, she has entirely rewritten it & hopes it will answer Mr. Griffin's purpose." She went on to offer the publisher her services in reading the biography of her father-in-law for, as she observed, "Sir William Hooker . . . is too busy to attend to such things."[40]

Frances, Lady Thomson made her secretarial role in Sir William's communication abundantly clear. She wrote some parts of the letters herself, included her own remarks and news, and transmitted her husband's scientific messages to his correspondents. When she wrote to George Darwin, for example, she introduced her husband's (sometimes dictated) messages, with a phrase like, "Sir William sends to tell you," or "Now for Sir William's message. . . ." What followed could be a lengthy message about tide gauges or thermometers. She did not find the technical language difficult but only the speed: "I hope this is legible," she apologized to George Darwin, "I have been expected to write as quick as a shorthand writer!" Scientists wishing to communicate with Thomson did not, for their part, hesitate to address their letters to his wife. Likewise Macmillan's, the publishing house, was accustomed to communicating with its nineteenth-century authors through a spouse, or sometimes a son or daughter.[41]

Correspondence was a common task for these household clerks—or "home secretaries"—but often women took on larger projects, like making fair copies (and later typescripts) of manuscripts for publisher or printer and reading galley proofs of the books and articles their brothers, husbands, or fathers were in the process of publishing. Catharine Paget read her father's article proofs, to prepare them for *Macmillan's Magazine*. Mary Church shared with Luke Paget the job of reading and correcting the proofs of her brother-in-law Francis Paget's biography. Hensley Henson's wife was a ready helper in the proofreading and indexing of his memoirs. During all of her husband's career as clergyman, biblical scholar, historian, man of letters, and bishop, Harriot Moule was, a friend observed, "her husband's right hand and helper." Her duties were often secretarial: "She wrote out or typed many of his sermons and books," and that was no mean task, for in his lifetime Handley Moule published forty books, twenty-six booklets and tracts, forty-nine articles and individual sermons, fourteen volumes of poetry, and fifty-four other items of varying length.[42]

Just as Constance Buxton was involved in Sydney's parliamentary campaigns, so was she a participant in his writing. In the middle of 1888 Sydney Buxton published a book on *Finance and Politics;* he dedicated it to his father-in-law, "at whose suggestion this work was begun," and to his wife, "without whose help and encouragement it would not have been accomplished." These nice words were no *pro forma* nod to his wife. Constance Buxton actively assisted his authorship. She edited and proofread the text at various stages. In March of 1888 she felt the great pressures of deadlines, she told her father, because the book "seems to me to want a tremendous lot of correcting & polishing up, & we are working so much against time that I feel afraid just the finishing touches may be wanting & so the book not really do itself justice."[43] They worked hard and by mid-April they were reading proof. Everywhere the record reveals that women's partnership in men's literary work went beyond copying and proofreading to substantive and substantial help. In 1854 Frances Hooker and her husband read her father's manuscript of a botany textbook, presumably to give him a critique of the work. Alice Stopford "taught herself Greek in order to help her father in his biblical studies." Young Winnie Talbot often traveled with her uncle and aunt, Archbishop and Mrs. Randall Davidson. On their trips she helped him with his letters and speeches. In 1911 she remembered that "we had a great 'travailing' over his Church Congress sermon . . . reading it over and re-writing." Mary Robinson Stokes, wife of the mathematician and physicist George Gabriel Stokes, heard or read all but the most "purely scientific of her husband's writings and offered suggestions for their improvement." T. H. and Netty Huxley went further. Her husband "invariably submitted his writings to the criticism of his wife before they were seen by any other eye." And Professor Huxley enjoyed it when his wife turned out to be right in her criticism. On one occasion when he ignored her advice, George Grove, *Macmillan's* editor, gave him the same suggestions; Huxley reported the fact back to her with some amusement. Catharine Thompson and Mary Church gave Stephen Paget substantive and editorial help in his life of Francis Paget, bishop of Oxford.[44]

Formal coauthorship between men and women was relatively rare, but it did happen occasionally among the upper-middle-class families studied here. Dawson and Mary Turner together produced *Outlines in Lithography* in 1840. J. R. and Alice Stopford Green were the coauthors of the 416–page *Short Geography of the British Islands*, which Macmillan published in 1879. Mary Dyson Hort and her brother A. F. Hort shared the credit for the edition of the Gospel according to St. Mark which they published in 1917. Mary Baird Smith's parents co-produced a book on Alpine natural history, he providing the illustrations and she writing the "botanical notes." Occasionally parents cooperated in a literary memorial to a child of theirs, dead before his or her time. A. C. Tait's colleague William Benham wove together and published a family memorial from A. C. and Catharine's recollections of their children and A. C. Tait's recollections of his wife. Similarly, Handley and Mary Moule wrote a memoir of their daughter, which he published in 1905.[45]

When a writer died with his work unfinished, he often left the task of completing his last essays or books to a student, younger colleague, or a brother. Or a female relative might carry out this work. To do so she had to be knowledgeable about the man's work and plans. Such female literary executorship indicates the full depth of female engagement in what we have thought was exclusively his career. Alice Stopford Green had learned historical methods under her husband's tutelage. As his health weakened "She completed . . . his *Conquest of England*" and published it the year he died. Jane Busk found her most important task of assistance at the time her father, George, was dying. He was in the midst of completing what has since been judged "his most important work," his *Report on the Polyzoa collected by H.M.S. Challenger,* when illness overtook him. He completed the two-volume work "with the assistance of his eldest daughter," and it was published in 1884 and 1886, the last years of his life. Eliza Cecilia Stainer, daughter of the organist and musicologist Sir John Stainer, helped him with his study of *Early Bodleian Music* (1898). Earlier she and her brothers had collaborated in compiling the *Catalogue of English Song Books* from their father's library. That volume had appeared in 1891. Alice Stopford Green edited and revised seven of her late husband's historical works. Louise Creighton performed similar work for her husband, churchman and historian Mandell Creighton. Both women, meanwhile, continued to write and publish their own historical and political works.[46]

Maud Paget Gadow offers a good example of literary executorship in science. Her husband died in 1928 and she subsequently arranged for colleagues and students to help prepare two of Gadow's works for publication. She carried a significant share of the work herself. One manuscript in progress was Gadow's study of the biological after-effects of the eruptions of Jorullo (a volcano in southern Mexico) that took place in the 1750s and 1760s. Maud asked Hans's friend and colleague A. C. Steward to write a preface and another, Philip Lake, to edit the work. Maud provided the illustration of the volcano that served as the frontispiece. In the case of Hans's study of *The Evolution of the Vertebral Column*, Maud called on J. F. Gaskell and H. L. H. Green to do the editing. From Hans Gadow's "rough sketches" Maud made the scientific illustrations for the book. She also worked on the "composition of the bibliography and index." Another woman, Mrs. H. S. Hacker, provided additional scientific illustrations for the book.[47]

The last act of piety and loyalty to a man of importance was the preparation of his "life and letters," a task often taken on by a colleague, a protégé, or a son. Frequently, however, that task was the last collaboration of a Victorian woman and her husband. As his marital colleague, his wife often knew as much about him and the conduct of the family's career as anyone. In a few instances a surviving sister or daughter was the author or editor of this memorial volume.

Given the involvement of clergymen's wives and daughters in ecclesiastical work at all levels, it is not remarkable that they often wrote their husbands' or fathers' memoirs or biographies. Mary Church, who remained single all her life, provided this service of "Life and Letters" for her father, R. W. Church, the dean of St. Paul's Cathedral from 1871 until his death in 1890. One of the many wives to perform this literary memorial task was Fanny Kingsley. She took up the work immediately after Charles Kingsley's death in 1875, and the volumes were in print by December of the next year. Many of these works done by women have been singled out for special praise for their completeness and their usefulness. Kingsley biographers and other scholars of the period have found Fanny's work on Charles "a treasure house of Kingsley material." Catharine Paget Thompson and her brother Stephen Paget cooperated in preparing a memorial volume for her husband, the Reverend H. L. Thompson, after his death in 1905. The volume contained a biography of Thompson written by Stephen and Catharine, together with a selection of his sermons.[48]

Elma Paget's biography of her husband Henry Luke, bishop of Chester, drew heavily on their close cooperation in the work of the church. Louise Creighton, wife of the bishop of London, wrote his biography. She earned special praise from his friends and colleagues for her work, particularly because they felt that his personal style had led many to misunderstand him. Of Creighton's memoir, Randall Davidson remarked: "I know of no instance in which the publication of a public man's biography has so greatly raised him in the estimation of good and thoughtful people."[49]

Women relatives of scientists, medical men, and lawyers, like those of clergymen and theologians, carried on the biographical last rites. Sir Charles Lyell's sister-in-law prepared the two-volume edition of his letters and journals. Similarly, Grace Anne Milne M'Call Prestwich wrote and edited her husband's biography, not hesitating to treat the geological as well as the social and familial features of her husband's life and career. Ethel Romanes prepared the life and letters of her scientist husband. When she encountered problems with scientific materials that she could not solve, she called on Mrs. St. George Reid, whose "scientific knowledge and ability" she found "simply invaluable." Among Victorian professional men in this circle, the lawyers are least well represented by biographical memoirs. Lucy Cohen's biography of her father, the barrister, is one of the rare exceptions to the silence that often prevailed in this field.[50]

A volume of "life and letters" may appear to be a simple matter to produce: select the letters to be included, put them in chronological order, write a line or two of introductory or explanatory text, and the work is done. Such work is not, of course, as simple as it may look. The ordering of the masses of material produced by active Victorian scholars, scientists, and clergymen and the selection of appropriate and representative writing were themselves demanding tasks. And then the editor very often had to present family background, childhood, and youth, weaving together and explaining letters, and offer a summation of a man's life and an account of his death, all the while avoiding unseemly controversy or offense to the living. In this way so-called "editors" contributed a substantial amount of writing to the work. To take as an example the first life mentioned here: Mary Church wrote about fifty-seven pages of her father's 422-page life and letters.[51] Many Victorian lives were much longer than Church's, running to two, occasionally three, volumes. The task was, in short, substantial. Some were undoubtedly pedestrian products. Others, such as those of Fanny Kingsley and Louise Creighton, were notable achievements.

PARTNERSHIP IN PROFESSIONAL LIFE

Victorian men used terms like "colleague" and "partner" to refer to wives, and their generalizations about shared work attest to the notion that professional life was not simply "man's work." Contemporaries testified, for example, to the good "influence of the clergy and their families" in the growth of local education and thus point to the cooperation of husbands and wives in parish work. Brothers and sisters who shared their homes also shared their work. The Reverend William Baird and his sister Jane Frances Baird worked together in his east London parish in the mid-Victorian years. She was "his devoted helper, and worked with him all through the terrible epidemic of cholera in 1865."[52]

The notion of shared work permeates every discussion of professional life. When the Taits moved to the See of London, "a great deal devolved upon . . . [Mrs Tait] in the direct furtherance of my episcopal work as Bishop of London," A. C. Tait observed. The couple sought advice from their predecessors there: the former bishop of London and Mrs. Blomfield gave the Taits "advice and information for the better discharge of her and my duties," Tait recalled. The rhetoric itself is revealing. Tait referred to "her and my duties." Other men spoke of "our new work" or "our duties." In either case, a professional man's appointments brought with them explicit responsibilities for his wife. Catharine Tait's earlier duties, as the wife of a cathedral dean, for example, included helping the poor and providing deanery hospitality, as well as assisting her husband with his particular tasks. In London the Taits made it their business to call on all the other episcopal couples and to develop friendships with them all. Exactly the same sort of female participation appears in the academic world. When Rose Thomson's husband moved from the Cavendish to the mastership of Trinity College, Cambridge, Rose had a new sphere of work and "her duties at Trinity," too.[53]

The specifics are revealing. Professional work often involved reading and research, and here wives played a regular and useful role—the kind of work professionals now pay research assistants to do. When Catharine and A. C. Tait were at Rugby School, she regularly took on the task, he reported, of "helping me to get up my history lessons." She helped him, too, by doing the research for his articles and lectures.[54]

When Elma Paget's husband became bishop of Chester, she often attended the meetings of committees that her husband, *ex officio*, belonged to or chaired. It may have been a simple way of conserving his energy, but it had the more important advantage that she could see that issues in which they had special interest were not shunted aside or decided without the bishop's control. Controversial issues (and they were common) were side-tracked by Mrs. Paget while her husband remained officially ignorant of the conflict, worked behind the scenes for their goals, and all the while sustained the peaceful surface of his administration of the diocese.[55]

The Taits' daughter Edith, as a cleric's wife, followed the pattern laid down in her parents' household. For example, when her husband, Randall Davidson, was bishop of Winchester, he founded a "Hostel for the training of young men for ordination." Edith Davidson "shared the bishop's interest in all that concerned the Hostel." In addition, she accompanied him whenever possible in his episcopal duties, "going to every opening of a church and as often as possible to confirmations."[56]

Sometimes we catch only glimpses of these couples working side by side. When Francis Paget was vicar of Bromsgrove, "He and Mrs. Paget did 'any amount of work': night-schools, classes, visits, choir practices, two services daily, and four on Sundays." Friends spoke of their work as "their duties." In another of those glimpses, we can see the bishop of Durham and Mrs. Moule going together to the scene of a colliery disaster in 1908 to bring the consolation of faith to the sufferers there. Although the Reverend McDougall was called to missionary life, his wife "had never formally proposed to undertake any direct missionary work." But her marriage brought problems and tasks to her attention that she considered her "duty" and these "she threw herself into . . . at once and pursued . . . with all her energy." As in any career, there were some tasks women liked better than others. Mrs. McDougall had, she admitted, a "great dislike to teaching," but the "mission needed a female school" and she took it up. The partnership might go so far as to bring the wife to the point of standing in for her husband in some of his specific private or public duties. When Archbishop Tait's health seemed to weaken, the queen agreed he should have a suffragan. Edward Parry, suffragan bishop of Dover, was chosen and, Tait recalled, "My wife made all the arrangements for the consecration in Lambeth Chapel."[57]

Husbands and wives sometimes shared a single task. Sometimes they divided the labor into her part and his. But these "separate spheres" were not the private sphere for her and the public for him. It was a division of labor based partly on custom, partly on talent, and partly on personal choice.

We could dismiss the partnership of clerical husbands and wives as a peculiarity of the church as a profession, were it not for the fact that such sharing took place in many spheres of upper-middle-class life. Take the case of banker Dawson Turner, an art collector and connoisseur. The Turner art collection included works by Titian, Gian Bellini, Reubens, Greuze, Cuyp, and

T. Phillips. The Turners' Yarmouth home was a veritable artistic and antiquarian workshop. Dawson Turner's major interests were architectural history and portraits (those of family, distinguished visitors, and friends). Under his direction, artist and teacher John Sell Cotman, among others, made drawings of Norfolk architectural antiquities. Mrs. Turner, one of the Turner daughters, and Cotman did the portraits. From these drawings, etchings or lithographs were prepared and prints produced for the Turners' published works or private studies. The books resulting from this family team of antiquarians and artists included *One Hundred Etchings* (1830), a series of one hundred portraits of the Turner family and their celebrated friends, published under Dawson Turner's name. Thirteen of the portraits in this volume were done by Cotman and some of the rest by other male artists, but most came from the pencils of the Turner women, principally Elizabeth Turner. She also did the etchings that appeared in the book. A second published volume appeared in 1840, under the title *Outlines in Lithography*. This work was an illustrated catalogue of the Turner art collection. Mrs. Turner wrote the descriptions of the paintings and other works, her husband provided comments on the "origin, price," and "peculiarities of each item." The Turner daughters Hannah Sarah and Mary Ann did the lithographs. In all, the Turner women produced thousands of drawings and etchings, and they testify to women's capacity for sustained artistic production and technical proficiency.[58]

In other families it was money or science, not art, that provided the arena for important wifely action. From the beginning of their married life Catharine Tait kept the household accounts—"she had a great capacity for business." Her work went beyond balancing the books. She kept tight control over expenditures and watched the income and outflow of the family's resources so that the projects and plans the Taits had in mind could be carried out without financial strain. At Rugby, where her husband was headmaster, Mrs. Tait took on independently an important part of the administration of the school: she took over all the financial accounts, both for his house and for the school as a whole. She reformed Rugby record-keeping and "set to rights the complicated finance" of the school. Her work did not stop when they left Rugby for ecclesiastical life in his post as dean of Carlisle. There, and also after his elevation to the dioceses of Winchester and then London, she continued this fiscal work. Her role as accountant continued after he was made archbishop of Canterbury in 1869. Bank officials in London knew of her involvement in church finance and complimented the Taits on her excellence as an account manager. Mrs. Tait also had policy power in money matters. From their Rugby days the Taits had abundant resources, her husband recalled, and "at Fulham and Lambeth, having the command and distribution of large revenues, she ever exercised a vigilant control over our expenditures."[59]

Maud Paget's husband, Hans Gadow, was a vertebrate paleontologist first at the British Museum and then, for the bulk of his career, in Cambridge. He traveled extensively in search of specimens of animal life, and Maud went with him. She was his colleague and research assistant in Mexico during two trips in 1904 and 1906. The couple had some mild adventures, and some pleasing days, but their first objective was work. "When one can loll in a chair on the verandah, with a cooling drink at one's elbow," Hans Gadow mused, "life in the tropics is delightful; but when one has a hundred odd jobs to do, besides the day's active work, life assumes an altogether different aspect." And, he assured his readers, "we were not lazy, because we had not come merely to amuse ourselves." The local wildlife the Gadows collected in Mexico included two boa constrictors, which they stored in wooden barrels in their private railroad car. One escaped. Two days later Maud came upon the beast when she was tidying up the car. She and Hans grappled, Laocoön-like, with the reptile until they could return it to the barrel-cage they had arranged. "It was easy enough, with patience, to recapture him," Gadow recalled, "but my wife and I had our hands full with the creature." Most of Maud's duties were not so exciting. Daily work included the gathering of examples of animal and insect life, "the pickling and labelling of specimens, and the making of notes" about the insects, reptiles, and animals they had caught. In the evening, the two "set . . . traps for various kinds of opossums and little rodents" that might be caught during the night.[60]

Zoological specimens aside, Maud and Hans Gadow's work together involved the books about their travels. He wrote two lengthy volumes, *In Northern Spain* (1897) and *Through Southern Mexico* (1908). He illustrated the works with his photographs, those of his colleagues in Spain and Mexico, and with sketches and watercolors. Hans did the drawings related to interior architecture and to the scientific specimens he had observed. The other illustrations came from Maud. For the Spanish volume she provided dozens of pen-and-ink drawings of the landscapes, exteriors of buildings, and camp sites. Twenty-four of her watercolors of Mexican scenery illustrate the book on Mexico.[61]

Even medical practice was not out of bounds for the Victorian gentlewoman. Rose Paget sometimes had responsibility for treating servants or family members, under her mother's or father's direction, when her parents were away. In Borneo Harriette McDougall took on medical practice, too. She began some rudimentary medical treatment during an outbreak of cholera that occurred while her doctor-husband was away. But the work continued after he returned: "The sick children now came to me to be doctored early every morning."[62]

When a professional man died, family and friends offered assessments of his career, and the occasion provided a chance for reflecting on the role of his wife as well. At the time of Canon Barnett's death, the bishop of Stepney wrote to Mrs. Barnett to express his sense of loss and his admiration for Barnett. In the process he described the working relationship that the couple had had: "He and you have stood side by side in it all, and all that is felt for him [by London's East End poor] is felt for you. Your wise and tender love for the poor; your confidence in them and faith in their best; your work and your power of inspiring them have made all the difference! The best that is being done now is very largely the immediate result of your labours, and the good that shall be done will bear the constant impression of your touch."[63] Note how the referent of the pronoun "you" became ambiguous, seeming to be singular at first, but moving to the plural, from his work to their work.

In the same way Archbishop Tait, after his wife's death, described Catharine Tait's active role: "in our social and official life she was a real power." He praised her for her loyal partnership: "Her heart was in all we had to do together, and in all my separate work," as well as "her own labours." The labels of "private" and "public" were not the distinguishing features of this female and male work. Instead, the Taits recognized three spheres: his, hers, and ours. In a similar vein the London *Times* reported on the work of Edith Davidson and her husband, the archbishop of Canterbury: from the day of their marriage, "the texture of Edith Davidson's life was so closely interwoven with that of her husband that it is difficult to tell where the work and influence of one ended and the other began." The Davidsons shared friendships and leisure activities, but most importantly they "shared . . . their spiritual life and their work." Louise Creighton illustrates just how thoroughly wives were integrated into professional careers. After Bishop Creighton's death, Mrs. Creighton served on international church committees and advised churchmen on Anglican affairs. Archbishop Davidson wrote to her after one conference, reflecting on the benefits derived from it and puzzling over "How we can make it all fruitful. . . . I shall ask for your help in trying to solve it. You are one of the very few who seem to me to combine the power of vision with the power of action in our present-day Church life."[64] Her knowledge of and influence in church affairs did not die when Bishop Creighton died, and she continued to play an important role in ecclesiastical affairs.

In the 1890s one observer of the Victorian professional scene articulated the relationship between men, women, and professional life. Miss Goodwin, daughter of the bishop of Carlisle, evaluated (and probably undervalued) Elizabeth Browne's contribution to the work of the church. She judged that Elizabeth Browne had helped Bishop E. H. Browne "by entering into his work." She did this "just from her sweet wifely sympathy," Miss Goodwin insisted, and "Not professionally, as is rather the plan now."[65] Perhaps the late Victorians made it a conscious plan that wives should enter professionally into their husbands' work: in fact, such cooperation had been going on for at least two generations—a partnership of husband and wife in their common life's work.

Recent social science scholarship has addressed itself to the "Incorporated Wife," the woman who, in late twentieth-century Oxbridge or corporate legal or medical life, is tied to her husband's career as a status symbol and decorative companion but who dares not enter into his professional life intellectually or politically. The authors argue, with good Whiggish logic, that what now exists in English society must only have been worse in the less enlightened Victorian age. Such critics join ranks with Lawrence Stone in criticizing Victorian marriage; Stone contrasts the companionate marriage of an earlier era, based on "personal qualities" and characterized by affection, with those later marriages that were contracted and conducted merely with a view to "worldly advancement." Peter Gay, more optimistic than Stone, recognizes that "bourgeois marriage" might be founded on the drive for money and status, but he finds many instances of what he considers the happy alternative, the union of "tenderness and passion."[66] The evidence provided here suggests another view.

This chapter began with George Eliot's *Middlemarch*. Let it end there as well. The marriages of Dorothea Brooke and Casaubon and of Rosamond Vincy and Lydgate foundered on the failures of these couples to establish marital partnerships in work. The well-bred Dorothea knew what she should do, but she chose the wrong man and hence her willing partnership met the blank wall of Casaubon's incompetence and fear. Rosamond, the daughter of a socially-rising businessman, thought decorativeness was enough, and she failed to provide her doctor-husband with the partner in life's work that he needed.[67]

In the upper-middle-class Victorian marriages examined here, the sentimental and the sexual were often joined by the intellectual and the occupational in marriages where tenderness, passion, and shared work were the potential—and potent—sources of marital unity. What we may have seen in the course of the twentieth century is a deterioration in marriage, as the partnership that once marked professional couples' relationship to work and to one another has disappeared. Companions in domestic life, the Victorian couples were also partners in careers. Shared work bound these Victorian spouses more than affection alone could do.

Conclusion

Catharine Spooner Tait's life held its false glories, like life in episcopal palaces that fell short of luxuries and long on their need for repairs. The social glories of moving in elite circles and the more personally defined glories of gratifying work and married life were hers as well. She also had staggering grief and a nearly unthinkable test of faith in the deaths of five little girls. Her faith carried her through, and, in the end, her husband judged that she had had a life of "congenial society, ample means, and abundant occupation."[1] Fortunately, most of the women of this study did not have to face quite the measure of pain that Catharine Tait did. But in other respects their lives were similar in that there were plentiful resources and a world of work to do. The Paget women and their circle show us that Victorian upper-middle-class women's lives were rich in experience of life and death and socially and intellectually productive.

Their childhood education could be rich and varied, and as adults they continued to learn. They read philosophy, history, and literature in their own language or in others. They might develop musical or artistic skills, depending on their own bent and on their parents' resources, connections, and preferences. And most of them led vigorous physical lives, walking, climbing, riding, and in youth at least, playing tennis, cricket, and hockey. Financial means and family environment alike allowed these gentlewomen a large degree of psychological and social independence.

But all was not a Victorian rose garden. They had to deal with money, servants, illness, and death—depressed and ailing husbands, children suffering, sometimes dying, from diphtheria, scarlatina, and tuberculosis. When gentlewomen went outside the home to find useful work to do, they confronted the fruits of poverty in the poor neighborhoods and slums of every Victorian town and city—vice, prostitution, pornography, wife-abuse, drunkenness. Victorian female delicacy was never a product of ignorance but of a Victorian ideal of what should be said in public, a matter of reticence in speech rather than repression of mind.

And these Victorian ladies did find useful work. Their charitable activities brought them into working contact with children and adults, and they dealt with their physical, intellectual, and social needs as well as their souls. As teachers with pupils of all ages and both sexes, they made a special contribution to the literacy and order of their society, the magnitude of which has not yet been measured. Beyond their nearly universal philanthropy and educational work, some followed individual interests that made them painters, and entomologists, and photographers. And they wrote. Many of them published useful books and pamphlets related to their work in charity or teaching or art. Some wrote poetry; others wrote fiction. The abundance of their writing on a range of subjects, from art to science, suggests that authorship was a standard of female behavior in their social rank—that writing and publishing were norms of gentlewomen's lives, not merely tolerable but positively expected.

Marriage did not end an upper-middle-class woman's participation in the life of her society. Indeed, marriage often opened new doors. As a married woman, she was a partner in the family's profession. She shared decision making and the work of professional socializing with students, colleagues, and clients. Victorian gentlewomen also acted as secretaries, research assistants, editors, accountants, and coauthors. They took on administrative tasks of all sorts. Partnership was the order of the day, as Victorian husbands and wives together did historical or zoological research, wrote books, managed the clergy and led the laity of a diocese, and in other respects shared their lives. This was the family economy of the upper-middle class.

Nothing more clearly establishes that the norms of the Paget women and their circle were the norms of much of the Victorian upper-middle class than the creation of organizations that reflect significant numbers of gentlewomen at work: the Mothers' Union, the Archbishop's License for Women Teachers of Theology, the Women's Horticultural and Agricultural International Union, and the Association of Women Musicians. Large numbers of Victorian ladies were doing as the women of this study did, engaging in effective action in a wide variety of arenas.

Out of all this comes a different view of Victorian marriage. In the cases we have seen, the central fact of marriage was parity and partnership between husband and wife. The sharing of both affection and work made for marriages that often appear more fully companionate than those in our own time. For both, the spousal roles and the work they did together were paramount. Parenthood came second. Such a configuration of priorities helps to make sense out of the recollections of the Victorians' children, that their parents were affectionate but distant. A new generation would develop new ideals of motherhood, perhaps as a reaction to their parents' style of family life, perhaps in compensation for diminishing women's roles outside the family for most of the twentieth century.

The wider implications of these findings take us to matters of how we have viewed Victorian society and women's role in it. First, women's involvement in teaching, social work, and the shared family career make utter nonsense of the idea that women's sphere was the private sphere and only men operated in public.[2] No such distinction existed for these couples. The evidence provided here points to the fact that Victorian gentlemen were involved in the private spheres of home and family, and nearly every chapter of this study has shown gentlewomen functioning in public. Whether in the classroom, the settlement house, the pages of periodicals, the streets of industrial towns, or at the site of a colliery disaster, these women went about their work. As a corollary, the much-vaunted notion of separate spheres demands some radical revision. A gentlewoman's place was in the home—and the library and the lecture hall, the laboratory, and the mountains of southern Mexico. Either we must abandon the private/public dichotomy, or we must redefine more narrowly the meaning of the public sphere.[3]

Secondly, gentlewomen had careers. In the family economy of the upper-middle class they had their place in the world of work. Their experiences in youth prepared them for it. Single women with adequate resources might exercise a wide variety of choices of useful work to do. If a woman married, the matter of life-work was a central issue for the couple, as a couple, during the courtship. Marriage meant sharing a life, of course. It also meant sharing work, doing work together. Within any shared career there were tasks that were customarily his. Others were entirely open to negotiation, and others yet were her duty. Victorians understood that his appointment to a post was her appointment, too, and they carried out their lives with that understanding. Couples arranged, according to personal preference, how they would work out the particulars of the distribution of labor. But there was never any doubt that the labor belonged to them both.

Gentlewomen did not live without restrictions, of course. For most of the nineteenth century, they could not be physicians. They could not be clerics or lawyers. And, although they shared the work, their husbands always won the primary credit. Why, then, did women not find this life stifling, unsatisfactory, and unrewarding, the trigger of social rebellion? Well, some did, of course, and out of the frustrations and anger of the Florence Nightingales, the Josephine Butlers, and the Vera Brittains of Victorian and Edwardian England, new social possibilities began to emerge. But the women studied here did not foment a social revolution; they did not press for work of their own but were satisfied with sharing "his" career. They were, apparently, reasonably content with the social order as it was.

The reasons for such relative contentment were three: first, a woman of this rank nearly always had the option to do something on her own, outside the boundaries of the family profession and unconnected to any of his duties. Secondly, the inequalities between the sexes, and even between husband and wife, were part of the larger pattern of English society. Victorian England was profoundly hierarchical. Englishmen might abandon inequalities behind the closed doors of a London club or in the confines of the Oxbridge senior common room (and perhaps even within the family, when no guests were present). But in company and in public no two people were ever equal, and Victorian ladies as well as gentlemen accepted such inequality as a fact of the social order and a fact of family order as well. Inequality was not a function of incompetence, nor did it lead *ipso facto* to oppression.

Finally, women did not resent a shared career because of another fundamental fact of Victorian social structure (one much neglected in the dazzling light of the Industrial Revolution and the so-called rise of class society). Victorian society was not "modernizing" as rapidly as we have until now believed. England was still largely (and especially for professionals and others of the upper-middle class) a traditional, status society (to use Max Weber's term), in which the basis of social identity was birth, rather than work, merit, or achievement.[4] The centrality of birth rather than professional achievement as a source of identity may explain why the husband and father of the professional family shared, with equanimity, "his work" with his wife (or sisters or daughters). His primary sense of himself as a man and as a social being came from his birth, not from what he did.

This fundamental principle of social structure would also explain why she could share "his profession" without insisting on her formal membership in it. Her primary identity, too, came from her birth, not from achievement or publicly recognized merit. Of course, at the same time, everyone in their circle knew that the law or the Church or medicine was the family's profession, and they also knew what role she might play in that profession. But she did not lose status by not having her own exclusive work. Both men and women drew their standing from their birth. They were who they were born to be.

The place and role of gentlewomen may help explain the strength and stability of English social structure. Men and women of the upper-middle class alike benefited from their differential access to resources and power in the society. They benefited at the expense of the new middle class (and other ranks) below them, but because women shared in the empowerment and privileges of their rank, they had no cause to challenge the social or the sexual order. Indeed, their access to lecture halls, laboratories, libraries, scientific societies, bishops' palaces, or political soirées was based on their gentle birth. Status mattered more than gender.

This system of family careers did not always work. For some women the avenues of sharing were closed by the death of a father or the absence of a brother or husband with whom to share life and work. If, at the same time, family funds were limited, a woman's individual options were also limited. The ordinary doors to a useful life were closed.

Women's access to useful work was also cut off in those socially rising families in which the culture of shared work, involvement, action, and usefulness was alien. Social mobility into the ranks of the middle classes had taught these newly arrived families the ethos of achievement as the source of their identity. For the women of these families, a shared career was impossible, for a man's achieved identity required the clear delimiting of *his* achievement in *his* work. What he did not do, he paid to have done, in a market arrangement that left him the sole author of his professional achievement. For the newly arrived members of this class, women had to be excluded from what could not be a family profession. For the woman without a viable family career, without a man, without money, the world had to change. She needed a vote and a career of her own.[5]

Victorian prosperity and social mobility brought into the middle classes men who had, indeed, achieved. They were not the sons of gentlemen, and their birth mattered *less* than what they had done. Their social identity rested squarely on their accomplishments, and thus they could not weaken it by sharing their work. Some families, as they rose socially, managed to adopt the attitudes and mentality of the urban gentry into whose ranks they moved. Others did not, and the new ideals of individual achievement that they brought to urban professional life began to shape the way women as well as men thought about work and identity. Those new ideas would shake the foundations of the English social order in the twentieth century.

Notes

PREFACE

1. Pat Jalland, *Women, Marriage and Politics 1860–1914* (New York: Oxford University Press, 1986); Edna Healey, *Wives of Fame: Mary Livingstone, Jenny Marx, Emma Darwin* (London: Sidgwick and Jackson, 1986); Martha J. Vicinus, *Independent Women: Work and Community for Single Women, 1850–1920* (Chicago: University of Chicago Press, 1985); Deborah Gorham, *The Victorian Girl and the Feminine Ideal* (Bloomington: Indiana University Press, 1983); Esther Shkolnik, *Leading Ladies: A Study of Eight Late Victorian and Edwardian Political Wives* [W. H. McNeill and Peter Stansky, eds., Modern European History Series] (New York: Garland, 1987).

2. For works that offer examples of the non-angelic Victorian woman see: Phyllis Rose, *Parallel Lives: Five Victorian Marriages* (New York: Knopf, 1983); Steven Mintz, *A Prison of Expectations: The Family in Victorian Culture* (New York: New York University Press, 1983); Lotte Hamburger and Joseph Hamburger, *Troubled Lives: John and Sarah Austin* (Toronto: University of Toronto Press, 1985). But these all treat their subjects as atypical or deviant. I first argued against the "angel" as a Victorian reality in: M. Jeanne Peterson, "No Angels in the House: The Victorian Myth and the Paget Women," *American Historical Review* 89:3 (June 1984): 677–708. The present book is built on that article but goes beyond to a much larger circle of people. Moreover this book moves away from the primarily negative argument of the article to present a new vision of Victorian gentlewomen. For a study of a different segment of the middle class, with very different conclusions, see: Leonore Davidoff and Catherine Hall, *Family Fortunes: Men and Women of the English Middle Class, 1780–1850* (Chicago: University of Chicago Press, 1987).

3. Notable works on Victorian English middle-class women that have appeared recently include Gail K. Malmgreen, ed., *Religion in the Lives of English Women, 1760–1930* (Bloomington: Indiana University Press, 1986); Vicinus, *Independent Women;* and Elaine Showalter, *The Female Malady: Women, Madness, and English Culture, 1830-1980* (New York: Pantheon, 1986). In *The Education of the Senses* and *The Tender Passion* [*The Bourgeois Experience: Victoria to Freud,* vols. 1 and 2] (New York: Oxford University Press, 1984, 1986), Peter Gay draws on much of the important research of the past two decades. His materials on Britain are limited, but his bibliographical essays are a mine of information on works about women in Europe and the United States.

Historians of the United States have long since begun to reconsider the place and character of American women. See, for example, Carl Degler, "What Ought to Be and What Was: Women's Sexuality in the Nineteenth Century," *American Historical Review* 79 (1974): 1467–90, and Degler, *At Odds: Women and the Family in America from the Revolution to the Present* (New York: Oxford University Press, 1980); Erna Olafson Hellerstein *et al.,* eds., *Victorian Women: A Documentary Account of Women's Lives in Nineteenth-Century England, France, and the United States* (Stanford: Stanford University Press, 1981), pp. 123–33; and Linda Kerber, *Women of the Republic: Intellect and Ideology in Revolutionary America* (Chapel Hill: Institute of Early American History and Culture, by University of North Carolina Press, 1980). But it is a mistake to assume that Victorian England and nineteenth-century America were identical.

4. Daniel Goleman, *Vital Lies, Simple Truths: The Psychology of Self-Deception* (New York: Simon and Schuster, 1985), deals with this issue. Goleman summarized

some of his findings in "Insights into Self-Deception," *New York Times Magazine*, May 12, 1985, pp. 36–43.

5. Lady Frances Balfour, *Ne Obliviscaris: Dinna Forget*, 2 vols. (London: Hodder and Stoughton, n.d.), ii, 117, 118.

6. For examples of works that assume (to some degree or other) the homogeneity of the middle classes, see: J. A. Banks, *Prosperity and Parenthood: A Study of Family Planning among the Victorian Middle Classes* (London: Routledge and Kegan Paul, 1954) and Patricia Branca, *Silent Sisterhood: Middle-Class Women in the Victorian Home* (London: Croom Helm, 1975). Banks sees the upper-middle class as the model of the whole middle class, while Branca focuses on the lower-middle-class woman as the prototypical middle-class female. Banks offers a corrective of his earlier view in: *Victorian Values: Secularism and the Size of Families* (London: Routledge and Kegan Paul, 1981), pp. 44–45.

ONE. BACKGROUNDS AND PERSONALITIES

1. Catharine Paget, Diary, January 2, 1871, MS. Res. c. 285, Bodleian Library, Oxford (hereafter Bodl. Lib.).

2. W. J. Reader, *Professional Men: The Rise of the Professional Classes in Nineteenth-Century England* (London: Weidenfeld and Nicolson, 1966), pp. 209–11, describes some of the difficulties in establishing their numbers. Income data are available for few of the families studied here, but their style of life suggests incomes (in most cases) above £700 a year; see Banks, *Prosperity and Parenthood*, pp. 48–51, passim. On images of women see, e.g.: *Punch* 20 (Feb. 1851): 57; *Illustrated London News*, July 22, 1854.

3. Some were evangelical in the early years of the nineteenth century, but few were low church Anglicans after about 1850. A few began as dissenters but none remained so for life. The families studied here had more contact with the elites of English Jewry than with dissenters, agnostics, or "free thinkers." Matthew Arnold, John Stuart Mill, and the Bloomsbury group alike fell outside their sphere.

4. About methods and sources: my initial guides to the Paget women's circle were two short diaries kept by Paget daughters in London and Cambridge, together with a handful of their letters (C. Paget, Diary, 1870, 1871; Rose Paget, Diary, 1874–78, and miscellaneous letters in the possession of David P. Thomson, London [hereafter Thomson MSS.]). These records report, *inter alia*, who visited whom and offer the first clues to the family's extensive network. A second set of clues came from the biographies of fathers and husbands. These men's records are less directly reliable as evidence of *women's* associations, but I proceeded on the assumption (supported by the diaries) that the men's professional associates, together with birth and family ties of both men and women, give substantial clues to women's networks. The sources for this study include, in the first place, the surviving writings of women themselves: letters, diaries, memoirs, essays, and the like, together with their wills. A few women were the subjects of a memoir by husband, offspring, or friend. Often, however, the only information about these women was to be found in the lives-and-letters of the men in their lives. Although some are too brief, some sanitized, these sources are often surprisingly rich in information about women. Other sources include the writings of fathers and husbands, newspapers and periodicals of the time, and the institutional records of the Victorian age.

5. Humphry Paget, "The Pagets of Great Yarmouth. 1800 to 1850. From the memoirs of the Rev. Alfred Tolver Paget, Rector of Kirstead, Norfolk" (Mimeographed, September 1937, Lord Mayhew's MS.), pp. 3–6, 62–68, 94–106.

6. Sir James Paget, *Memoirs and Letters of Sir James Paget*, ed. Stephen Paget

(London: Longmans, Green, 1901), pp. 1–9; H. Paget, "Pagets of Great Yarmouth," pp. 5–7, 19–20, 84–87.

7. J. Paget, *Memoirs and Letters,* p. 7; Sarah Elizabeth Paget to George Paget, February 26, 1832, as quoted in: J. Paget, *Memoirs and Letters,* p. 31; Tom Tolver to Sarah Elizabeth Paget, August 18, 1816, as quoted in: H. Paget, "Pagets of Great Yarmouth," pp. 40–41.

8. J. Paget, *Memoirs and Letters,* pp. 8–9; H. Paget, "Pagets of Great Yarmouth," pp. 86–87.

9. H. Paget, "Pagets of Great Yarmouth," pp. 64, 68, 81.

10. Sir Julian Paget, Bt., "Paget Family Tree" (unpublished manuscript, 1963, Sir Julian Paget's MS.), p. 5; H. Paget, "Pagets of Great Yarmouth," pp. 103–19.

11. H. Paget, "Pagets of Great Yarmouth," pp. 119, 123; Stephen Paget, Memoir, Pt. 2, "Pinner," pp. 1–4 (Lord Mayhew's MS.); George Paget to James Paget, October 8, 1844, and April 3, 1845, Paget MSS. 158 and 159, Wellcome Institute for the History of Medicine, London (hereafter W.I.H.M.).

12. S. Paget, Memoir, Pt. 2, "Pinner," pp. 3–5.

13. S. Paget, Memoir, Pt. 2, "Pinner," pp. 7, 8.

14. H. Paget, "Pagets of Great Yarmouth," pp. 113–19, 123; S. Paget, Memoir, Pt. 2, "Pinner," pp. 6, 8–9, 13, 10, 12.

15. S. Paget, Memoir, Pt. 2, "Pinner," pp. 8–9, 10, 12.

16. S. Paget, Memoir, Pt. 2, "Pinner," pp. 11, 10–11, 13, 15.

17. J. Paget, "Family Tree," p. 6; H. Paget, "Pagets of Great Yarmouth," pp. 63, 84, 123; and personal communication from Oliver Paget.

18. J. Paget, *Memoirs and Letters,* pp. 1–10. On the "paraphernalia of gentility" see Banks, *Prosperity and Parenthood,* pp. 48–51.

19. S. Paget, Memoir, Pt. 3, "My Mother's People," p. 2.

20. Lydia North to James Paget, February 2, 1841, and July 31, 1840, Paget MSS. 120 and 107, W.I.H.M.

21. Lydia North to James Paget, February 11, 1837, and October 9, 1839, Paget MSS. 22 and 100, W.I.H.M.

22. Lydia North to James Paget, February 6, 1837, Paget MS. 19, W.I.H.M.

23. Samuel Paget to Rev. Henry North, October 24, 1836 [copy], and Lydia North to James Paget, July 11, 1839, Paget MSS. 10 and 90, W.I.H.M.

24. Lydia North to James Paget, August 4, 1838, and October 9, 1839, Paget MSS. 60 and 100, W.I.H.M. (emphasis hers). For another superficially obedient woman, see Mrs. Bradshaw in: Elizabeth Gaskell, *Ruth* [1853] (Oxford: Oxford University Press, 1985).

25. Lydia North to James Paget, October 9, 1839, and March 25, 1843, Paget MSS. 100 and 135, W.I.H.M.

26. S. Paget, Memoir, Pt. 1, "Harewood Place," p. 46. Zuzanna, Lady Shonfield, *The Precariously Privileged: A Professional Family in Victorian England* (Oxford: Oxford University Press, 1987), pp. 145, 180, hints at conflict between the Marshall and Paget women.

27. Will of Emma Clara Anne Fardell, proved 1874 (Principal Registry of the Family Division, Somerset House, London [hereafter Somerset House]). About Clara's husband, see: Royal College of Physicians of London, *Lives of the Fellows of the Royal College of Physicians, 1826–1925,* comp. G. H. Brown (London: Royal College of Physicians, 1955), s.v. George Edward Paget.

28. Clara Paget to Rose Paget, n.d.; same to same, n.d.; same to same, April 7, [n.y.], Thomson MSS.

29. Clara Paget to Rose Paget, [July 1880], and R. Paget, Diary, August 30, 1874, Thomson MSS.

30. Maud Paget to Rose Paget, n.d. [1880?], Thomson MS.

31. Clara Paget to Rose Paget, June 9, 1876, Thomson MS.

32. Clara Paget to Rose Paget, April 17 [n.y.], Thomson MS.

33. Henry Lewis Thompson, *Four Biographical Sermons on John Wesley and Others: With a Memoir,* ed. Catharine P. Thompson and S. Paget (London: Henry Frowde, 1905), pp. 16–17, 26, 46–47. The account in the *Dictionary of National Biography* (hereafter *D.N.B.*), s.v. James M. Thompson, differs slightly as to dates.

34. C. Paget, Diary, January 8, 1871.

35. Stephen Paget and J. M. C. Crum, *Francis Paget. Bishop of Oxford* (London: Macmillan, 1912), pp. 16, 26, 34–35, 20n.; C. Paget, Diary, January 17, 1871.

36. C. Paget, Diary, August 2, January 20, 1870; S. Paget, Memoir, Pt. 3, "My Mother's People," pp. 8–9.

37. *D.N.B.*, s.v. R. W. Church; S. Paget and J. Crum, *Francis Paget,* p. 74. Helen Bennett's father was a cleric and squire.

38. Elma K. Paget, *Henry Luke Paget: Portrait and Frame* (London: Longmans, 1939), pp. 159ff.

39. J. Paget, "Family Tree," pp. 10, 15; private communication from Mrs. J. M. Thompson; *Burke's Peerage, Baronetage and Knightage,* 105th ed. (London: Burke's Peerage, 1970) (hereafter *B.P.B.&K.*), s.v. "Paget of Harewood Place"; "Miss [Mary Maud] Paget" [obituary], *The Times* (London), June 25, 1945, p. 6. For a negative view of Mary see: Jeannette Marshall, Diary, June 24, December 7, 1885, December 13, 1886. My thanks to Lady Shonfield for these references.

40. "Dr. H. F. Gadow" [obituary], *The Times* (London), May 18, 1928, p. 21; J. Paget, "Family Tree," p. 8.

41. Maud Paget to Rose Paget, n.d., Thomson MSS.; will of Clara Maud Gadow, proved 1950, Somerset House.

42. R. Paget, Diary, February 12, June 16, September 27, October 3, November 8, 1874, July 20, 31, 1874, May 17, 1875, August 30, 1874; see also, August 17, 1874, April 17, 1875; Charles E. Paget to Rose Paget, May 29, 1878, Thomson MSS.; *Oxford English Dictionary,* s.v. "missish" and Robert J. Strutt, 4th Baron Rayleigh, *Life of J. J. Thomson* (Cambridge: Cambridge University Press, 1942).

43. "Mr. J. H. Batty" [obituary], *The Times* (London), January 23, 1946, p. 7; personal information from the late Mrs. James M. Thompson, Oxford; J. Paget, "Family Tree," p. 8; John Venn, comp., *Alumni Cantabrigienses: A Biographical List of All Known Students, Graduates and Holders of Office at the University of Cambridge, from the Earliest Times to 1900.* Part 2. *From 1752–1900,* 5 vols. (Cambridge: Cambridge University Press, 1940–54) (hereafter *Alum. Cantab.*), s.v. C. S. Roy.

44. Private information from Mr. David Thomson, London; J. Paget, "Family Tree," p. 8; M signifies date of marriage; dates of birth and death are unknown.

45. A. M. Hyamson, *David Salomons* (London: Methuen, 1939), genealogy following p. 132; also p. 107; Chaim Bermant, *The Cousinhood: The Anglo-Jewish Gentry* (London: Eyre and Spottiswoode, 1971); R. Paget, Diary, August 29, 14, 1877. The Pagets were acquainted with the Goldsmids, the Cohens, and other members of the Anglo-Jewish elite.

46. R. Paget, Diary, August 14, 1877; Stella Paget to Rose Paget, July 19, 1878, and December 16, 1878, Thomson MSS.

47. H. Paget, "Pagets of Great Yarmouth," p. 123; S. Paget, Memoir, Pt. 2, "Pinner," pp. 16–17, 19–20. Stephen thought her independence came with Kate's death in 1885; I suspect that money she inherited from a brother in 1874 was equally important.

48. J. Paget, *Memoirs and Letters,* p. 14; Sydney D. Kitson, *The Life of John Sell Cotman* (London: Faber and Faber, 1937), pp. 161–62, 171; Joseph Dalton Hooker,

A *Sketch of the Life and Labours of Sir William Jackson Hooker, K.H.* (Oxford: Clarendon Press, 1903), pp. xxii, xii, xxiv.

49. *Burke's Landed Gentry,* ed. Peter Townend, 18th ed., 3 vols. (London: Burke's Peerage, 1965) (hereafter *B.L.G.*), s.v. "Turner *formerly* of Mulbarton"; Gwenllian F. Palgrave, *Francis Turner Palgrave: His Journals and Memories of His Life* (London: Longmans, Green, 1899), pp. 12, 16. After Mary Turner's death, Dawson married widow Rosamund Matilda Duff.

50. F. T. Palgrave, Journal, March 2, 1882, as quoted in: Palgrave, *Palgrave,* p. 167.

51. S. Paget, Memoir, Pt. 3, "My Mother's People," p. 3.

52. *D.N.B.*, s.v. W. J. Hooker; Kitson, *Cotman,* p. 162.

53. *D.N.B.*, s.v. Joseph Dalton Hooker; *Alum. Cantab,*, s.v. J. D. Hooker; W. B. Turrill, *Joseph Dalton Hooker: Botanist, Explorer and Administrator* (London: T. Nelson, 1963), p. 163; Dorothy Middleton, *Victorian Lady Travellers* (London: Routledge and Kegan Paul, 1965), pp. 54–55; Marianne North, *A Vision of Eden: The Life and Work of Marianne North* (New York: Holt, Rinehart and Winston, 1980). The latter is an edition of: Marianne North, *Recollections of a Happy Life, being the Autobiography of Marianne North,* ed. Mrs. J. A. [Janet C.] Symonds, 2 vols., 2d ed. (London: Macmillan, 1892).

54. Eleanor Ormerod, *Eleanor Ormerod, LL.D., Economic Entomologist: Autobiography and Correspondence,* ed. Robert Wallace (London: John Murray, 1904), pp. 56, 57, 73, 225, 19; *B.L.G.*, s.v. "Ormerod"; *D.N.B.*, s.v. Eleanor Ormerod; and *The Times* (London), August 9, 1900, p. 5; will of Susan Mary Ormerod, proved 1896, Somerset House.

55. Ormerod, *Ormerod,* pp. 16, 91, 92–93, 88.

56. *B.L.G.*, s.v. "Busk *formerly* of Ford's Grove"; *D.N.B.*, s.v. George Busk, Rachel Harriette Busk, and William Pitt Byrne.

57. *B.L.G.*, s.v. "Sir John Lubbock"; C. Paget, Diary, January 9–11, and July 15ff., 1871; *B.P.B.&K.*, s.v. "Avebury"; H. G. Hutchinson, *Life of Sir John Lubbock, Lord Avebury,* 2 vols. (London: Macmillan, 1914). Lubbock became the first Lord Avebury in 1900 and Alice's father was the heir of the 2nd Baron Rivers, closer links to the aristocracy than most families in this study. This George Grove was not the Grove of *Macmillan's Magazine.*

58. Constance Lubbock Buxton to Sir John Lubbock, [April 1884], Add. MS. 49647, f. 38, British Library; *D.N.B.*, s.v. Sydney Buxton.

59. M. Jeanne Peterson, *The Medical Profession in Mid-Victorian London* (Berkeley: University of California Press, 1978), pp. 44–48.

60. J. B. Atlay, *Sir Henry Wentworth Acland, Bart., K.C.B., F.R.S., Regius Professor of Medicine in the University of Oxford: A Memoir* (London: Smith, Elder, 1903), pp. 9–11; Sir Thomas Dyke Acland, *Memoir and Letters,* ed. A. H. D. Acland (London: Privately printed, 1902), pp. 12, 121, 191, 177, 94–96, 140ff., 148.

61. *B.L.G.*, s.v. "Acland of Oxford"; *B.P.B.&K.*, s.v. "Sir Henry Wentworth Acland"; Atlay, *Acland,* pp. 106, 327; "Miss Sarah Acland" [obituary], *The Times* (London), December 4, 1930, p. 18.

62. James Paget to H. W. Acland, December 26, 1896, and same to Sarah Angelina Acland, November 12, 1890, and January 7, 1891, MS. Acland d. 64, f. 233, d. 162, f. 36 and 38, Bodl. Lib.; John Ruskin, *Diaries of John Ruskin,* sel. and ed. Joan Evans and J. H. Whitehouse, 3 vols. (Oxford: Clarendon Press, 1957–59), October 30, 1873, November 24, 1874; will of Sarah Angelina Acland, proved 1931, Somerset House.

63. *B.L.G.*, s.v. "Acland of Columb, Devon"; "Acland of Oxford"; and "Cropper of Ellergreen"; Eleanor Acland, *Goodbye for the Present. The Story of Two Child-*

hoods. Milly: 1878–88 & Ellen: 1913–24 (London: Hodder and Stoughton, 1935), pp. 19, 23, 196, 199; and George Trevelyan, "Introduction," in: ibid., p. 9.

64. C. Paget, Diary, e.g., January 2, 3, 4, 5, 6, 15, and July 14, 1871; *B.P.B.&K.*, s.v. "Sir William Withey Gull"; Ethel Romanes, *Life and Letters of George John Romanes* (London: Longmans, Green, 1896); *Who Was Who, 1916–28* (hereafter *W.-W.W.*), s.v. Ethel Romanes.

65. *D.N.B.*, s.v. G. M. Humphry and G. G. Stokes; *Burke's Landed Gentry of Ireland*, ed. L. G. Pine, 4th ed. (London: Burke's Peerage, 1958) (hereafter *B.L.-G.I.*), s.v. "Stokes *formerly* of Askive," and Miss [Margaret] Stokes to H. W. Acland, January 9, 1897, MS. Acland, d. 80, f. 135, Bodl. Lib.

66. C. Paget, Diary, January 25, 1871; *D.N.B.*, s.v. Sir Thomas Smith; Shonfield, *Precariously Privileged*, pp. 5, 7, 145, 180.

67. *W.W.W.*, *1897–1915*, s.v. William Thomson, Lord Kelvin; Harold I. Sharlin with Tiby Sharlin, *Lord Kelvin: The Dynamic Victorian* (University Park: Pennsylvania State University Press, 1979), pp. 3–4, 124–25.

68. Sir Charles Lyell, *Life, Letters and Journals of Sir Charles Lyell, Bart.*, ed. Mrs. Lyell, 2 vols. (London: John Murray, 1881); Grace Anne Milne M'Call Prestwich, *Life and Letters of Sir Joseph Prestwich, M.A., D.C.L., F.R.S., Formerly Professor of Geology in the University of Oxford* (Edinburgh: William Blackwood, 1899); *D.N.B.*, s.v. Lister, Huxley; *B.L.G.*, s.v. "Lawrence of Ealing Park"; R.C.P., *Lives*, s.v. Sir George Burrows and Alfred Willett.

69. *Alum. Cantab.*, s.v. Penrice; Kitson, *Cotman*, p. 290; Palgrave, *Palgrave*, pp. 12, 16; *B.L.G.*, s.v. "Turner *formerly* of Mulbarton."

70. J. Paget, *Memoirs and Letters*, pp. 88, 123; and S. Paget, Memoir, Pt. 3, "My Mother's People," pp. 4, 15–18.

71. Lydia North to James Paget, August 4, 1838, with a note from Sarah North, and Sarah North to James Paget, July 31, 1840, Paget MSS. 60 and 108, W.I.H.M.; S. Paget, Memoir, Pt. 3, "My Mother's People," pp. 3–5, 15–22.

72. S. Paget, Memoir, Pt. 3, "My Mother's People," pp. 13–15.

73. J. G. Lockhart, *Charles Lindley Viscount Halifax*, 2 vols. (London: Geoffrey Bles, Centenary Press, 1935), i, 217, 260–61, 105–107.

74. C. J. Bunyon, *Memoirs of Francis Thomas McDougall, 1817–1886, D.C.L., F.R.C.S., Sometime Bishop of Labuan and Sarawak and of Harriette, His Wife* (London: Longmans, Green, 1889), pp. 18, 19; Mary Bramston, *An Early Victorian Heroine: The Story of Harriette McDougall* (London: S.P.C.K., 1911).

75. Henrietta Barnett, *Canon Barnett, His Life, Work, and Friends*, 2 vols. (London: John Murray, 1918), i, 38, 123.

76. Barnett, *Barnett*, i, 35, 30.

77. Barnett, *Barnett*, i, 37–38. Her biography of her husband is a model of such bluntness.

78. William Benham, ed., *Catharine and Craufurd Tait, Wife and Son of Archibald Campbell, Archbishop of Canterbury: A Memoir* (New York: Macmillan, 1880), pp. 13, 21, 72, 52–53, 14.

79. G. K. A. Bell, *Randall Davidson: Archbishop of Canterbury*, 2 vols. (London: H. Milford, Oxford University Press, 1935), i, 69, 122–23.

80. Bell, *Davidson*, i, 43–44, 122, 37–41.

81. Bell, *Davidson*, i, 123, 69, 122, 171, 50, 713; Francis Paget to Bernard Paget, February 2, 1911, as quoted in: ibid., i, 713; [G. K. A. Bell], "Lady Davidson of Lambeth: An Appreciation," *The Times* (London), July 1, 1936, p. 18.

82. *D.N.B.*, s.v. Mandell Creighton; Louise Creighton, *Life and Letters of Mandell Creighton, D.D. Oxon. and Cam., Sometime Bishop of London*, 2 vols. (London: Longmans, Green, 1904), i, 1, 77n, 133, 139, 185, 188, 200, 381; *D.N.B.*, s.v. Edward White Benson, Margaret Benson; Arthur C. Benson, *Life and Letters*

of Maggie Benson (London: John Murray, 1918), pp. 19, 9, 24, 90–92; Mary Eleanor Benson, *Streets and Lanes of the City,* with a Brief Memoir by her Father [E. W. Benson] (London: Privately printed, 1891), pp. vii-xviii.

83. Gwendolyn Stephenson, *Edward Stuart Talbot, 1844–1934* (London: Society for the Propagation of Christian Knowledge, 1936), p. 3; J. G. Lockhart, *Cosmo Gordon Lang* (London: Hodder and Stoughton, 1949), pp. 88, 89; Herbert Hensley Henson, *Retrospect of an Unimportant Life,* 3 vols. (London: Oxford University Press, 1942), i, 67; *D.N.B.,* s.v. H. H. Henson. Mrs. Talbot was the only daughter of the first Lord Wharncliffe.

84. Olive Parker, *For the Family's Sake: A History of the Mothers' Union, 1876–1976* (Folkestone: Bailey Brothers and Swinfen, 1975), pp. 1–2, 4, 21; *W.W.W., 1897–1916,* s.v. G. H. Sumner; *D.N.B.,* s.v. James Fraser (1818–85).

85. Arthur Engel, *From Clergyman to Don: The Rise of the Academic Profession in Nineteenth-Century Oxford* (New York: Oxford University Press, 1983).

86. *D.N.B.,* s.v. E. H. Browne; G. W. Kitchin, *Edward Harold Browne, D.D., Lord Bishop of Winchester, and Prelate of the Most Noble Order of the Garter: A Memoir* (London: John Murray, 1895), pp. 61, 62, 66, 166; R. Paget, Diary, February 26–29, 1876, November 23, 1877.

87. *D.N.B.,* s.v. Charles Kingsley; Susan Chitty, *The Beast and the Monk: A Life of Charles Kingsley* (London: Hodder and Stoughton, 1974); R. Paget, Diary, e.g., May 31, 1874.

88. *D.N.B.,* s.v. George Kingsley and Mary Henrietta Kingsley; Katherine Frank, *A Voyager Out: The Life of Mary Kingsley* (Boston: Houghton Mifflin, 1986), pp. 39, 44, 18, 20, 27, 21, 43, 51; and Mary Henrietta Kingsley, *Travels in West Africa: Congo Francais, Corisco and Cameroons* [1897], 5th ed. (London: Virago, 1982). Also see: M. H. Kingsley, *West African Studies,* 2d ed. (London: Macmillan, 1901), and Middleton, *Victorian Lady Travellers,* pp. 149ff.

89. Arthur Fenton Hort, *Life and Letters of Fenton John Anthony Hort, D.D., D.C.L., LL.D., Sometime Hulsean Professor and Lady Margaret's Reader in Divinity in the University of Cambridge,* 2 vols. (London: Macmillan, 1896), ii, 172; Arthur Westcott, *Life and Letters of Brooke Foss Westcott, D.D., D.C.L., Sometime Bishop of Durham,* 2 vols. (London: Macmillan, 1903), i, 7; *D.N.B.,* s.v. B. F. Westcott.

90. *B.L.G.I.,* s.v. "Pilkington *formerly* of Tore"; *Alum. Cantab.,* s.v. George Phillips, Henry Lionel Pilkington, and Henry Mulock Pilkington; Emily Pilkington to Rose Paget, August 2, 1877; Charity Pilkington to same, December 10, 1877, Thomson MSS.; "Lady Reichel" [obituary], *The Times* (London), November 13, 1911, p. 11, and June 25, 1931, p. 16. A third daughter, Katharine (b. 1868), was too young to share the activities of her adolescent sisters and their friends in these years.

91. Felicia Mary F. Skene to H. W. Acland, May 16, 1898, MS. Acland d. 80, f. 84, Bodl. Lib.

92. *D.N.B.,* s.v. Edward Bouvier Pusey (1800–81), H. G. Liddell (1811–98). By special vote, college fellows were occasionally exempted from the rule against marriage.

93. *B.L.G.,* s.v. "Moberly"; *D.N.B.,* s.v. George Moberly; and *W.W.W., 1929–40* (London: 1941), s.v. Charlotte E. Moberly.

94. J. B. Harford and F. C. MacDonald, *Handley Carr Glynn Moule, Bishop of Durham: A Biography* (London: Hodder and Stoughton, 1922), pp. 5, 6, 72, 84, 86.

95. *D.N.B.,* s.v. George Grote.

96. Harriet L. Grote, *The Personal Life of George Grote,* 2d ed. (London: John Murray, 1873), pp. 4, 12–13.

97. H. Grote, Memoir, quoted in: Elizabeth, Lady Eastlake, *Mrs. Grote: A Sketch* (London: John Murray, 1880), pp. 27, 29, 31, 36; also pp. 6–7, 13.

98. Mary F. Smith, *Arthur Lionel Smith, Master of Balliol (1916–1924): A Biogra-*

phy and Some Reminiscences (London: John Murray, 1928), pp. 39, 92ff.; *D.N.B.*, s.v. George Grote, John Richard Green; ibid., s.v. A. L. Smith, Alice Sophie Stopford Green; J. R. Green, *Letters of J. R. Green*, ed. Leslie Stephen (London: Macmillan, 1902), pp. 1, 51.

99. Kitson, *Cotman*, p. 162; F. T. Palgrave, Journal, July 28, 1874, as quoted in: Palgrave, *Palgrave*, p. 138; ibid., pp. 1, 2; *D.N.B.*, s.v. Francis Palgrave. Palgrave began life as Francis Cohen but, on Dawson Turner's insistence, converted to Christianity and took Palgrave, his mother-in-law's maiden name, as his own.

100. *B.L.G.*, s.v. "Turner *formerly* of Mulbarton."

101. Lucy Cohen, *Arthur Cohen: A Memoir* (London: Privately printed, 1919), pp. 117, 118; *Alum. Cantab.*, s.v. H. Pollock; *D.N.B.*, s.v. Sir William Bovill and Malins; J. Foster, *Men-at-the-Bar* (London: Reeves and Turner, 1885), s.v. T. G. Fardell; "Sir T. G. Fardell" [obituary], *The Times* (London), March 13, 1917, p. 9; *W.W.W.*, *1916–28*, s.v. T. G. Fardell. Arthur Cohen was also a cousin of Stella Salomons Paget, Clara's daughter-in-law; see Hyamson, *Salomons*, genealogy facing p. 132, 135.

102. *D.N.B.*, s.v. F. T. Palgrave, John Lough, and George Grove.

103. For further comments on the "urban gentry," see: Peterson, "No Angels in the House," p. 692, and M. Jeanne Peterson, "Gentlemen and Medical Men: The Problem of Professional Recruitment," *Bulletin of the History of Medicine* 58:4 (1984): 457–73; see Banks, *Prosperity and Parenthood*, passim, on the economic and material parameters of rank. George Kitson Clark's "new gentry" (*The Making of Victorian England: Being the Ford Lectures Delivered before the University of Oxford* [London: Methuen, 1962], pp. 252ff.) is more distinctly rooted in landed society than the "new urban gentry" described here.

Two. Ladies Learning

1. George Gissing, *In the Year of Jubilee* [1893] (New York: Dover, 1982), pp. 13, 49, 48, 132, 133. Miss Lord was the best (although pathetic) version of this type; Mrs. Peachey and Fanny French exemplify the pretentious and ambitious daughters of the commercial classes in the same novel. For another sort see Polly Neefit in: Anthony Trollope, *Ralph The Heir* [1870–71] (New York: Dover Press, 1978).

2. For stereotypes of female education as trivial or mancatching in its orientation: Gorham, *Victorian Girl*, p. 165; Lee Holcombe, *Victorian Ladies at Work: Middle-Class Working Women in England and Wales, 1850–1914* (Newton Abbott: David and Charles, 1973), p. 24. Also see: Phyllis Stock, *Better than Rubies: A History of Women's Education* (New York: Putnam, 1978), pp. 127, 176; and Janet H. Murray, *Strong-Minded Women: And Other Lost Voices from Nineteenth-Century England* (New York: Pantheon, 1982), pp. 195, 197. A Victorian woman with a good education is labeled "exceptional."

3. M. F. Smith, *A. L. Smith*, pp. 46, 85.

4. F. J. A. Hort to Miss March Phillipps, October 28, 1871, as quoted in: Hort, *Hort*, ii, 149–50. The *Saturday Review* was known for its opposition to women's rights. For male views similar to Hort's, see: Palgrave, *Palgrave*, p. 130, and Shonfield, *Precariously Privileged*, p. 19.

5. J. Paget, *Memoirs and Letters*, p. 6; Lydia North to James Paget, July 16, 1839, Paget MS. 91, W.I.H.M.; C. Paget, Diary, e.g., February 2, 1870; S. Paget, Memoir, Pt. 1, "Harewood Place," pp. 14, 16–17, 32–37; M. F. Smith, *A. L. Smith*, pp. 43–45, 48; Shonfield, *Precariously Privileged*, pp. 15–16.

6. Kitson, *Cotman*, p. 161; M. F. Smith, *A. L. Smith*, p. 44; T. D. Acland *Memoir and Letters*, p. 95.

7. Ormerod, *Ormerod*, pp. 3–5, 78; S. Paget, Memoir, Pt. 1, "Harewood Place," p. 14.

8. C. Paget, Diary, 1870, passim; Lydia North to James Paget, July 16, 1839, Paget MS. 91, W.I.H.M.

9. Ormerod, *Ormerod*, p. 95; Shonfield, *Precariously Privileged*, pp. 15–17; Parker, *For the Family's Sake*, p. 2; M. F. Smith, *A. L. Smith*, pp. 43–45.

10. S. Paget and J. Crum, *Francis Paget*, p. 74; *D.N.B.*, s.v. Rachel Harriette Busk; Isaac W. North, *A Brief Memoir of the Rev. Henry North . . . Late Assistant Minister of Welbeck Chapel* (London: Hatchard, 1839), pp. 5–6, 33–34; Lydia North to James Paget, February 6, 1837, and [November 16, 1838], Paget MSS. 19, 64, W.I.H.M.; T. D. Acland, *Memoir and Letters*, pp. 147, 210. The record does not specify the children's gender. I assume he taught girls and boys, or the record would say "sons." For a detailed record of one girl's education, see: Anne (Grenville) Hadaway, School Report Book, 1861–65, Stowe MS. (ST. 356), Huntington Library, San Marino, CA. Despite the title I think this manuscript records a girl's education with a governess rather than in a school. Also see: Shonfield, *Precariously Privileged*, pp. 14, 19.

11. T. D. Acland, *Memoir and Letters*, p. 210; Hort, *Hort*, ii, 23–26; Harford and MacDonald, *Moule*, pp. 87, 88; Sir George Paget to Rose and Violet Paget, June 30, 1872; same to Rose Paget, July 7, 1872, May 17, 1874, July 21, 1876, Thomson MSS; [Beatrice Creighton] as quoted in: Creighton, *Creighton*, i, 259; also p. 257.

12. F. J. A. Hort to Ellen Hort, June 24, 1871, as quoted in: Hort, *Hort*, ii, 146, and ii, 210, 223–26, 279; see also, ii, 188, 219. Cf. a similar letter to Hort's son Frank, August 20, 1876, in: Hort, *Hort*, i, 214f. Also see: Frank, *Voyager Out*, p. 25.

13. Sir George Paget to Rose Paget, July 6, 1873, May 10, 1874, July 2, 1876, Thomson MSS.; Hort, *Hort*, ii, 227.

14. Sir George Paget to Rose Paget and Violet Paget, June 30, 1872, and to Rose Paget, July 5, July 3, 1878, Thomson MSS.

15. J. Paget, *Memoirs and Letters*, p. 8; Kitson, *Cotman*, pp. 155, 158, 161; Ormerod, *Ormerod*, p. 16 (also p. 18 re their mother); *D.N.B.*, s.v. Mary St. L. Harrison.

16. Frederick Corder, *History of the Royal Academy of Music from 1822 to 1922*, (London: Corder, 1922), pp. 44–45; C. Paget, Diary, February 24, 28, June 2, July 13, 1870; R. Paget, Diary, October 16, 1875, April 29; October 13, 1876, and Maud Paget to Rose Paget, July 31, [1878], Thomson MSS. Two of Rose's teachers were Cambridge men: *Alum. Cantab.*, s.v. Richard Dacre Hodgson (*post* Archer-Hind) and William Amps; re Wiles see: Algernon Graves, comp., *A Dictionary of Artists Who Have Exhibited Works in the Principal London Exhibitions from 1760–1893*, 3d ed. [1901] (Bath: Kingsmead Reprints, 1970), s.v. William Wiles. Boguet and Steinhilper were probably emigrés, native speakers of French and German respectively.

17. S. Paget and J. Crum, *Francis Paget*, p. 75. For other examples see: George Gissing, *The Whirlpool* [1897] (London: Hogarth Press, 1984); and Harriet Martineau, *Autobiography, with memorials by M. W. Chapman*, 3d ed., 3 vols. (London: Smith Elder, 1877), i, 43, 53–55.

18. E. Acland, *Goodbye*, p. 151; Hort, *Hort*, ii, 216, 232; M. F. Smith, *A. L. Smith*, pp. 50, 60, 68.

19. Lydia North to James Paget, December 24, 1836, Paget MS. 12, W.I.H.M.; J. Paget, *Memoirs and Letters*, p. 255; *D.N.B.*, s.v. J. R. Macculloch; Grote, *Grote*, p. 28; the surgeon Thomas Hodgkin gave lectures on physiology which women attended.

20. C. Paget, Diary, March 25, April 5, June 3, 1870; R. Paget, Diary, e.g., May

5, October 12, 1875; Sir Martin Conway, as quoted in: E. V. Lucas, *The Colvins and Their Friends* (New York: Scribners, 1928), pp. 27–28; Hastings Rashdall, November 18, 1877, as quoted in: P. E. Matheson, *Life of Hastings Rashdall* (London: Milford, 1928), p. 32.

21. Elizabeth King, ed., *Lord Kelvin's Early Home* (London: Macmillan, 1909), pp. 99–100, as quoted in: Sharlin, *Kelvin*, p. 6; Emily Pilkington to Rose Paget, December 10, 1877, and R. Paget, Diary, October 16, 1875, Thomson MSS.

22. R. Paget, Diary, May 5, October 12, November 2, 1875, February 2, 1876, November 23, 27, 30, 1877; Lucas, *The Colvins*, pp. 27–29; and Rayleigh, *Thomson*, p. 34. Also see the account by Rose's son George P. Thomson, *J. J. Thomson and the Cavendish Laboratory in His Times* (London: Nelson, 1964), pp. 77, 92; *W.-W.W.*, *1929–40*, s.v. Charlotte Anne Elizabeth Moberly; *D.N.B.*, s.v. Eleanor Mildred Sidgwick and Mary St. L. (Kingsley) Harrison; S. Paget, Memoir, Pt. 5, "October 5, 1925," p. 17; James Paget to H. W. Acland, June 3, 1885, MS. Acland, d. 64, f. 210. For other upper-middle-class women at the Slade, see: Germaine Greer, *The Obstacle Race: The Fortunes of Women Painters and Their Work* (New York: Farrar, Straus, and Giroux, 1979), pp. 52, 53, 63, 319.

23. S. Paget, Memoir, Pt. 1, "Harewood Place," p. 32. Publication data on all the women's readings discussed here are drawn from the British Museum (now Library) *Catalogue* (hereafter *B.M.Cat.*), unless otherwise noted.

24. Frank, *Voyager Out*, p. 24.

25. H. Paget, "Pagets of Great Yarmouth," p. 115; M. North, *Vision of Eden*, p. 18; Edward White Benson to Mrs. Benson, his mother, October [?], 1849, as quoted in A. C. Benson, *The Life of Edward White Benson, Sometime Archbishop of Canterbury*, 2 vols. (London: Macmillan, 1899), i, 82.

26. Ormerod, *Ormerod*, p. 53; Benham, *Catharine and Craufurd Tait*, p. 10; Sharlin, *Kelvin*, p. 4; Emily Pilkington to Rose Paget, December 10, 1877, Thomson MS.

27. C. Paget, Diary, 1870 and 1871, frontispiece and November 2, 1870; Maud Paget to Rose Paget, n.d., and n.d., Thomson MSS. It is not clear whether Catharine read Lanfrey in French or English; the English translation appeared between 1871 and 1875. *Vikram . . .* was adapted from the *Baital-Pachisi* by Richard Burton (London: Longmans, 1870). I have been unable to trace the authors of the apparently religious books Maud read.

28. W. Talbot as quoted in: Bell, *Davidson*, i, 585, presumably referring to Thomas Martin Lindsay's *A History of the Reformation*, 2 vols. (Edinburgh: Clark, 1906, 1907) and T. B. Macaulay's *History of England, from the Accession of James II*, 5 vols. (London: Longman, 1849–61), vol. 5 edited by Lady Trevelyan; Frank, *Voyager Out*, pp. 30–32, 15, 24, 35, 42, 28.

29. C. Paget, Diary, frontispiece, and May 12, 1870, April 15, 12, and February 9, 1871; Frank, *Voyager Out*, p. 28. Florence Wilford published twenty books between 1858 and 1895; *B.M.Cat.*, s.v.

30. Eastlake, *Grote*, pp. 41, 42, 44; Creighton, *Creighton*, i, 80.

31. Eastlake, *Grote*, pp. 44–45, 143–44.

32. M. F. Smith, *A. L. Smith*, pp. 85, 89; *Ancient Classics*, ed. W. Lucas Collins, 31 vols. (Edinburgh: Blackwood, 1870–1932); Butcher and Lang, *The Odyssey of Homer* (London: Macmillan, 1879) with new eds. in 1887, 1924, and 1930; William John Grayson, *Friends in Council: Reply to Professor Hodge, on the "State of the Country,"* (Charleston, S.C.: Evans and Cogswell, 1861); MacCarthy's *History* was reissued in 1881–85 in 7 vols., and again in 1882–97 in 5 vols., as well as in abridged versions.

33. Benham, *Catharine and Craufurd Tait*, p. 14; Barthold G. Niebuhr, *Collected Lectures on Roman History: Ancient History, Including the History of Greece, An-*

cient Ethnography, and Geography, 8 vols., trans. and ed. by Leonhard Schmitz (London: Walton and Maberly, 1852–53); F. J. A. Hort to Ellen Hort, December 20, 1880, as quoted in: Hort, *Hort,* ii, 282.

34. Hort, *Hort,* ii, 22, 28, 18, 27, 43, 298, 40–41. Anne Grenville studied spelling, reading, writing, grammar, "Sums," "Numeration," geography, history, "Tables," music, "Drilling," dancing, "Catechism," and hymns. She also received marks on "Deportment," "Order," and "Temper." Anne (Grenville) Hadaway, School Report Book, January 9, 1861, Stowe MS., Huntington Lib. In 1863 French and verse were added to her curriculum.

35. Hort, *Hort,* i, 7.

36. C. Paget, Diary, June 24, 1870, and unnumbered separate ledger at end of vol.; J. Paget, *Memoirs and Letters,* p. 7; C. Paget, Diary, June 30, July 15, October 8, November 23, 1870; and R. Paget, Diary, March 13, 1877, November 22, 1876. The Thomson MSS. are full of such references.

37. Gorham, *Victorian Girl,* p. 104; Holcombe, *Victorian Ladies at Work,* p. 24; Carol Dyehouse, *Girls Growing Up in Late Victorian and Edwardian England* (London: Routledge and Kegan Paul, 1981), p. 40; Greer, *Obstacle Race,* pp. 248–49; Kitson, *Cotman,* p. 157. See especially Greer's oddly contemptuous remarks about female artists: *Obstacle Race,* p. 249.

38. J. Paget, *Memoirs and Letters,* pp. 7–8; Kitson, *Cotman,* pp. 244, 162, 155; Palgrave, *Palgrave,* pp. 12, 13, 158, 161; *D.N.B.,* s.v. James Sowerby and William C. Edwards. Louisa Gurney, later Mrs. Samuel Hoare, also studied with Crome. Cotman's other female pupils included Lucy Brightwell, Katherine Cholmely, and Eliza Brightwen (Edmund Gosse's stepmother); Cotman had male pupils in Yarmouth, as well; Kitson, *Cotman,* pp. 89, 301, 243.

39. Hooker, *Hooker,* pp. lxxxvi and xxiv; Kitson, *Cotman,* p. 161; Bunyon, *McDougall,* p. 18; *D.N.B.,* s.v. Cornelius Varley and Henry Gastineau. For examples of Mary Turner's work see: A litho portrait (profile) of Fs. Douce, Esq., by Mary Turner, B.L. Add. MS. 43645, f. 6b, and Litho portrait of the Rev. T. F. Dibdin, 1821, B.L. Eg. 2974, f. vi. b.

40. Ormerod, *Ormerod,* pp. 18, 16; *D.N.B.,* s.v. Eleanor Ormerod, John Flaxman, A. V. C. Fielding, and William Henry Hunt; Hunt exhibited regularly at the Royal Academy and his patrons included the earl of Essex and the duke of Devonshire. Some of the Ormerod women's work is reproduced in Ormerod, *Ormerod,* passim.

41. M. North, *Vision of Eden,* pp. 18, 235; Middleton, *Victorian Lady Travellers,* p. 55; *Australian Dictionary of Biography,* 10 vols. (Melbourne: Melbourne University Press, 1966–86), vol. 4, s.v. R. H. Dowling; *D.N.B.,* s.v. George Busk. North also took lessons in etching on copper.

42. Algernon Graves, *The Royal Academy of Arts: A Complete Dictionary of Contributors and Their Work from Its Foundation in 1769 to 1904,* 8 vols. in 4 (East Ardsley: S. R. Publishers, 1905) [Bath: Kingsmead Reprint, 1970), 6:39; and S. Paget, Memoir, Pt. 2, "Pinner," p. 20; Christopher Wood, *Dictionary of Victorian Painters* (Woodbridge, Suffolk: Antique Collectors' Club, 1971), s.v. Elise Paget. Some of her paintings were donated to the Bodl. Lib. by the late Mrs. J. M. Thompson; I have been unable to ascertain the nature of Netty Huxley's art education.

43. Graves, *Dictionary of Artists,* s.v. Elise Paget and Henry Wiles; Clara Maud Paget to Rose Paget [a series of fifteen letters from Dresden, 1878–79]; same to same, December 8, 1878; R. Paget, Diary, January 21, 1875; Maud Paget to Rose Paget, July 13, 1880, August 31, and n.d., [1880], Thomson MSS.; Sir John Stainer to S. A. Acland, January 15, 1895, MS. Acland d. 160, f. 53, Bodl. Lib. On the importance of drawing from life for Victorian women's art education, see: Greer, *Obstacle Race,* p. 319.

44. *D.N.B.*, s.v. Mary St. L. Harrison and Sir Edward Poynter; James Paget to H. W. Acland, June 3, 1885, MS. Acland d. 64, f. 210, Bodl. Lib.; and S. Paget, Memoir, Pt. 5, "October 5th, 1925," p. 17. See chap. 5 below for the alternative direction Mary Harrison's efforts took.

45. "Miss Sarah Acland" [obituary], *The Times* (London), December 4, 1930, p. 18. Copies of her portraits may be seen in: MS. Don. d. 14, Bodl. Lib. Rosalind Sydie, "Women Painters in Britain: 1768–1848," *Atlantis* 5 (1979): 144–75.

46. Untitled MS. music book, n.d., in the possession of Dr. Oliver Paget, Vienna.

47. J. Paget, *Memoirs and Letters*, p. 255; Stanley Sadie, ed., *New Grove Dictionary of Music and Musicians*, 20 vols. (London: Macmillan, 1980), s.v. Crotch, Gaetano Crivelli, Anderson, Pinsuti, Leslie, and Sainton-Dolby; C. Paget, Diary, February 24, 28, March 10, 14, 21, April 4, June 2, July 13, 1870. Marianne North also studied voice with Sainton-Dolby; see *D.N.B.*, s.v. M. North.

48. S. Paget and J. Crum, *Francis Paget*, p. 75; Harford and MacDonald, *Moule*, p. 84; Palgrave, *Palgrave*, p. 78; Sadie, *New Grove Dictionary of Music*, s.v. Sir William Sterndale Bennett. Mary J. Smith (later Mrs. Benjamin Ward Richardson) also studied with Sterndale Bennett; Arthur S. MacNalty, *Biography of Sir Benjamin Ward Richardson* (London: Harvey and Blythe, 1950), pp. 13, 29; *Alum. Cantab.*, s.v. William Amps.

49. Charles Hallé, *The Autobiography of Charles Hallé: With Correspondence and Diaries*, ed. Michael Kennedy. (New York: Barnes and Noble, 1972), pp. 121–22; also p. 126, and Gissing, *Whirlpool*, chap. 4. The market for musicians' services may have been constricted enough to drive some to teaching even untalented amateurs. The willingness of women of modest talents to enroll in music classes resulted in wider support for art and artists in their communities.

50. J. Paget, *Memoirs and Letters*, p. 255; Corder, *Royal Academy of Music*, pp. 40, 45; Lydia North to James Paget, [November 16, 1838], December 24, 1836, and February 3, 1837, and James Paget to Lydia North, January 4, 1837, Paget MSS. 64, 12, 17, and 14, W.I.H.M.; S. Paget, Memoir, Pt. 5, "October 5th 1925," pp. 35–36, 41; and J. H. Newman to Lady Paget, January 9, 1879, MS. Autogr. b. 13, ff. 378–79, Bodl. Lib. The archives of the Royal Academy of Music from this period have not survived.

51. S. Paget, Memoir, Pt. 1, "Harewood Place," p. 33; C. Paget, Diary, February 24, 28, March 10, 14, 21, April 4, June 2, July 13, 1870; and R. Paget, Diary, January 11, 14, December 15, 18, 1874, February 8, 1875; Ormerod, *Ormerod*, p. 95; Bunyon, *McDougall*, p. 18.

52. S. Paget, Memoir, Pt. 1, "Harewood Place," pp. 22, 23. Sadie, *New Grove Dictionary of Music*, s.v. Janotha. Amateur musicianship among men has been thoroughly ignored in Victorian cultural history; among the Pagets, James played the flute, sons Luke and Stephen played the concertina, and all had some musical education (S. Paget, ibid., pp. 33–34). George Grote studied the violoncello (Grote, *Grote*, p. 11).

53. Hallé, *Autobiography*, pp. 116–17, 126; C. Paget, Diary, July 11, June 10, December 1, January 14, 1870 (also, February 19, March 24, June 6, 1870); Sadie, *New Grove Dictionary of Music*, xi, 188, s.v. "London," para. vi, 3 (also, "Bach Revival. England," i, 886). Catharine went to concerts two or three times a week. For a photograph of women playing in an orchestra, see: Gordon Winter, *A Country Camera, 1844–1914* (Harmondsworth: Penguin, 1973), p. 70.

54. Sadie, *New Grove Dictionary of Music*, s.v. "Society of Women Musicians"; also see: Valerie O'Brien, "Living British Women Composers: A Survey," in: *The Musical Woman: An International Perspective, 1983*, ed. J. L. Zaimont (Westport, Conn.: Greenwood Press, 1984), p. 209.

55. S. Paget, Memoir, Pt. 2, "Pinner," pp. 10–11; Palgrave, *Palgrave*, pp. 13–16,

35; Lydia North to James Paget, February 6, [1837], Paget MS. 19, W.I.H.M.

56. Sharlin, *Kelvin*, p. 9; Harford and MacDonald, *Moule*, pp. 84–85, 333.

57. R. Paget, Diary, January 21, 1875, February 14, April 19, 1876; Sir John Stainer to S. A. Acland, January 15, 1895, MS. Acland d. 160, f. 53, Bodl. Lib.; Francis Paget to Catharine Paget, August 2, 1874, as quoted in: S. Paget and J. Crum, *Francis Paget*, p. 35; and C. Paget, Diary, November 28, July 12, January 11 and 31, 1870; S. Paget, Memoir, Pt. 1, "Harewood Place," p. 46. Frank was referring to J. A. W. Neander, *Allgemeine Geschichte der christlichen Religion und Kirche*, 6 vols. (Hamburg, 1825–52).

58. S. Paget and J. Crum, *Francis Paget*, pp. 75, 84; Frank, *Voyager Out*, pp. 36, 23, 24, 31; Parker, *For the Family's Sake*, p. 2; T. D. Acland, *Memoir and Letters*, p. 379; "Miss Sarah Acland" [obituary], *The Times* (London), December 4, 1930, p. 18; Ormerod, *Ormerod*, p. 78.

59. Charlotte Mary Yonge, *The Daisy Chain: or, Aspirations: A Family Chronicle* [1856] (London: Macmillan, 1876), p. 20; Grote, *Grote*, p. 6; Palgrave, *Palgrave*, pp. 3, 14–16, for clues that Elizabeth Turner Palgrave knew Latin and Greek; T. D. Acland, *Memoir and Letters*, pp. 5, 12; E. W. Benson to Mrs. Benson [his mother], October ?, 1849, as quoted in: Benson, *Edward White Benson*, i, 82; Clara Paget to Rose Paget, April 22, [1878?], Thomson Papers; S. Paget, Memoir, Pt. 1, "Harewood Place," p. 14; W. G. Rutherford to [Mary] Paget, November 1, 1893, MS. Autogr. b. 13, f. 209 Bodl. Lib.; and Sir Alfred Milner to Miss [Mary] Paget, June 30, 1896, MS. Autogr. b. 14, f. 229, Bodl. Lib. Also see: Martineau, *Autobiography*, i, 43, re her Latin studies. For other clues to Latin learning see: Ethel Romanes to William Ewart Gladstone, June 15, 1894, B.L. Add. MS. 44518, f. 233.

60. Rose Paget, Diary, October 16, 1875; *D.N.B.*, s.v. Henry W. Cookson; Emily Pilkington to Rose Paget, July 5, 1880; *D.N.B.*, s.v. Alice S. S. Green; Francis Paget to Catharine Paget, n.d., and same to same, n.d., as quoted in: S. Paget and J. Crum, *Francis Paget*, pp. 18–19, 26; and Maud Paget to Rose Paget, n.d. [1878–79], Thomson MSS.; C. Paget, Diary, January 8, 1870. For other examples of girls' classical language study, see: Emily Shirreff, *Intellectual Education and Its Influence on the Character and Happiness of Women* (London: J. W. Parker, 1858), pp. 65ff.; Gorham, *Victorian Girl*, pp. 26, 130; and Helen Heinemann, *Restless Angels: The Friendship of Six Victorian Women: Frances Wright, Camilla Wright, Harriet Garnett, Frances Garnett, Julia Garnett Pertz, Frances Trollope* (Athens, Ohio: Ohio University Press, 1983), pp. 3, 10.

61. T. D. Acland, *Memoir and Letters*, p. 379; Eliot, *Middlemarch*, chap. 7; Frank, *Voyager Out*, pp. 24, 45.

62. Maud Paget to Rose Paget, July 13, 1880; R. Paget, Diary, March 23, 1877, Thomson MS.; Shonfield, *Precariously Privileged*, p. 16; Maud Paget to Rose Paget, June 23, June 22, 1880, Thomson MSS.; Frank, *Voyager Out*, pp. 15, 24, 28, 35, 42.

63. Ormerod, *Ormerod*, p. 17. Women naturalists were not unheard of; see: D. E. Allen, "The Women Members of the Botanical Society of London, 1836–1856," *British Journal for the History of Science* 13 (1980): 240–54. Allen finds women's involvement in the BSL "joltingly at variance with . . . stereotypes" of women but then maintains that the stereotypes are otherwise "broadly true" except at "the margins," presumably where the BSL might be found (p. 241).

64. Roy MacLeod and Russell Moseley, "Fathers and Daughters: Reflections on Women, Science and Victorian Cambridge," *History of Education* 8:4 (1979): 321–33, found that over 400 women (or about 18 percent of all women examinees) passed the honors examinations in science in the period 1881 to 1916 (p. 325). About 54 percent of those who passed the Natural Sciences Tripos went into school teaching; another 25 percent went into university teaching or medicine. Over 60 percent

of the successful examinees never married. These women were exceptional—a tiny portion of one late Victorian generation. Also see: Rita McWilliams-Tullberg, *Women at Cambridge: A Men's University—Though of a Mixed Type* (London: Gollancz, 1975).

65. Rayleigh, *Thomson*, pp. 34, 275; and J. J. Thomson to Rose Paget, October 15, 1888, as quoted in Thomson, *Thomson*, p. 77; Ethel Sidgwick, *Mrs. Henry Sidgwick: A Memoir* (London: Sidgwick and Jackson, 1938), pp. 9, 21, 71–72, 77. Rose Paget married Thomson in 1890. He later won the Nobel Prize in physics, as did their son George.

THREE. SEX, FRIENDSHIP, AND LOVE

1. J. Marshall, Diary, [1892], as quoted in: Shonfield, *Precariously Privileged,* p. 199.

2. Steven Marcus, *The Other Victorians: A Study of Sexuality and Pornography in Mid-Nineteenth-Century England* (New York: Basic Books, 1966), pp. 18, 21; William Acton, *Functions and Disorders of the Reproductive Organs in Childhood, Youth, Adult Age, and Advanced Life,* 3d American ed. from the 5th London ed. (Philadelphia: Lindsay and Blakiston, 1871), p. 62; Gay, *Education of the Senses* and *Tender Passion;* and Edward Shorter, *A History of Women's Bodies* (New York: Basic Books, 1982); Jane Lewis, *Women in England 1870–1950: Sexual Divisions and Social Change* (Bloomington: Indiana University Press, 1984), p. 118. For an alternative view of women's sexuality, see: M. Jeanne Peterson, "Dr. Acton's Enemy: Medicine, Sex, and Society in Victorian England," *Victorian Studies* 29:4 (1986): 569–90.

3. Harriet Grote, Autobiography, as quoted in: Eastlake, *Mrs. Grote,* pp. 29–30; also pp. 30, 31; David Rubinstein, *Before the Suffragettes: Women's Emancipation in the 1890s* (New York: St. Martin's Press, 1986), dates women's growing athleticism from the 1890s, but, as we can see, women were physically active much earlier. Susan P. Casteras, *The Substance or the Shadow: Images of Victorian Womanhood* (New Haven: Yale Center for British Art, 1982), has many illustrations of women's athletic activity, but she continues to see the Victorian woman as "placid" (pp. 40–41).

The athletic aristocratic woman has long been known to Victorian scholars, but less is known of the upper-middle-class woman's activities. Deborah Gorham found them vigorous; *Victorian Girl,* p. 94. But Paul Atkinson contrasted the "'sickly' Victorian lady of the . . . upper-middle classes" with new schemes for women's physical education in the 1880s; Paul Atkinson, "Fitness, Feminism and Schooling," in: S. Delamont and L. Duffin, eds., *The Nineteenth-Century Woman: Her Cultural and Physical World* (London: Croom Helm, 1978), pp. 92, 93.

4. Lydia North to James Paget, December 24, 1836, July 28, 1839, March 17, 1843, Paget MSS. 12, 94, 134, W.I.H.M.; Emily Pilkington to Rose Paget, March 11 and 14, 1879, and R. Paget, Diary, e.g., July 11, 27, August 9, 22, 1876; Maud Paget to Rose Paget, e.g., September 25, 1879, June 26, 1880, June 24, [1880], Thomson MSS.; C. Paget, Diary, July 11, August 4, September 23, 1870. Compare Vicinus, *Independent Women,* pp. 12, 14, 19–20.

5. C. Paget, Diary, August 12, 24, 25, 1870. The highest peak in the Snowdon group is Moel-y-Wyddfa, at 3,560 feet. The peak closest to their residence, Tal-y-fan, was 2,001 feet high.

6. Maud Paget to Rose Paget, June 16, 1880, Thomson MS.; A. C. Benson, *Maggie Benson,* pp. 89–90; E. W. Benson, "Memoir," in M. E. Benson, *Streets and Lanes,* p. 89; R. Paget, Diary, August 16, 1874.

7. Lydia North to James Paget, April 1, March 17, 1843, Paget MSS. 138, 134, W.I.H.M.; Prestwich, *Life and Letters,* pp. 221–22; Emily Pilkington to Rose Paget,

August 2 and October 18, 1877, Thomson MSS.; "Miss F. M. Skene" [obituary], *The Times* (London), October 10, 1899, p. 4; A. C. Benson, *Maggie Benson*, p. 81; R. Paget, Diary, July 19, July 4, 1877. Jehu, a king of Israel, was known for the fury of his chariot-driving. By "Minshi," Isaac presumably meant Nimshi, Jehu's grandfather. For illustrations of women driving carriages, see: Winter, *Country Camera*, p. 112, and *Punch*, September 29, 1877, p. 142, and August 31, 1878, p. 94.

8. C. Paget, Diary, August 26, 1870; R. Paget, Diary, August 27, 1877.

9. C. Paget, Diary, September 12 and 15, 1870 (emphasis hers); E. W. Benson, "Memoir," in: M. E. Benson, *Streets and Lanes*, p. ix. For a photograph of girls playing cricket, see: Winter *Country Camera*, p. 71.

10. C. Paget, Diary, January 29 and February 12, 1870; M. F. Smith, *A. L. Smith*, p. 98. For pictures of women skating and playing hockey, see: *Punch*, 1850, pp. 54. 231.

11. Mary Maud Paget to James Paget, July 19, 1899, MS. Eng. lett. c. 496, f. 77b, Mary Maud Paget, Diary of Travel, 1899, Bodl. Lib.; "Miss Margaret Benson. A Versatile Writer and Artist" [obituary], *The Times* (London), May 15, 1916, p. 4. Miss DuCane was probably the daughter of Sir Edmund DuCane (1830–1903), prison reformer and army officer; *D.N.B.*, s.v.

12. Hans Gadow, *In Northern Spain* (London: A and C Black, 1897), pp. viii, 12, 223, 16, 73, 75; and Hans Gadow, *Through Southern Mexico: Being an Account of the Travels of a Naturalist* (London: Witherby, 1908). It is impossible to know how much horseback riding and walking Maud did on these trips, but I would guess it was hundreds of miles.

13. Gadow, *Mexico*, pp. v, 63, 21, 24, 65, 61, 67. See map of travels facing p. 1.

14. Ibid., pp. 489, 492–94.

15. Ibid., pp. 494–95, 497, 499, 493.

16. Middleton, *Victorian Lady Travellers*, p. 153. Middleton also reports on another Victorian woman, Isabella Bird, not a member of this circle, who traveled eight hundred miles on horseback in North America. For a popular account of women travelers, see: Mary Russell, *The Blessings of a Good Thick Skirt: Women Travellers and Their World* (London: Collins, 1986).

17. Benham, *Catharine and Craufurd Tait*, p. 21; C. Paget, Diary, July 14 and August 17, November 18 and 22, August 30 (Mrs. Gull), 1870; R. Paget, Diary, July 3 and 4, 1877; Bunyon, *McDougall*, pp. 330, 328, 332; Huxley, *Huxley*, i, 127.

18. Banks, *Prosperity and Parenthood*, p. 5; J. Paget, "Family Tree," p. 6; Bell, *Davidson*, p. 82; *B.L.G.*, s.v. "Moberly"; *D.N.B.*, s.v. Sydney Buxton; S. Paget and J. Crum, *Francis Paget*, p. 167; Hutchinson, *John Lubbock*, i, 165–66.

19. George E. Paget to Rose Paget, May 25, 1880, Thomson MS. (emphasis his); Lydia North to James Paget, [May 14, 1839], August 2, 1839, [February 2, 1841], Paget MSS. 88, 95, 120, W.I.H.M.; and C. Paget, Diary, February 3, 23, March 24, April 21, May 3, 1870; also July 7 and August 4, 1870. Another man knew about women's menstrual periods; see the crosses, moons, and other notations that John Chapman entered in his diary to record the menstrual cycles of his wife and other women with whom he was intimate; Gordon S. Haight, *George Eliot & John Chapman, with Chapman's Diaries* (New Haven: Yale University Press, 1940), pp. 131, 131n, 183, 194, 227, 235, 242, 250.

20. J. Paget, *Memoirs and Letters*, pp. 145–46; Ormerod, *Ormerod*, pp. 77, 84, and 325.

21. James Paget to Henry W. Acland, December 26, 1890, MS. Acland d. 64, f. 233, Bodl. Lib.; Barnett, *Barnett*, i, 67; "Miss Sarah Acland" [obituary], *The Times*, December 4, 1930, p. 18; Jalland, *Women, Marriage and Politics*, p. 261; Harford and MacDonald, *Moule*, p. 87; Hort, *Hort*, ii, 56.

22. Will of Elise Paget, proved 1889, Somerset House; S. Paget, Memoir, Pt. 2, "Pinner," p. 20.

23. A. C. Benson, *Maggie Benson*, pp. 8–10, 24, 398, 409–10.

24. Benham, *Catharine and Craufurd Tait*, p. 23. For other clues to Victorian children's knowledge of sex see: E. Acland, *Goodbye*, p. 145; Stephen Paget, *Adolescence* (London: Macmillan, 1917). Eleanor Acland thought her parents were too reticent about sex, and in her book she perpetuates (or perhaps helps generate) some of the stereotypes of Victorian prudery; see e.g., p. 143. They might have been reticent *with her* without being Victorian prudes.

25. M. F. Smith, *A. L. Smith*, p. 43. Mary was seven or eight at this point. Compare Lucy Bland, "Marriage Laid Bare: Middle–Class Women and Marital Sex, 1880s–1914," in Jane Lewis, ed., *Labour and Love*, pp. 124–25.

26. M. E. Benson, *Streets and Lanes*, p. 177; Bell, *Davidson*, i, 113–115; Elma K. Paget, *The Story of Bishop Patteson* [Children's Heroes Series, 13] (London: Jack, 1907), p. 26; [C. L. H.] "Retrospect and Reform," and Elma K. Paget, "Hints, Suggestions, and Experiments," in: E. K. Paget, ed., *New Methods in the Mothers' Meetings* (London: Longmans, Green, 1915), pp. 5, 16–17. Also see: Benham, *Catharine and Craufurd Tait*, p. 27.

27. Samuel Barnett to Henrietta Rowland, April 7, 1872, as quoted in: Barnett, *Barnett*, i, 40, 40n, and 123.

28. "Miss [Felicia] Skene" [obituary], *The Times* (London), October 10, 1899, p. 4; M. F. Smith, *A. L. Smith*, pp. 105–106. Ann R. Higginbotham, "The Unmarried Mother and her Child in Victorian London," Ph.D. diss., Indiana University, Bloomington, 1985, makes clear the rescue workers' sympathy and compassion for the unmarried mother, as well as their knowledge of sexual behavior.

29. Eliot, *Middlemarch*, chap. 3.

30. H. Paget, "Pagets of Great Yarmouth," pp. 6–7, 21; Sarah North to James Paget, February 6, 1837, Paget MS. 21, W.I.H.M. Also see: Lydia North (with a postscript by Sarah North) to James Paget, February 11, and April 6, 1837, Paget MSS. 22, 33; compare Hannah North's letter, H. North to J. Paget, February 6, 1837, Paget MS. 20, W.I.H.M.

31. J. R. Green to Louise von Glehn, March 6, 1871, as quoted in: Green, *Green*, pp. 373, 380; also pp. 67–68; S. Paget and J. Crum, *Francis Paget*, pp. 105–107, 112.   First names were not supplied; Miss Lightfoot was probably a relative of Joseph Barber Lightfoot, bishop of Durham, and Miss Lawrence was either Louisa Elizabeth or Mary Wilhelmina, one of the two surviving daughters of surgeon Sir William Lawrence and his wife, the former Louisa Senior. For more information on these see *D.N.B.*, s.v. J. B. Lightfoot; *B.P.B.&K.*, s.v. "Lawrence of Ealing Park"; will of Dame Clara Paget, proved 1899; will of Sarah Angelina Acland, proved 1931; will of Hannah Sarah Brightwen, proved 1882; Somerset House. Austen Leigh was a cleric.

32. F. M. Skene to H. W. Acland, November 29, 1897, February 11, 1898, March 16 [1898?], MS. Acland d. 89, ff. 161, 163, 165; same to same, February [?], and April 7, 1899, MS. Acland, d. 80, ff. 79 and 81; same to same, March 1 [189?], MS. Acland d. 174, f. 183, Bodl. Lib.

33. Eastlake, *Mrs. Grote*, pp. 48n, 94–95, 78; Ormerod, *Ormerod*, pp. 80, 81; *D.N.B.*, s.v. J. O. Westwood. Wallace used the term "mentor" about Westwood. In her forties and after, Mary Paget apparently acted as mentor and friend to several younger men; personal communication from Mrs. James M. Thompson; I have been unable to verify the details.

34. Harford and MacDonald, *Moule*, p. 316; Lord Houghton to F. T. Palgrave, December 13, [1863], as quoted in: Palgrave, *Palgrave*, p. 86; C. Paget, Diary, January 31, January 11, July 12, November 28, 1870; *A Calendar of the Correspondence*

of *Charles Darwin, 1821–1882*, ed. F. Burckhardt, S. Smith, and D. Kohn (New York: Garland, 1985), s.v. Henrietta Huxley; he had several other women friends: s.v. Fanny Biddulph, Sarah Haliburton, and Mary Butler.

35. "Miss [Sarah] Acland," [obituary], *The Times*, London, December 4, 1930, p. 18; J. Paget to H. W. Acland, January 14, 1882, MS. Acland d. 64, f. 190; J. Paget to S. A. Acland, May 12, 1887, August 31, 1894, February 1, 1892, January 12, 1898, MS. Acland d. 162, ff. 29, 49, 40, and 58, Bodl. Lib.

36. Ruskin, *Diaries*, ii, 764, 765, 769; iii, 824, 829, 848, 871, 1087. (The earliest entry about Angie was November 13, 1868, the latest November 12, 1884.) Catharine Paget, Diary, June 5, 1871; "Miss [Sarah] Acland" [obituary], *The Times*, London, December 4, 1930, p. 18; George Richmond to S. A. Acland, January 28, 1885, March 12, 1888, February 21, 1898, MS. Acland d. 160, ff. 35–38; W. H. Smith to S. A. Acland, November 6, 1890, MS. Acland d. 174, f. 234, Bodl. Lib.; see also ff. 201–34. John Ruskin, *The Brantwood Diary of John Ruskin*, ed. and annota. Helen Gill Viljoen (New Haven: Yale University Press, 1971), p. 559, says Angie was Ruskin's godchild, but I have found no evidence of this. The Ruskin editors variously (and incorrectly) identify Sarah Angelina Acland as "Angelina" or "Sarah Angeline."

37. Miss M. Stokes to H. W. Acland, January 21, 1878, May 23, 1880, MS. Acland d. 80, ff. 125, 129, Bodl. Lib.; Bramston, *Victorian Heroine*, p. 7.

38. Bell, *Davidson*, i, 584–85.

39. Corder, *Royal Academy of Music*, p. 49; S. Paget, Memoir, Pt. 1, "Harewood Place," p. 17; Lydia North to James Paget, February 2, 1841, Paget MS. 120, W.I.H.M. (emphasis hers).

40. Maud Paget to Rose Paget, n.d. [1878?], same to same, May 15 [1880]; same to same, February 7 [1879], Thomson MSS.; C. Paget, Diary, May 29, 1870.

41. M. F. Smith, *A. L. Smith*, p. 109. Cf. the impact of rescue work on W. E. Gladstone.

42. Kitchin, *Browne*, p. 63; Westcott, *Westcott*, i, 8; Lydia North to James Paget, December 30, 1836, October 9, 1839, Paget MSS. 13, 100, W.I.H.M.; Caroline Gull to S. A. Acland, December 26, [1887?], MS. Acland d. 143, f. 147, Bodl. Lib.

43. Lydia North to James Paget, February 3, 1837 and James Paget to Lydia North, March 11, 1837, Paget MSS. 17 and 28, W.I.H.M. See also: Hort, *Hort*, i, 353–54; Ellen K. Rothman, *Hands and Hearts: A History of Courtship in America* (New York: Basic Books, 1984).

44. James Paget to Lydia North, February 5, 1837, Paget MS. 16, W.I.H.M.

45. James Paget to Lydia North, May 23, 1839, March 25, 1843; Lydia North to James Paget, April 1, 1843; James Paget to Lydia North, July 20, 1838, Paget MSS. 89, 136, 57, W.I.H.M. Bland, "Marriage Laid Bare," deals with the sexual views of radicals, feminists, and career women in the late nineteenth century.

46. C. Paget, Diary, May 15 and June 21, 1871. Presumably this was A. B. Donaldson; see *W.W.W., 1951–60*, s.v. his son Leonard Andrew Boyd Donaldson.

47. Charles Kingsley to Frances Grenfell, October [?] and October 24, 1843, as quoted in: Chitty, *The Beast and the Monk*, p. 82. Also see: Jalland, *Women, Marriage and Politics*, pp. 105, 106, 110, 116, 120, 221.

48. Chitty, *The Beast and the Monk*, p. 17; Frank, *Voyager Out*, p. 7, shares this view.

49. For another illustration of the linking of sexuality and sacrament see: Richard L. Nettleship to H. Scott Holland, July 29 and September 4, 1868, as quoted in: S. Paget, ed., *Henry Scott Holland* (London: John Murray, 1921) pp. 26–28.

50. See, for example, Anthony Trollope, *Kept in the Dark* [1882] (New York: Dover, 1978), which deals entirely with broken engagements and the resultant suffering; *Punch*, August 19, 1871, p. 67.

51. Sarah E. Paget to Samuel Paget, n.d. [1815?], as quoted in: H. Paget, "Pagets of Great Yarmouth," pp. 37, 38.

52. Bunyon, *McDougall*, p. 53; Betty Askwith, *Two Victorian Families* (London: Chatto and Windus, 1971), p. 128.

53. S. Paget, Memoir, Pt. 1, "Harewood Place," pp. 28–29, 15, 31; and James Paget to Lydia Paget, July 6, 1857, Paget MS. 182, W.I.H.M. Stephen also tickled his aunt Sarah's foot. See also: Jalland, *Women, Marriage and Politics*, pp. 120–21, 129.

54. Lawrence Stone, *The Family, Sex and Marriage in England, 1500–1800*, abr. ed. (New York: Harper and Row, 1979), pp. 422, 423; Mintz, *Prison of Expectations*, pp. 126, 128–29, 198–99.

55. H. Paget, "Pagets of Great Yarmouth," pp. 22–23.

56. S. Paget, Memoir, Pt. 3, "My Mother's People," pp. 8–10.

57. S. Paget, Memoir, Pt. 3, "My Mother's People," pp. 13–14, 5–7; Sharlin, *Kelvin*, p. 4. Many of these marriages may have "worked" for the parties involved, however unpleasant they may have seemed from the outside. Sometimes needs or neuroses, when matched, made for a solid (if not always beautiful) marriage.

58. R. Paget, Diary, April 7, 14, October 9, 1874; April 1, 5, October 1, 1875; March 31, September 30, 1876; March 23, September 21, 1877; June 10, 1875, May 23, June 11, 1877; July 28, August 19, 1875; August 9, 24, 1876, July 1, 12, 1877; September 21, 23, 1875; and Clara Paget to Rose Paget, April 17 [n.y.], Thomson MS. No correspondence between Clara and George survives.

59. Clara Paget to Rose Paget, September 7, [n.y.], and June 9, 1876, Thomson MSS.

60. Samuel Paget to Sarah E. Paget, May 11, 1836, Paget MS. 9, W.I.H.M.; Sarah E. Paget to Samuel Paget, n.d. [1815?], as quoted in: H. Paget, "Pagets of Great Yarmouth," pp. 37–38; S. Paget, Memoir, Pt. 5, "October 5th, 1925," p. 19. Also see: Dina Copelman, "'A New Comradeship between Men and Women': Family, Marriage and London's Women Teachers, 1870–1914," in: Jane Lewis, ed., *Labour and Love*, pp. 175–93.

61. S. Paget, Memoir, Pt. 3, "My Mother's People," p. 2; James Paget to Lydia Paget, December 5, 1855, and July 19, 1863, Paget MSS. 190 and 195, W.I.H.M. See Bunyon, *McDougall*, p. 285, for similar expressions of feelings.

62. James Paget to Lydia Paget, December 5, 1855, Paget MS. 190, W.I.H.M.

63. Palgrave, *Palgrave*, pp. 79, 103, 221ff.; will of William Jackson Hooker, proved 1865, Somerset House.

64. James Paget to Lydia North, February 18, 1837, Paget MS. 23, W.I.H.M.; Hort, *Hort*, i, 353–54.

65. T. Huxley to [Ethel] Romanes, November 1, 1892, as quoted in: Romanes, *Romanes*, p. 287; Westcott, *Westcott*, i, 33, 94, 138, 394, 395–96, 431–32, 435–36.

66. Harford and MacDonald, *Moule*, p. 86; Westcott, *Westcott*, i, 8; G. G. Stokes to Mary Robinson, June 13, 1854, as quoted in: George Gabriel Stokes, *Memoir and Scientific Correspondence of the Late Sir George Gabriel Stokes*, 2 vols., arr. J. Larmor (Cambridge: Cambridge University Press, 1907), i, 71.

67. Bunyon, *McDougall*, pp. 51, 343; Ethel Romanes to W. E. Gladstone, June 15, 1894, B.L. Add. MS. 44518, f. 241.

68. M. F. Smith, *A. L. Smith*, p. 72; Rev. James M. Hussey, *Home* (London: H. L. Barrett, n.d.), pp. 29–32, implies that the worst fate that can befall a family is the destruction of the marriage; the second worst sorrow is the death of children. The author was vicar of a North Brixton parish and Hon. canon of Rochester. Victorian mourning customs also point to the primacy of the wife-husband relationship. Mourning for a husband or wife lasted two years or longer; mourning

for a dead parent or child lasted one year; Sybil Wolfram, *In-Laws and Out-laws: Kinship and Marriage in England* (New York: St. Martin's Press, 1987), pp. 54–55.

FOUR. OTHER FACTS OF FAMILY LIFE

1. Harriette McDougall to [her brother?], June 11, 1854, as quoted in: Bunyon, *McDougall,* p. 96.

2. Peter Cominos, "Late Victorian Sexual Respectability and the Social System," *International Review of Social History* 8 (1963): 18–48, 216–50; and Peter Cominos, "Innocent Femina Sensualis in Unconscious Conflict," in: M. J. Vicinus, ed., *Suffer and Be Still: Women in the Victorian Age* (Bloomington: Indiana University Press, 1972), pp. 155–72.

3. Jonathan Gathorne-Hardy, *The Unnatural History of the Nanny* (New York: Dial Press, 1973); Stanley Weintraub, *Victoria: An Intimate Biography* (New York: Dutton, 1987), pp. 150, 224; Mintz, *Prison of Expectations,* pp. 51, 59, 118; Lewis, *Women in England,* p. 129.

4. Lydia North to James Paget, April 15, 1843, Paget MS. 141, W.I.H.M.; M. F. Smith, *A. L. Smith,* p. 44 (name omitted in the original). Lydia's relative indifference to small children seems to have been no special disadvantage to her own six sons and daughters; they had strong sibling relationships and family feeling; S. Paget, Memoir, Pt. 1, "Harewood Place," pp. 26–27.

5. J. Paget, "Family Tree," pp. 5, 10, 8; *B.L.G.,* s.v. "Turner *formerly* of Mulbarton," and "Acland of Oxford." I am discussing here only given names; the use of the mother's maiden name as a second name may have been an attempt to link the offspring (usually a son) to a maternal network of useful connections.

6. H. McDougall to [her brother?], June 11, 1854, as quoted in: Bunyon, *McDougall,* p. 96; H. Paget, "Pagets of Great Yarmouth," pp. 50–51; Benham, *Catharine and Craufurd Tait,* p. 212.

7. Clara Paget to Rose Paget, June 9, 1876, and Clara Paget to Rose and Maud Paget, April 22, [1874?], Thomson MSS.

8. R. Paget, Diary, August 25, December 29, 1877; Edmund Paget to Rose Paget, December 3, 1878, Stella Paget to Rose Paget, January 4, 1879, Thomson MSS.

9. R. Paget, Diary, August 19, December 23, 1875, January 12, 13, February 14, March 31, May 5, 1876, January 31, 1877, January 23, 1878; S. Paget, Memoir, Pt. 2, "Pinner," pp. 2, 14; Louisa Howard to Rose Paget, May 23, 1879, Charles Paget to Rose Paget, November 19, 1878, Thomson MS.; Joan Jacobs Brumberg, *Fasting Girls: The Emergence of Anorexia Nervosa as a Modern Disease* (Cambridge, Mass.: Harvard University Press, 1988); J. R. Reynolds, "Hysteria," in: Reynolds, ed., *A System of Medicine,* 3 vols. (Philadelphia: Lea, 1879–80), i, 631 [orig. pub. London: Macmillan, 1866–79].

10. Clara's actions may have been sound from a modern medical point of view: she removed her daughter from the necessity of daily contact with her mother and their troubled relationship. But this does not excuse Clara's apparently callous behavior. Clara's own mother may have treated her badly, too; see: will of Emma Clara Anne Fardell, proved 1874, Somerset House, for hints of tension between them.

11. *D.N.B.,* s.v. A. L. Smith; David Williams, *Genesis and Exodus: A Portrait of the Benson Family* (London: Hamish Hamilton, 1979), pp. 47, 56–57; also see: A. C. Benson, *Maggie Benson,* pp. 12–13.

12. E. Acland, *Goodbye,* pp. 31–32, 74, 196. Eleanor's memoir of her daughters may be a harbinger of the new view of motherhood.

13. G. E. Paget to Rose Paget, July 4, 1880, and Clara Paget to Rose Paget, n.d., Thomson MSS.; Benham, *Catharine and Craufurd Tait*, p. 178.

14. Lydia Paget to James Paget, December 5, 1855, Paget MS. 190, W.I.H.M.; Kitchin, *Browne*, pp. 74–75. The most virulent form of scarlet fever disappeared after about 1870. The available evidence does not allow for a diagnosis of Alice's ailment.

15. Stone, *Family, Sex and Marriage*, p. 423–24.

16. *B.L.G.*, s.v. "Turner *formerly* of Mulbarton"; Francis T. Palgrave, Journal [July 1870], as quoted in: Palgrave, *Palgrave*, pp. 132–33; Bramston, *Victorian Heroine*, p. 20; *B.P.B.&K.*, s.v. Sir William Gull; and S. Paget, Memoir, Pt. 5, "October 5th, 1925," p. 18. The Horts lost one child; Hort, *Hort*, ii, 9, 188.

17. H. Paget, "Pagets of Great Yarmouth," p. 20, and J. Paget, "Family Tree," p. 5; *B.L.G.*, s.v. "Turner *formerly* of Mulbarton." After the deaths of three Samuels, no other children were given that name. In the end Sam and Betsey had seventeen children in twenty-five years; of these, eleven died as infants or young adults and six survived to middle or old age.

18. Hort, *Hort*, i, 9, 7; George G. Stokes to Mary Robinson, February 7, 1857, as quoted in: Stokes, *Memoir and Scientific Correspondence*, i, 60; R. Paget, Diary, January 24, 1876.

19. Thompson, *Four Biographical Sermons*, p. 26. See also: Westcott, *Westcott*, i, 300n, re the death of their little girl Grace.

20. Kitchin, *Browne*, p. 75; Bunyon, *McDougall*, pp. 16, 43, 51, 54, 55; H. McDougall to C. J. Bunyon, February 6, 1850, as quoted in: ibid., p. 55. McDougall, himself a physician, found there was nothing he could do to help his children.

21. T. D. Acland, *Memoir and Letters*, p. 144.

22. Benham, *Catharine and Craufurd Tait*, pp. 152, 158. The children's names were: Catharine Anna (Catty), b. March 15, 1846; Mary Susan (May), b. June 20, 1847; Craufurd, b. June 22, 1849; Charlotte (Chatty), b. September 7, 1850; Frances Alice Marion, b. June 29, 1852; Susan Elizabeth Campbell, b. August 1, 1854; and the baby, Lucy Sydney Murray, b. February 11, 1856.

23. Benham, *Catharine and Craufurd Tait*, pp. 174, 175–76, 177.

24. Ibid., pp. 178, 179.

25. Ibid., pp. 179, 180; the date was March 6, 1856.

26. Ibid., pp. 182, 190, 194; the date was March 11, 1856.

27. Ibid., pp. 196, 197.

28. Ibid., pp. 198, 201–202, 203, 206, 207, 208.

29. Ibid., pp. 211, 212, 215. Presumably the doctors thought the disease would be milder because of its having "spent itself" on the other children.

30. Ibid., pp. 215, 216, 218.

31. Ibid., pp. 220, 230, 221–22, 225, 236–37.

32. Ibid., pp. 235, 237, 242.

33. Ibid., pp. 242. The infant was protected because of natural immunity. The Taits went on to have two more children.

34. Bunyon, *McDougall*, p. 94; Kitchin, *Browne*, pp. 74–75; *D.N.B.*, s.v. Sydney Buxton; H. Paget, "The Pagets of Great Yarmouth," p. 54.

35. Benham, *Catharine and Craufurd Tait*, pp. 96–97, 100–102, 108; *D.N.B.*, s.v. A. C. Tait; *B.L.G.*, s.v. "Moberly"; and Henry L. Thompson, *Henry George Liddell* (New York: Holt, 1899), p. 257. It is not clear what Craufurd Tait died of; it was some chronic disease, most probably an infection or a cancer. Leukemia and tuberculosis are also possible diagnoses, but the record is not full enough to allow for any certainty.

36. Shorter, *History of Women's Bodies*; Peter Stearns, *Be a Man! Males in Modern Society* (New York: Holmes and Meier, 1979), pp. 50–54.

37. Hort, *Hort,* i, 92; Kitchin, *Browne,* p. 85; F. Kingsley to [G.?] Macmillan, August 19, 1852, B.L. Add. MS. 54912, f. 2; Thompson, *Four Biographical Sermons,* pp. 20, 26n; Bunyon, *McDougall,* p. 273; and E. A. Ormerod to G. W. Ormerod, February 21, 1884, MS. Eng. lett. d. 220, f. 142, Bodl. Lib.

38. J. Paget, *Memoirs and Letters,* pp. 79, 244; Bunyon, *McDougall,* p. 332; M. North, *Vision of Eden,* p. 14. Paget (p. 190) also had pneumonia six times between 1851 and 1870.

39. Bell, *Davidson,* p. 24; Westcott, *Westcott,* i, 63, 93. Davidson also suffered from ulcers when he was bishop of Rochester.

40. Kitchin, *Browne,* p. 85, 148, 501; Hort, *Hort,* i, 92, 244, 377, 378; Green, *Green,* pp. 8, 393; J. R. Green to Alice Stopford, April 4 and 5, 1877, as quoted in: ibid., pp. 456, 457. Some Victorian doctors called this sort of breakdown or enfeeblement in men "Hypogastria." See J. Paget, "Sexual Hypochondriasis," in: James Paget, *Selected Essays and Addresses,* ed. Stephen Paget (London: Longmans, Green, 1902) pp. 34ff.; and Reynolds, "Hysteria," in: Reynolds, *System of Medicine,* i, 631.

41. Atlay, *Acland,* pp. 22–23, 25, 27, 29–30, 45, 46, 43–44, 71–73, 79. For clues to James Paget's depressive personality see: James Paget to Lydia North, July 19, 1863, July 29, 1867, Paget MSS. 195, 196, W.I.H.M.; *D.N.B.,* s.v. E. W. Benson, H. C. G. Moule. There is little evidence of psychosis among the families studied here; Charles Paget and Mr. Bagnall seem to have suffered serious mental disorder.

42. Gissing, *Whirlpool,* chap. 6; Showalter, *Female Malady,* passim.

43. C. Paget, Diary, February 6, 8, 1871; J. Paget, *Memoirs and Letters,* pp. 244–45.

44. C. Paget, Diary, February 21, 10, 14, 1871.

45. C. Paget, Diary, February 9, April 25, 1871.

46. C. Paget, Diary, February 10, 16, March 8, 1871.

47. C. Paget, Diary, February 11, 12, March 11, 12, 17, 1871.

48. C. Paget, Diary, March 23, 24, 1871.

49. C. Paget, Diary, March 14, 21, 25, 1871.

50. See, for example, M. Jeanne Peterson, "The Victorian Governess: Status Incongruence in Family and Society," *Victorian Studies* 14 (1970): 9–10.

51. Yonge, *The Daisy Chain,* p. 25; S. Paget, Memoir, Pt. 2, "Pinner," pp. 1–2; E. K. Paget, *Henry Luke Paget,* p. 39.

52. Lydia North to James Paget, [November 16, 1838], Paget MS. 64, W.I.H.M.; S. Paget, Memoir, Pt. 3, "My Mother's People," p. 2.

53. C. Paget, Diary, March 28, 1870, and unnumbered ledger section (emphasis hers); Ormerod, *Ormerod,* p. 84. For more on Catharine's earnings, see her diary, unnumbered ledger section, December 1870. I believe Vicinus goes too far in placing *earning* at the heart of single women's activism; she is closer to the mark with her recognition of the value of work; *Independent Women,* pp. 6, 14.

54. Lydia North to James Paget [November 16, 1838], Paget MS. 64, W.I.H.M.; I. North, *A Brief Memoir,* p. 34; and S. Paget, Memoir, Pt. 3, "My Mother's People," p. 8. Only much later did Lydia's son and daughter-in-law raise doubts about Rev. North's attitude: S. Paget, Memoir, Pt. 3, "My Mother's People," pp. 1–2, and E. K. Paget *Henry Luke Paget,* p. 39 (perhaps illustrating how the Victorians' children might have created myths about their parents).

55. Lydia North to James Paget, [November 16, 1838], [November 17, 1838?], and October 9, 1839, Paget MSS. 64, 65, and 100, W.I.H.M.; S. Paget, Memoir, Pt. 3, "My Mother's People," p. 19; C. Paget, Diary, October 31, November 7, December 23, 1870.

56. Ormerod, *Ormerod,* p. 84; Mary Kingsley to Miss [Emily Maud] Bowdler-

Sharpe, January 3, 1896, and February 2, 1897, B.L. Add. MSS. 42181, ff. 74, 75; H. W. Winston to Miss Bowdler–Sharpe, October 2, 1905, B.L. Add. MS. 42181, f. 76. Later Miss Bowdler-Sharpe was employed at the British Museum.

57. C. Paget, Diary, 1871, unpaginated ledger section at end of volume; wills of: George Ormerod, proved 1873, Arthur Stanley Ormerod, proved 1884, and Marianne North, proved, 1890, Somerset House; Eleanor Ormerod to G. W. Ormerod, March 7, 1884, MS. Eng. lett. d. 220, f. 149, Bodl. Lib. Both Ormerod women left sizable estates: Eleanor's £51,921, and Georgiana's £34,621. All inheritance sums are rounded off to the nearest whole pound.

58. Settlement on the marriage of James J. Morier and Harriet Grenville, 1820, STG Personal Box 21 (3), Huntington Library, San Marino, CA. Women could not enter into contracts with husbands, but families circumvented the law by arranging the contract between the husband and the bride's father; Lee Holcombe, *Wives and Property: Reform of the Married Women's Property Law in Nineteenth-Century England* (Toronto: University of Toronto Press, 1983), pp. 159–60. See also: *Oxford English Dictionary,* s.v. "pin money." Jalland, *Women, Marriage and Politics,* pp. 58–72, discusses settlements among upper-class subjects.

59. Wills of: Archibald Campbell Tait, proved 1883; Sir William Withey Gull, proved 1890; and Sir George Burrows, proved 1888.

60. J. Paget, *Memoirs and Letters,* p. 8.

61. James Paget to Lydia North, February 5, 1837, Paget MS. 18; also see: James Paget to Lydia North, July 23, 27, 1840, Lydia North to James Paget, March 17, 1843, Paget MSS. 104, 105, 134, W.I.H.M.

62. James Paget, [Visiting Lists], 1856–96, 41 vols., Paget MSS., Library, Royal College of Surgeons of England; S. Paget, Memoir, Pt. 1, "Harewood Place," p. 39.

63. C. Paget, Diary, January 19, February 22, 1870; and Maud Paget to Rose Paget, June 25, [n.y.], Thomson MS.; Benham, *Catharine and Craufurd Tait,* p. 72; M. F. Smith, *A. L. Smith,* pp. 133, 140.

64. Prerogative Court of Canterbury, *Calendar of the Grants of Probate and Letters of Administration in the Probate Registers of the High Court of Justice in England. . . , 1844* (London: P.C.C., 1844), Principal Registry of the Family Division, Somerset House, London (hereafter P.C.C., *Calendar*), s.v. Charles Paget; P.C.C., *Calendar, 1900,* s.v. Sir James Paget; wills of Charles Paget, proved 1844, James Paget, proved 1900, Somerset House; P.C.C., *Calendar, 1883,* s.v. A. C. Tait, and will of A. C. Tait, proved 1883; P.C.C., *Calendar, 1900,* s.v. Sir Henry Wentworth Acland, and will of H. W. Acland, proved 1900; wills of Edward Ormerod, proved 1873, Arthur S. Ormerod, proved 1884, George Ormerod, proved 1873, J. S. Henslow, proved 1861, Lord Halifax, proved 1896, and T. H. Huxley, proved 1895, Somerset House.

The annual printed *Calendar* (with manuscript additions) provides information on the value of a testator's personal estate, the names of executors, and the date of probate. For details of bequests one must consult the will itself. The Prerogative Court of Canterbury was the agency responsible for most wills and probate until 1971; now it is the Principal Probate Registry of the Family Division. Both wills and probate records are to be found in Somerset House, London.

65. P.C.C., *Calendar, 1929,* s.v. George Edmund Paget, and *1892,* s.v. Sir George Edward Paget, Kt.; wills of George Edmund Paget, proved 1929, Sir George Edward Paget, proved 1892, Sir John R. Paget, Bt., proved 1938; and Rose Paget, Diary, August 11, 14, 20, 29, 1877.

66. P.C.C., *Calendar, 1881,* s.v. Isaac W. North; *1885,* s.v. Jacob North; *1937,* s.v. Henry Luke Paget; *1862,* s.v. Alfred Paget; *1912,* s.v. Francis [Paget], bishop of Oxford; *1905,* s.v. Henry Lewis Thompson; and *1926,* s.v. Stephen Paget. For

other instances of women administrators of men's estates, with dates of probate and estate values, see: P.C.C., *Calendar, 1868,* s.v. Frederick Paget to Sarah Lucy Paget (under £800); *1927,* s.v. Charles Edward Paget to Ethel Paget (£8,627); *1927,* s.v. Alfred J. Meyrick Paget to Christobel Paget (£1,383); and *1928,* s.v. Hans Gadow to Clara Maud Gadow (£2,703). Women who named women executors include (with date of probate): Julia Byrne to her daughter and three others (1894), Georgiana Ormerod to her sister and two brothers (1896), Felicia Skene to her niece and great-nephew (1899), Sarah Angelina Acland to her niece and nephew (1931).

67. P.C.C., *Calendar, 1940,* s.v. Sir Joseph J. Thomson, Kt.; *1865,* s.v. William Jackson Hooker; *1866,* s.v. George Busk; *1896,* s.v. George M. Humphry; *1890,* s.v. Sir William Withey Gull; *1891,* s.v. Richard W. Church; *1896,* s.v. William Jacobson; and *1913,* s.v. Alfred Willett, Somerset House.

68. P.C.C., *Calendar, 1870* and *1882,* s.v. Thomas Brightwen and Hannah Sarah Brightwen, respectively; also wills of Hannah Sarah Brightwen, proved 1882, and Thomas Brightwen, proved 1870.

69. *The Times* (London), August 5, 1871, p. 5; also see: Lockhart, *Halifax,* i, 107, 217, ii, 28; Henry Parry Liddon to Mrs. [Emily] Meynell Ingram, November 24, 1889 [copy], Liddon MS., Pusey House, St. Cross College, Oxford. For extensive records of one Scottish widow's management of her large inheritance (an engine and boiler works), see: Financial Records of John Elder & Co., Engine and Boiler Works, 1869ff.; Mrs. Elder's memoir of her life after her husband's death in September 1869, p. 1; Mrs. Isabel Elder, Letterbooks; and *The Elder Park* (Glasgow: Privately printed, 1891); all of these in the Glasgow University Archives. My thanks to Derek Dow for bringing these materials to my attention.

70. *The Times* (London), August 5, 1871, p. 5; August 9, 1900, p. 5; and "Lady Davidson's Estate," ibid., August 13, 1936, p. 13; will of George Grote, proved 1871, Somerset House.

71. Wills of: Alfred Willett, proved 1913; Sir Henry Wentworth Acland, proved 1900 (valued at £56,606); Sarah Angelina Acland, proved 1931, Somerset House. See also: will of W. J. Hooker, proved 1865.

72. Wills of: Sir William Withey Gull, proved 1890; and A. C. Tait, proved 1883, Somerset House.

73. Wills of: William Jackson Hooker, proved 1865; William Jacobson, proved 1884; Alfred Willett, proved 1913; Hans Busk, proved 1862; George Grote, proved 1871; A. C. Tait, proved 1883; Sir George Edward Paget, proved 1892; Somerset House.

74. Wills of: Dawson Turner, proved 1858; Hans Busk, proved 1862, Somerset House. For more on trusts see Holcombe, *Wives and Property,* pp. 39–42.

75. Gerald Dworkin, "Estate Taxation in Great Britain," in: *Estate and Gift Taxation: A Comparative Study,* rev. and ed. George S. H. Wheatcroft [British Tax Review Guides, No. 3] (London: Sweet and Maxwell, 1965), pp. 55–82.

FIVE. GENTLEWOMEN AT WORK

1. Susan Siefert, *The Dilemma of the Talented Heroine: A Study in Nineteenth Century Fiction* [Monographs in Women's Studies, ed. Sherri Clarkson] (Montreal: Eden Press, 1977), p. 1; Lewis, *Women in England,* pp. 114, 118, 78.

2. Vicinus, *Independent Women,* pp. 6, 14, 11.

3. Hort, *Hort,* ii, 232.

4. Alfred Spender, as quoted in: Barnett, *Barnett,* i, 309.

5. T. D. Acland, *Memoir and Letters,* p. 379; Lydia North to James Paget, December 30, 1836, Paget MS. 13, W.I.H.M. District visiting brought to city neighborhoods the oversight and responsibility exercised by the country lady for rural tenants.

See: Jessica Gerard, "Lady Bountiful: Women of the Landed Classes and Rural Philanthropy," *Victorian Studies* 30:2 (1987): 183–210.

6. *D.N.B.*, s.v. Felicia Mary Skene; Benham, *Catharine and Craufurd Tait*, p. 10; there is no clue to the nature of the "difficulties." For a description of visiting see, e.g., Lucy Lyttelton Cameron, *The Life of Mrs. Cameron: Partly an Autobiography*, ed. by her son [Charles Cameron] (London: Darton, [1862], 2d ed., 1873), p. 11.

7. *Parochial Visiting & Provident Society* (Oxford: H. Cooke, 1835), Pusey MS., Pusey House, Oxford. Miss Pusey, who used this book, did not conform to the standards of the editors; she collected only part of the data the volume provided for. She recorded visits to thirty-two families. Prochaska found another example in the British Library; *Women and Philanthropy*, p. 112.

8. Yonge, *Daisy Chain*, pp. 24–25; Mary (Mrs. Humphry) Ward, *Marcella* [1894] (London: Virago, 1984) chap. 8.

9. Kitchin, *Browne*, pp. 121, 358. A richly detailed source on visiting is: Miss Bibby et al., with a letter from Mrs. Humphry Ward, *The Pudding Lady: A New Departure in Social Work* (London: Stead's, for the St. Pancras School for Mothers, [1912]). More research needs to be done on women's work as deaconesses and "mission women." (See hints in Kitchin, p. 359.) Vicinus, concerned with separate institutions for single women, focuses on "Sisterhoods and Deaconesses' Houses" in *Independent Women*, chap. 2.

10. C. Paget, Diary, e.g., February and June 1870, October 10, 11, 15, 1870; Prochaska, *Women and Philanthropy*, pp. 98–100, calls these "visiting societies" and thinks they were run by men. Louisa Twining was the most famous Victorian workhouse visitor.

11. *D.N.B.*, s.v. Felicia Mary Skene; Henry W. Acland, *Memoir on the Cholera at Oxford in the Year 1854* (London: Churchill, 1856); "Lady Davidson of Lambeth" [obituary], *The Times* (London), June 27, 1936, p. 16.

12. Ormerod, *Ormerod*, p. 31; Constance Mary Lubbock Buxton to Sir John Lubbock, March 23, 1883, B.L. Add. MS. 49646, f. 35.

13. E. K. Paget, *Henry Luke Paget*, p. 132; "Miss [Mary Maud] Paget," [obituary], *The Times* (London), June 25, 1945, p. 6; Barnett, *Barnett*, i, 185, 186; Harford and MacDonald, *Moule*, pp. 332–33. See also: Brian Harrison, "For Church, Queen and Family: The Girls' Friendly Society, 1874–1920," *Past and Present* 61 (1973): 107–38.

14. S. Paget, Memoir, Pt. 2, "Pinner," p. 14; Catharine Thompson to [?], October [?], 1913, Bodl. Lib.; Violet Paget Roy to George Paget Thomson, May 2, 1898, Thomson MS.; Barnett, *Barnett*, i, 123. Many Oxford colleges established missions or settlement houses in the East End. See: Standish Meacham, *Toynbee Hall and Social Reform* (New Haven: Yale University Press, 1987).

15. *D.N.B.*, s.v. Felicia Mary Skene; Harford and MacDonald, *Moule*, pp. 333, 225. For a detailed examination of women's rescue work with unwed mothers see: Higginbotham, "The Unmarried Mother."

16. Prochaska, *Women and Philanthropy*, pp. 146, 147, and 222; Martha Westwater, *The Wilson Sisters: A Biographical Study of Upper Middle-Class Victorian Life* (Athens, Ohio: Ohio University Press, 1984), pp. 186, 185; Vicinus, *Independent Women*, pp. 211–13. Vicinus is primarily concerned with the settlement house movement of the 1880s and after, with the organized and corporate agencies of women's service.

17. Lydia North to James Paget, December 30, 1836, Paget MS. 13, W.I.H.M. (emphasis mine).

18. C. Paget, Diary, March 15 and 17, 1870; Maud Paget to Rose Paget, [July 5, 1880], Thomson MS., London; M. F. Smith, *A. L. Smith*, pp. 71, 72.

19. Barnett, *Barnett*, i, 123.

20. M. F. Smith, *A. L. Smith*, pp. 105–106.

21. Barnett, *Barnett*, p. 123. Also see: M. E. Benson, *Streets and Lanes*, a memoir of the poor she knew; Melvin Richter, *The Politics of Conscience: T. H. Green and His Age* (Cambridge: Harvard University Press, 1954). Only Harriet Grote, of all the women studied here, openly opposed charity.

22. Holcombe, *Victorian Ladies at Work*, chaps. 2 and 3; Joyce Senders Pedersen, "Reform of Women's Secondary and Higher Education: Institutional Change and Social Values in Mid and Late Victorian England," *History of Education Quarterly* 19:1 (1979): 61–91; Pedersen, "Some Victorian Headmistresses: A Conservative Tradition of Social Reform," *Victorian Studies* 24:4 (1981): 463–88; McWilliams-Tullberg, *Women at Cambridge*.

23. Lydia North to James Paget [November 16, 1838], Paget MS. 64, W.I.H.M.; S. Paget, Memoir, Pt. 3, "My Mother's People," pp. 16–17; Sidgwick, *Mrs. Henry Sidgwick*, pp. 38ff.; *W.W.W.*, *1929–40*, s.v. Charlotte Anne Elizabeth Moberly. The most recent treatment of this part of women's educational history is Vicinus, *Independent Women*, chap. 4.

24. S. J. Curtis, *History of Education in Great Britain*, 7th ed. London: University Tutorial Press, 1967; H. C. Dent, *1870–1970: Century of Growth in English Education* (London: Longman, 1970); Asher Tropp, *The School Teachers: The Growth of the Teaching Profession in England and Wales from 1800 to the Present Day* (New York: Macmillan [1956]); Holcombe, *Victorian Ladies at Work*, chap. 3; E. G. West, *Education and the Industrial Revolution* (New York: Barnes and Noble, 1975); and H. J. Keisling, "Nineteenth-Century Education according to West—A Comment and Note," *Economic History Review* 36:3 (1983): 416–25. Vicinus, *Independent Women*, p. 11, seems to dismiss charity education, perhaps because it was unpaid work, and sees Sunday school teaching as an extension of domestic duties, not public work at all. A notable exception to this neglect of charity education is: Thomas W. Laqueur, *Religion and Respectability: Sunday Schools and Working Class Culture, 1780–1850* (New Haven: Yale University Press, 1976).

25. Prochaska, *Women and Philanthropy*, does not explore teaching; he alludes to women teaching "domestic skills to paupers" (p. 148; also p. 150); Ron Walton, *Women in Social Work* (London: Routledge and Kegan Paul, 1975).

26. See chapter 2 above for examples of mothers teaching their own children; Benham, *Catharine and Craufurd Tait*, p. 13. Also see: Sharlin, *Kelvin*, p. 4.

27. Laqueur, *Religion and Respectability*, p. xi; Marion Johnson, *Derbyshire Village Schools in the Nineteenth Century* (New York: Kelley, 1970), p. 77.

28. Harford and MacDonald, *Moule*, p. 6; Lydia North to James Paget, December 24, 1836, February 3 and 11, 1837, Paget MSS. 12, 17, and 22, W.I.H.M.; M. F. Smith, *A. L. Smith*, pp. 71–72.

29. Benham, *Catharine and Craufurd Tait*, pp. 10, 13; A. Twining to Mary Twining, November 20, 1843, B.L. Add. MS. 39932, f. 128 (emphasis hers); C. Paget, Diary, 1870, passim. The Burlington School records give no hint of the existence of volunteer teachers. The records show only two paid teachers who taught domestic subjects; Burlington School, Board of Governors Minute Book, 1870, et seq., Burlington Danes School Library MS. If the Burlington School records are at all typical, a wholesale reassessment of Victorian education may be necessary.

30. Bunyon, *McDougall*, p. 44; Bramston, *Victorian Heroine*, pp. 68, 95. Also see: *Church Quarterly Review*, 1890, p. 383. See M. F. Smith, *A. L. Smith*, pp. 98, 100, 111, 145, for another woman who cared little for teaching but felt the pressure to do it.

31. Barnett, *Barnett*, i, 32, 42, 102, 103, 116–17.

32. Sir William Rumbold, *Recollections of a Diplomatist*, ii, 176f., as quoted in: Lockhart, *Halifax*, i, 61. Also see: Barnett, *Barnett*, p. 43.

33. Jean Russell-Gebbett, *Henslow of Hitcham: Botanist, Educationalist and Clergyman* (Lavenham, Suffolk: Terence Dalton, 1977), p. 83; C. L. H., "Origins," in: E. K. Paget, *New Methods*, p. 1; Parker, *For the Family's Sake*, p. 8.

34. Barnett, *Barnett*, i, 100–102; E. K. Paget, *New Methods*, passim.

35. Richard W. Church, *Life and Letters of Dean Church*, ed. Mary C. Church (London: Macmillan, 1895), p. 165; Parker, *For the Family's Sake*, pp. 10–11; E. W. Benson, "Memoir," in: M. E. Benson, *Streets and Lanes*, p. ix. For women teaching gentlemen, see: Harford and MacDonald, *Moule*, p. 102, where women addressed men at Ridley Hall, Cambridge. Women also taught fiancés or husbands: Westcott, *Westcott*, i, 10; T. D. Acland, *Memoir and Letters*, pp. 241, 287, 349. Acland also took instruction from an unidentified "Miss F."

36. E. K. Paget, *The Woman's Part* (London: 1914) (not in the British Library); E. K. Paget, ed., *Studies and Discussions for the Women's Fellowship and Reformed Mothers' Meeting* (London: Longmans, 1918); and her *New Methods*. See: *B.M.Cat.*, s.v. Jane King, Mary Sumner. The average length of King's books was over 160 pages. Jane King may have been a relative of Edward King, bishop of Lincoln.

37. Bell, *Davidson*, i, 501. By 1935, 170 women had received the diploma, 115 of whom were teaching, some in England, some abroad (p. 501n).

38. West, *Education*; Keisling, "Nineteenth-Century Education."

39. Allen, "The Women Members of the Botanical Society of London," found that 6 to 10 percent of the members of the BSL were women, their mean age 42.7. Women who achieved some distinction in botany included Elizabeth Twining and Annie Lorraine Smith (a volunteer at the British Museum's Natural History Section from 1888 on). According to Allen, the Zoological Society of London admitted women in 1827, the Ornithological Society after 1880, the Geological Society in 1904, and the Linnean Society in 1919.

40. J. D. Hooker to Mary Kingsley, August 29, 1894, B.L. Add. MS. 41299, f. 184; Marianne North to A. R. Wallace, 23 April [1890], B.L. Add. MS. 46436, f. 224; Mary Kingsley to Miss E. M. Bowdler-Sharpe, January 3, 1896, B.L. Add. MS. 42181, f. 74. Both Kingsley and North had plants named for them. For women naturalists who were friends of Charles Darwin, see: *A Calendar of Darwin Correspondence*, s.v. Elizabeth Watts (editor and author of works on "gardening & country living") and Mary Anne Theresa Whitby ("Silk producer" and author of a book on silkworms).

41. Ormerod, *Ormerod*, pp. 53–54; *D.N.B.*, s.v. Charles Giles Bridle Daubeny.

42. Ormerod, *Ormerod*, p. 54; Eleanor Ormerod to G. W. Ormerod, March 7, 1884, MS. Eng. lett. d. 220, f. 149, Bodl. Lib.

43. *D.N.B.*, s.v. Westwood. Ormerod, *Ormerod*, p. 53, links the Ormerods to Daubeny of Oxford.

44. Ormerod, *Ormerod*, pp. 59ff., 65, 127, and unnumbered back sheet. Fitch may have been Sir Joshua Girling Fitch, inspector of schools (see *D.N.B.*, s.v.). I have found no clue to Preston's identity. Ormerod also published some papers on South African pests; Ormerod, *Ormerod*, unnumbered back sheet, and *D.N.B.*, s.v. Eleanor Ormerod.

45. Ormerod, *Ormerod*, pp. 79, 226, 65, 282; *D.N.B.*; Eleanor Ormerod to G. W. Ormerod, December 16, 1882, and May 17, 1883, MS. Eng. lett. d. 220, ff. 171, 173, Bodl. Lib. (emphasis hers). She won prizes for her entomological work. She also studied meteorology and was the first woman elected a fellow of the Meteorological Society.

46. Ormerod, *Ormerod*, pp. 83, 84.

47. Ibid., pp. 215, 227, 275ff., 279–81, 282n, 256n, 278, 224–25; also 279–80.

48. See the *B.M.Cat.*, London, III: s.v. Women's Farm and Garden Union, and s.v. Lady Warwick College, for publications of these organizations. Ladies founded the school; their apparent object was the training of poor women for farm management.

49. *W.W.W.*, *1929–40*, s.v. Mrs. Thomas Fisher; *D.N.B.*, s.v. Sir Charles Lyell; Rayleigh, *Thomson*, pp. 34, 275, 77; Cavendish Laboratory, *A History of the Cavendish Laboratory, 1871–1910* (London: Longmans, Green, 1910), pp. 324–34, 63, 65, 69, 70, 288, 289; Sidgwick, *Mrs. Henry Sidgwick*, pp. 9, 21, 71–72, 77, 103. Most of the other women workers were affiliated with one of the women's colleges. The Cavendish history may understate the number of women, for the list was generated retrospectively, by a mail questionnaire, and the women who married and changed their names and addresses may have been impossible to locate.

Lest anyone be tempted to trivialize Rose Paget's research on soap bubbles, it is worth noting that the famous physicist James Clerk-Maxwell also studied them (*Cavendish Lab.*, p. 281).

50. McLeod and Moseley, "Fathers and Daughters," Table 1, pp. 327, 321. Women also read mathematics in growing numbers in this period. Annie Scott Dill Maunder published two books about astronomy; see: *B.M.Cat.*, s.v. Annie Scott Dill Maunder.

51. Benham, *Catharine and Craufurd Tait*, pp. 50–51. Catherine Gladstone took responsibility for the orphaned boys.

52. Kitchin, *Browne*, pp. 471–72; Parker, *For the Family's Sake*, pp. 8–10, 12–18. Parker gives Sumner less credit for this work, attributing most initiative to men.

53. "Lady Davidson of Lambeth" [obituary], *The Times* (London), June 27, 1936, p. 16; and Benham, *Catharine Tait*, pp. 50–51; Harford and McDonald, *Moule*, pp. 225, 333; will of Eleanor Paget, proved 1933, Somerset House. The organization and administration of girls' schools and women's colleges also required these skills.

54. Anthony Huxley, Introduction to: North, *Vision of Eden*, pp. 26–27, 12–13.

55. Eleanor Ormerod to the Editor, *Natural Science*, August 32, 1896, B.L. Add. MS. 4251, f. 218; Lady Hooker, as quoted in: Ormerod, *Ormerod*, p. 74; also Ormerod, *Ormerod*, pp. 283–84. See Georgiana's drawings of architecture and antiquities in her sister's biography. Eleanor did her own entomological illustrations, but some newspapers and her biographer incorrectly attribute the illustrations in the *Annual Reports* to Georgiana.

56. S. Paget, Memoir, Pt. 2, "Pinner," p. 19; Wood, *Dictionary of Victorian Painters*, s.v. Elise Paget; Elise Paget, "Old Crome," *The Magazine of Art*, 5 (1882): 221–26; Russell–Gebbett, *Henslow*, p. 111; *D.N.B.*, s.v. George Grote.

57. *B.M.Cat.*, s.v. "Ismay Thorn"; Hans F. Gadow, *Amphibia and Reptiles* [Cambridge Natural History, vol. 7, ed. S. F. Harmer and A. E. Shipley] (Cambridge: Cambridge University Press, 1900), p. v; *W.W.W.*, *1941–50*, s.v. M. E. Durham. Durham also illustrated a Latin text. Of the 16,000 artists who exhibited at the Royal Academy between 1760 and 1893, 27.7 percent were women; Sydie, "Women Painters," p. 148. My special thanks to Anka Ryall for her help in identifying Miss Durham.

58. "Miss Sarah Acland" [obituary], *The Times* (London), December 4, 1930, p. 18. The Acland MSS. e.g., d. 160 and d. 165, Bodl. Lib., provide examples of Angie Acland's wide acquaintance. A collection of her photographs may be found in MS. Don. d. 14, Bodl. Lib.

59. "Miss Sarah Acland" [obituary], *The Times* (London), December 4, 1930, p. 18; S. A. Acland, *The Spectrum Plate—Theory, Practice; Result* (London: 1900); *Cassell's Cyclopaedia of Photography*, ed. B. E. Jones (London: Cassell, 1911), p.

467. *Cassell's* makes no reference to Acland. Sanger–Shepherd owned a photographic company, and he published extensively on photographic processes.

Historians of color photography link Acland and Sanger-Shepherd in these developments, but they do not explore the details of their working relationship; e.g., E. J. Wall, *The History of Three Color Photography* (Boston: American Photographic Pub. Co., 1925), pp. 445, 453 n.12, and 682. Acland's book is referred to in Wall's history. It is not listed in the *B.M.Cat.* or the *N.U.C.*

60. G. W. Norton to S. A. Acland, 25 February 1899, MS. Acland d. 166, f. 3; Mary Paget to Sarah A. Acland, March 7, [1899], MS. Acland d. 166, f. 40; Felicia Mary Skene to S. A. Acland, March 4, [1899], MS. Acland d. 166, f. 48; Margaret Stokes to S. A. Acland, March 6, 1899, MS. Acland d. 166, f. 48; Cecilia Stainer to M. M. Paget, November 3, 1896, MS. Eng. lett. c. 495, f. 65, Bodl. Lib. Jalland, inexplicably, misses this public and productive side of Acland's life; *Women, Marriage and Politics*, pp. 260–63.

61. E. Paget, "Old Crome"; Mary Turner, *One Hundred Etchings* (?Yarmouth, ?1825); Mary Anne Turner, *Practical Hints on the Revived Art of Crewel and Silk Embroidery* (London: n.p., 1877). This Mary Anne Turner may not have been Mrs. M. Turner's daughter.

62. [Mary Maud Paget], "Henry Purcell," *Temple Bar* 107 (1895): 593–603; "Henry Lawes," ibid. 109 (1896): 24–33; and "John Bull," ibid. 111 (1897): 398–407; "Dr. Arne," ibid. 117 (1899): 111–27.

63. Sadie, *New Grove Dictionary of Music*, 18:57–58, s.v. Sir John Stainer (re Cecilia Stainer). I have been unable to locate her contributions.

64. Compiled from: *Sir* George Grove, *Grove's Dictionary of Music and Musicians*, ed. J. A. Fuller-Maitland, 6 vols. (New York: Macmillan, 1904–20). When no clues suggested otherwise, I have assumed the authors to be male.

65. Fanny Aitkin-Kortwright to W. E. Gladstone, February 10, [1870], B.L. Add. MS. 44424, f. 273; "Miss F. M. Skene" [obituary], *The Times* (London), October 10, 1899, p. 4. See also: *D.N.B.*, s.v. Felicia Mary Skene. Aitkin-Kortwright's works were published "for circulation among her friends." She had published "about 20 works of fiction" by that date.

66. *B.M.Cat.*, s.v. Mary Senior, *afterward* Simpson; *D.N.B.* s.v. Charles Kingsley and Mary St. Leger Harrison; "Lucas Malet" [obituary of Mary St. Leger Harrison], *The Times* (London), October 29, 1931, p. 14; *B.M.Cat.*, s.v. "Lucas Malet" and Mary St. Leger Harrison.

67. *B.M.Cat.*, s.v. C. E. Pollock (Ismay Thorn), Emily Acland, A. E. Moberly, and Lucy G. Moberly. Page numbers are included to suggest volume and to point out that these items were larger than pamphlets. See also Anne Crawford, et al., eds., *The Europa Biographical Dictionary of British Women: Over 1000 Notable Women from Britain's Past* (Detroit: Gale Research, 1983), s.v. "Lucas Malet," and *B.L.G.*, s.v. "Moberly." There is no entry for Lucy G. Moberly in the *D.N.B.* or *W.W.W.*

68. *D.N.B.*, s.v. Harriet Grote; [anon.], "Aber Waterfall," *Temple Bar* 58 (1880): 388.

69. E. Acland, *Goodbye*, pp. 155–56 (re Cropper); E. K. Paget, *Bishop Patteson*; Constance Mary Buxton, *Side Lights on Bible History* (London: Macmillan, 1892); *B.M.Cat.*, s.v. C. M. Buxton, E. K. Paget, M. E. Sumner, Mary Hort Chitty. Cropper's book is not listed in the *B.M.Cat.*

70. *B.M.Cat.*, s.v. Chitty, Acland, Creighton.

71. *B.M.Cat.*, s.v. Harriet Gunn, F. M. Skene; E. K. Paget, *In Praise of Virginity* [Marriage and Morality, Series 1, No. 4] (London: Longmans, Green, 1916), and *The Claim of Suffering: A Plea for Medical Missions* (London: Society for the Propagation of the Gospel, 1912).

72. Mary Benson to W. E. Gladstone, November 27, 1891, B.L. Add. MS. 44513, f. 280.

73. *D.N.B.*, s.v. Julia Clara Byrne; *B.M.Cat.*, s.v. M. A. Turner; M. F. Smith, *A. L. Smith*, p. 48. Julia Clara Byrne published thirteen books. An author identified as "J. C. Byrne" published four travel books, all of which won readers' praise and went into many editions. Another member of the extended Busk clan, Mary Margaret (Blair) Busk (1779–1863), published sixty–four articles, notices, and reviews in the *Foreign Quarterly Review* in her lifetime; see: *Wellesley Index to Victorian Periodicals*, ed. Walter Houghton, 3 vols. (Toronto: University of Toronto Press, 1966–79), s.v. M. M. Busk.

74. *B.M.Cat.*, s.v. Sumner, McDougall; C. P. [Catharine Paget], "The Pleasures of Hotel-Bills. By a Traveller," *Macmillan's Magazine* 23 (1870): 159–60, and C. P., "The Traveller's Calendar," *ibid.* 28 (1873): 184–92; Bunyon, *McDougall*, pp. 27, 329–30 (Mrs. McDougall's original *Letters* was reprinted in 1924). C. Paget's use of initials is not, I would argue, an attempt at complete anonymity. Rather, initials allowed one's authorship to be known in one's own circle, while protecting one's privacy vis-à-vis strangers. My thanks to Thomas Prasch for his suggestive comments on this point.

75. *D.N.B.*, s.v. Harriet Lewin Grote, Alice Stopford Green; *B.M.Cat.*, s.v. Louise Creighton, Alice Stopford Green, Harriet Lewin Grote, Mary Eleanor Benson.

76. *B.M.Cat.*, s.v. Rachel Harriette Busk; Busk also wrote on Roman politics. Clara Paget, *Extracts from "The Kalevala,"* tr. J. M. Crawford (Cambridge: Privately printed, 1892); *King Bele of the Sogn District, Norway, and Jarl Angantyr of the Orkney Islands* (Cambridge: Privately printed, 1894); *The Northmen in Wales* (Cambridge: Privately printed, 1896); and *Some Ancient Stone Forts in Carnarvonshire* (Cambridge: Privately printed, 1896). These pamphlets are available in the Cambridge University Library, most of them not in the B.L.

77. *B.M.Cat.*, s.v. Agnes G. Grove, Margaret Benson. Grove's study of health statistics does not appear in the *B.M.Cat.*; she also published a travel book: *Seventy-One Days' Camping in Morocco* (London: Longmans, 1902). For clues to social science and criticism written by women not in this circle see: Westwater, *Wilson Sisters*, pp. 40–41, 47.

78. *Wellesley Index*, s.v. Pollock; Frank, *Voyager Out*, p. 42; Constance Mary Lubbock Buxton to Sir John Lubbock, April 29, 1884, B.L. Add. MS. 49647, f. 36; also see "C.M.B.," [Letter to the editor headed "Steele or Congreve?"], *The Spectator*, April 26, 1884, p. 550.

79. Huxley, *Huxley*, i, 36; *B.M.Cat.*, s.v. Elizabeth Sabine; C. Paget, Diary, January 31, 1870. Sabine's authors were F. P. Vrangel, H. W. Dove, and F. H. A. von Humboldt. I have been unable to find Catharine Paget's translation in print.

80. Turrill, *Hooker*, p. 63. See also: *Calendar of Darwin Correspondence*, s.v. M. E. H. Lyell; Elizabeth Eastlake's translation of G. F. Waagen, *Treasures of Art in Great Britain* (1854–57), 4 vols. My thanks to David Kohn for his help with Sabine and Darwin.

81. G. Guerini, *Fireside Entertainments; Or a Series of Interesting Tales*, tr. A. Acland, Mrs. William Barnet et al. (London: n.p., 1874); *B.M.Cat.*, s.v. Mary C. M. Senior, *afterward* Simpson, and M. S. H. Stokes. My thanks to Moureen Coulter for bringing this item to my attention. Mary Senior Simpson also published many articles of her own; see *Wellesley Index*, s.v.

82. *D.N.B.*, s.v. Rachel Busk, E. Ormerod, Lucas Malet.

83. *B.M.Cat.*, s.v. "Ismay Thorn"; "Miss F. M. Skene" [obituary], *The Times* (London), October 10, 1899, p. 4; Westcott, *Westcott*, ii, 225. Miss Bunyon may have been a relative of Harriette Bunyon McDougall. Mrs. Henry Wood edited volumes 5–42 of *The Argosy* before 1901; see *B.M.Cat.*, s.v. *Argosy*. Fanny Aikin-Kortwright

edited *The Court Suburb Magazine;* F. Aikin-Kortwright to William Ewart Gladstone, February 10, [1870], B.L. Add. MS. 44424, f. 273. For others see: Annie Scott Dill Maunder, who edited the *Journal of the British Astronomical Society* from 1923, and Elizabeth Watts, who edited the *Poultry Chronicle.*

84. Mary Kelley, *Private Women, Public State: Literary Domesticity in Nineteenth-Century America.* (New York: Oxford University Press, 1984), p. 127. In this circle there seems to have been none of the ambivalence about writing that Gilbert and Gubar found in their writers; Sandra Gilbert and Susan Gubar, *Madwoman in the Attic: The Woman Writer and the Nineteenth-Century Literary Imagination* (New Haven: Yale University Press, 1979) argue that women wrote in spite of deep cultural repression and deep ambivalence in them. The women of the present study did not.

85. "Lady Davidson of Lambeth" [obituary], *The Times* (London), June 27, 1936, p. 16.

SIX. "TWO WORKING TOGETHER FOR A COMMON END"

1. Eliot, *Middlemarch,* chaps. 3 and 6; Anthony Trollope, *Barchester Towers* [1857], ed. J. R. Kincaid (New York: Oxford University Press, 1980), chap. 3; Lewis, *Women in England,* p. 78. The *Saturday Review* (November 1859) called marriage women's "business" (as quoted in: Vicinus, *Independent Women,* p. 3).

2. Lockhart, *Halifax,* i, 94, 150, 157, 264. S. Paget and J. Crum, *Francis Paget,* pp. 16, 26, 34–35. Also see: Kitchin, *Browne,* p. 96; Harford and MacDonald, *Moule,* p. 84.

3. E.g., Lydia North to James Paget, November 8, 1839, Paget MS. 101, W.I.-H.M.; F. T. Palgrave to W. E. Gladstone, April 1890, as quoted in: Palgrave, *Palgrave,* p. 223; Hort, *Hort,* i, 353; ii, 77; Barnett, *Barnett,* ii, 29; Westcott, *Westcott,* ii, 337; Bell, *Davidson,* i, 629. For examples of Westcott sharing his ideas with his wife, see: Westcott, *Westcott,* i, 394, 395–96, 431–32, 435–36. Also see: Bell, *Davidson,* i, 79, re the Ponsonbys.

4. Kitchin, *Browne,* p. 362; Benham, *Catherine and Craufurd Tait,* p. 93; Henson, *Retrospect,* i, 44, 45. Also see: Kitchin, *Browne,* p. 237.

5. Samuel Barnett to Henrietta Rowland, March 30, 1872, as quoted in: Barnett, *Barnett,* p. 40, also p. 37; Stephenson, *Talbot,* p. 17; Benham, *Catharine and Craufurd Tait,* pp. 6–7; also p. 11, 12; Mandell Creighton to Louise von Glehn, May 17, 1871, as quoted in: Creighton, *Creighton,* i, 79.

6. M. F. Smith, *A. L. Smith,* p. 85.

7. Brooke Foss Westcott to Mary Whittard, Trinity Sunday, 1851, and 21 Dec. 1851, as quoted in Westcott, *Westcott,* i, 167, 168.

8. MacLeod and Moseley, "Fathers and Daughters," pp. 321–33.

9. F. Paget to Lord Victor Seymour, August 1885, as quoted in: S. Paget and J. Crum, *Francis Paget,* p. 88; H. L. Thompson to R. M. Gawne, March 1879, December 1882, and April 1884, as quoted in: Thompson, *Four Biographical Sermons,* pp. 28, 30. Also see: Westcott, *Westcott,* i, 120.

10. B. F. Westcott to his sons, 29 May [1901], and B. F. Westcott to J. Ll. Davies, 29 June 1901, as quoted in: Westcott, *Westcott,* ii, 339, 341; Henson, *Retrospect,* i, 66; Eastlake, *Mrs. Grote,* p. 19.

11. My thanks to Ann R. Higginbotham for participating in the development of these ideas about the 'family economy.'

12. It is a mark of the degree of our conditioning that we cannot get away from calling the work *his* career. He was, of course, the official representative of the family at work.

13. J. Paget, *Memoirs and Letters*, pp. 13, 31, 67, 89; Clara Paget to Rose and Maud Paget, April 22, [1874?], Thomson MS.

14. Kitchin, *Browne*, pp. 66, 96; B. F. Westcott, Diary, 1 January 1847, as quoted in: Westcott, *Westcott*, i, 50. The Brownes later moved to Kenwyn.

15. Bunyon, *McDougall*, p. 19.

16. Lydia North to James Paget, February 14 and 23, 1839, Paget MSS. 86 and 87, W.I.H.M.; Sharlin, *Kelvin*, pp. 45, 78; Catharine Tait to the Speaker [J. Evelyn Denison], September 9, 1864, B.L. Add. MS. 36722, f. 471; *D.N.B.*, s.v. Anthony Panizzi.

17. Eastlake, *Mrs. Grote*, pp. 72, 73, 74–77.

18. Constance Mary Buxton to Sir John Lubbock, November 10, 1885, B.L. Add. MS. 49648, f. 135–36. Also see: same to same, September 19, 1885, B.L. Add. MS. 49648, f. 107; Frederick Haynes McCalmont, *McCalmont's Parliamentary Poll Book, British Election Results, 1832–1918*, 8th ed., J. Vincent and M. Stenton, eds. (Brighton, Sussex: Harvester, 1971) Pt. ii, 241, 198; Constance Mary Lubbock Buxton to Sir John Lubbock, Bt., November 13, 1885, B.L. Add. MS. 49648, f. 138–40; Sydney Buxton to Sir John Lubbock, June 18, 1886, B.L. Add. MS. 49649, f. 73. For more of Mrs. Buxton's efforts on behalf of her husband, see: Constance Mary Buxton to Sir John Lubbock, January 13 and 16, 1886, B.L. Add. MS. 49649, f. 11 and 17 (emphasis hers). For aristocratic women's political work see: Jalland, *Women, Marriage and Politics*, pp. 189–210, and chap. 8.

19. Sydney Buxton to Sir John Lubbock, June 18, 1886, B.L. Add. MS. 49648, f. 138–40 (emphasis mine); Constance Mary Buxton to Sir John Lubbock, July 6 and 9, 1886, B.L. Add. MS. 49649, f. 84 and 85. Eastlake, *Mrs. Grote*, pp. 74, 75–76, 77, offers other examples of "we."

20. Bell, *Davidson*, i, 62; also 378–79, and 179; Jalland, *Women, Marriage and Politics*; F. J. A. Hort to Mrs. Fraser, February 9, 1884, as quoted in: Hort, *Hort*, ii, 307; Benham, *Catharine and Craufurd Tait*, p. 61; Kitchin, *Browne*, p. 452; for more detail see: Bell, *Davidson*, i, 58–59. Gladstone and Mrs. Browne discussed Browne's career again a decade later; W. E. Gladstone to Mrs. E. H. Browne, December 12, 1891, B.L. Add. MS. 42581, f. 1. Also see Henson, *Retrospect*, i, 44–45. Mrs. Maclagan, observing her husband's failing "mental powers," engineered his resignation as archbishop of York. She enlisted Randall Davidson's help; Bell, *Davidson*, i, 580–81. The fictional Mrs. Quiverful's intervention on her husband's behalf over the appointment to Hiram's Hospital makes complete sense in this context; Trollope, *Barchester Towers*, chaps. 25, 26, and 43.

21. Margaret Thomson to William Thomson, 1 April 1867, Kelvin MS., Glasgow University Library; Victor Horsley to Mrs. Shafer, [December?], 1883, as quoted in: Stephen Paget, *Sir Victor Horsley: A Study of His Life and Work* (London: Constable, 1919), p. 49.

22. Leonore Davidoff, *The Best Circles: Women and Society in Victorian England* (Totowa, N.J.: Rowman and Littlefield, 1973), pp. 41–46; Hort, *Hort*, ii, 77; Alfred Paget, Letter book, 1835–47, Res. col., Bodl. Lib., includes a collection of calling cards from A. Paget's undergraduate days at Cambridge.

23. C. Paget, Diary, May 7, June 29, May 10, and May 12, 1870.

24. C. Paget, Diary, May–June, 1870. I excluded dinners and evening parties because they are known to be mixed-sex affairs, and it is the "woman's work" of social visiting that I am most interested in examining here.

25. Kitchin, *Browne*, p. 114; "Lady Thomson" [obituary], *The Times* (London), June 2, 1951, p. 8.

26. Bell, *Davidson*, i, 255, 252; Benham, *Catharine and Craufurd Tait*, pp. 37–38, 64. See also: Peterson, *Medical Profession*, pp. 88, 98, 109, 143–45, 165–66.

27. Bell, *Davidson*, i, 570; Kitchin, *Browne*, p. 84, 126.

28. Peterson, *Medical Profession*, p. 268; J. Paget, *Memoirs and Letters*, p. 306.

29. Kitchin, *Browne*, 1895, pp. 84, 126; S. Paget and J. Crum, *Francis Paget*, pp. 96, 99.

30. Sir Walford Davies, as quoted in: Bell, *Davidson*, i, 70.

31. H. Paget, "Pagets of Great Yarmouth," p. 12.

32. B. F. Westcott to Mrs. F. J. A. Hort, 19 October 1869, as quoted in: Westcott, *Westcott*, i, 328–29; W. E. Gladstone to Mrs. Catharine Tait [copy], 9 February 1870, B.L. Add. MS. 44424, f. 272; Lewis M. Owen to Elizabeth Browne, November 8, 1876, as quoted in: Kitchin, *Browne*, pp. 433–34.

33. Benham, *Catharine and Craufurd Tait*, p. 59; Bell, *Davidson*, i, 285. Compare Mrs. Tait's similar pouring of oil on troubled waters during the discussions over the disestablishment of the Irish church; Benham, p. 63.

34. Queen Victoria to the archbishop of Canterbury, May 4, 1883, as quoted in: Bell, *Davidson*, i, 63; Bishop of Llandaff to W. E. Gladstone, February 16, 1870, B.L. Add. MS. 44424, ff. 310–313; see also W. E. Gladstone to Connop Thirlwall (bishop of St. David's), February 14, 1870, and Connop Thirlwall to W. E. Gladstone, February 14, 1870, ibid., f. 301, 302.

35. Bell, *Davidson*, i, 711. Modern professions may operate on the basis of merit and certifiable expertise, but in the Victorian period much professional patronage was exercised on the basis of family and connection; Peterson, *Medical Profession*, pp. 143–44, 147–48, 155, and passim.

36. Examples include Mrs. Benson, in: Bell, *Davidson*, i, 63. It is tempting to see the beginnings of the transformation of secretarial work from a male province to a female one in these domestic clerical arrangements.

37. Lydia North to James Paget, February 11, 1837, Paget MS. 22, W.I.H.M.; *D.N.B.*, s. v. John Richard Green; B. F. Westcott to Katie Westcott [1873?], as quoted in: Westcott, *Westcott*, i, 341. For a fictional example see Dorothea Brooke, first offering to help her uncle, then working with Casaubon, in George Eliot, *Middlemarch*, chaps. 3 and 4.

38. Hooker, *Hooker*, p. xxxiii; *D.N.B.*, s.v. W. J. Hooker. Elizabeth Sabine had a similar record of scientific assistance; see *D.N.B.*, s.v. Sir Edward Sabine.

39. See e.g., the letter from James Paget to [Ernest] Hart, 1867?, Huntington Library MS., probably written by Lydia or Catharine Paget.

40. Biographical notice [of Joseph Dalton Hooker] with letter from his wife [to Messrs. Richard Griffin, Publishers], 1860, B.L. Add. MS. 2850, f. 246.

41. Frances, Lady Thomson to George Darwin, July 2, August 15, August 20, and September 27, 1879, and January 17, 1881; James Joule to Mrs. [Margaret Crum] Thomson, November 2, 1858, Kelvin MSS.; the Macmillan Archive, B.L., passim.

42. C. Paget, Diary, November 14, 1870; S. Paget and J. Crum, *Francis Paget*, p. vi; Henson, *Retrospect*, i, vi; Harford and MacDonald, *Moule*, pp. 86, 364–71.

43. Sydney Buxton, *Finance and Politics: An Historical Study, 1783–1885*, 2 vols. (London: Murray, 1888), i, v; Constance Lubbock Buxton to Sir John Lubbock, March 15, 1888, and April 6, 1888, B.L. Add. MS. 49651, ff. 24–25, 37–38.

44. Russell-Gebbett, *Henslow*, p. 51; *D.N.B.*, s.v. Alice S. Green; Bell, *Davidson*, i, 585; Stokes, *Memoirs and Scientific Correspondence*, i, 17, also i, 36; Huxley, *Huxley*, i, 301; S. Paget and J. Crum, *Francis Paget*, p. vii. Lucy Toulmin Smith (a friend of Mary Kingsley) was her father's assistant in his research on such subjects as "geology, constitutional law, public health, and parish rights and duties," until his death in 1870 (Frank, *Voyager Out*, p. 42). Frank's sister-in-law Mary Church helped him, too; she lived with Frank and reared her nephews and nieces after her sister Helen Church Paget's death.

45. Dawson Turner and Mary Turner, *Outlines in Lithography* (?Yarmouth: Pri-

vately printed, 1840); *B.M.Cat.*, s.v. Bible, Mark, A. F. Hort and M. D. Hort; M. F. Smith, *A. L. Smith*, p. 48; Benham, *Catharine and Craufurd Tait*, p. 2, passim; Harford and MacDonald, *Moule*, pp. 172, 178; H. C. G. Moule, *The School of Suffering: A Brief Memorial of Mary E. E. Moule* . . . (London: Christian Knowledge Society, 1908). Mrs. Moule's coauthorship is asserted by the Rev. Moule's biographer but not shown in the library catalogues. Benham's volume includes A. C. Tait's recollections of his wife and of Craufurd, together with her recollections of their children.

46. *D.N.B.*, s.v. J. R. Green, George Busk. Cf. MacLeod and Moseley, "Fathers and Daughters," pp. 321–333; Sadie, *New Grove Dictionary of Music*, s.v. Sir John Stainer; *B.M.Cat.*, s.v. Alice Stopford Green, John Richard Green, Louise Creighton, and Mandell Creighton.

47. H. F. Gadow, *Jorullo: The History of the Volcano of Jorullo and the Reclamation of the Devastated District by Animals and Plants* (Cambridge, 1930), pp. ix, vii; Gadow, *The Evolution of the Vertebral Column: A Contribution to the Study of Vertebrate Phylogeny* (Cambridge: Cambridge University Press, 1933), p. v.

48. Church, *Life and Letters;* Frances E. Kingsley, *Charles Kingsley: His Letters and Memories of His Life*, 2 vols. (London: Henry S. King, 1877); S. Chitty, *The Beast and the Monk*, p. 16; Thompson, *Four Biographical Sermons*, pp. 1–63. Some suppose that Kingsley's student John Martineau helped. I wonder.

49. E. K. Paget, *Henry Luke Paget;* R. Davidson, as quoted in: Bell, *Davidson*, i, 359; Creighton, *Creighton;* Also see: Mary Sumner, *Memoir of George Henry Sumner, D. D., Bishop of Guildford* (Winchester: Warren, 1912).

50. Lyell, *Life, Letters;* Prestwich, *Life and Letters*, e.g., p. 311; Romanes, *Romanes*, p. viii; Cohen, *Cohen*. Mrs. Reid had been a student at Newnham. Lucy Cohen published other biographies as well.

51. Church, *Life and Letters*. This constitutes some 13.5 percent of the work.

52. Johnson, *Derbyshire Village Schools*, p. 77; M. F. Smith, *A. L. Smith*, p. 37.

53. Benham, *Catharine and Craufurd Tait*, pp. 40, 37, 31–32; "Lady Thomson" [obituary], *The Times*, London, June 2, 1951, p. 8.

54. Benham, *Catharine and Craufurd Tait*, pp. 13, 35; Hort, *Hort*, ii, 282. Their friend Mrs. Wordsworth helped her husband "collate . . . MSS" in Rome on a research trip there in 1883.

55. Minutes of the Chester Diocesan Association for the Promotion of Social Purity, October 26, 1925, September 28, October 24, 1924, April 30, 1926, November 14, 1927, Cheshire Record Office.

56. Bell, *Davidson*, i, 250, 252.

57. S. Paget and J. Crum, *Francis Paget*, p. 84; Harford and MacDonald, *Moule*, p. 231; Bunyon, *McDougall*, p. 44; Benham, *Catharine and Craufurd Tait*, p. 70.

58. Palgrave, *Palgrave*, p. 13; Kitson, *Cotman*, pp. 159–81, 175–76, 179, 173, 180–81. Art historian S. Kitson tracked these down in his search for Cotman's works.

59. *D.N.B.*, s.v. A. C. Tait; Benham, *Catharine and Craufurd Tait*, p. 72; Harriette McDougall also kept accounts at the mission school as well as serving as the mission's provisioning officer; Bramston, *Victorian Heroine*, pp. 73, 68.

60. Gadow, *Through Southern Mexico*, pp. 82–83. Cf. MacLeod and Moseley, "Fathers and Daughters," p. 332, who imply that women gave up science when they married, even if they married scientists. Middleton, *Victorian Lady Travellers*, p. 3, says, "Nearly always [lady travellers] went alone." This is not so among the women studied here. Most went as part of a couple. When they went alone, they wrote their own accounts of their travels and were, as a result, more visible. Anka Ryall's forthcoming study will shed light on this question.

61. Gadow, *In Northern Spain*, passim, and Gadow, *Through Southern Mexico*, passim. In each case Maud Gadow's works are identified by her initials, "C.M.G."

in the first volume and "M.G." in the second volume. Eleanor Ormerod helped her brother with his scientific research; that was how her own interests began. Similar family scientific collaborations may be found in the work of Professor A. M. Low, scientist and inventor, and his mother, Mrs. J. W. Low, who "helped him with his early experiments." See: "Mrs. J. S. Low" [obituary], *The Times* (London), August 5, 1939, p. 14. Also see: *D.N.B.*, s.v. Sir Edward Sabine.

62. Clara Paget to Rose Paget, April 7 [n.y.], and August 30 [n.y.], and G. E. Paget to Rose Paget, July 4, 1880, Thomson MSS.; Bramston, *Victorian Heroine*, pp. 64, 68, 74. For an example (outside the Paget circle) of a woman's work in medical matters, consider Mrs. Radford who, together with her surgeon husband, rebuilt the Manchester Lying-In Hospital (where he was a staff member) in the 1840s and 1850s; John V. Pickstone, *Medicine and Industrial Society: A History of Hospital Development in Manchester and Its Region, 1752–1946* (Manchester: Manchester University Press, 1985), pp. 114–15. Also see pp. 121, 217–18ff.

63. Henry Luke Paget [bishop of Stepney] to Henrietta Barnett, n.d., as quoted in: Barnett, *Barnett*, ii, 382.

64. Benham, *Catharine and Craufurd Tait*, pp. 59, 21–22; "Lady Davidson of Lambeth" [obituary], *The Times* (London), June 27, 1936, p. 14; Archbishop of Canterbury to Mrs. [Mandell] Creighton, September 10, 1908, as quoted in: Bell, *Davidson*, i, 582; see also i, 717; Harford and MacDonald, *Moule*, p. 327n.

65. Miss Goodwin, as quoted in Kitchin, *Browne*, p. 501. Few families were so self-conscious about shared family roles as the A. L. Smiths in Oxford: he participated in child care and she, in turn, "shared his wider interests." H. Barnett observed and recorded this partnership in: *Barnett*, i, 304. For most, some such sharing was the standard organization of family life.

66. Hilary Callan and Shirley Ardener, eds., *The Incorporated Wife*, (London: Croom Helm, 1984), chap. 1; Stone, *Family, Sex and Marriage*, p. 234; Gay, *Tender Passion*, p. 398, for an example.

67. Eliot, *Middlemarch*, e.g., chaps. 36, 42, 58.

CONCLUSION

1. Benham, *Catharine and Craufurd Tait*, p. 21. With the exception of public office-holding, no corner of Victorian life seems to have been closed to the gentlewoman in the sense of action and doing; she did not have the title, but she often had the role. And by the 1870s political life began to open to women, first at the local level.

2. M. Rosaldo, "The Use and Abuse of Anthropology: Reflections on Feminism and Cross-Cultural Understanding," *Signs* 5:3 (1980), 389–417, raises questions about the relation of public and private. In any case, philanthropy was driving women into local government as early as the 1860s: see Patricia Hollis, *Ladies Elect: Women in English Local Government, 1865–1914* (Oxford: Clarendon, 1987).

3. It may be that the only truly public sphere was Parliament.

4. Max Weber, *From Max Weber: Essays in Sociology*, tr. and ed. H. H. Gerth and C. W. Mills (New York: Oxford University Press, 1966), chap 7.

5. Such women were among the first feminists and suffragists; see Olive Banks, *Becoming a Feminist: The Social Origins of "First Wave" Feminism* (Athens: University of Georgia Press, 1987), pp. 33–44, 88–92. But Banks gives her data a different reading than I would. See also: Andrew Rosen, *Rise Up, Women: The Militant Campaign of the Women's Social and Political Union, 1903–1914* (London: Routledge and Kegan Paul, 1974), pp. 1–15.

Bibliography

MANUSCRIPTS:

THE BODLEIAN LIBRARY, Oxford:
    MSS. Acland
    MSS. Autograph
    MSS. Don
    MSS. Eng. lett.
    MSS. Eng. misc.
    Res. coll. (including material formerly in the possession of Mr. and Mrs. James M. Thompson)
THE BRITISH LIBRARY, London: All of the following are Add. MSS.
    Avebury MSS. [the Lubbock family]
    Eg. MSS.
    Gladstone MSS.
    The Macmillan Archive
    Sherborne Autographs
    Twining Papers
    Wallace Papers
CHESHIRE RECORD OFFICE, Cheshire:
    Minutes of the Chester Diocesan Association for the Promotion of Social Purity.
GLASGOW UNIVERSITY ARCHIVES:
    Elder MSS.
GLASGOW UNIVERSITY LIBRARY:
    Kelvin MSS.
HUNTINGTON LIBRARY, San Marino, CA.:
    Stowe MSS.
PUSEY HOUSE, St. Cross College, Oxford:
    Liddon MSS.
    Parochial Visiting and Provident Society. Oxford: H. Cooke, 1825, with MS. additions.
ROYAL COLLEGE OF SURGEONS OF ENGLAND, London:
    Paget MSS.
SOMERSET HOUSE, London: Principal Registry of the Family Division, (formerly the Prerogative Court of Canterbury):
    Calendar of the Grants of Probate and Letters of Administration in the Probate Registers of the High Court of Justice in England. . . . (London: various years).
    Wills (proved after 1858).
WELLCOME LIBRARY FOR THE HISTORY OF MEDICINE, London:
    Paget MSS.
PRIVATE MANUSCRIPT COLLECTIONS:
    Burlington Danes School, London. Board of Governors Minute Book.
    Lord Mayhew's MS:
        Paget, Humphry. "The Pagets of Great Yarmouth. 1800 to 1850. From the memoirs of the Rev. Alfred Tolver Paget, Rector of Kirstead, Norfolk" (Mimeographed, September 1937).
    Sir Julian Paget: "Paget Family Tree" (unpublished manuscript, 1963).
    Oliver Paget MS.: [Sarah Elizabeth Paget], Untitled music book, n.d.

Thompson MS. (in the possession of Mrs. Alice Thompson):
Paget, Stephen. Memoir (typescript, n.d.).
Thomson MSS. (in the possession of David P. Thomson, London):
Rose Paget, Diary, 1874–78
Letters, mainly to Rose Paget, 1870–1899

PRINTED PRIMARY AND SECONDARY WORKS:

This bibliography does not include the works (other than biographical and autobiographical works) published by the women of this study, nor the books they read as part of their education and discussed in chapter 2.

Acland, Eleanor. *Goodbye for the Present: The Story of Two Childhoods: Milly: 1878–88 & Ellen: 1913–24*. London: Hodder and Stoughton, 1935.

Acland, *Sir* Henry Wentworth. *Memoir on the Cholera in Oxford in the Year 1854*. London: Churchill, 1856.

Acland, *Sir* Thomas Dyke. *Memoir and Letters*. Edited by A. H. D. Acland. London: Privately printed, 1902.

Acton, William. *Functions and Disorders of the Reproductive Organs in Childhood, Youth, Adult Age, and Advanced Life*. 3d American ed. from the 5th London ed. Philadelphia: Lindsay and Blakiston, 1871.

Allen, D. E. "The Women Members of the Botanical Society of London, 1836–1856." *British Journal for the History of Science* 13:3 (1980): 240–54.

Alum. Cantab. See Venn.

Alum. Oxon. See Oxford University.

Askwith, Betty. *Two Victorian Families*. London: Chatto and Windus, 1971.

Atkinson, Paul. "Fitness, Feminism and Schooling." In *The Nineteenth-Century Woman: Her Cultural and Physical World*, edited by S. Delamont and L. Duffin. London: Croom Helm, 1978.

Atlay, J. B. *Sir Henry Wentworth Acland, Bart., K.C.B., F.R.S., Regius Professor of Medicine in the University of Oxford: A Memoir*. London: Smith, Elder, 1903.

Australian Dictionary of Biography. 10 vols. Melbourne: Melbourne University Press, 1966–86.

Balfour, *Lady* Frances. *Ne Obliviscaris. Dinna Forget*. 2 vols. London: Hodder and Stoughton, n.d.

Banks, J. A. *Prosperity and Parenthood: A Study of Family Planning among the Victorian Middle Classes*. London: Routledge and Kegan Paul, 1954.

———. *Victorian Values: Secularism and the Size of Families*. London: Routledge and Kegan Paul, 1981.

Banks, Olive. *Becoming a Feminist: The Social Origins of "First Wave" Feminism*. Athens: University of Georgia Press, 1987.

Barnett, Henrietta. *Canon Barnett, His Life, Work, and Friends*. 2 vols. London: John Murray, 1918.

Bell, G. K. A. *Randall Davidson: Archbishop of Canterbury*. 2 vols. London: H. Milford, Oxford University Press, 1935.

Benham, William, ed. *Catharine and Craufurd Tait, Wife and Son of Archibald Campbell, Archbishop of Canterbury: A Memoir*. New York: Macmillan, 1880.

Benson, Arthur C. *Life and Letters of Maggie Benson*. London: John Murray, 1918.

———. *The Life of Edward White Benson, Sometime Archbishop of Canterbury*. 2 vols. London: Macmillan, 1899.

Benson, Mary Eleanor. *Streets and Lanes of the City, with a Brief Memoir by her Father* [E. W. Benson]. London: Privately printed, 1891.

Bermant, Chaim. *The Cousinhood: The Anglo-Jewish Gentry*. London: Eyre and Spottiswoode, 1971.

Bibby, Miss, et al. *The Pudding Lady: A New Departure in Social Work*. London: Stead's, for the St. Pancras School for Mothers, [1912].

Boase, Frederick. *Modern English Biography*. 6 vols. London: Frank Cass, 1965.

Bramston, Mary. *An Early Victorian Heroine: The Story of Harriette McDougall*. London: S.P.C.K., 1911.

Branca, Patricia. *Silent Sisterhood: Middle-Class Women in the Victorian Home*. London: Croom Helm, 1975.

British Museum [now Library], Department of Printed Books. *General Catalogue of Printed Books*. 263 vols. London: Trustees of the British Museum, 1965. [*B.M.Cat.*]

Brumberg, Joan Jacobs. *Fasting Girls: The Emergence of Anorexia Nervosa as a Modern Disease*. Cambridge, Mass.: Harvard University Press, 1988.

Bunyon, Charles J. *Memoirs of F. T. McDougall . . . and of Harriette, His Wife*. London: Longmans, 1889.

Burke's Landed Gentry. Edited by Peter Townend. 18th ed., 3 vols. London: Burke's Peerage Ltd., 1965. [*B.L.G.*]

Burke's Landed Gentry of Ireland. Edited by L. G. Pine. 4th ed. London: Burke's Peerage Ltd., 1958. [*B.L.G.I.*]

Burke's Peerage, Baronetage and Knightage. 105th ed. London: Burke's Peerage Ltd., 1970. [*B.P.B.&K.*]

Buxton, Sydney. *Finance and Politics. An Historical Study, 1783–1885*. 2 vols. London: Murray, 1888.

A Calendar of the Correspondence of Charles Darwin, 1821–1882. Edited by Frederick Burckhardt et al. [Garland Reference Library of the Humanities, vol. 369]. New York: Garland, 1985.

Callan, Hilary, and Shirley Ardener, eds. *The Incorporated Wife*. London: Croom Helm, 1984.

Cameron, Lucy Lyttelton. *The Life of Mrs. Cameron: Partly an Autobiography*. Edited by her son [Charles Cameron]. London: Darton, [1862].

Cassell's Cyclopaedia of Photography. Edited by B. E. Jones. London: Cassell, 1911.

Casteras, Susan P. *The Substance or the Shadow: Images of Victorian Womanhood*. New Haven: Yale Center for British Art, 1982.

Cavendish Laboratory. *A History of the Cavendish Laboratory, 1871–1910*. London: Longmans, Green, 1910.

Chitty, Susan. *The Beast and the Monk: A Life of Charles Kingsley*. London: Hodder and Stoughton, 1974.

Church, Richard W. *Life and Letters of Dean Church*. Edited by Mary C. Church. London: Macmillan, 1895.

Church Quarterly Review (London).

Clark, George Kitson. *The Making of Victorian England: Being the Ford Lectures Delivered before the University of Oxford*. London: Methuen, 1962.

Cohen, Lucy. *Arthur Cohen: A Memoir*. London: Privately printed, 1919.

Cominos, Peter. "Innocent Femina Sensualis in Unconscious Conflict." In *Suffer and Be Still: Women in the Victorian Age*, edited by M. J. Vicinus. Bloomington: Indiana University Press, 1972, pp. 155–72.

———. "Late Victorian Sexual Respectability and the Social System." *International Review of Social History* 8 (1963): 18–48, 216–50.

Copelman, Dina, "'A New Comradeship between Men and Women': Family, Marriage and London's Women Teachers, 1870–1914." In *Labour and Love*, edited by Jane Lewis, q.v., pp. 175–93.

Corder, Frederick. *History of the Royal Academy of Music from 1822 to 1922*. London: Corder, 1922.

Crawford, Anne, et al., eds. *The Europa Biographical Dictionary of British Women: Over 1000 Notable Women from Britain's Past*. Detroit: Gale Research, 1983.

Creighton, Louise. *Life and Letters of Mandell Creighton, D.D.Oxon. and Cam., Sometime Bishop of London*. 2 vols. London: Longmans, Green, 1904.

Curtis, S. J. *History of Education in Great Britain*. 7th ed. London: University Tutorial Press, 1967.

Darwin, Charles. See *A Calendar . . . .*

Davidoff, Leonore. *The Best Circles: Women and Society in Victorian England*. Totowa, N. J.: Rowman and Littlefield, 1973.

———, and Catherine Hall. *Family Fortunes: Men and Women of the English Middle Class, 1780–1850*. Chicago: University of Chicago Press, 1987.

Degler, Carl. *At Odds: Women and the Family in America from the Revolution to the Present*. New York: Oxford University Press, 1980.

———. "What Ought to Be and What Was: Women's Sexuality in the Nineteenth Century." *American Historical Review* 79 (1974): 1467–90.

Dent, H. C. *1870–1970: Century of Growth in English Education*. London: Longman, 1970.

Dictionary of National Biography. Edited by *Sir* Leslie Stephen and *Sir* Sidney Lee. 22 vols. and supplements. London: Oxford University Press, 1949–50 [repr.]. [*D.N.B.*]

Dworkin, Gerald. "Estate Taxation in Great Britain." In *Estate and Gift Taxation: A Comparative Study*, revised and edited by George S. H. Wheatcroft. [British Tax Review Guides, no. 3]. London: Sweet and Maxwell, 1965, pp. 55–82.

Dyehouse, Carol. *Girls Growing Up in Late Victorian and Edwardian England*. London: Routledge and Kegan Paul, 1981.

Eastlake, [Elizabeth] Lady. *Mrs. Grote: A Sketch*. London: John Murray, 1880.

Eliot, George. *Middlemarch: A Study of Provincial Life* [1871–72]. London: Oxford University Press, 1947.

Engel, Arthur. *From Clergyman to Don: The Rise of the Academic Profession in Nineteenth-Century Oxford*. New York: Oxford University Press, 1983.

Foster, J. *Men-at-the-Bar: A Biographical Hand-List of the Members of the Various Inns of Court. . . .* London: Reeves and Turner, 1885.

Frank, Katherine. *A Voyager Out: The Life of Mary Kingsley*. Boston: Houghton Mifflin, 1986.

Gadow, Hans. *Amphibia and Reptiles*. [Cambridge Natural History, vol. 7, ed. S. F. Harmer and A. E. Shipley]. Cambridge: Cambridge University Press, 1900.

———. *In Northern Spain*. London: A and C Black, 1897.

———. *Jorullo: The History of the Volcano of Jorullo and the Reclamation of the Devastated District by Animals and Plants*. Cambridge: Cambridge University Press, 1930.

———. *Through Southern Mexico: Being an Account of the Travels of a Naturalist*. London: Witherby, 1908.

Gaskell, Elizabeth. *Ruth* [1853]. Oxford: Oxford University Press, 1985.

Gathorne-Hardy, Jonathan. *The Unnatural History of the Nanny*. New York: Dial Press, 1973.

Gay, Peter. *The Education of the Senses* [*The Bourgeois Experience: Victoria to Freud*, vol. 1]. New York: Oxford University Press, 1984.

————. *The Tender Passion* [*The Bourgeois Experience: Victoria to Freud*, vol. 2]. New York: Oxford University Press, 1986.

Gerard, Jessica. "Lady Bountiful: Women of the Landed Classes and Rural Philanthropy." *Victorian Studies* 30:2 (1987): 183–210.

Gilbert, Sandra, and Susan Gubar. *The Madwoman in the Attic: The Woman Writer and the Nineteenth-Century Literary Imagination*. New Haven: Yale University Press, 1979.

Gissing, George. *In the Year of Jubilee* [1893]. New York: Dover, 1982.

————. *The Whirlpool* [1897]. London: Hogarth Press, 1984.

Goleman, Daniel. "Insights into Self-Deception." *New York Times Magazine*, May 12, 1985, pp. 36–43.

————. *Vital Lies, Simple Truths: The Psychology of Self-Deception*. New York: Simon and Schuster, 1985.

Gorham, Deborah. *The Victorian Girl and the Feminine Ideal*. Bloomington: Indiana University Press, 1983.

Graves, Algernon, comp. *A Dictionary of Artists Who Have Exhibited Works in the Principal London Exhibitions from 1760–1893*. 3d ed. [1901]. [Bath: Kingsmead Reprints, 1970].

————. *The Royal Academy of Arts: A Complete Dictionary of Contributors and Their Work from Its Foundation in 1769 to 1904*. 8 vols. in 4. East Ardsley: S. R. Publishers, 1905. [Bath: Kingsmead Reprint, 1970].

Green, J. R. *Letters of J. R. Green*. Edited by Leslie Stephen. London: Macmillan, 1902.

Greer, Germaine. *The Obstacle Race: The Fortunes of Women Painters and Their Work*. New York: Farrar, Straus, and Giroux, 1979.

Grote, Harriet L. *The Personal Life of George Grote*. 2d ed. London: John Murray, 1873.

Grove, *Sir* George. *Grove's Dictionary of Music and Musicians*. Edited by J. A. Fuller-Maitland. 6 vols. New York: Macmillan, 1904–20.

Grove's Dictionary of Musicians, new edition. See Sadie.

Haight, Gordon. *George Eliot & John Chapman, with Chapman's Diaries*. New Haven: Yale University Press, 1940.

Hallé, *Sir* Charles. *The Autobiography of Charles Hallé: With Correspondence and Diaries*. Edited by Michael Kennedy. New York: Barnes and Noble, 1972.

Hamburger, Lotte, and Joseph Hamburger. *Troubled Lives: John and Sarah Austin*. Toronto: University of Toronto Press, 1985.

Harford, J. B., and F. C. MacDonald. *Handley Carr Glynn Moule, Bishop of Durham: A Biography*. London: Hodder and Stoughton, 1922.

Harrison, Brian. "For Church, Queen and Family: The Girls' Friendly Society, 1874–1920." *Past and Present* 61 (1973): 107–38.

Healey, Edna. *Wives of Fame: Mary Livingstone, Jenny Marx, Emma Darwin*. London: Sidgwick and Jackson, 1986.

Heinemann, Helen. *Restless Angels: The Friendship of Six Victorian Women: Frances Wright, Camilla Wright, Harriet Garnett, Frances Garnett, Julia Garnett Pertz, Frances Trollope*. Athens, Ohio: Ohio University Press, 1983.

Hellerstein, Erna Olafson, *et al.*, eds. *Victorian Women: A Documentary Account of Women's Lives in Nineteenth-Century England, France, and the United States*. Stanford: Stanford University Press, 1981.

Henson, Herbert Hensley. *Retrospect of an Unimportant Life*. 3 vols. London: Oxford University Press, 1942.

Higginbotham, Ann R. "The Unmarried Mother and Her Child in Victorian London." Ph. D. diss., Indiana University, Bloomington, 1985.

Holcombe, Lee. *Victorian Ladies at Work: Middle-Class Working Women in England and Wales, 1850–1914*. Newton Abbot: David and Charles, 1973.

————. *Wives and Property: Reform of the Married Women's Property Law in Nineteenth-Century England*. Toronto: University of Toronto Press, 1983.

Hollis, Patricia. *Ladies Elect: Women in English Local Government, 1865–1914*. Oxford: Clarendon Press, 1987.

Hooker, Joseph Dalton. *A Sketch of the Life and Labours of Sir William Jackson Hooker, K.H.* Oxford: Clarendon Press, 1903.

Horn, Pamela. *Education in Rural England: 1800–1914*. New York: St. Martin's Press, 1978.

Hort, Arthur Fenton. *Life and Letters of Fenton John Anthony Hort, D.D., D.C.L., LL.D., Sometime Hulsean Professor and Lady Margaret's Reader in Divinity in the University of Cambridge*. 2 vols. London: Macmillan, 1896.

Houghton. See *Wellesley Index*.

Hussey, James M. *Home*. London: H. L. Barrett, n.d.

Hutchinson, H. G. *Life of Sir John Lubbock, Lord Avebury*. 2 vols. London: Macmillan, 1914.

Huxley, Leonard. *Life and Letters of Thomas Henry Huxley*. 2 vols. London: Macmillan, 1900.

Hyamson, A. M. *David Salomons*. London: Methuen, 1939.

Illustrated London News (London).

Jalland, Pat. *Women, Marriage and Politics 1860–1914*. New York: Oxford University Press, 1986.

Johnson, Marion. *Derbyshire Village Schools in the Nineteenth Century*. New York: Kelley, 1970.

Keisling, H. J. "Nineteenth-Century Education according to West—A Comment and Note." *Economic History Review* 36:3 (1983): 416–25.

Kelley, Mary. *Private Women, Public State: Literary Domesticity in Nineteenth-Century America*. New York: Oxford University Press, 1984.

Kerber, Linda. *Women of the Republic: Intellect and Ideology in Revolutionary America*. Chapel Hill: Institute of Early American History and Culture, by University of North Carolina Press, 1980.

Kingsley, Frances E., ed. *Charles Kingsley: His Letters and Memories of His Life*. 2 vols. London: Henry S. King, 1877.

Kingsley, Mary Henrietta. *Travels in West Africa: Congo Français, Corisco and Cameroons* [1897]. 5th ed. London: Virago, 1982.

————. *West African Studies*. 2d ed. London: Macmillan, 1901.

Kitchin, G. W. *Edward Harold Browne, D.D., Lord Bishop of Winchester, and Prelate of the Most Noble Order of the Garter: A Memoir*. London: John Murray, 1895.

Kitson, Sydney D. *The Life of John Sell Cotman*. London: Faber and Faber, 1937.

Laqueur, Thomas W. *Religion and Respectability: Sunday Schools and Working Class Culture, 1780–1850*. New Haven: Yale University Press, 1976.

Lewis, Jane. *Women in England, 1870–1950: Sexual Divisions and Social Change*. Bloomington: Indiana University Press, 1984.

————, ed. *Labour and Love: Women's Experience of Home and Family, 1850–1940*. Oxford: Basil Blackwell, 1986.

Lockhart, J. G. *Charles Lindley Viscount Halifax*. 2 vols. London: Geoffrey Bles, Centenary Press, 1935.

————. *Cosmo Gordon Lang*. London: Hodder and Stoughton, 1949.

Lucas, E. V. *The Colvins and Their Friends*. New York: Scribners, 1928.

Lyell, *Sir* Charles. *Life, Letters and Journals of Sir Charles Lyell, Bart.* Edited by Mrs. [K. M.] Lyell. 2 vols. London: John Murray, 1881.

McCalmont, Frederick Haynes. *McCalmont's Parliamentary Poll Book: British Election Results, 1832–1918.* Edited by J. Vincent and M. Stenton. 8th ed. Brighton, Sussex: Harvester, 1971.

MacLeod, Roy, and Russell Moseley. "Fathers and Daughters: Reflections on Women, Science and Victorian Cambridge." *History of Education.* 8:4 (1979): 321–33.

MacNalty, Arthur S. *Biography of Sir Benjamin Ward Richardson.* London: Harvey and Blythe, 1950.

McWilliams-Tullberg, Rita. *Women at Cambridge: A Men's University—Though of a Mixed Type.* London: Victor Gollancz, 1975.

Malmgreen, Gail K., ed. *Religion in the Lives of English Women, 1760–1930.* Bloomington: Indiana University Press, 1986.

Marcus, Steven. *The Other Victorians: A Study of Sexuality and Pornography in Mid-Nineteenth-Century England.* New York: Basic Books, 1966.

Martineau, Harriet. *Autobiography, with Memorials by M. W. Chapman.* 3d ed., 3 vols. London: Smith, Elder, 1877.

Matheson, P. E. *Life of Hastings Rashdall.* London: Milford, 1928.

Meacham, Standish. *Toynbee Hall and Social Reform.* New Haven: Yale University Press, 1987.

Middleton, Dorothy. *Victorian Lady Travellers.* London: Routledge and Kegan Paul, 1965.

Mintz, Steven. *A Prison of Expectations: The Family in Victorian Culture.* New York: New York University Press, 1983.

Murray, Janet H. *Strong-Minded Women: And Other Lost Voices from Nineteenth-Century England.* New York: Pantheon, 1982.

North, Isaac W. *A Brief Memoir of the Rev. Henry North . . . Late Assistant Minister of Welbeck Chapel.* London: Hatchard, 1839.

North, Marianne. *A Vision of Eden: The Life and Work of Marianne North.* New York: Holt, Rinehart and Winston, 1980 [an edition of: M. North, *Recollections of a Happy Life, Being the Autobiography of Marianne North*, ed. Janet C. (North) Symonds, 2 vols., 2d ed. London: Macmillan, 1892].

O'Brien, Valerie. "Living British Women Composers: A Survey." In *The Musical Woman: An International Perspective, 1983,* edited by J. L Zaimont, pp. 209–34. Westport, Conn.: Greenwood Press, 1984.

Ormerod, Eleanor. *Eleanor Ormerod, LL.D., Economic Entomologist: Autobiography and Correspondence.* Edited by Robert Wallace. London: John Murray, 1904.

Oxford English Dictionary; Being a Corrected Reissue with an Introduction. . . . Edited by J. A. H. Murray et al. 13 vols. Oxford: Clarendon, 1933. [*O.E.D.*]

Oxford University. *Alumni Oxonienses: The Members of the University of Oxford, 1715–1886: Their Parentage, Birthplace, and Year of Birth, with a Record of Their Degrees* [1891]. Arranged by Joseph Foster. 2 vols. Nendeln: Kraus Reprint, 1968. [*Alum. Oxon.*]

Paget, Elma K. *Henry Luke Paget: Portrait and Frame.* London: Longmans, 1939.

———. *The Story of Bishop Patteson.* [Children's Heroes Series, 13]. London: Jack, 1907.

———, ed. *New Methods in the Mothers' Meetings.* London: Longmans, Green, 1915.

Paget, *Sir* James. *Memoirs and Letters of Sir James Paget.* Edited by Stephen Paget. London: Longmans, Green, 1901.

———. *Selected Essays and Addresses*. Edited by Stephen Paget. London: Longmans, Green, 1902.

Paget, Stephen. *Adolescence*. London: Macmillan, 1917.

———. *Sir Victor Horsley: A Study of His Life and Work*. London: Constable, 1919.

———, ed. *Henry Scott Holland . . . Regius Professor of Divinity in Oxford, Canon of St. Paul's: Memoir and Letters*. London: John Murray, 1921.

———, and J. M. C. Crum. *Francis Paget: Bishop of Oxford*. London: Macmillan, 1912.

Palgrave, Gwenllian F. *Francis Turner Palgrave: His Journals and Memories of His Life*. London: Longmans, Green, 1899.

Parker, Olive. *For the Family's Sake: A History of the Mothers' Union, 1876–1976*. Folkestone: Bailey Brothers and Swinfen, 1975.

Pedersen, Joyce Senders. "Reform of Women's Secondary and Higher Education: Institutional Change and Social Values in Mid and Late Victorian England." *History of Education Quarterly* 19:1 (1979): 61–91.

———. "Some Victorian Headmistresses: A Conservative Tradition of Social Reform." *Victorian Studies* 24:4 (1981): 463–88.

Peterson, M. Jeanne. "Dr. Acton's Enemy: Medicine, Sex, and Society in Victorian England." *Victorian Studies* 29:4 (1986): 569–90.

———. "Gentlemen and Medical Men: The Problem of Professional Recruitment." *Bulletin of the History of Medicine* 58:4 (1984): 457–73.

———. *The Medical Profession in Mid-Victorian London*. Berkeley: University of California Press, 1978.

———. "No Angels in the House: The Victorian Myth and the Paget Women." *American Historical Review* 89:3 (June 1984): 677–708.

———. "The Victorian Governess: Status Incongruence in Family and Society." *Victorian Studies* 14 (1970): 3–26.

Pickstone, John V. *Medicine and Industrial Society: A History of Hospital Development in Manchester and Its Region, 1752–1946*. Manchester: Manchester University Press, 1985.

Prestwich, Grace A. M. M. *Life and Letters of Sir Joseph Prestwich, M.A., D.C.L., F.R.S., Formerly Professor of Geology in the University of Oxford*. Edinburgh: William Blackwood, 1899.

Prochaska, F. K. *Women and Philanthropy in Nineteenth-Century England*. Oxford: Clarendon Press, 1980.

Punch (London).

Rayleigh, Robert J. Strutt, 4th Baron. *Life of J. J. Thomson*. Cambridge: Cambridge University Press, 1942.

Reader, W. J. *Professional Men: The Rise of the Professional Classes in Nineteenth-Century England*. London: Weidenfeld and Nicolson, 1966.

Reynolds, J. R., ed. *A System of Medicine*. 3 vols. Philadelphia: Lea, 1879–80. [Orig. pub. London: Macmillan, 1866–79].

Richter, Melvin. *The Politics of Conscience: T. H. Green and His Age*. Cambridge: Harvard University Press, 1954.

Romanes, Ethel. *Life and Letters of George John Romanes*. London: Longmans, Green, 1896.

Rosaldo, M. Z., "The Use and Abuse of Anthropology: Reflections on Feminism and Cross-Cultural Understanding." *Signs* 5:3 (1980): 389–417.

Rose, Phyllis. *Parallel Lives: Five Victorian Marriages*. New York: Knopf, 1983.

Rosen, Andrew. *Rise Up, Women: The Militant Campaign of the Women's Social and Political Union, 1903–1914*. London: Routledge and Kegan Paul, 1974.

Rothman, Ellen K. *Hands and Hearts: A History of Courtship in America*. New York: Basic Books, 1984.

Royal College of Physicians of London. *Lives of the Fellows of the Royal College of Physicians, 1826–1925*. Compiled by G. H. Brown. London: Royal College of Physicians, 1955.

Rubinstein, David. *Before the Suffragettes: Women's Emancipation in the 1890s*. New York: St. Martin's Press, 1986.

Ruskin, John. *The Brantwood Diary of John Ruskin*. Edited and annotated by Helen Gill Viljoen. New Haven: Yale University Press, 1971.

————. *Diaries of John Ruskin*. Selected and edited by Joan Evans and J. H. Whitehouse. 3 vols. Oxford: Clarendon Press, 1957–59.

Russell, George W. E. *Edward King: Sixtieth Bishop of Lincoln. A Memoir*. New York: Longmans, Green, 1912.

Russell, Mary. *The Blessings of a Good Thick Skirt: Women Travellers and Their World*. London: Collins, 1986.

Russell-Gebbett, Jean. *Henslow of Hitcham: Botanist, Educationalist and Clergyman*. Lavenham, Suffolk: Terence Dalton, 1977.

Sadie, Stanley, ed. *New Grove Dictionary of Music and Musicians*. 20 vols. London: Macmillan, 1980.

Sharlin, Harold I., with Tiby Sharlin. *Lord Kelvin: The Dynamic Victorian*. University Park: Pennsylvania State University Press, 1979.

Shirreff, Emily. *Intellectual Education and Its Influence on the Character and Happiness of Woman*. London: J. W. Parker, 1858.

Shkolnik, Esther. *Leading Ladies: A Study of Eight Late Victorian and Edwardian Political Wives*. [Modern European History Series, edited by W. H. McNeill and Peter Stansky]. New York: Garland, 1987.

Shonfield, Zuzanna. *The Precariously Privileged: A Professional Family in Victorian England*. Oxford: Oxford University Press, 1987.

Shorter, Edward. *A History of Women's Bodies*. New York: Basic Books, 1982.

Showalter, Elaine. *The Female Malady: Women, Madness, and English Culture, 1830–1980*. New York: Pantheon, 1986.

Sidgwick, Ethel. *Mrs. Henry Sidgwick: A Memoir*. London: Sidgwick and Jackson, 1938.

Siefert, Susan. *The Dilemma of the Talented Heroine: A Study in Nineteenth Century Fiction*. [Monographs in Women's Studies, ed. Sherri Clarkson]. Montreal: Eden Press, 1977.

Smith, Mary F. *Arthur Lionel Smith, Master of Balliol (1916–1924): A Biography and Some Reminiscences*. London: John Murray, 1928.

Stearns, Peter. *Be A Man! Males in Modern Society*. New York: Holmes and Meier, 1979.

Stephenson, Gwendolyn. *Edward Stuart Talbot, 1844–1934*. London: Society for the Propagation of Christian Knowledge, 1936.

Stock, Phyllis. *Better than Rubies: A History of Women's Education*. New York: Putnam, 1978.

Stokes, Sir George Gabriel. *Memoir and Scientific Correspondence of the Late Sir George Gabriel Stokes*. Selected and arranged by J. Larmor. 2 vols. Cambridge: Cambridge University Press, 1907.

Stone, Lawrence. *The Family, Sex and Marriage in England, 1500–1800*. Abridged edition. New York: Harper and Row, 1979.

Strutt. See Rayleigh.

Sydie, Rosalind. "Women Painters in Britain: 1768–1848." *Atlantis* 5 (1979): 144–75.

The Times (London).

Thompson, Henry Lewis. *Four Biographical Sermons on John Wesley and Others: With a Memoir*. Edited by Catharine P. Thompson and S. Paget. London: Henry Frowde, 1905.

———. *Henry George Liddell, D.D. Dean of Christ Church, Oxford: A Memoir.* New York: Holt, 1899.

Thomson, George P. *J. J. Thomson and the Cavendish Laboratory in His Times.* London: Nelson, 1964.

Trollope, Anthony. *Barchester Towers* [1857]. Edited by J. R. Kincaid. New York: Oxford University Press, 1980.

———. *Kept in the Dark* [1882]. New York: Dover, 1978.

———. *Ralph the Heir* [1871]. New York: Dover 1978.

Tropp, Asher. *The School Teachers: The Growth of the Teaching Profession in England and Wales from 1800 to the Present Day.* New York: Macmillan, [1956].

Turrill, W. B. *Joseph Dalton Hooker: Botanist, Explorer and Administrator.* London: T. Nelson, 1963.

Venn, John, comp. *Alumni Cantabrigienses: A Biographical List of All Known Students, Graduates and Holders of Office at the University of Cambridge, from the Earliest Times to 1900.* Part 2. From 1752–1900. 5 vols. Cambridge: Cambridge University Press, 1940–54. [*Alum. Cantab.*]

Vicinus, Martha J. *Independent Women: Work and Community for Single Women, 1850–1920.* Chicago: University of Chicago Press, 1985.

———, ed. *Suffer and Be Still: Women in the Victorian Age.* Bloomington: Indiana University Press, 1972.

Wall, E. J. *The History of Three Color Photography.* Boston: American Photographic Pub. Co., 1925.

Walton, Ron. *Women in Social Work.* London: Routledge and Kegan Paul, 1975.

Ward, [Mary] Mrs. Humphry. *Marcella* [1894]. London: Virago, 1984.

Weber, Max. *From Max Weber: Essays in Sociology.* Translated and edited by H. H. Gerth and C. W. Mills. New York: Oxford University Press, 1966.

Weintraub, Stanley. *Victoria. An Intimate Biography.* New York: Dutton, 1987.

Wellesley Index to Victorian Periodicals. Edited by Walter Houghton. 4 vols. Toronto: University of Toronto Press, 1966–87.

West, E. G. *Education and the Industrial Revolution.* New York: Barnes and Noble, 1975.

Westcott, Arthur. *Life and Letters of Brooke Foss Westcott, D.D., D.C.L., Sometime Bishop of Durham.* 2 vols. London: Macmillan, 1903.

Westwater, Martha. *The Wilson Sisters: A Biographical Study of Upper Middle-Class Victorian Life.* Athens, Ohio: Ohio University Press, 1984.

Who Was Who. 7 vols. and index. London: Adam and Charles Black, 1966–81. [*W.-W.W.*].

Williams, David. *Genesis and Exodus: A Portrait of the Benson Family.* London: Hamish Hamilton, 1979.

Winter, Gordon. *A Country Camera, 1844–1914.* Harmondsworth: Penguin, 1973.

Wolfram, Sybil. *In-Laws and Outlaws: Kinship and Marriage in England.* New York: St. Martin's Press, 1987.

Wood, Christopher. *Dictionary of Victorian Painters.* Woodbridge, Suffolk: Antique Collectors' Club, 1971.

Yonge, Charlotte Mary. *The Daisy Chain: or, Aspirations: A Family Chronicle* [1856]. London: Macmillan, 1876.

Index

(ordinary, but extraordinary —
she can't decide

(False unity —
doesn't cohere)

155 — women of the group published
poetry only rarely. What does that
mean? We're not interested in this group

what the conclusion? Gentlewomen didn't write poetry?
or these gentlewomen didn't? So what?

A catalogue —
156-158 — what
people wrote — where's the analysis?
remarkably few did a or b —

So what?

we know their accomplishments
what we don't know is how it
was incorporated into their
everyday.